Wireless Network Hacks & Mods For Dummies®

Cheat Sheet

Wireless LAN Glossary

802.11: The general standard developed by the IEEE for wireless local area networks. Within the 802.11 standard are various substandards, including 802.11b (11 Mbps using the 2.4 GHz spectrum), 802.11a (54 Mbps using the 5 GHz spectrum), and 802.11g (54 Mbps using the 2.4 GHz spectrum).

802.11e: A forthcoming addition to the 802.11 family of standards, 802.11e is *not* a physical standard like 802.11b/g/a, but instead describes a series of QoS (Quality of Service) mechanisms the performance of 802.11 networks for delay- or bandwidth-sensitive applications (Wi-Fi Multimedia) includes some, but not all, of the QoS mechanisms

802.11i: The IEEE standard for enhanced security in a Wi-Fi ne other enhancements to Wired Equivalent Privacy (WEP) and W *Equivalent Privacy* and *Wi-Fi Protected Access*.) WPA2 systems

802.1X: 802.1X is an IEEE standard for network authentication. In a ... network, users can access only the authentication system (a single network *port*) until ... ve been authenticated by the authentication server. (*See also* RADIUS and AAA.)

AAA (Authentication, Authorization, and Accounting): An AAA system (like RADIUS servers, but not limited to that protocol) is used to control access to a network like a wireless LAN. AAA systems are used for WPA-Enterprise Wi-Fi networks and are also used to secure access to many hot spot networks.

access point (AP): A wireless LAN base station that connects a wired network (like the wired Ethernet connection on a broadband modem) to the wireless network. The AP contains a radio transceiver, which transmits and receives radio signals, and many APs contain a router, which reads the addresses within data packets and directs them to the appropriate networked computer.

Bluetooth: A standard system for wireless Personal Area Networks (or PANs). Bluetooth provides speeds of up to 723 Kbps at short ranges (typically less than 10 meters). PAN technologies such as Bluetooth are complementary to LAN technologies (like 802.11) and are typically used to connect peripheral devices together (like keyboards to computers, or wireless headsets to mobile phones).

dBm: The decibel milliwatt, or dBm, is used in radio communications as a measure of signal strength. It is a logarithmic measure, with 0 dBm being equivalent to 1 milliwatt of power. An addition of 3 dBm is roughly equivalent to a doubling in power, whereas a decrease of 3 dBm is roughly equivalent to a halving of power. dBm is most commonly used when examining signal strength relative to the receive sensitivity of a wireless network device.

Ethernet: A standard data communications protocol for computers and computer peripheral devices such as printers. The most common variation of Ethernet found in home networks is the 100 Mbps 100BaseT variant, but dozens of other variations exist with speeds up to 10,000 Mbps (10GB Ethernet).

IP address: The "phone number" of the Internet, the IP address is used to identify computers and devices connected to the Internet and allows traffic to be routed across the Internet. Most home wireless networks have two types of IP addresses: a *public* IP address (used by your modem and access point or router) that identifies your network to other computers on the Internet, and a set of *private* IP addresses used only within your network. Your access point (or separate router, if you have one) translates between your public and private IP addresses to send data to the right computer within your network.

LAN (local area network): A computer data communications network used within a limited physical location, like a house.

For Dummies: Bestselling Book Series for Beginners

Wireless Network Hacks & Mods For Dummies®

Cheat Sheet

network adapter (also Network Interface Card, or NIC): A device that connects to an internal bus in a PC, which provides an interface between the computer or device and the LAN. For wireless networks, network adapters typically connect to the PC Card bus, or the USB bus of the device being networked.

Network Address Translation (NAT): A process performed within your access point (or separate router, if you use one) to translate (or create a tie) between your internal network's "private" IP addresses and the public IP address assigned to your network by the ISP. A NAT router is a device which performs this translation and which lets devices on your network using non-routable private IP addresses communicate with devices on the Internet.

RADIUS (Remote Access Dial-in User System): RADIUS is a protocol for AAA (*see also* AAA) for controlling access and use of a network. WPA-Enterprise uses a RADIUS server to authenticate and authorize users on the network. You can create your own RADIUS server (with PC software or a special hardware device), or use a "hosted" RADIUS server on the Internet.

receive sensitivity: Receive sensitivity is a measure of the minimum signal strength and quality that a Wi-Fi device (like a network adapter in a PC) can accept while still maintaining a specific level of performance. 802.11 systems have multiple receive sensitivities — with lower signal level requirements equating to lower speed connections.

Service Set Identifier (SSID): Also referred to as ESSID (or Extended SSID, when referring to a network with an AP or base station), network name, and other terms, this is the name that identifies a specific wireless LAN. In order to connect to a network, a device must "know" the SSID of the network. The SSID is usually broadcast by the base station, but this broadcast may be turned off (as a *very* weak security measure).

signal-to-noise ratio (SNR): A measure of the overall strength of a radio signal (like Wi-Fi) compared to the background and ambient noise (or radio interference). A higher SNR (measured in decibels, dB) means a better quality signal, all else being equal.

Wi-Fi Protected Access (WPA): An improvement to WEP, WPA adds, among other changes, a key (TKIP, or temporal key integrity protocol) that changes dynamically over time, which eliminates the greatest shortcoming of WEP. WPA is the minimum level of security you should choose if at all possible. WPA-Enterprise adds in 802.1X authentication to make the network even more secure.

Wi-Fi Protected Access 2 (WPA2): WPA2 (*see also* 802.11i) adds even further enhancements to WPA, including AES (Advanced Encryption Standard), which makes the encryption key almost impervious to current cracker attacks.

Wired Equivalent Privacy (WEP): The encryption system used by wireless LANs to provide security on the network. WEP uses an encryption *key* (which can be 40 or 108 bits long — these are often referred to as 64- and 128-bit keys, due to some extra bits used in the WEP system) to encrypt data flowing across the network. WEP is considered an insecure protocol because the encryption key can easily be "broken" using free tools downloaded from the Internet.

Wireless Distribution System (WDS): A system within 802.11 networks that enables APs and other devices to operate as repeaters and bridges. WDS is designed to extend your wireless signal from a main base station (AP) to relay base stations (which extend the signal to other base stations) or to remote base stations (which rebroadcast the signal to client devices).

wireless Ethernet Bridge: A device that connects to an Ethernet port on a networked device (like a PC, game console, or networked audio system) and provides network adapter functionality for that device.

wireless LAN repeater: A device that extends the range of a wireless LAN by receiving signals from an access point (and other devices on a wireless LAN) and retransmitting them. A wireless LAN repeater is often placed in a separate part of the house and is used to allow devices that are too far from the access point to "get onto" the wireless LAN. Repeaters are usually part of a WDS distribution system.

For Dummies: Bestselling Book Series for Beginners

Wireless Network Hacks & Mods FOR DUMMIES®

by Danny Briere and Pat Hurley

WILEY

Wiley Publishing, Inc.

Wireless Network Hacks & Mods For Dummies®

Published by
Wiley Publishing, Inc.
111 River Street
Hoboken, NJ 07030-5774

www.wiley.com

Copyright © 2005 by Wiley Publishing, Inc., Indianapolis, Indiana

Published by Wiley Publishing, Inc., Indianapolis, Indiana

Published simultaneously in Canada

For general information on our other products and services, please contact our Customer Care Department within the U.S. at 800-762-2974, outside the U.S. at 317-572-3993, or fax 317-572-4002.

For technical support, please visit www.wiley.com/techsupport.

Wiley also publishes its books in a variety of electronic formats. Some content that appears in print may not be available in electronic books.

Library of Congress Control Number: 2005923793

ISBN-13: 978-0-7645-9583-7

ISBN-10: 0-7645-9583-0

Manufactured in the United States of America

10 9 8 7 6 5 4 3 2 1

1B/RV/QZ/QV/IN

WILEY

About the Authors

Danny Briere founded TeleChoice, Inc., a telecommunications consulting company, in 1985 and now serves as CEO of the company. Widely known throughout the telecommunications and networking industry, Danny has written more than one thousand articles about telecommunications topics and has authored or edited nine books, including *Internet Telephony For Dummies, Smart Homes For Dummies, Wireless Home Networking For Dummies,* and *Home Theater For Dummies*. He is frequently quoted by leading publications on telecommunications and technology topics and can often be seen on major TV networks providing analysis on the latest communications news and breakthroughs. Danny lives in Mansfield Center, Connecticut, with his wife and four children.

Pat Hurley is a consultant with TeleChoice, Inc., who specializes in emerging telecommunications technologies, particularly all the latest access and home technologies, including wireless LANs, DSL, cable modems, satellite services, and home-networking services. Pat frequently consults with the leading telecommunications carriers, equipment vendors, consumer goods manufacturers, and other players in the telecommunications and consumer electronics industries. Pat is the coauthor of *Internet Telephony For Dummies, Smart Homes For Dummies, Wireless Home Networking For Dummies,* and *Home Theater For Dummies*. He lives in San Diego, California, with his wife, daughter, and two smelly dogs.

Dedication

Pat: I would like to dedicate this book to my baby daughter, Annabel, who gives me improbable faith in my own genes. Thanks for making me smile every time you pooter.

Authors' Acknowledgments

Pat Hurley

I want to thank my wife, Christine, for putting up with yet another book, another set of deadlines, and another life disruption. Thanks, Chrissy, for not following through on your threats — I couldn't do anything at all without your help and support. And I especially want to thank Emily Silady, "AB's PA," who has filled this home office worker's long empty role of "coworker." Thanks, Emily, for enabling my caffeine addiction, facilitating the pursuit of chicken mole burritos, and just for making the workday a bit more fun every day. Hope you'll be around 'til AB is in college.

Danny Briere

I want to thank my wife, Holly, and all our kids, Nick, Emily, Maddie, and Chris, for their infinite patience with everything that does not work electronically around the house, and particularly Holly for her continued support of my tinkering and testing despite the fact that connectivity to the Internet disappears at the worst possible time due to something I unplugged without telling her. Writing books like this takes a lot of time invested in installing and uninstalling just about every conceivable device we can get our hands on, and that usually means that the network is "challenged" about half the time. Now that it has crept into the last bastion of network privacy, the car, Holly is totally without a haven from connectivity problems. I can only say that at least she can now use her iPod on all sorts of devices around the house, and that's got to be worth something.

With any book there are a boatload of people to thank, and some are always missed. Having said that, we simply must single out the following people for their assistance with testing, reviewing, installing and understanding some very cool wireless products:

Mehrshad Mansouri and Lisa Hawes from Sterling PR representing NETGEAR, Mike Chen and Melody Chalaban from Belkin, Darek Connole from D-Link, Dana Brzozkiewicz representing ZyXEL, Michale Gulledge from Wireless Extenders, Suzanne Hawley with Digital Antenna, Marcia Simon, who represents Parrot, Inc., Christine Atalla who represents Canary Wireless, Trisha King with SMC Networks, Tommy Fradenburgh from Rockford Corporation, and (last only by random choice) Jeff Paine and Andy Tennille of UTStarcom.

Finally, thanks to Ed Ferris, our IT guru (and coauthor on our next wireless book), who provides our sanity checks where and when needed; to Linda Morris, our project editor, who showed nearly infinite patience and a keen eye for our grammatical shortcomings; and to Melody Layne, our Wiley champion and favorite Las Vegas conference lunch date.

Publisher's Acknowledgments

We're proud of this book; please send us your comments through our online registration form located at www.dummies.com/register/.

Some of the people who helped bring this book to market include the following:

Acquisitions, Editorial, and Media Development

Project Editor: Linda Morris

Acquisitions Editor: Melody Layne

Copy Editor: Linda Morris

Technical Editor: Mike Williams

Editorial Manager: Carol Sheehan

Media Development Supervisor: Richard Graves

Editorial Assistant: Amanda Foxworth

Cartoons: Rich Tennant
(www.the5thwave.com)

Composition Services

Project Coordinators: Adrienne Martinez, Shannon Schiller

Layout and Graphics: Andrea Dahl, Lauren Goddard, Joyce Haughey, Stephanie D. Jumper, Barry Offringa, Melanee Prendergast, Heather Ryan, Julie Trippetti

Proofreaders: Leeann Harney, Jessica Kramer, Carl William Pierce, TECHBOOKS Production Services

Indexer: TECHBOOKS Production Services

Publishing and Editorial for Technology Dummies

Richard Swadley, Vice President and Executive Group Publisher

Andy Cummings, Vice President and Publisher

Mary Bednarek, Executive Acquisitions Director

Mary C. Corder, Editorial Director

Publishing for Consumer Dummies

Diane Graves Steele, Vice President and Publisher

Joyce Pepple, Acquisitions Director

Composition Services

Gerry Fahey, Vice President of Production Services

Debbie Stailey, Director of Composition Services

Contents at a Glance

Table of Contents

Introduction

Welcome to *Wireless Network Hacks & Mods For Dummies.* This book was written to help you get the most out of your wireless network. Whether you've got one access point that you'd like to do more with, or a whole house full of wireless gear, you can do a lot to boost your performance and extend the core wireless functionality. Whatever your situation, we're here to help you supercharge your wireless network.

Wireless Network Hacks & Mods For Dummies is *not* an electronics mod or software hacker's guide to wireless gear. As intricate as these devices have gotten these days, if you think you know how to retool a motherboard for performance, you don't need us to tell you what to do. Second, more and more off-the-shelf software can now help you accomplish what used to require backdoor hacking.

Our focus is on helping you use the current equipment on the market, with the current software tools and design techniques, to put together the most comprehensive and high-performance home wireless network you can possibly get. You're not going to pry open your wireless access point and start soldering high-performance chips onto its motherboard (at least not under our guidance).

Wireless Network Hacks & Mods For Dummies picks up where our more beginner-level book, *Wireless Home Networking For Dummies,* published by Wiley, left off. If you have not installed a network yet, you might consider buying both books so that you can cover the more basic installation issues at the same time you read about how to broaden and optimize that network's performance after it is installed.

About This Book

If you've installed some level of wireless capability in your home and want to take it to the next level, or are thinking of purchasing a wireless computer network and want a high-powered setup from the get-go, this is the book for you. Here's the bottom line: If you want to (or have) cut the cord, we want to help you improve your network.

If you have a wireless network, you have probably realized that performance can vary wildly around your home. What's more, you might be trying to add additional gear onto your network, only to find it does not seem to solve the problems you set out to fix. You're not alone — many of those who have mastered the first stage of getting a wireless network up and running have wondered how they can simply get more out of it. Towards that end, this book helps you get the most out of your network over the long term.

With this book in hand, you'll have all the information that you need to know about the following topics:

- Planning a wireless network that can cover your whole home, including in your car and outside the walls of the house
- Evaluating and selecting advanced wireless networking equipment for installation in your home
- Installing and configuring multiple wireless networking devices that work together seamlessly
- Understanding the issues surrounding boosting your wireless signals to increase the range and throughput of your network
- Securing your wireless network from nosy neighbors and hackers
- Playing computer games over a high-performance wireless network and across the Internet
- Connecting your audio-visual gear to your wireless network and sharing MP3, video files, DVDs, and more around the whole house
- Talking with people worldwide, for free, over your wireless network
- Protecting your home with wireless surveillance
- Using your wireless gear on the road
- Setting up your own hot spot to share wireless access with others
- Outfitting your car with a wireless network
- Discovering devices that you'll be able to connect to your wireless home network in the future

System Requirements

There are no minimum requirements from a wireless equipment or computer perspective for this book. Just about any computer will work over a wireless connection, as long as it has some sort of networking capability (which covers most of the computers still working today).

If your home network is anything like ours, you want to end up with a wireless network that connects old and new computers and devices, newer and older operating systems, Windows and Mac-affiliated devices, and a whole lot more. *Wireless Network Hacks & Mods For Dummies* will help you get there.

That having been said, the newest versions of Windows and Mac OS do the best job of helping you quickly and painlessly optimize your wireless network. Much of the sophistication in wireless networking has occurred relatively recently. Most of the advanced wireless gear and software, as well as most of the newer wireless audio/visual, gaming, and similar gear, have been designed around the latest operating systems and hardware interface capabilities. So if your computer does not have USB ports, Windows Wireless Networking, or other similarly "modern" computer conveniences, you're likely to be at a huge disadvantage in trying to adopt at least some of the ideas and recommendations in this book.

As a result, we mostly cover optimizing wireless networks that connect PCs running the Windows operating system (Windows 95 or later) or the Mac OS (Mac OS 9 or later) — with a particular focus on Windows XP and Mac OS X. Although wireless networking is also popular among Linux users, Linux-specific instructions are not provided in this book.

How This Book Is Organized

This book is organized into several chapters that are grouped into five parts. The chapters are presented in a logical order — flowing from an intense tutorial on wireless technologies, to installing, optimizing, and using your wireless home network — but feel free to use the book as a reference and read the chapters in any order that you want.

Part 1: Making Your World Wireless

The first part of the book is an in-depth primer on networking and on wireless networking. If you are not overly familiar with the concepts of networking a computer, this part of the book provides a quick foundation on wireless gear, standards, and concepts, so that you can appreciate the advice provided in the rest of the book. Chapter 1 presents a total view of all the devices we intend to help you wirelessly network; Chapter 2 discusses the state of standards and important technology trends that affect the operation, optimization, and future-proofing of your network; Chapter 3 provides an overview of the key elements of a home wireless network; and Chapter 4 introduces you to the key broadband Internet access technologies that your wireless home network uses to connect outside your home and gives you the information you need to connect the two networks (wireless and Internet access) together.

Part II: Boosting Performance on Your Wireless Network

The second part of the book helps you plan your extended and expanded wireless home network. It helps you understand how to create a whole home wireless footprint; how to link your wireless network with other wired technologies in your home; how to track and maintain the operation of your entire home network; how to optimize your network's overall performance; and how to secure your wireless network. This is the part to turn to if you want to learn how to measure the performance of your wireless network and what to do to improve that performance.

Part III: Wireless on the Go

Part III discusses how to use your wireless network on the road. It helps you understand how you can access the Internet from remote wireless access sites called *hot spots* in coffee shops, hotels, airports, and other public locations. We tell you how to keep your communications safe from eavesdroppers while on the road, and even how to put wireless connectivity in your car. The last chapter in this part covers how to set up your own wireless hot spot, so you can help others communicate wirelessly on the road too.

Part IV: Cool Wireless Toys

After you get your wireless home network running in perfect shape, now comes the fun. Part IV of the book presents many cool things that you can do over a wireless network, including playing multi-user computer games, connecting your audio-visual equipment, viewing rooms via wireless surveillance (even over the Internet!), and talking over your wireless network to anyone in the world. What's the fun of a high-powered wireless network without cool toys?

Part V: The Part of Tens

Part V provides a couple of top-ten lists that we think you'll find interesting — ten great online sources for specific areas of high-performance networking and the ten most frequently-asked security questions about Wi-Fi security (a topic that puzzles even the most experienced users sometimes).

Icons Used in This Book

All of us these days are hyper-busy people, with no time to waste. To help you find the especially useful nuggets of information in this book, we've marked the information with little icons in the margin. The following icons are used in this book:

As you can probably guess, the Tip icon calls your attention to information that can save you time or maybe even money. If your time is really crunched, you might try just skimming through the book and reading the tips.

The little bomb in the margin alerts you to pay close attention and tread softly. You don't want to waste time or money fixing a problem that could have been avoided in the first place.

This icon is your clue that you should take special note of the advice that you find there . . . or that this paragraph reinforces information that has been provided elsewhere in the book. Bottom line: You will accomplish the task more effectively if you remember this information.

Face it, computers and wireless networks are high-tech toys — we mean *tools* — that make use of some pretty complicated technology. For the most part, however, you don't need to know how it all works. The Technical Stuff icon identifies the paragraphs that you can simply skip if you're in a hurry or you just don't care to know.

Where to Go from Here

Where you should go next in this book depends on what you know and what you are trying to accomplish. If you are still relatively new to wireless technologies and networking in general, we recommend that you start at the beginning with Part I. When you feel comfortable with networking terminology, or you just get bored with the lingo, move on to the chapters about monitoring and boosting your network in Part II. If you've got your network operation well in hand, check out Part III to help you extend this on the road. Part IV gives you the most useful and fun ways to use your network — this lets you get the most bang for your wireless buck.

When you are done with this book, you should have a highly optimized and extensive wireless network that covers your needs from the pantry to the pool! And if you don't have a pool, we'll help you cover that part of your yard where you dream about putting one. How's that for future-proofing your wireless home network?

Part I
Making Your World Wireless

The 5th Wave   By Rich Tennant

"Why am I modding my wireless network?
I pimped my Xbox, my fish tank, and my
Water Pik. This was next."

In this part . . .

*W*ireless gear touches our lives in surprising ways. It's not just computers and phones these days — there's wireless in everything from TVs and audio systems to planes, trains, and automobiles. To help you wrap your mind around the expanse of wireless, we take the time in this Part to lay out a vision of the wireless world. We talk about where you find wireless and what flavor of wireless you can expect to find in each device and place.

Then we spend some time looking at the nitty-gritty details about the standards and certifications — explaining key concepts like 802.11 and Wi-Fi — so that you'll understand exactly which pieces of wireless gear work together, and which don't.

We also review the pieces and parts that make up a wireless network. If you've already got a wireless network in place, you can skim through this quickly — it's always there for you to refer back to if you want. Finally, we review the equipment and services you need to connect your wireless networks to the Internet. Don't underestimate the importance of this step — the value of your networks increases exponentially as they are connected to other networks.

Chapter 1

Wireless Inside Everything!

In This Chapter

▶ Understanding the wireless world around you

▶ Tapping into wireless at home . . . and away

▶ Encountering wireless everywhere

▶ Getting a handle on the many uses of wireless

*W*e recently read the following quote by a pundit commenting on the sorry state of fast food in America: "You can have cheap, good, and fast — pick any two." Up until very recently, you could say something similar about the situation in the world of electronic devices: Cheap, portable, and network-connected — pick any two.

The combination of inexpensive, small, and networked just didn't happen all that often — devices that were portable usually required a cable to work (think about a PDA that needs to be docked), or they cost a fortune but worked wirelessly (think about early "smartphones").

Luckily, there's been a revolution. That's not just marketing-speak or hyperbole — the world has gone mad for wireless, and now it's time for all of us to catch up. In *Wireless Network Hacks & Mods For Dummies,* we are going to help you do just that — catch up and move right to the head of the wireless line. And in this chapter, we begin that trek by giving you the lay of the land.

Remember: *Wireless Network Hacks & Mods For Dummies* was written to help those of you who want to achieve high performance with your wireless network. We're going to help you boost your signals, attach more devices, and in general, do a whole lot more of everything wireless. Although we won't help you rewrite the operating code for a D-Link Internet camera or splice into a MIMO antenna, we are going to help you maximize your wireless network based on off-the-shelf gear and software. This first Part of the book introduces many of the concepts that you need to know to do what we suggest in Parts II through IV. If you consider yourself pretty adept at everything wireless already, feel free to skip to Part II and get right to the nitty-gritty of boosting your performance.

Wireless Networks Are Everywhere

Where can you find the wireless *networks,* or electronic "highways," to connect all of your devices? The answer is simple: everywhere.

Wireless networks are an increasingly ubiquitous part of our existence. Satellite networks blanket the entire globe, touching just about everywhere that people live, and most places that they don't (excepting only the North and South Poles). Closer to earth, *terrestrial* (ground-based) networks of all sorts cover homes, buildings, cities, and even wider areas.

Wireless networks let you stay in contact, online, connected, entertained, and informed, no matter where you go.

Feeling at home with wireless

The main focus of *WNH&M For Dummies* (we're abbreviating the name to save a few micrometers of cartilage in our typing fingers) is on wireless networks that you would install or access from within your home.

We're not going to waste your time talking about "old style" wireless networks, like regular old-fashioned cordless phones here. We stick to the newfangled networks like Wi-Fi, Bluetooth, UWB, and ZigBee. (Don't worry if these names aren't familiar: We explain them all!)

So what can you do in your home wirelessly? The sky's the limit — anything you can do over a wired network in the home can be done wirelessly these days. Here are just a few of the cool ways you can use your wireless network:

- **Data transfer:** This one is a no-brainer — we bet you're already doing this, or planning on it. Simply put, wireless networks are a great way to transfer data (PC files, Web pages, e-mail, digital pictures, and the like) among computers in a home, and between a computer in the home and a destination on the Internet. Today, data transfers are the most common use for home wireless networks; tomorrow, data will continue to be a huge driver of wireless networking, but its relative share of network usage will decrease as newer uses for wireless networking come into being.

- **Audio:** Audio usage is exploding on many wireless networks. Just look at the millions of people buying iPods and downloading MP3 and other digital music files to them via the PCs in the home. Wireless networks take this music from the PC and send it to the home stereo or any location in the house. In Chapter 13, we tell you more about audio distribution and wireless networks.

✔ **Voice:** We're willing to bet that every single reader of this book is currently using some sort of wireless network for voice communications (also known as phone calls). Between cordless phones in the house and cellphones everywhere, we bet you've got this covered. What's new (and to us more interesting) is how voice calls will soon become part of the unified home wireless network — traveling over the same connections that data, audio, and video do, and then converging onto your home's broadband connection. The end result (we tell you how to do this in Chapter 15) allows you to gain control over your "phones" and save money at the same time. We can see Pauly Shore saying, "Whoa, that's thrifteee."

✔ **Audio and video conferencing:** You don't have to limit yourself to just voice calls either. With a wireless network and a broadband Internet connection, you can move up to that *Jetsons*-esque fantasy — video phone calls. Wireless connections to laptops as well as "standalone" wireless conferencing units enable you to see and be seen, as well as heard, when you talk to far-flung friends and relatives. We tell you more about this subject in Chapter 16!

✔ **Home control:** This application is near and dear to our hearts, and not only because we wrote *Smart Homes For Dummies* — we're basically lazy and like to make our house work for us, instead of vice versa. With a wireless network backbone in your home, you can control lights, HVAC (heating, ventilation, and air conditioning), drapes, sprinklers, garage doors . . . basically anything, from the comfort of, well, anywhere you want to be lounging. We talk about this in Chapter 14.

✔ **Security and monitoring:** A wireless network doesn't just enable sloth-like and lazy behavior — it can also make you (or at least your home) safer and more secure. Wireless networks within the home can be connected to wireless networks outside the home (or with your "wired" broadband connection) and combined into one super-duper security and monitoring system. This system lets you see who's at the front door while you're at work, turn off the alarm when the nanny's there, or just let a monitoring company watch it all for you. We tell you how to do this in Chapter 14.

Offices

Wireless networks aren't just for home use — an ever-increasing number of offices and businesses are using wireless networks too. In fact, the whole concept of wireless networking was originated for business and not residential users — some of the original (and still biggest) suppliers of wireless networking gear developed their systems for providing communications in large business workplaces like warehouses and factory floors.

In the work setting, wireless networks provide services such as

- **Data connections to workspaces:** One of the most obvious uses of wireless networks within the office is to replace (or avoid the installation of) wired data connections to PCs. As more and more workers use laptop computers and handheld computers and work in more flexible settings, the "access it anywhere" nature of wireless is a big advantage. Of course, wireless will probably *never* completely replace wired networks — for an ironic example, the engineers who design all this cool wireless gear will probably still rely on super-fast wired networks to transfer their gigantic drawings, schematics, and plans across the network in a shared workspace environment. For most of us, however, the wireless state of the art is sufficient for us to "pull the plug" on wired networks.

- **Network access in conference/meeting rooms:** Many businesses deploy wireless networks specifically in conference and meeting rooms, with the thought that even if employees have wired access at their desks, they need to be wireless to be productive in meetings and group collaborations in these public spaces. Some of the newer wireless equipment we talk about throughout *WNH&M For Dummies,* such as Wi-Fi–enabled projectors, makes it easier to hold meetings, give presentations, and do all that boring stuff you have to do to pay the mortgage. We can't make it fun, but we can make it easier!

- **Guest access for Internet:** Many businesses are also creating their own "hot spots" (discussed in the next section of this chapter) for their guests, partners, and even for their own employees. Public spaces such as lobbies, outdoor areas, and even the cafeteria are being set up for Wi-Fi access to the Internet — providing an open "Wild West" Internet connection that's completely separated from the corporate network for security purposes. In Chapter 12, we talk about how to create a secure "zone" on your network for similar purposes at your home or neighborhood or for a small business.

- **Factory floor automation and monitoring:** One of the original applications that drove technology companies to develop wireless networks in the first place was to monitor, control, and automate production processes — like manufacturing processes on a factory floor. If you've ever been to a factory, you've probably noticed that most are big and spread-out. Even small factories, however, are not typically wired up with network cabling — wireless provides the perfect means for tying together the data communications from each workstation and control point on the assembly line.

- **Warehouse control and inventory tracking:** Another group of business structures that tends to be large, spread-out, and unwired are warehouses, distribution centers, and the like. Many of the original vendors of wireless gear (folks like Symbol Technologies, www.symbol.com) specialize in things like wireless bar code scanners and ruggedized handheld devices for use in logistics operations. Take a look next time you get a package delivered: Chances are good that your delivery person is using a wirelessly-enabled handheld, and that many more were used as your box of CDs from Amazon.com made its way across the country.

✔ **Wireless voice and PBX:** The next big thing in business wireless is the use of Wi-Fi wireless networks for voice communications (just as they are being adapted for this use in the home). With wirelessly networked handsets (or cellphones with additional Wi-Fi functionality built in), workers are able to access all of the functionality of a corporate PBX system, with its voicemail, extension dialing, conferencing, and the like, without cables.

✔ **Security monitoring:** Wireless networks are also being used for security monitoring and alarm systems. Wireless cams are being installed in office buildings, warehouses, distribution centers, retail stores, and malls, and even in very distributed applications, such as alongside pipelines.

✔ **Hundreds of specialized applications:** Almost nothing in the business world is *not* moving towards wireless. For example, hospitals are installing wireless networks that can provide *Star Trek*–like wireless voice communications via cool little "press to talk" lapel pins.

 Our focus in this book is mainly on the home. We don't have a separate section of chapters in the book that specifically talk about all of these business applications (but we *do* sprinkle in business-specific information where it's appropriate). However, there's not a lot of difference between, for example, wireless security monitoring in the home and in your small business. So you can pretty much directly translate *WNH&M For Dummies* to your business. If your business is bigger, work with your IT staff to implement wireless networks — that's beyond our scope here.

Hot spots and beyond

Wireless networks don't just end at the walls of a home, office, or factory — they extend to the outdoors as well. Wireless networks of various sorts blanket the globe, providing you with opportunities to be online without wires almost anywhere you go.

One particularly cool trend is the development of the Wi-Fi hot spots. If you've ever stepped foot in a Starbucks or Barnes & Noble (or one of several other retail locations who've gotten into wireless networking big-time), you've already been in a hot spot. Simply put (and we add in the details in Chapters 9 and 12), a *hot spot* is an area with publicly available high-speed Internet access via a Wi-Fi network.

Depending upon who's counting and what exactly they are counting (some folks only count "for-pay" or "official" hot spots), anywhere from tens to hundreds of thousands of hot spots exist in the U.S., and more worldwide. Just as

Wi-Fi has become a common term that just about everyone knows, so too has the term *hot spot* become a part of the zeitgeist.

Hot spots can be found in some of the most unusual places. (There's one in Pat's town at a beach on the San Diego coastline. Check out `www.parks.ca.gov/?page_id=662` for pictures of San Elijo State Beach Park, where you can surf the Web and the waves!)

You might find hot spots in interesting locations near you as well. Here are some locations where you can commonly find hot spots:

- **Personal hot spots (open access points):** Power to the people — seriously! A lot of folks are community-minded (or maybe they just want to stick it to the Man by helping other folks get online for free) and have opened up their personal wireless networks to all comers. In Chapter 9, we give you some tips for finding these networks — they can be anywhere that has power and a broadband connection!

- **Retail:** This is your archetypal café/restaurant/bookstore hot spot location. When most people think of hot spots, they think of a room full of small round tables, an espresso machine hissing away in the background, and maybe some latter-day beatnik at the open mic. This is where the hot spot revolution gained steam (no latté pun intended) and became corporate (some really big companies got involved with the Starbucks hot spot deployments, which now number in the thousands).

- **Libraries:** As you're probably aware, many libraries have taken to the Internet age in a big way — providing Internet terminals for customers to use, putting their card catalogs online, and even digitizing big chunks of their collections (wherever those pesky and annoying copyright lawyers don't try to stop them). It should probably come as no surprise that many libraries have begun to offer free hot spots for their patrons.

- **Hospitality:** The hotel industry earns a big chunk of its money from business travelers (who usually pay more per room than vacationers who book six months in advance on special rates). Every road-warrior type needs high-speed Internet access — many hotels have begun to offer hot spots in their lobbies, meeting rooms, and even some guest rooms.

- **Airports:** Another "hot" location for providing hot spot access to business travelers is the airport terminal, lounges, and other common areas (such as restaurants).

- **Convention centers:** Keeping the theme of supporting business travelers (who have expense accounts to use) in mind, you won't be surprised that convention centers are being outfitted with wireless network gear as a matter of course. The hardest part about putting together one of these networks is finding a system that can support the thousands of connections that a busy conference may demand.

Beyond the hot spot we find the *hot zone* — a wireless network that covers a few square miles instead of just a few hundred feet. Hot zones can use a variety of different network technologies — most use the familiar Wi-Fi technologies that we explain in depth in Chapter 2 (and which we discuss throughout the book), but you may also find hot zones that use special proprietary wireless technologies (and therefore require special *network adapters* or wireless "modems") to get connected.

Yes, we know that *Hot Zone* is also the name of a book and movie about a horrifying Ebola virus outbreak. We agree that it's an unfortunate name — but we decided *not* to make up our own term for it that no one else in the world would ever use!

Like hot spots, hot zones can be found just about anywhere, but here are some locations that you might run into:

- **Universities:** Many universities — we can almost say *most* these days — have built campuswide networks, usually using Wi-Fi equipment, to provide network access to students, staff, and faculty. We know this first-hand — both of our wives work on university campuses, and both access the university hot zones quite frequently. Universities are hotbeds of hot zone and hot spot action.

- **Corporate campuses:** Many of the largest corporations, such as Microsoft, operate not just in a single building, but in a *campus* of interconnected or adjoining buildings. Many of these same enterprises have spent money installing huge wireless hot zones for their employees, partners, customers, and guests. If you're in luck, they give you a password and let *you* on their network too!

- **Economic zones:** Just as many countries set up regions which are "free trade zones" or "economic development zones," so too have many municipalities looked at wireless hot zones as a tool to stimulate the economy in parts of their cities. An example is Long Beach, California — a really pretty town with a big port and a closed Navy base that needed a little boost. The city leaders there have "unwired" a big chunk of the city, providing a free Wi-Fi hot zone to bring businesses, customers, and tourists downtown.

- **Municipal networks:** On a wider scale, many cities are considering citywide hot zones (usually using Wi-Fi) as a municipal service and as a means of stimulating development. The most famous of these is being developed in the City of Brotherly Love (Philadelphia, home of the famous Pat's cheese steaks), but scores of smaller cities are doing the same thing. The only thing that's holding this movement back is the local telephone and cable companies, who — in what we think is the mother of all negative PR moves — are fighting these networks tooth and nail.

Wireless Gear: The New Standard

Of course, all of these wireless networks won't mean a thing if your electronic gear and gizmos don't have the ability to "talk" wirelessly. It'd be like going to a skinny-dipping party without your swimsuit . . . oh, never mind. Anyway, having the proper wireless equipment built into your gear is important.

The good news here is that electronic gizmos with wireless networking already built in are becoming commonplace; adding built-in wireless to equipment that hasn't got it already is a snap; and it's getting to be darn near impossible to be totally blocked out of the wireless world.

In this section, we take a 50,000-foot view of the electronics world and explain how wireless networks are (or soon will be) touching just about every part of your life.

In computers

The most obvious place to look for wireless networking capabilities is within the realm of computers. (We're known for our fantastic grasp of the obvious.) Computers were the first use of wireless networking technology that allowed users to cut the cord, and today, computers are the most "unwired" of all devices (next to cellphones, of course).

We're talking desktop computers, laptops, and notebooks, as well as hand-held ("palm" or "pocket") PCs here. Almost all of the new models have been enabled for wireless networking, and — as a matter of fact — wireless networks have basically become standard equipment for almost any kind of computer. Almost the only exceptions we can think of are supercomputers, high-powered workstations (the kind engineers and designers often use), and super-high-capacity network *server* computers that are used for things like Web sites, e-mail hosting, or file storage. These kinds of computers transfer so much data that they need the fastest of the fast networked connections, which means wired.

Otherwise, "It's all wireless, baby!" as Dick Vitale would say. Among the wireless networking systems and technologies making their home in computers are the following:

> ✔ **Wi-Fi:** The most common type of network technology is *Wi-Fi*, the computer wireless Ethernet networking system that we talk about in detail in Chapter 2. Wi-Fi is built into almost every new laptop computer and most new desktops today (as well as literally hundreds of millions of other devices including computer peripherals, handhelds, and more).

✔ **Bluetooth:** Another common network connection (although less prevalent than Wi-Fi) is *Bluetooth,* which we discuss in Chapter 2. This is a *PAN* (or personal area network) technology, which is designed for low-speed connections among peripherals (such as keyboards, mice, cell-phones, and so on). Bluetooth is designed to take the place of all the extra cables hanging off the back of your PC. It's already common to see wireless keyboards and mice using Bluetooth to "connect" to desktops wirelessly. In the near future, this system may very well be replaced by one or more emerging wireless technologies, such as *UWB* (ultra wide-band) or even the proposed *wireless USB* system. But for today's computers, Bluetooth is where it's at.

✔ **Wireless WANs:** There are also many wireless *WANs* (or wide area networks, which are networks that extend outside the home or office and cover extended territory). These network connections are usually found in mobile computers (laptop or handheld) and are designed to provide connectivity anywhere. Some of the most common (or important) of these connections include

- EV-DO: This is the high-speed variant of *CDMA* (code division multiple access), the wireless technology pioneered by Qualcomm for cellphones. This is the fastest wireless WAN technology in the U.S. right now, offered by Verizon and Sprint, among others.

- GPRS/EDGE: The competitor to CDMA is a European system called *GSM.* (Global System for Mobile is the current expansion of that acronym, although it has changed over time and taken on a life of its own.) The high-speed WAN version of GSM is GPRS (offered by Cingular in the U.S.). The next version (slightly faster than GPRS, although still slower than EV-DO) is called *EDGE.*

- WiMax: Competing with both of these systems is an emerging WAN technology called WiMax. When it hits the street, WiMax will replace cable and DSL modems, but in the long term, it will become a mobile technology to provide high-speed connections for anybody on the move.

In TVs

Believe it or not, wireless networks are moving to the big screen. No, not the silver screen (although there's no reason to think that you won't also see some sort of wireless technology in cinemas in the near future — if nothing more than some sort of antiwireless technology to shut down that annoying guy's cellphone in the middle of the movie). We're talking about the big screen TV in your family room!

If you've ever hooked up a TV, especially an HDTV, you know what a pain in the patoot it really is. Trust us on this one: We wrote *HDTV For Dummies.* (More importantly, we've tried to help relatives do this over the phone!)

TVs are now being made with wireless built right in to make the hook-up process as simple as just turning everything on. The power cord is the only cable you have to worry about! The TV auto-configures with your stereo equipment and other gear in your home. Cool, huh?

Here's how it all shakes out:

- ✔ **Wi-Fi:** This is available today. Several televisions — small, portable, LCD flat panels on one end of the spectrum, and big-screen, front projector systems on the other end — have built-in Wi-Fi networks. Depending upon the system, this either provides a hookup to a base station/set-top box type of device, or it provides a PC connection. Either way, it lets you watch the tube without connecting the wires.

- ✔ **ZigBee:** ZigBee is a new technology that's not quite on the market yet, but it will hit the streets soon. (The manufacturers of the ZigBee "chips" are ramping up their production.) ZigBee is designed as a low-speed, inexpensive networking technology to replace all of today's proprietary control systems. A ZigBee TV will be easier to control remotely, will work with any ZigBee remote, and will "play nice" with your other components.

- ✔ **UWB:** This is where it really gets cool. Universal wideband will provide instant high-speed connections for your HDTV (or regular old tube) that allow you to send all of your surround sound audio, high-definition video, and even the control signals that ZigBee wants to carry. This is a big deal: The Wi-Fi that's currently built into some TVs is iffy on its ability to carry HDTV. Technically, it *should* work, but in practice, it doesn't always, so most vendors don't support it with their products.

In A/V equipment

Just as TVs are getting the wireless treatment, so is all of the audio and video equipment that sits on the shelf next to the TVs in our entertainment centers.

Surround-sound receivers, DVD players, satellite TV receivers, and so on — all of these gizmos are getting wireless network connections and cutting their cords too!

How are they doing this? Ponder these wireless networks:

- ✔ **Wi-Fi:** Ah, good old Wi-Fi. Yep, it's being built into this stuff too. As you probably already know, and as you'll see throughout *WNH&M For Dummies*, Wi-Fi is *everywhere.* Sorta like the old Decon Foregone ads with Muhammad Ali, only with Wi-Fi cards instead of bugs. (Tell us you don't remember the champ in those ads!)

✔ **ZigBee:** Like TVs, other A/V gear can benefit from the ubiquity of ZigBee, and from the fact that it uses radio waves (which can penetrate objects like walls) instead of infrared light.

✔ **UWB:** Once again, UWB comes riding in on its silver wireless horse to save the day. This technology is going to let us throw away all those monstrous cables we have to deal with. (No offense to the good folks at Monster cable, who really do make good cables!)

Keep in mind the fact that you don't *need* to have built-in wireless to make any of these devices wireless. We'll talk extensively in several parts of *WNH&M For Dummies* about how to make these wireless connections for your existing gear. No sense throwing all that good stuff out just to go wireless, huh?

We're good guys who want to save your money! If your spouse or partner is berating you for buying a book just to help you figure out how to spend more money on electronics, tell him or her that we've got *their* back too, and we're gonna help you economize this time!

In cellphones

To say that wireless technology is used in cellphones sounds like the dumbest statement ever written in a *For Dummies* book (which are *not* for actual dummies, by the way — we have found out over the years that *For Dummies* readers often ask the best and hardest to answer questions of anyone we know). A wireless network client device (a cellphone) has wireless networking built in. Well, duh!

But we've got a point to make here, and it's kind of important: Cellphones are being filled up with network connections beyond just their primary WAN connections back to the cellphone company.

In particular, you can find cellphones with the following connections:

✔ **Wi-Fi:** A few cellphones are beginning to hit the market with built-in Wi-Fi hardware. This feature lets you use your mobile phone as a Voice over IP (VoIP) "cordless" phone, making free or low-cost calls over a Wi-Fi Internet connection in your home, office, or in a hot spot (see Chapter 15) instead of paying for "minutes" on the cell network. If your phone has a Web browser or e-mail program, you can also "surf" or check your messages over a mega-fast Wi-Fi connection, instead of using the cell network for those functions.

- **Bluetooth:** This is the most common "extra" network connection on cell-phones. You can do a ton of different things over a Bluetooth network, but here are the big three:

  - Sync your phone with your PC: Keep the address book on your mobile phone and that on your PC or Mac in perfect sync, all of the time, without a docking cord or cradle.

  - Use your cellphone as a modem: While you're on the road, connect your computer to the Internet wirelessly by using your cellphone's high-speed WAN connection.

  - Go hands-free: Use a Bluetooth headset (or even a Bluetooth-enabled car) to leave your hands free to drive, write, or even eat more French fries while you yak away.

A bit of a three-way battle is brewing between the folks who make cellphones, the folks who run cellphone companies, and the folks who actually use cellphones (all of us, in other words). We want cellphones that we can use however we like. For example, if we take pictures on the cellphone, we want to use Bluetooth (for example) to transfer them to our computers.

The folks who run cellphone companies, however, want us to pay to use their networks to e-mail the pictures to ourselves, so they make the cellphone manufacturers disable functions like this. The manufacturers want to sell a lot of phones, so they design neat new features, but they have to do what *their* customers (the phone companies) want them to do.

This is annoying, but not the end of the world, except for this: You often don't know until after you've already bought the phone and the service plan that features have been turned off. This is *really* annoying and has brought people to the point of multiparty class action suits (against both the vendor and the cellphone companies). Ugh!

Our advice is to read some good online sources *before* you buy any phone with Bluetooth or Wi-Fi to find out if wireless capabilities are truly enabled or not.

In cars

So far we've talked about some relatively small devices. (Not withstanding a huge-screen TV, most of the wirelessly-enabled gizmos we've discussed in this section could fit in a pocket or a box.) But how about making something bigger than a bunch of bread boxes connect to the wireless network?

We're talking about your car. Heck, we're even talking *really* big, for you SUV drivers out there. You don't have to just talk about gizmos and gadgets when you think about wireless. Wireless truly is going everywhere!

Now, we know you've already got wireless network equipment in your car — no doubt, cellphones are coming with you when you drive or ride. But in fact, wireless is being built right into cars. Some cars come with cellphones built into them. They also are sporting new wireless *telematics* systems, such as OnStar, www.onstar.com, which connect your car to a satellite and cellphone network to provide services like remote door unlocking and accident reporting.

Telematics services are generally proprietary and not all that "open" to uses outside of their specific service plans. But some network connections that you can build into your car let you do your own thing, such as

- **Wi-Fi:** A lot of car manufacturers are developing "connected" cars that can use Wi-Fi for a variety of information and entertainment purposes. You don't have to wait for them, though — in Chapter 11, we talk about how to do this yourself. Imagine updating your car MP3 and video files wirelessly every time you park in the garage!

- **Bluetooth:** In the world of Bluetooth, car manufacturers have gone beyond planning and are already offering Bluetooth-enabled cars. If you want the ultimate in integrated cellphone systems in your car, you need to go Bluetooth — you don't even have to take your phone out of your briefcase to accept phone calls. In Chapter 11, we also talk about how you can add Bluetooth to your existing car. (Look, now we're saving you the car payments you would incur by upgrading! *WNH&M For Dummies* can pay for itself in savings!)

On planes

Nope, we aren't making this one up (although you probably won't be installing this one yourself). Airlines, aircraft manufacturers (Boeing in particular), and networking equipment vendors have begun to install wireless hot spots in airliners. It's not cheap (nearly $30 a flight at present), but it's immeasurably cool. Imagine checking your e-mail, surfing the Web, or even having an iChat AV video conference at 35,000 feet!

To Wireless Infinity and Beyond!

Wireless does *NOT* stop here. Literally thousands of engineers worldwide are working on wireless technologies of all sorts. In this chapter, we've already discussed one emerging technology that's going to make your wireless networks all the more powerful — UWB.

Here are a few trends that we think will make all wireless networks faster, cheaper, more reliable, and just plain better over the next few years:

- **UWB:** This technology has a lot of promise, but also some challenges. The promise is to move beyond the ultra short-range "connector cable" replacement being promised for first-generation UWB systems (replacing things like the cables between a DVD player and a TV) and to extend throughout the home with super high-speed (hundreds of megabytes per second). The challenge revolves around some competing groups of technology companies — at least two different groups want to "own" the standard for UWB — and this competition is causing a Betamax versus VHS-style war. We won't know for a while how this will turn out, but we still maintain high hopes for UWB.

- **Wireless USB:** If UWB *doesn't* pan out, one reason may be that the infighting between the different groups hasn't been resolved before a working *wireless USB* standard has been put into place. A bunch of companies are working on this technology, which extends USB 2.0 (480 Mbps) beyond the cable and into the airwaves. If it works out, USB may beat out UWB in the battle of TLAs (three-letter acronyms).

- **802.11somethingnew:** The 802.11 technologies (also known as Wi-Fi) are ruling the roost of wireless networks today. Hundreds of millions of Wi-Fi–enabled devices have been built in the past few years, and Wi-Fi is still going strong. Many pundits wonder, however, if the technology will be overcome by newer technologies like WiMax or UWB, with their longer range (WiMax) or higher speeds (UWB). That isn't beyond the realm of possibility, but we have a sneaking suspicion that the next few generations of 802.11 (like the forthcoming 802.11n, which we discuss in Chapter 2) will keep the technology in its current leading position.

- **Software-defined radios:** This isn't a specific wireless standard or system (like Wi-Fi or UWB), but instead a really cool underlying technology. Most wireless gear today uses hardware that is purpose-built to work with one or another kind of radio signal. Software-defined radios (*SDRs*), however, are more general-purpose, with software allowing the same bit of radio hardware to work with completely different radio frequencies, transmission standards, data compression methods, and the like. SDR is a big focus for the defense industry, where it might reduce the huge number of radios that the military needs to load onto Hummers, tanks, planes, and ships. If you're in the military, this will be handy — if you're not, don't fear, as the technology should quickly cross over to civilian wireless networking uses quickly. How could it be used? Suppose your cellphone radio worked with your cell company, Wi-Fi, Bluetooth, and other signals, depending on what application you were running. That would cut costs and improve your ability to enhance your phone over time without doing a "trash can upgrade," which is what we call upgrading by buying a new cellphone.

Chapter 2

Wireless Network Basics

A s much as it pains us to tell you this, we really have to get this out of the way: If you're going to get into wireless networking, you're going to have to spend at least some time digging into (and figuring out) wireless *standards* and *protocols* (which are commonly agreed-upon specifications for how wireless network devices communicate with each other).

Like many other computer and networking-related systems, wireless networks rely on these standards to ensure that disparate pieces and parts work together smoothly. These standards are part of everyone's daily life — ranging from the standards that make your HDTV work to standards that underlie the Internet itself.

Most of the time, you can safely ignore the standards and just assume that they are there, working in the background for you (when was the last time you had to worry about your long distance provider's implementation of MGCP in their interoffice switching?). But when it comes to designing, choosing components for, building, and operating a wireless network, standards come to the fore.

Introducing the 802.11s

Most of the wireless networks we discuss throughout *WNH&M For Dummies* are based upon a set of standards (called *802.11,* explained below) set by a group called the *IEEE* (or Institute of Electrical and Electronic Engineers — insiders call them the "I triple E"). The IEEE is one of the three main groups in the networking industry that create standards governing how different pieces of networked equipment talk to each other (the other two are the *ITU,* or

International Telecommunications Union, and the *IETF,* or Internet Engineering Task Force).

The IEEE's 802 LAN/MAN Standards Committee has a large task force of engineers (who don't work for the IEEE itself, but instead are employees of various technical companies who make software, computer chips, and networking equipment) working on various *LAN* (local area network) and *MAN* (metropolitan area network) issues. Each of these issues has its own working groups — including (pay attention to this one!) the 802.11 Working Group, which is focused on wireless LANs.

Within 802.11 (which is the overarching wireless LAN working group) are a number of smaller working groups, each of which is identified by a letter appended to the end of the 802.11 name — for example, 802.11*b* (we added the italic for emphasis). These working groups are tasked with developing specific enhancements and variants to the basic 802.11 standards.

Why are we bothering to tell you all of this? For several reasons:

- ✔ If you haven't already, you *will* hear some of these 802.11 terms as you move forward with your wireless LAN. We guarantee it. You *can* build a simple wireless LAN without knowing all of this stuff, but as you get more complex, 802.11 something-or-other pops up.

- ✔ 802.11 and wireless networks in general are constantly moving forward. Knowing the 802.11 variants (and we talk not only about current variations, but also future ones) keeps you in the loop.

- ✔ If you know about the IEEE and the 802.11 working group, you can keep track of all this online. Most of the (admittedly very technical) documents of the various 802.11 working groups are available online at the following URL:

```
http://grouper.ieee.org/groups/802/11/
```

Beyond the IEEE, another group is "watching over" wireless LAN standards — the Wi-Fi Alliance (discussed later in this chapter in the section titled "Oh my, Wi-Fi"). These folks are responsible for testing and certifying interoperability between vendors — in other words, making sure things actually work in the real world.

Easy as a, b, g

The IEEE has a *lot* of 802.11 working groups, and therefore a lot of 802.11 *something* standards. But at the most basic, you absolutely need to know something about only three of them to build and operate your wireless LAN. These are 802.11b, 802.11g, and 802.11a — the three current standards for the physical layer (PHY) of the network.

The physical layer is one part (Layer 1) of the seven-layer *OSI networking model,* which defines everything from the physical media to the applications in a network. If you're curious, you can learn more about the OSI model at the following URL:

```
http://en.wikipedia.org/wiki/OSI_model
```

The physical layer defines how the bits and bytes of data are transferred to and from the physical medium of the network — in this case, the *electromagnetic spectrum* (or radio waves) of the wireless LAN. The physical layer standard defines all of the important details of how your wireless network takes the data you're sending across it and converts it to the radio waves that bounce around your home.

This physical layer process is really a basic underlying task in a wireless network — two pieces of wireless networking gear can "talk" with each other only if they share a common physical layer implementation.

The three 802.11 standards that are used for nearly all wireless LAN gear you can buy today (802.11a/b/g) each use different PHYs. The PHYs in 802.11b and g systems use the same *spectrum* (or range of radio frequencies) — in the 2.4 GHz band — whereas 802.11a uses a different set of frequencies in the 5 GHz band. This means that 802.11b and g systems have at least a fighting chance of talking to each other in a network (and in fact, they *can* talk to each other), but neither of these systems can connect to an 802.11a system.

Your wireless friend — the electromagnetic spectrum

Nothing is more fundamental to the concept of wireless networking than the electromagnetic spectrum — the radio waves that carry signals around your house, your neighborhood, or even your town. Understanding a little bit about this concept can be very useful as you think about wireless networks.

A warning: We aren't physics instructors, and we're not trying to help your SAT scores here — just a little high-level overview is all we want to provide.

The electromagnetic spectrum is simply a continuum of electromagnetic radiation ranging from low-frequency radio waves on up to x-rays and

gamma rays, encompassing electrical power, radio waves, and even light waves. Any particular spot on this spectrum is defined by its wavelength and frequency — two characteristics that are actually tightly related (longer wavelengths have lower frequencies).

A big chunk of the middle of the electromagnetic spectrum (from about 3 to 30 billion *hertz* — Hz, a measure of frequency) is the radio frequency spectrum. All of the wireless networking gear we discuss in this book uses radio frequencies to communicate — and all of the gear is somehow defined by, or limited to, a specific smaller range of frequencies (called a *band* or *channel*).

Even if two PHYs use the same spectrum (as do 802.11b and 802.11g), there's no guarantee that they are *compatible* and can "network" with each other. In the case of 802.11g and b, the engineers deliberately made decisions to allow this.

If the concept of spectrum is a bit alien to you, read the sidebar titled "Your wireless friend — the electromagnetic spectrum" to get yourself up to speed.

802.11b: The old standby

When wireless networks hit the big-time a few years ago, it was in the form of networking equipment conforming to the 802.11b standard. You can really think of 802.11b as the baseline for wireless LANs — the lowest (but not least) common denominator. Most wireless LANs you run into (at the office, in your friend's home, at a coffee shop, or other hot spot) are 802.11b-based.

So what's 802.11b all about? We've already mentioned that it uses spectrum in the 2.4 GHz band, which is an *unlicensed* band (the government — in the U.S., the Federal Communications Commission, or FCC — won't require you to get a radio operator's license like a ham radio operator to use these frequencies). This means that *anyone* can use equipment that operates in the 2.4 GHz frequency range without asking permission from anyone.

The people who build the equipment used in wireless networks *do* have to get permission — or approval — from the FCC (and other regulatory bodies in other countries) to ensure that their equipment works within the "rules." Basically, these certifications verify that the equipment doesn't crank out too much power or stray too much onto other frequencies. When you see wireless network accessories (such as antennas) that are marketed specifically for certain pieces of equipment and not for general use, it's usually because those are the only devices for which the accessory has been certified.

The fact that 2.4 GHz is an unlicensed band is good for you because you can build a wireless network without any interference from the Man, but it's also (potentially, at least) bad because everyone around you can do the same thing. And not just wireless networks use the 2.4 GHz band — cordless telephones, Bluetooth systems, baby monitors, wireless speaker systems, and other devices use it too. All of which adds up to *spectrum scarcity* (in other words, a situation where radio signals interfere with each other).

802.11b defines more than just the frequencies used for the wireless LAN. It also defines how those radio waves behave. In particular, 802.11b adopted a system called *DSSS* (or direct sequence spread spectrum). In a DSSS system, the radio spectrum is divided up into a number of channels. The wireless networking gear uses a single one of those channels to transmit and receive data. A competing system (known as frequency hopping spread spectrum — FHSS, if you feel like getting fancy) divides up the spectrum into a larger number of smaller channels and uses them all (no surprise here), hopping from frequency to frequency.

The very first wireless LAN systems (just plain 802.11 — no b, a, or g — LANs, which you *never* run into these days) could use either of these two modulation techniques. (*Modulation* is the technical word for describing how the data is added to the radio waves — *demodulation* is the reverse process, where radio waves are turned back into data packets. *Modem* stands for *modulate/demodulate*.) Generally speaking, DSSS was faster, whereas FHSS was more immune to interference.

As the folks at the IEEE worked on developing a standard that was faster than the very slow first generation 802.11 wireless LANs, they benefited from advances in engineering that let them have the best of both worlds — DSSS systems that were faster than FHSS, but nearly as immune to interference. This advance was a modulation scheme known as *CCK* (complementary code keying). The 802.11b system with CCK modulation has a theoretical maximum speed of 11 Mbps — as fast as the 10 Mbps Ethernet networks used by many homes and small businesses at the time (the late 1990s).

The real *throughput* (or actual speed) of any wireless LAN system is less than the maximum speed of the standard. Most 802.11b networks max out at about 5 Mbps in real throughput. This is faster than the Internet connections in most homes, but not really fast enough to handle bandwidth-intensive network applications such as music and video. Part II of *WNH&M For Dummies* focuses on how to get your real throughput as close to the theoretical maximum as you can.

The DSSS modulation used for 802.11b divides the 2.4 GHz frequency spectrum into 14 total channels — when you set up your wireless network, you can manually set which of these channels you want to use (or let the equipment do the choosing itself, automatically).

In the U.S., only 11 of these 14 channels can be used (1–11) due to FCC regulations. Some other countries are similarly restricted. Because most of our readers are in the U.S. (as are we — and all the equipment we use, for that matter), we refer to channels 1 to 11 throughout the book. If you live elsewhere, you're not missing out on anything — but just check with your equipment vendor and local wireless experts to find out exactly which channels you can use!

Although 11 (or 14, if you're lucky enough to be able to use all the channels) seems like a pretty good number of choices, it's actually a relatively limited number because the channels are *overlapping*. Each channel is defined by its *center* frequency (like 2.412 GHz, for channel 1), and each channel assignment is 5 MHz apart (so channel 2 is 2.417 GHz). The problem arises from the fact that each channel is about 22 MHz wide (11 MHz on either side of the center frequency). This means that signals in channel 1 are actually using some of the same radio frequencies as channels 2, 3, 4, and even 5.

Figure 2-1 shows this phenomenon graphically.

Figure 2-1:
Channels in
an 802.11b
system step
on each
other's feet.

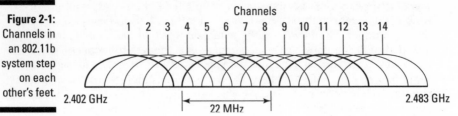

In an 802.11b radio system, only three channels (channels 1, 6, and 11) are *non-overlapping* or completely incapable of interfering with each other. If you're using multiple access points (if this term is unfamiliar to you, we talk about the different pieces and parts of wireless networks in Chapter 3), or if you're in a crowded location like an office, dorm, or apartment where other people's networks may be within a few hundred feet of each other, this can be an issue. We deal with the issue in Chapter 5.

802.11g systems, which we discuss in the very next section, use the same channel assignments and therefore suffer from the very same problem.

To sum things up, 802.11b

✔ Uses the 2.4 GHz frequency spectrum

✔ Contains 14 total channels (11 can be used in the U.S.)

✔ Has only three channels that are non-overlapping

✔ Uses the CCK variant of DSSS modulation

✔ Has maximum speeds of 11 Mbps

✔ Has real-world speeds (throughput) of no more than about 5 Mbps

802.11g: The new champ

802.11b, as we mentioned earlier, works pretty well when it's connected to a cable or DSL modem that maxes out at 2 or 3 Mbps — even a pokey (in the absolute sense) 4 Mbps network connection can handle Internet sharing for your home or small office.

But as soon as you start getting a bit more complex than that — trying to, for example, stream a video file from your PC to your TV, or even just trying to access your iTunes music store purchases from another computer on your network — 802.11b starts to come up a bit short. The folks who make wireless gear (and the folks at the IEEE who come up with new standards) all realized that something faster and more capable of handling advanced networking applications was in order, so they stirred their cauldrons and brewed up 802.11g.

802.11g is nothing more or less, when you get down to the essence of it, than a new, improved, fancier, souped-up version of 802.11b. 802.11g uses the same frequencies — the 2.4 GHz band — and the same channel assignments (with the same overlaps and same three non-overlapping channels). 802.11g even includes the DSSS and CCK modulation from 802.11b — which means that any 802.11g system is backwards-compatible with 802.11b and fits perfectly into any 802.11b network.

The reverse is also true — 802.11b systems can be used in an 802.11g network, but in almost all cases, this slows down the 802.11g network to 802.11b speeds. Typically, the 802.11g clients and access points slow down to a lower speed (like 22 Mbps) while still allowing the 802.11b clients to operate on the network — with some APs you can configure the AP to *not* allow the 802.11b clients on the network in order to maintain the highest possible speeds.

The real breakthrough for 802.11g is a new modulation scheme known as *OFDM,* or *orthogonal frequency division multiplexing. Orthogonal* is a mathematics term that relates to things being at right angles — or, more generally, refers to things that are independent and well-separated. In the wireless world, this means that the data is sent across the airwaves in a series of well-separated frequency modulations that, in essence, can be jam-packed into the airwaves but still distinct enough to be demodulated at the far end.

The net result is a much greater amount of data being sent across the wireless network — five times as much data can be sent simultaneously across an 802.11g network as can travel across an 802.11b one. That's a big deal if you're trying to send audio signals — or the home movie you just created in iMovie — across the network in real time.

Of course, as with 802.11b — and all wireless networks — there's a difference between the theoretical maximum (in this case, 54 Mbps) and the actual throughput you get in the real world. It's not unreasonable to expect upwards of 20 Mbps throughput in an 802.11g network — which gives you enough bandwidth to handle even an HDTV channel's worth of data.

The combination of backwards compatibility and significantly higher throughput have made 802.11g the top dog of the wireless world today.

Most of the wireless LAN gear you can buy today (or that you might get "included" with devices such as digital media adapters) uses 802.11g.

802.11a: Still hanging in there

The limited number of non-interfering channels (just three of them!), when combined with the large amount of gear (like cordless phones) can cause 802.11b and g networks to face interference that causes decreased range (meaning that users have to stay close to the base station or access point) and poor performance.

One way of getting around this issue is to use a different, less crowded set of frequencies. That's exactly what systems based on the 802.11a standard do — they move from the crowded city streets of the 2.4 GHz band on out to the relatively unexplored frontier of the *U-NII* (Unlicensed National Information Infrastructure) band. U-NII is in the 5 GHz range of frequency spectrum, where relatively few other devices operate (a few cordless phones are the only devices operating at this frequency that we've seen on the marketplace).

Besides having few other devices contending for scarce spectrum, the U-NII band has the big advantage of just being a bigger chunk of frequencies than the 2.4 GHz band used for 802.11b and g. This provides some big benefits:

✔ More room for data on each channel — the channels assigned in 802.11a are "bigger" (they use a wider swath of frequencies) than those in 802.11b or g.

✔ There are more channels — 14 versus 11 (although 4 are designated for outdoor use).

✔ Most importantly, there are more non-overlapping channels than 802.11b and g — 8 versus 3.

This leaves you with a much lower chance of interference and, typically, greater throughput. So 802.11a wireless LANs — which, by the way, use the same OFDM modulation scheme as do 802.11g LANs — can reach maximum speeds of 54 Mbps (the same as 802.11g), and in the real world, often reach speeds in the vicinity of 30 Mbps. This makes 802.11a networks the fastest for many folks.

Figure 2-2 shows the channels in 802.11a.

So what's the downside? Why aren't we all using 802.11a? The biggest reason is inertia — 802.11a is *not* compatible with 802.11b, and therefore won't work with a lot of the legacy wireless network equipment found in homes, offices, and public locations throughout the world. 802.11g *does* provide this compatibility, which makes it a safer choice.

As we discuss in Chapter 3, where we talk about choosing equipment, many wireless networking devices these days are *dual mode* and can support both 802.11g and 802.11a. (Many vendors advertise these as 802.11a/b/g access points.)

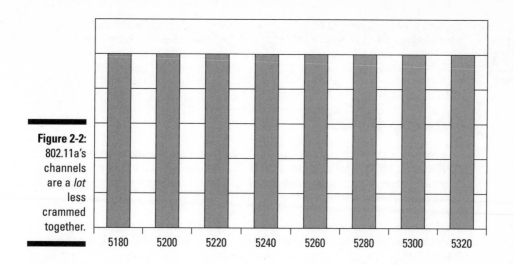

Figure 2-2:
802.11a's
channels
are a *lot*
less
crammed
together.

5180   5200   5220   5240   5260   5280   5300   5320

The other reason why 802.11a has been less popular than 802.11b and g has to do with range. If you think back to your physics classes in college and high school, you might recall a concept called *attenuation* — this is simply the reduction in signal strength of an electrical signal over a distance. In the world of electromagnetic radiation (radio waves), signals attenuate faster when they are higher in frequency.

802.11a uses higher frequencies than do 802.11b and g — and for that reason, it tends to suffer from greater attenuation than do those other standards. So where an 802.11b or g network might have a range of 200 or 300 feet from the base station, an 802.11a network might only reach 65 to 100 feet.

a, b, and g compared

Deciding among the three standards (802.11b/a/g) isn't really all that hard. The first step is to look at 802.11b — and eliminate it if you're building a new LAN. Buying the older 802.11b equipment offers only a negligible cost savings and a big performance deficit — we think you should consider 802.11b only if you're buying gear to fit into an existing network (and even then, you might consider moving your network — or part of it — to a faster standard).

Choosing between 802.11g and 802.11a networks is a bit more difficult, but shouldn't require too much brain-wrangling. If your situation requires you to use your gear within an 802.11b network (like going to a coffee shop that offers wireless Internet access), you're probably better off with an 802.11g network.

On the other hand, if you have a lot of interference issues (with an existing or older wireless LAN, or with your 2.4 GHz phone system), you might want to try 802.11a.

If you are considering 802.11a, our advice is to get a dual mode system — which gives you the best of both worlds. You may also consider having two separate networks in your home or office, with the 802.11a network dedicated to certain high bandwidth applications (like video distribution).

Oh my, Wi-Fi

As you peruse the various variants of 802.11, you'll also run into the term *Wi-Fi* (short for Wireless Fidelity). In fact, chances are good that you're more familiar with this term than with the 802.11 standards we've discussed throughout this chapter.

Indeed, Wi-Fi has become, in some circles at least, an almost genericized name, but in fact, it means something very specific: a certification by the Wi-Fi Alliance (www.wi-fi.org). This certification means a lot — it's a guarantee that a piece of wireless LAN gear was tested and proven to work with any other piece of equipment with the same certification.

The original Wi-Fi certifications were for 802.11b equipment, but the Alliance now does certifications for not just 802.11b, but also for 802.11a and g equipment, as well as for wireless security protocols (see the section later in this chapter titled, "Get an "i" for security," for more details).

Although the standards themselves are designed to provide interoperability between different pieces of wireless equipment (and across vendors), they're not enough. That last *n*th degree of engineering is always required to make sure that everything works together properly. The certification gives you the assurance that the *n*th degree has been applied to your product — all certified equipment of the same standard works together regardless of vendor, which is nice to know! Look for a logo like the one in Figure 2-3.

Figure 2-3:
Look for the
Wi-Fi label
when you
want
compatibility
you can
count on.

Throughout *WNH&M For Dummies,* we often use the term *Wi-Fi* ourselves, if for no other reason than we hate typing "802.11a, b, and g" over and over.

Get an "i" for security

The biggest advantage of wireless networks — the fact that you don't have to be tied down to a cable — is also the root of wireless network's biggest Achilles heel: security. We won't get into the who, what, where, why, and whens here, but suffice to say that wireless networks can't be contained inside your house or office the way that a wired network can.

Every time you turn on your wireless network, consider it the equivalent of having a network outlet for a wired network out in the front lawn, available for all passers-by.

We talk about security protocols and standards for Wi-Fi networks in this chapter at a very general level. We're not talking about how to secure your network in detail — that's something that we discuss in detail in our *other* wireless book, *Wireless Home Networking For Dummies,* also published by Wiley. You should also consult your equipment's user's manuals to figure out how to implement security in your network.

The original 802.11b networks used a system called *WEP* (Wired Equivalent Privacy) to provide a means for doing two things:

- ✔ Keeping people whom you don't want on your network off of it so that they can't access your file servers, Internet connection, and so on. This is done by requiring users to provide a password to get "attached" to the wireless network.

- ✔ Keeping people from intercepting and "reading" the data traveling over your network. This is done by *encrypting* or scrambling your data as it travels wirelessly.

WEP is better than nothing, but it turns out to be a not particularly good way of securing a network. The *keys* used to scramble data in WEP are not all that robust, and it didn't take hackers (the good guys interested in figuring out how things work) and crackers (the bad guys who want to get into your business) long to figure out how to "break" the key and therefore defeat WEP.

There are two efforts to remedy this problem that you should be aware of. Both the IEEE — with a new standard called 802.11i — and the Wi-Fi Alliance — with a protocol called WPA — have stepped in to fill the security gap:

- ✔ **802.11i:** Ratified in late 2004, 802.11i is the IEEE's newest and most robust security standard. The name can confuse some folks — because it's an 802.11*x* standard, many assume that it's another PHY standard like 802.11b or g. In fact, 802.11i only covers the security portions of the wireless LAN and can be used (if the equipment allows it) with 802.11b, g, or a networks.

802.11i provides a lot of security improvements, but the biggest ones revolve around the improved encryption keys used — either *TKIP* (Temporal Key Integrity Protocol) or *AES* (Advanced Encryption Standard). AES is the stronger of these two protocols — it's used by the U. S. government for its own communications, so you can feel pretty confident that no bad guy is going to be able to eavesdrop on your Wi-Fi network.

As we write this book, 802.11i-certified gear is starting to hit the streets, mainly focused on enterprise wireless equipment, not for the home.

✔ **WPA:** As the IEEE was completing the 802.11i standard, the folks at the Wi-Fi Alliance put together a security standard called *WPA* (or Wi-Fi Protected Access) that provided an interim improvement over WEP by using the more secure TKIP encryption key. Now that 802.11i has been finalized, the Alliance has come up with a new version of WPA — called WPA2 — which provides the full level of security provided by the AES standard in 802.11i.

The WPA standards include both *personal* and *enterprise* variants of the standard. The personal variants (the kind you find on any home Wi-Fi gear) let you set the encryption key by means of a shared password (one that you make up yourself and share with anyone who is on the network), whereas the enterprise variants use a separate system called *802.1x* (which uses a special server to ascertain a user's identity and provide her with the encryption key).

At a bare minimum, you should always turn on WPA on your wireless network (unless you're deliberately sharing access publicly, as we describe in Chapter 12). If you're buying new equipment, make sure it supports WPA2.

Gimme an "e" for service quality

Besides security, another wireless LAN shortcoming has been the lack of a *QoS* (or quality of service) mechanism in any of the standards. Sounds like some sort of techie mumbo-jumbo, no? It is, but it's important: QoS is what allows your wireless LAN to "look" at the data being sent across the network and decide which bits and bytes need to be *prioritized* and which don't.

Ultimately, a QoS system should be able to, for example, make sure that the VoIP (Voice over Internet Protocol) phone call you're making gets the highest priority, and that the iTunes music stream gets the next highest priority, and so on down the line (all the way down to the real low priority stuff, like that e-mail from your mother-in-law).

802.11a/b/g wireless LANs don't, by nature, have any QoS mechanism. All the data you send across your network carries the same priority, no matter what type of traffic it is. This isn't really a problem for most data applications, such as e-mail and Web surfing, but it can be a real issue for multimedia uses of the network such as audio, video and voice. As you'll see throughout *WNH&M For Dummies,* these multimedia applications are where all the cool wireless networking fun begins!

The IEEE and the Wi-Fi Alliance are both on top of the problem, with standards efforts to add QoS mechanisms into wireless LAN gear. Like the 802.11i/WPA efforts we discussed in the previous section, these efforts are designed to work *with* rather than replace existing wireless LAN standards like 802.11a/b/g.

Two related QoS efforts are in place, one you can use today, and one that you have to wait for:

✓ **802.11e:** This is the IEEE standard for Wi-Fi QoS. As we write, this is still a *draft* standard — meaning it's close to being finalized, but it is not yet an official standard. What this means to you is simply this: You can buy equipment that incorporates the draft standard, but it's possible that the final standard, when it comes out, will be changed in some unanticipated way that makes your *pre-standard* equipment non-compliant.

Your pre-standard equipment won't quit working the day the new standard is finally finalized — all this really means is that you may not be able to mix new pieces and parts into your network and expect QoS to work properly. It may also not work across vendors.

✓ **WMM:** As they did with 802.11i and WPA, the Wi-Fi Alliance didn't wait around for the standard to be finalized before they took action to solve the QoS issue. The result is *WMM* (Wi-Fi Multimedia) — a standard based on the draft 802.11e specifications drawn up by IEEE. WMM is designed to provide multiple levels of data packet prioritization based upon the packet type:

- Voice: The highest prioritization level, designed to ensure that VoIP phone calls work properly and without delays on a Wi-Fi network.

- Video: The second highest prioritization level, designed to ensure smooth, flicker-free video pictures.

- Best effort: Designed for "regular" data traffic, like Web surfing sessions, that don't need any special prioritization, but which perform better without long delays.

- Background: The lowest level of priority, designed for data like print jobs that are completely unaffected by slight delays.

WMM-certified equipment began to appear on the market at the end of 2004, and we expect it to become widely available over the next few years.

The bottom line on WMM is that it's needed for wireless LANs. Unfortunately, Wi-Fi networks don't behave in a predictable way — scheduling of transmissions is based upon "collisions" between bits of data coming from different network clients and randomly retransmitting around these collisions. So *true*

QoS, where the network elements all work together to ensure that data gets through with adequate bandwidth and minimal latency, probably won't happen even with WMM. But WMM can help, and if you're choosing between two systems that are otherwise equal, WMM is a good choice.

"n" for the future

One final standard worth mentioning in this chapter is what may end up being the replacement for 802.11a/b/g — *802.11n.* This is the IEEE's next-generation wireless LAN standards working group, formed (in the IEEE's own words) for "investigating the possibility of improvements to the 802.11 standard to provide high throughput" (meaning greater than 100 Mbps).

802.11n will take wireless LANs to the next level in performance — bringing enough bandwidth to support things that aren't supported today. For example, an 802.11n network would, theoretically, be able to support multiple HDTV (high definition TV) channels at the same time — something none of today's networks can handle.

The 802.11n standard is a long way from being fully baked — it still needs to be mixed up and hasn't gone in the oven yet. But there are two camps of vendors proposing 802.11n technologies to the working group — *TGn Sync* and *WWiSE.* Each group consists of a number of vendors, and each has a slightly different "take" on what technology will make the best next-generation wireless LAN — and both are fighting it out tooth and claw to get the working group to select their technology as the next standard. So far, this fight has the makings of another BetaMax versus VHS war.

One element that is common to both approaches is something called *MIMO,* or Multiple Input/Multiple Output. What MIMO does, in a nutshell, is expand the number of antennas that a wireless system uses — sending data out simultaneously over several antennas and signal paths. This can effectively double (or more) the throughput and range of a wireless LAN system.

You may see non-MIMO Wi-Fi gear that has two antennas attached to it. These devices don't actually use two antennas at the same time — instead, they use one or the other of their antennae, depending upon signal strength and other factors.

You see a lot of "pre-standard 802.11n" gear on the market — none of it is truly 802.11n compatible (there's not even a draft standard to build to). Instead, this is 802.11g gear that incorporates MIMO systems. Yes, it is, or can be, faster than regular 802.11g gear — when used in conjunction with other "pre-N" gear from the same vendor — but it does not work with equipment from different vendors, and is not compatible or upgradeable to 802.11n when it is ratified.

Actually, the really important compatibility issue with these so-called "turbo" modes is the manufacturer of the Wi-Fi chipsets inside your Wi-Fi device. Many vendors use 802.11 chips from the same vendor, and those chips enable the turbo mode. So you could have an AP from vendor X (say, NET-GEAR) and a network adapter from vendor Y (say, D-Link), and as long as both had a turbo chip from the same chip vendor (say, Atheros), they would work together. To confirm this, dig into the marketing material of the vendors to see which chips they are using.

The bottom line on 802.11n is that it promises to be a great step forward for Wi-Fi, when it happens. As we write in 2005, it's simply too soon to predict how long it will take for a standard to be decided upon and equipment built and sold on the market. For now, we can only wait in anticipation.

Chapter 3

Wireless LAN Infrastructure

- -

In This Chapter

▶ Sorting through wireless LAN equipment

▶ Getting to the base of things

▶ Routing your traffic

▶ Connecting devices

▶ Building bridges

- -

Staying current with the wireless world isn't easy: The technologists driving the development of equipment are constantly improving wireless gear. The pace of change in wireless is probably among the fastest in all the sectors of consumer electronics.

A quick look down any wireless gear aisle in a department store is enough to make your head swim. Switches, routers, bridges . . . what is all this stuff? If you don't know, this is the chapter for you.

In order to truly appreciate the content and advice in this book, you need a good grasp of baseline wireless gear fundamentals. We can't talk about enhancing your network if we don't establish what that network looks like.

So in this chapter, we discuss the basic elements of your wireless LAN. In the rest of the book, we build upon this foundation, so if you are not familiar with terms like DHCP and TCP/IP, be sure to read this chapter and the next (Chapter 4, which covers broadband Internet connections). If you feel you know LAN basics well enough, feel free to refer back to this chapter later if you have any questions.

What's in Your Network?

Your wireless gear at home composes a wireless computer *network*. A network is merely a collection of devices that are interconnected using a common language or *protocol*. The common protocol used in almost all home networks is called *Ethernet*. You don't need to know how Ethernet works; just be aware that your home network uses it, as do most businesses in the world.

The network that connects devices in a particular physical location, such as in a home or in a single office site, is often called a *local area network* (LAN). Conversely, the network outside your home that connects you to the Internet and beyond is called the *wide area network* (WAN). You will likely see LAN and WAN Ethernet connections on your gear.

You connect to your WAN connections — often provided by cable modem, digital subscriber line (DSL), or other Internet access services — via an Ethernet cable that plugs into *ports* in your gear. These ports support a standardized plug called an *RJ-45* connector.

You don't need to know too much about WAN networking except where the *demarcation* (often called a *demarc*) is between your home network and your Internet service provider's *(ISP)* network. That demarc is the point where your ISP's responsibility stops and your responsibility starts. This differs by provider and what you are buying from them. If you are buying a bundled home networking gateway that has a wireless component to it, your ISP helps you manage and troubleshoot problems with that wireless gateway. On the other hand, if you just have a plain old cable modem in your house, you are responsible for the operation of all the LAN gear that connects to that. Demarcation is different for each person and can change over time as you buy more services from your ISP. If you don't know where your demarc is located, call your ISP.

We talk more about the WAN Internet connections in Chapter 4.

Jacking into Your Network

As the wireless market matures, more and more functionality is converging together into fewer devices. Whereas you used to need a switch, a router, and an access point to support your home wireless network, these devices have all converged together so that you can now buy a wireless router with an integral switch. (If you don't know these terms, that's okay: The point we're making is about convergence. Read on and we define them all!)

Convergence is great if you are buying equipment for the first time, but many of us have bought gear as it comes out. Because a good hub may work for six or more years without a problem, we're not likely to replace it for the sake of convergence.

In this chapter, we cover the underlying functionality of wireless devices. Remember, however, that this functionality can be in its own device or combined with other functionality into another device. Wireless functionality is going into all sorts of form factors, ranging from set-top boxes to electrical wall outlets. In this chapter, the important walk-away for you is to understand the functionality you need to complete your network, regardless of what it looks like.

The discussion that follows is a bit generic — it's mainly focused specifically on Wi-Fi equipment because the vast majority of wireless networks are built around Wi-Fi, but many of the concepts (like network adapters) can apply across any sort of wireless LAN.

I see your (access) point

Without question, the most common piece of wireless gear is the access point — a special form of wireless station that receives radio transmissions from your wireless transmitter and from other stations on the wireless network, and forwards these signals on to the rest of the network.

Access point functionality can be in a stand-alonedevice, in a computer that contains a wireless network adapter along with special access point management software, or bundled into other network devices such as routers, cable modems, DSL modems, and so on. You can see a stand-alone AP in Figure 3-1.

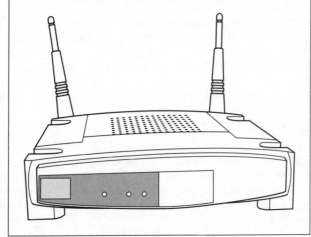

Figure 3-1:
Stand-alone
access
points can
be very
small yet
cover a big
area.

If you've ever visited a friend in New York City or some other densely populated area and tried to log onto a wireless access point, you might have been blown away by the sheer number of wireless networks in the ether around you. The smart people in the standards bodies anticipated this and put in place the right identification and security parameters to make sure you log onto the right network.

Wireless networking has three main parameters you need to know about:

✔ **Network name:** You assign your wireless network a unique name when you install it. This network name can also be referred to as the *Service Set Identifier (SSID)* or perhaps *Extended Service Set Identifier (ESSID)*. When you first enter your AP through your setup software, you might see that the manufacturer has assigned it a name already, such as *Linksys* or *NETGEAR*. Note that each manufacturer's APs ship named this way, and you should rename it something unique so that you can differentiate that network from others in the area.

All stations and APs on a given wireless network must have the same network name to ensure that they can communicate.

✔ **Channel:** When you set up your wireless network, your setup software assigns a channel to the AP. The channel is the signal frequency over which the AP sends and receives signals. Because the wireless spectrum used by 802.11 access points is a shared spectrum, other users may be transmitting on the same channel, which can cause interference if not properly handled. Really good APs monitor (or "sniff") the airwaves for existing signals from other wireless devices and determine which is the best channel to use to avoid interference.

The number of channels available with your access point varies depending on what country you live in and what standard (802.11a/b/g) you are using. We discuss Wi-Fi channels in more detail in Chapter 2.

It doesn't really matter what channel you pick when you initially set up your network — a wireless station scans all available channels looking for a signal from an AP. When it finds one, it negotiates a connection to the AP over that channel. As your network gets more advanced and you start tweaking the performance of your network (or if you have *multiple* networks in the same area), you may very well want to manually configure your channels. We discuss this in Chapter 5.

✔ **Encryption key:** Because the wireless network's name is usually broadcast "in the clear" so that anyone can see it (you can turn this feature off with most APs), anyone — including crackers — can log on unless you have wireless security implemented. APs ship from the factory with the ability to enter a secret *encryption key*, a password of sorts that prevents anyone from logging into your wireless network unless they know the secret key code.

You may hear about security for your wireless network called *Wired Equivalent Privacy, WEP encryption protocol, Wi-Fi Protected Access (WPA)*, or if you are really up on technology, *WPA2*, which are topics we cover in a lot more detail in Chapter 2 — and throughout Parts II and III, where appropriate. For now, just know that these are various forms of encryption technologies that use encryption algorithms, combined with a private key phrase or series of characters, to encrypt everything sent over your wireless network. Any device wanting to connect to your network has to have this key or it can't access the network.

Changing your network name to something other than the factory-assigned setting does nothing to protect your network from determined crackers, nor does broadcasting over a specific channel. These measures are like the window locks in your house: They keep your friends out, but not determined bad guys. Most APs now ship with the security features enabled to protect new users from crackers.

Tonight, I'll be your server . . .

Your wireless network has lots of attached devices communicating with the access point(s). In computer parlance, each attached computer (even if wirelessly attached) is called a *station,* also sometimes referred to as a *workstation* or *client* computer.

If you have a Windows-based network, workstations are grouped together on the same local area network in a *workgroup.* Workstations in the same workgroup can share files and printers; you can see the computers and devices available within your workgroup by looking in the Network Neighborhood (or My Network Places) on your PC.

If you have an Apple Macintosh OS-based network, you find something similar — all the computers are grouped into a network *neighborhood.*

A station can also be a *server.* More and more, you're also likely to find servers on your network. Servers provide special services to other devices on the network. A server can be its own device, or functionality resident in a device that does other things as well. You might find servers like these on your network:

- **File server:** A *file server* offers lots of hard disk storage available to the various devices on the network. File servers focused on storing

audio and video files are often called *media servers.* You can find file and media servers throughout our product discussions in Part IV.

- **Print server:** A *print server* makes it possible for network-based computers to share one or more printers. Whereas some newer printers are network-enabled, meaning they can be seen as a network device on the network, most printers at home are only seen on a network as attached to another PC. More and more wireless networking equipment has an integrated print server built in.

- **E-mail server:** An *e-mail server* sends e-mail to users on the network. E-mail servers are staple items on any corporate network, but at home, these are rarely seen. Most home users have network-based e-mail from their ISP, such as AOL or Yahoo!

- **DHCP server:** A *Dynamic Host Configuration Protocol* (DHCP) server acts like the Sorting Hat in *Harry Potter,* automatically telling each computer on the network what its network address is. Because computers are constantly coming on and off the network, this is quite an active server on the network. You almost have always DHCP functionality bundled into other devices (such as APs or routers), not as a stand-alone unit.

Network interface adapters for client stations

In order to take part in a wireless network, each station on the network needs to be able to send and receive the wireless radio signals. To do this, each needs a radio, which is usually found in a network interface card or adapter. In the typical home wireless network, laptop computers use a slide-in wireless card, and PCs a USB wireless network adapter.

The fact that each computer has some sort of network interface card for wireless is no different than with wired home networks. To get on an Ethernet home network based on cabling, each computer has to have some sort of Ethernet card to plug the Ethernet cabling into.

Wireless network interface cards can come in many different form factors. Sometimes you won't see it at all — the card is embedded in your laptop or other device. Other times, an adapter is plugged into expansion slots in your device's PC or PC Card. Some adapters use your USB or other external interface ports to plug in external radios to do the trick.

Figure 3-2 shows a USB-based wireless networking adapter — you can carry this around with you and always have the ability to log any USB-enabled device onto a compatible wireless network. Look at how small that USB radio is — now that's portable!

Figure 3-3 shows a wireless networking adapter card designed to be installed inside your computer, inside one of the available PCI expansion slots. In the past few years, the computer manufacturers have made it disgustingly easy to install new internal cards — in most cases, you don't even need a screwdriver anymore.

Figure 3-2:
With a USB wireless network adapter, any USB port is an on-ramp to wireless.

Figure 3-3:
Open your
PC, slide in
this network
interface
card, and
you're
all set.

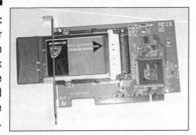

Figure 3-3:
Open your
PC, slide in
this network
interface
card, and
you're
all set.

Wireless adapters come in a large variety of *form factors* — sizes, shapes, and styles, in other words — in order to support the vast and variegated (there's a good SAT word for you!) array of devices that can be wirelessly enabled. Here are the general types of wireless network adapters you are likely to run into:

✔ **PC Cards:** The most common form of adapters for laptop computers (or at least those *without* embedded Wi-Fi) is the *PC Card* (formerly called PCMCIA, but no one could actually pronounce that acronym). These are the credit card-sized and -shaped devices that slide into a slot on the side of your laptop. Most wireless PC Cards have an external antenna segment on the card that sticks outside of the card slot (and sometimes makes it hard to use the second PC Card slot on your laptop, if you've got one). Figure 3-4 shows a typical PC card Wi-Fi adapter.

If you're clumsy or have kids running around near your computers, consider a PC Card with a removable antenna. If one of your kids zooms by and breaks off your antenna, you'll need to buy a whole new card.

Figure 3-4:
A PC Card
wireless
network
adapter.

What else is on your network?

As more devices become wireless-capable, you can find all sorts of workstations/clients on your network. If you don't have these yet, you probably soon will:

✔ **Gaming consoles:** Sony's PlayStation 2 (www.playstation.com), Microsoft's Xbox (www.xbox.com), and Nintendo's GameCube (www.nintendo.com) each have wireless adapters so you can link to the 'Net for multiplayer gaming.

✔ **Wireless network cameras:** Network cameras enable you to pan, tilt, scan, zoom, and record video from around your home. Not just still action shots, but true color video where and when you want it. D-Link (www.dlink.com) offers almost 20 different versions of wireless Internet cameras, including outdoor models for checking the perimeter of your property! Chapter 14 scans your options for network cameras.

✔ **VoIP phones:** Wireless-enabled VoIP (Voice over Internet Protocol) phones allow you to call anywhere in the world. In the near future, VoIP phones will swarm into your home, providing home office lines, teen lines, and even your main phone line. All the major brand-name telephone manufacturers are getting into the act, as are all the major department stores and office supply chains. We talk about VoIP phones in Chapter 15.

✔ **MP3 players:** Network-enabled MP3 servers will serve up your favorite album anywhere within your wireless footprint, enabling you the same portability at home that you used to only get with a portable radio. In Chapter 13, we lay out your options for media servers in your home.

These devices are just a start. Expect most of the consumer goods in your home to log on to your home network sometime soon. Network-enabling such devices allows them to be monitored for breakdowns, software upgrades, and so forth, just like your virus checker on your computer stays current on new definition files. So don't be surprised if you get a message from your microwave informing you that it needs a new LCD display. (Does this mean we have to give our dishwashers an allowance?)

✔ **PCI cards and Mini PCI cards:** Desktop computers typically use internal PCI cards — these are the standard PC internal cards also used for extra video cards, memory controllers, wired network adapters (like Ethernet adapters), and the like. A smaller variant of PCI, appropriately named *Mini PCI,* is often used for small form factor computers and laptops. You usually don't put Mini PCI cards in yourself: They are typically factory-installed.

✔ **Compact Flash adapters:** Some handheld computers (like PocketPCs) use a variant of flash memory known as *Compact Flash* (or CF). Some wireless adapter vendors have reduced the size of their wireless network adapters to fit in these tiny little slots. Figure 3-5 shows a CF network adapter.

Figure 3-5:
A Compact
Flash
wireless
network
interface
card.

Just because your handheld has a CF card slot doesn't mean you can jam a CF Wi-Fi adapter in there and expect it to work. You need to ensure that your specific handheld can support Wi-Fi at all, and then ensure that there are *drivers* (or device-specific software) that work for the CF Wi-Fi card you've chosen.

CF is the most common type of memory slot in handhelds, but there are a number of other types (like SD, SDIO, Memory Stick, and so on — we get dizzy just trying to keep up with the profusion of memory card standards). Vendors have (or soon will) come out with Wi-Fi cards for just about every form factor.

✔ **USB adapters:** Just about every computer these days has a profusion of *Universal Serial Bus* (or USB) ports on the front, back, side, and anywhere else they fit. (USB ports are really handy because they're . . . well, universal and almost every computer peripheral uses them.) So wireless network adapter vendors have cleverly created Wi-Fi and Bluetooth adapters in keychain form factors (like the little portable thumb- or pen-sized flash memory sticks many people carry these days). Some have even kept the flash memory in the same device, so you can carry your files *and* your network connection on your keychain! The device pictured in Figure 3-2 is a USB adapter.

For higher speed networks (like 802.11a or g), you need a *high-speed* USB 2.0 adapter plugged into a suitable high-speed USB 2.0 port on your computer. That's because USB 1.x speeds top out at 12 Mbps.

✔ **Sleds and docks:** For some devices, wireless adapters of the forms listed above just aren't in the cards (pun definitely intended!). For example, the latest version of the super hot Palm OS Treo handheld/smartphone, the 650, doesn't (at the time of this writing) support any Wi-Fi cards in its SD memory slot. Manufacturers know a hot market when they see it and have developed proprietary sled devices. A *sled* is nothing more than a portable dock for a handheld device (or phone) that contains a network adapter and (usually) an extra battery. You slide the handheld into the sled and you're set for Wi-Fi access. The real big disadvantage is just that Handheld + Sled = Real Big and Heavy.

✔ **Proprietary internal cards:** Sometimes equipment vendors just want to make your life a little bit more difficult — or they want to make it easier, but more expensive — so they don't use a standard PC, PCI, Mini PCI, or what have you card for their wireless adapters. Instead, they create a custom form factor themselves. A prime example here (may Steve Jobs strike us down if we're lying) is Apple computer. The Apple AirPort and AirPort Extreme cards are the company's 802.11b and 802.11g network adapters (respectively), which are basically kinda like PCI cards, but then again, they're not. Neither fish nor fowl (nor pork nor beef!), these cards are *proprietary:* You buy them only from the vendor and they fit only in the vendor's products. Luckily, everything else about them is standardized, and they communicate with wireless network infrastructures from any vendor.

✔ **Embedded wireless:** Finally, we get down to the easiest form of wireless adapters: Those that have been designed-in, factory installed, and *embedded* into wireless devices. If you're buying a new PC, a new handheld, a new network media adapter (see Chapter 13), a new, well, whatever, it's probably got wireless already built in. Embedded wireless systems often use a Mini PCI slot built into the motherboard of the device, but, increasingly, wireless is being built right in at the chip level, as companies such as Intel look to include Wi-Fi, Bluetooth, and even WiMax (see Chapter 4 for more on this technology) right into their chipsets. The great thing about embedded wireless is that you don't have to mess with anything. Turn on the device, configure the network access, and you're done!

Routers and gateways

If you want to connect your wireless network to the WAN (wide area network, or to the Internet, in other words), you need some sort of device to act as the traffic cop between your Internet connection and your wireless network (and any other networks you might have in your home — like a wired Ethernet network).

These devices are known as *routers* or *Internet gateways.*

You may find these routers or gateways sold as *DSL routers* or *cable routers,* or even *DSL/cable routers,* simply because most users hook them up to a DSL or cable modem connection.

In many cases, you buy a single device that incorporates both the access point we discussed earlier and the router we're discussing here. You often hear the term *access point* used generically to include access points that are actually routers or gateways.

Depending on who you ask (meaning there's a lot of fuzziness throughout the market), the term *gateway* is often used to refer to a router that has the broadband modem (for cable or DSL Internet) built right in. This isn't always the case, and we're not going to be sticklers about that point either way. Just make sure you verify that a "gateway" you are buying really has the built-in modem if you're planning to use it that way.

A router (we use that terminology throughout the course of *WNH&M For Dummies* to describe both routers and gateways*)* performs two primary functions:

✔ Translates between your home's *public* IP address (we discuss this in detail in Chapter 4 — it's the IP address that identifies your network to the rest of the computers and networks on the Internet) and all of the *private* IP addresses within your wireless network.

✔ Acts as a traffic cop within your home, directing data between the computers and devices connected to your home's networks, and also sending data to and from the Internet connection when required.

The first of these two functions — the translation — is known as *Network Address Translation,* or NAT. In fact, many home or small office routers are called *NAT routers* to distinguish them from the so-called "big iron" routers used by large enterprises, phone and cable companies, and Internet service providers.

Whenever you shop for a home router or gateway, ensure that it supports NAT as a bare minimum. You can pretty much rest assured that any product that calls itself a gateway or router does indeed support NAT. However, you'll also want to look for other features, including some of the following:

✔ **Firewall:** By its very nature, a NAT router hides internal IP addresses from the external public Internet, and in doing so, makes it difficult for rogue programs (such as viruses, Trojans, and worms) to communicate to and from your wirelessly-networked PCs to the Internet, and for crackers to sneak onto your network to do nefarious things. All routers claim to provide *firewall* functionality (a firewall does, essentially, just what we described in the previous sentence), but to help keep things exceptionally secure, you might consider a *SPI* (stateful packet inspection) firewall. A SPI firewall looks at every packet of data flowing through the router and applies firewall rules (logical tests that your firewall applies to different types of traffic) to them — a SPI firewall keeps you more secure than just plain NAT.

NAT really does make you *very* safe. SPI just adds some additional protection for some very specialized kinds of attacks. (These attacks aren't all that likely — but never say never. . . .) Don't freak out if your router doesn't have SPI, but don't avoid the feature either.

✔ **Port forwarding and routing:** Many routers let you configure rules for specific ports. In this context, *ports* are application-specific destinations within an IP address — for example, HTTP or World Wide Web traffic travels across port 80. Normally, a NAT router sends incoming traffic to the computer that specifically requested it, so if the Macintosh on IP address 192.168.0.101 requests a Web page, the router sends the Web page HTML code directly to that computer's IP address — incoming traffic that hasn't been "requested" is discarded. With port forwarding, the router sends all incoming traffic of a certain type to a particular computer based on the traffic's port or application type, rather than its destination IP address. For example, all VoIP calls on a specific port number are routed to the VoIP phone, and all Xbox Live gaming traffic is routed to the Xbox. You might see this sometimes in an IP address: 192.168.0.101:92. In this example, 92 (separated from the rest of the IP address with a colon) is the destination port associated with that IP address. Why bother to have port forwarding, you might ask? Port forwarding basically "fixes" applications that get "broken" by NAT routers. Port forwarding enables Internet traffic to find its way through your NAT so that it can get to the software or hardware endpoint it is looking for.

Firewalls use the same concept of ports, but instead of forwarding, they *filter* or block specific ports to keep traffic off of your network. Sometimes you need to *open* or *allow* ports on your router's firewall to enable certain applications to function correctly — we talk about this in a bunch of different places throughout the book, whenever the need to open ports arises!

Another related concept is the *DMZ* or demilitarized zone, which routes all packets bound for a certain port directly to a specific computer without connecting that computer to the rest of the devices on your network. Port forwarding creates a sort of "mini" DMZ for a specific application. Your computer is in a DMZ for that application (like port 80, if you have a Web server), but otherwise a normal part of the rest of your network.

✔ **Gaming support:** Some routers have specialized port forwarding and firewall settings designed to support certain video games right out of the box, without any need to get too fancy with firewall settings and port configuration.

✔ **UPnP support:** The easiest of all routers to set up, with regards to games and other port forwarding and firewall issues, are those that use a system called *UPnP* (Universal Plug'n'Play). The UPnP system is designed for computers, routers, gaming consoles, and related devices, as well as applications such as game software and VoIP software. It allows them all to "talk" to each other without your intervention, determining the right settings and configurations they require to play nicely with each other. If your router supports UPnP, for instance, it can automatically set up port forwarding and configure your firewall. You just sit back and enjoy a nice cold one!

✔ **QoS support:** A few routers, like D-Link's DGL-4300 Gaming Router (games.dlink.com), examine the data packets on your network not only for firewall and port forwarding purposes, but also for the type of application. On certain applications (in this case, gaming), the router applies *QoS* (Quality of Service) prioritization to the packets, making sure that they are sent across the network before any others. No longer will your kid's homework project download interfere with your ability to blow people away in your favorite FPS (first-person shooter) game! Gotta have priorities in life, no?

In the near future, we expect that you'll see more and more QoS-enabled routers as broadband service providers try to extend their own network QoS into your home and across your local area network!

✔ **Switch ports:** Most home routers and gateways include a few wired Ethernet ports for connecting devices that aren't wirelessly enabled. If you've got a separate router and access point, you actually use these wired ports to connect your router to the access point. Look for a router with a wired *switch* (not *hub*) with a speed of at least 100 Mbps (100BaseT), and perhaps even Gigabit Ethernet (1000BaseT) speed for the best performance for your old-fashioned wired gear.

We're talking about physical ports (or jacks) on your router here, not the IP ports we discussed a few bullet points earlier. We didn't decide to use the same term for software and hardware applications; we just write about it!

✔ **Print server:** You may have a big honking networked laser printer at your disposal at work, but at home, most of us get by with compact and inexpensive USB inkjet printers. These printers do a great job of printing documents and even photos, but they typically end up connected to only a single computer at a time. With the right router, however, you can utilize a *print server* that accepts print jobs from any computer on your network; this means they don't have to be directly wired to the printer to use it. You don't need to have your print server built in to your router either. For example, Pat has his printer hidden in a little cubby far from the main router/broadband modem/primary access point. In an instance like this, you can buy a wireless print server device that connects to your network and can go anywhere in your house.

✔ **POE:** Some routers are equipped with a system called *POE* (Power over Ethernet) that can be really handy when building a wireless network. POE lets you connect a remote access point with only a network cable (a *CAT-5e* or *CAT-6* cable, to use the official terminology), and no power cable. (The power travels over the network cable because the device does not require much energy to run.) POE is great when you're sticking an access point somewhere far from electricity: It's a heck of a lot easier to run a network cable yourself than it is to wire in an new electrical outlet! All you need on the far end is a POE-enabled access point.

✔ **Attached storage:** In Chapter 13, we talk about networked servers designed specifically for holding media files (music and video). You may also want to have a big ol' hard drive attached to your network somewhere for general file storage. A new trend in routers is a bit of built-in software combined with a USB port, which allows you to add your own USB hard drive (or even a USB *flash* or keychain memory card) to your network — for access from any location in your wireless coverage area. An example of this is the NETGEAR's 108 Mbps Storage Router (`www.netgear.com/products/details/WGT634U.php`).

✔ **Configuration and management:** Finally, you should always take a look at how a router can be configured and managed. Some routers require you to install a management program on your computer, but most allow you to simply enter an IP address in your favorite Web browser to review all of your settings (browser-based management is a must if you've got a mixture of Mac, Linux, and Windows computers on your network). Also, look for a router that allows secure remote access for management. In Chapter 6, we talk about some software that monitors your wireless network and also takes care of router management and monitoring.

We've introduced a lot of router concepts here that you'll see again and again throughout *WNH&M For Dummies.* In certain cases, we've mentioned specific chapters where you can skip ahead to see more, but for some of these concepts, we discuss them so often, in so many chapters, that we would almost have to create a complete index to give you all the cross references. So prepare to see some of these concepts pop back up throughout the book!

Network bridges

In this chapter, we've discussed the three most common elements of a wireless network infrastructure: the *access points,* which connect wireless devices together (and back to the "wired" parts of your network); the *network adapters,* which provide radio communications capabilities to the devices themselves; and the *router,* which moves data between your private wireless network and public networks like the Internet.

One other element of network infrastructure that we've not touched on much so far is worth discussing: network *bridges,* which — yes, we love using a word in its own definition, despite what we learned in English class — form a bridge between two different sections of networks.

The big difference between a bridge and a router is that a bridge is not "aware" of what's going on with IP addresses — it doesn't look at the IP addresses of traffic in a network to make IP routing decisions. That kind of decision-making is performed by a router. The bridge handles its "traffic cop" role at a lower level (on the MAC layer). What's important to remember is that a bridge and a router play different roles. You need a bridge to go between, for example, a wired and wireless network; you need a router to connect between the public IP network (your Internet connection) and your private home network.

A bridge may do its bridging between different kinds of network media — in fact, an access point, in its purest form (without a router), bridges between wired and wireless networks. A bridge may also bridge between two separate segments of the same type of network (for example, between the wireless network in your home and the separate wireless network in your guest house/garage/studio/pool cabana/what have you).

In a simple wireless network, the only bridge is the access point itself. As your wireless network gets more complex and expands, however, you may find a need to — sorry, we can't help ourselves — build bridges!

Wireless bridges usually work in one of the following modes:

- ✔ **Point-to-point:** In this mode, two bridges "talk" to each other and connect two segments of a network. In this mode, the bridges don't communicate with any nearby wireless clients (like PCs), so this mode is usually used to span across areas connecting two wired networks (such as the home-to-guest-home example we used earlier). You can still connect another access point to the wired location in a remote location if you need wireless connectivity there.

- ✔ **Point-to-multipoint:** In this mode, several wireless bridges talk to each other (one bridge is boss, controlling all the communications). Like point-to-point mode, in this type of connection, the bridges are used only for the interbridge communications, and won't talk to nearby wireless clients. This kind of network bridging mode isn't very common in home or small office networks.

- ✔ **Wireless repeater:** In this mode, a remote wireless bridge connects back to the other segment of the network, and *also* talks to local wireless clients. This is a very common bridging scenario found in home networks. The big advantage of using a repeater is economic — you have to buy less wireless gear. The disadvantage is performance — because you are effectively sending data twice over the same airwaves and frequencies (once from the original base station or bridge, and again from the repeater), your data throughput is reduced in half.

The repeater mode uses a wireless protocol called *WDS* or Wireless Distribution System.

When you're looking to set up a bridged wireless network, you usually have a choice of buying specialized bridging gear or simply using access points that can be configured in one or another bridging modes. You can even, in many cases, use some of the access points and routers that you've already got in place — at a minimum, you should be able to use the "primary" access point that you've got built in to your router or connected directly to your stand-alone router via Ethernet cables for one end of your bridge.

Most of the "dedicated" wireless bridge devices on the market are designed for specialized uses in enterprise networks for large businesses — and they are pretty much overkill for even a very sophisticated home wireless network. You can get everything you need and save money by skipping over these bridges and just buying access points that have a bridging "mode" instead.

Now that we've said that, let's contradict ourselves by saying this: For very specific purposes (like connecting an Xbox or PS2 to your wireless network), an inexpensive "dedicated" wireless-to-Ethernet bridge (like the D-Link DWL-810 shown in Figure 3-6) is a great way to go, simply because they are compact, cheap, and take almost no effort to set up and configure.

Figure 3-6:
Bridging
Ethernet
and Wi-Fi on
the cheap
with a
D-Link
DWL-810.

Chapter 4

Wi-Fi and Broadband Connections

· ·

In This Chapter

▶ Deciding on broadband

▶ Tapping into phone lines with DSL

▶ Getting into cable broadband

▶ Going wireless all the way

· ·

*W*ireless networks are a great way of sharing content and connecting devices within the home — for getting music from your file server to your stereo, for example, or for accessing work files on your home office PC using a laptop on the back patio. But for most of us, the fundamental "killer app" for wireless networks is sharing a broadband connection throughout the home.

In this chapter, we give you a quick overview of the broadband (high speed) Internet access options available to most people. We can't guarantee that all of these options are available to you, but chances are, you'll have your choice of at least a couple.

Even if you already have a broadband connection, you should at least skim this chapter because new options and packages are coming out all the time. If you are sitting behind a five-year-old cable or DSL modem, you might be surprised at the alternatives that are on the market, even if your broadband connection is fine today. New bundling packages from the telephone and cable industries make it probable that you might be able to get a better deal by doing a little research. But if you're a supercharged computer user and you know all about broadband, you can proceed directly to the next chapter and collect $200 for passing Go.

Extending Broadband into the Home

Before we get into the specific who, what, and where of broadband services, we thought we'd kick off with a brief discussion of "why." Although broadband now finds its way into somewhere between a quarter and a third of

American homes (the exact number depends upon who you ask and how they define broadband), a fairly significant number of *potential* broadband users just haven't taken the plunge yet.

Excepting the five percent or so who truly can't get access, there are really only three reasons why an Internet user (especially an Internet user with a wireless network) wouldn't have broadband yet:

- **They don't know they can get broadband:** We help solve that issue in this chapter with some good online tools for finding service.

- **They don't think they can afford it:** We tell you how broadband is much more affordable than you ever imagined.

- **They don't think they need it:** We explain the benefits of broadband and the almost absolute *necessity* of broadband for a wireless network.

So let's take these issues on one at a time, shall we?

Availability

Not that long ago, high-speed Internet services were hard to find in all but a few select neighborhoods. Luckily, that is no longer true in most places. Between cable modem providers and telephone companies (with DSL high-speed Internet), most states have broadband available to 80 percent or more of their households. Add in wireless broadband — especially satellite broadband, which essentially covers the "lower 48" in their entirety — and more than 90 percent of all homes have broadband available to them.

So how do you figure out what's available to you? Here are a couple of resources on the Web:

- **Broadband Reports:** The folks at Broadband Reports have taken their Web publication (originally called *DSL Reports*) from a small site that was mainly focused on the trials and tribulations of getting DSL service installed and have transformed it into a super site for news, reviews, and information about all kinds of broadband. It's truly a labor of love — and a great resource. Check out their Find Service function, which lets you track down any number of DSL providers in your area, as well as consumer reviews, speed tests, and more. Find it at `www.broadbandreports.com`.

- **CNET:** CNET is one of the most venerable and reliable Internet news sites out there — with coverage of a huge variety of service, networking, and computer news. CNET is perhaps best known for its comparison reviews and Editor's Choice awards, and their broadband coverage is no exception. You can use CNET to find their recommendations on broadband services, and then use their service finder to locate the cable or DSL providers who service your home. Find it at `www.cnet.com`.

✔ **DSL Prime:** You can find out what any DSL provider worldwide is working on at DSL Prime, a true insider's resource for reading about the latest happenings in DSL. This is considered a must-read by those in the DSL industry, and if you like reading about what is going to happen soon in your territory, here's a good place to start. Visit www.dslprime.com.

✔ **Local service provider Web sites:** You should always also check on the Web sites of your local telephone company and cable company. At the very least, you'll probably find a service area map that explains exactly where broadband is and is not available. In most cases, you can enter your phone number or address into a form on the Web page to find out exactly what you can and can't receive.

These are just a few of the sites you can use for tracking down broadband services — if you visit our book's companion Web site at www.digital dummies.com, you'll find links to even more!

Affordability

Let's get to the big issue for many people — broadband Internet just plain costs more than dial-up access. Unfortunately, we can't change the laws of economics — this is just plain true. Building a broadband network is more expensive (although not a lot more expensive) than providing low-speed dial-up Internet access over the existing telephony network.

The good news is this: The price differential between broadband and dial-up is decreasing every day as the big investments that broadband providers have made in their networks pay off — allowing them to lower their prices. But you should still expect to pay more for broadband than you do for dial-up: Whereas "full-service" dial-up services like AOL or Earthlink cost $20–$25 a month, broadband services start off at about $10 more a month, and can run over $50 a month for premium super-high-speed services.

You get a lot more for your dollar with broadband — if you were to use a purely economic measure, you'd see that you get ten or more times the speed for only 50 percent more money, which is a good deal in our book. (And hey, this *is* our book!) If you are using a dedicated second phone line for your dial-up modem, just getting broadband in the first place would be cheaper.

If you want to save some money on broadband, it really pays to shop around. Here are some tips:

✔ Generally, DSL is cheaper than cable Internet services — usually $10 or $15 a month cheaper (although in some areas, cable companies are lowering their prices to compete).

✔ Look for promotional pricing — often half off or more for the first six months or a year. This lets you try broadband without breaking the bank.

✔ Look for a broadband provider who gives away the "modem" for the service for free — so you don't have to put any up-front money into the service. Similarly, look for free "self-install" packages — no sense paying them money to "flip a switch" in their office.

✔ Consider a bundled service — most cable and phone companies give you significant discounts if you also buy TV, local, and long distance phone services (or even mobile phone services) from them at the same time. With a bundle like this, you can get your broadband bill down to $30 or so a month — and get discounts on the other service to boot!

So you see, although we can't tell you that broadband is going to be cheaper than dial-up, you can make it only a little bit more expensive. Combine that with the absolute benefits of broadband we're about to discuss in the next section, and we think that we've made a home-run economic case for upgrading!

Who really needs broadband anyway?

We hear this all the time: Yeah, I can get broadband at my house now, and yeah . . . it's not too expensive, and it would be nice to have, but I don't really *need* it, so I'm not going to bother. Usually, these folks don't really use their Internet connection much due to the shortcomings of dial-up, not because they wouldn't appreciate what broadband offers. Now as a couple of guys who have been involved in the broadband world since its early days, this is a discouraging thing to hear — but not so discouraging that we haven't got a snappy comeback. So let us state this up front: If you've got a wireless network in your home, and you can possibly get it and fit it into your budget, you *need* to have broadband. Why? Here are just a few of the reasons:

Will I ever need dial-up again?

You betcha, you will. Here are two important uses for dial-up services:

✔ On the road: As we discuss in detail in Part III of this book, when you are on the road, you can't always rely on broadband or wireless being available. Sometimes you need to dial up a connection to the Internet and brave the slow speeds to check e-mail and surf.

✔ As backup: Many routers have dial-up backup access built into them in case your broadband connection goes down. Again, as you get hooked on always-on, ubiquitous Internet access, you'll always want to be able to get online, even if it is slow access service.

So, when you buy your broadband service, be sure to see if they have complementary (and complimentary) dial-up service!

✔ Dial-up is hard to share. You have to buy extra hardware if you want to easily share a dial-up connection. Only a couple of wireless access points accept dial-up modem connections, and the list gets smaller every year. That makes it much more difficult — although not impossible — to even set up Internet sharing with a dial-up connection. Not only is it difficult to share — but be warned — it may actually cost you more (when you factor in equipment) than just going to broadband.

✔ Broadband is *always on*. You never get a busy signal, and you never have to wait to dial in — and you never get bumped off the line by an incoming call. 'Nuf said.

✔ Broadband is fast enough to support a home network. Dial-up bogs down with *one* user, so imagine four or five.

✔ Broadband supports the applications you'll want to use on a souped-up wireless network. If you want to share photos, download music and movies, and conduct wireless VoIP conferences, you *must have* broadband.

We're not going to spend too much more time convincing you — we suspect that 95 percent of you are already convinced and many probably already have broadband. We hope we've converted the 5 percenters. Read on for more information about specific broadband options and how they might interact with your wireless networks.

What to Look for in Broadband Service

Regardless of the *media* (be it phone lines, airwaves, cable connections or even fiber optic cables), broadband connections all share certain common characteristics and features. As you're choosing a broadband service to connect your wireless network to the Internet (and to broadband service providers for things like music and movies), you should consider some of the following characteristics:

✔ **Dynamic IP addresses:** Most home broadband connections provide users with what is known as a *dynamic IP address* (if you're not familiar with IP addresses, check out the sidebar "IP addresses for me and you" elsewhere in this chapter). The key here is the *dynamic* part — your IP address changes occasionally. Usually, it doesn't change very often, but change it does — so you can't rely on having the same IP address all the time for accessing your home network from remote locations. If you're planning on running servers on your network that you'll frequently access remotely (like FTP, Web, or e-mail servers), you may wish to get a fixed IP address (discussed in the next bullet point).

You can use a *dynamic DNS* service — like the one at www.dyndns.org — to remotely find your dynamic IP addressed network.

✔ **Fixed IP addresses:** In some cases, you can get a broadband connection with a *fixed* IP address — one that never changes, no matter what. This is what you want if your wireless network contains those servers we mentioned previously, or if you want to use certain applications (like some videoconferencing apps) that just work better with a "known" IP address. Expect to pay a bit more to get a fixed IP address.

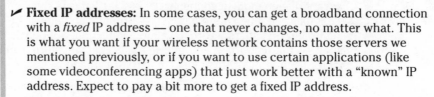

If your preferred provider offers both fixed and dynamic IP addresses, you can always start off with a dynamic address and a dynamic DNS service, and then upgrade later, if needed.

✔ **PPPoE:** Instead of simply providing your network router or gateway with an IP address, some broadband providers get complicated by using a network *protocol* or communications system known as *PPPoE* (or Point to Point Protocol over Ethernet) that requires you to use a special bit of client software and provide a username and password to get your network online. This can be a bit of a pain in the rear end as you need to make sure your router or access point can "talk" PPPoE (check the specifications, it'll be explicitly listed) and then spend time setting things up. PPPoE used to be a big pain to configure and use with home networks, but today almost all routers can be configured to deal with it in just a few moments' time, so it's not something to worry about.

✔ **Upstream and downstream bandwidth:** The big selling point (and marketing focal point) for broadband services is, of course, the speed, or *bandwidth,* of the connections. Most service providers advertise their *downstream* connection speed (the speed of the connection from the Internet to your network) pretty heavily, but do not spend as much time discussing the *upstream* speed (from your network back to the Internet) — mainly because downstream speeds are usually *much, much* higher. Pay attention to both speeds — ask the question if the upstream speed is not listed.

Upstream speeds are really important for things like videoconferencing, VoIP (Voice over Internet Protocol), and, increasingly, for common applications like uploading digital photos. If you can find an affordable broadband service that offers better than the usual 384 or so Kbps, consider it.

✔ **Service Level Agreement (SLA) guarantees:** Most broadband services offered to residential environments (your home, in other words) are what the industry terms "best-effort services" — which is super-secret insider code for "no effort at ensuring service quality." This is beginning to change as residential users — like those who are considering super-charged wireless networks — get more sophisticated. Look for providers who utilize some sort of *Quality of Service* (QoS) system to prioritize traffic on the network, and who then provide you with SLAs — which you may find in the form of guaranteed bandwidth, uptime (lack of network failures, in other words), and the like. Ideally, a provider would refund some of your monthly service fees if there were excessive failures to meet the SLA terms in your service contract.

✔ **Support for services:** This one is a bit more nebulous, but worth investigating if you're going to be doing some more sophisticated stuff with your wireless network — like setting up your own e-mail server, or creating a private Web site on a computer attached to your network (check with your provider to make sure they allow this). Some service providers block out this kind of traffic unless you get a "business-class" (translation: more expensive) account. Check the TOS (terms of service) for your preferred provider, or look on sites like Broadband Reports for other users' experiences.

✔ **Other stuff:** Finally, look at the catchall category we call "other stuff" that might be offered by a service provider — things like multiple e-mail accounts, Web site space, 24-hour customer service, virus protection software, and so on. As providers compete, they tend to throw some of this stuff in as freebies (it usually costs them very little money to provide to you), and some of it is worth your while.

Also keep an eye out for the "other stuff" gotchas — some providers have sneaky terms of service that begin to cut off your service or charge you more if you use your "unlimited" service too much. Yeah, it's a dirty trick, and we recommend you avoid providers who do this — let them earn someone else's business.

As Mike Williams, our oh-so-helpful technical editor, points out, many ISPs offer "extras" that provide genuine value (like spyware filters), but come at a cost; namely, a performance hit for your connection. It's sort of like when you implement a spam filtering system for your e-mail that effectively reduces the amount of spam you receive, but makes your e-mail take an extra five minutes to arrive. Not the end of the world, but always beware the law of unintended consequences.

We're not trying to give you *everything* you need to know when you're picking out a broadband service provider here. First off, we figure you probably know a lot of this — because you're reading *WNH&M For Dummies,* you're probably an advanced user. Also, we just haven't got the space to get into this subject in great detail. Check out *Internet For Dummies,* 9th edition, by John Levine, Margaret Levine Young, and Carol Baroudi (published by Wiley) if you need more details about choosing a service provider.

IP addresses for me and you

The most basic identification system for computers attached to the Internet (or to any *IP*, or Internet Protocol, network) is the *IP address* — basically, your computer's "phone number" on the Internet. Every computer, printer, server, network router, access point, or what-have-you that's attached to the Internet must have an IP address.

IP addresses take the form of a set of four bunches of one- to three-digit numbers — between 0 and 256 — separated by periods. A typical IP address might be something like 66.102.7.147 (which is an IP address for one of Google's Web servers).

When an IP address is hard-coded to a particular device, it's a fixed IP address; dynamic IP addresses are assigned using a system called *Dynamic Host Configuration Protocol,* or DHCP.

Most IP addresses have a corresponding *host name* using (almost) plain English — this is the familiar construct you see when typing in Web addresses (www.google.com) or assigning e-mail server addresses in your e-mail client program (pop-server.san.rr.com, for example). The Internet system that assigns and maintains the database linking IP addresses to host names is called the *DNS* (Domain Name Servers) system.

You'll typically deal with two sets of IP addresses in a wireless network: *public* IP addresses (those IP addresses that are "facing" the Internet — the address your router or access point will use) and *private* addresses (used only within your network — so they can be reused in other people's networks without causing confusion). In Chapter 5, we talk more about this topic, and we explain something called *NAT,* or Network Address Translation, which directs traffic between public and private IP addresses.

Picking a Technology

For the most part, we're pretty agnostic regarding *how* broadband services are delivered — as long as they *are* delivered. We wouldn't care if someone ran a length of barbed wire to our homes, as long as it got us fast Internet access for our wireless networks. (We've actually seen DSL running over barbed wire, as a matter of fact!)

Having said that, there *are* some substantive differences between different Internet technologies — not only in how they are delivered, but also in *what* they deliver.

The following is a general guideline to what's out there, and how these services typically differ from each other.

Don't get too caught up in the generic differences between different technologies. It's entirely possible that in *your* town, what we say for cable applies to DSL and vice versa!

Wither DSL with 802.11?

As we've mentioned throughout this chapter so far, two primary technologies are used to provide broadband network services to homes — DSL and cable. DSL (or *Digital Subscriber Line*) is the telephone company's main entry into the broadband world (although many are moving to fiber optic connections — see the sidebar titled "Fiber comes home" elsewhere in this chapter for more information).

DSL services use a common copper telephone line, combined with some very sophisticated "modems" using digital signal processing (DSP) devices that can cram a lot more data across a phone line than a conventional analog modem can. There actually isn't a single "DSL" technology out there — there's a huge range of DSL variants, each with its own specific characteristics.

These variants (or *line codes*) are named by simply adding a letter to the beginning of the letters DSL (replacing the *x* in *x*DSL). There are many forms of DSL (some defunct, some used for very specialized purposes that you'll never see), including the following common variants:

- ✔ **ADSL:** This is the most common variant of DSL. The "A" stands for asymmetric, which means that the upstream speed is significantly less than the downstream. ADSL is a relatively low-speed solution — maximum speeds reach 8 Mbps downstream, and real-world speeds are well below that — but because it can serve customers over existing telephone wiring up to three miles in length, ADSL is widely deployed throughout the world. ADSL was the first consumer version of DSL on the market.

- ✔ **ADSL2/2+/2++:** These are the newest developments of ADSL, designed to increase both the speed and reach of the older ADSL technology. The equipment for ADSL2/2+/2++ has been developed, is in production, and is slowly being deployed by telephone companies. Under ideal conditions, it can provide speeds downstream of around 20 Mbps, and upstream speeds of a few megabits per second.

- ✔ **SDSL:** *Symmetric* DSL offers equal speeds in both directions and is mainly used for business connections at speeds of up to 1.1 Mbps. The newest variants use a technology called G.shdsl to bump the speeds up over 2 Mbps.

- ✔ **VDSL and VDSL2:** Very high-speed DSL! What a great name. Makes us happy! VDSL is indeed the fastest of the DSL variants and can provide downstream speeds as fast as 50 Mbps — but only at very short distances (a few thousand feet of phone line, at most). VDSL is most typically deployed in areas where fiber optic cables run to the neighborhood, but *not* directly to the home. VDSL2 is the almost (as we write) approved upgrade to VDSL, designed to provide higher speeds at longer distances. We can't wait!

Because the *vast* majority of DSL lines in place everywhere in the world but Japan and Korea are ADSL lines, we discuss that variant of DSL here:

✔ **Speed:** Most DSL services offer downstream speeds between 1 and 3 Mbps, with higher speeds occasionally available for premium pricing. The downstream speed typically ranges from 128 Kbps to 1 Mbps. Most DSL services are slightly slower than similar cable services.

DSL speeds are highly distance-sensitive — the further away your home is from the local phone company office (or the outdoor "remote terminal" where your DSL circuit terminates), the slower your speed is, all other things being equal. The speed you get may not be the speed you think you bought!

✔ **Price:** DSL is (in the U.S. and Canada at least) usually the most inexpensive broadband connection available. Telephone companies got off to a slightly slow start compared to their competitors at the cable companies and are trying to make up ground with lower prices and good bundling deals. You can get a basic DSL line from many telephone companies for about $35 a month, but the price can vary depending upon how long a contract term you agree to and how many other services you purchase from the phone company. This is about $10 a month less than most cable companies charge for their basic service (generally speaking, cable companies choose to offer more speed at a higher price).

✔ **Availability:** Most phone companies have extended their networks enough so that 80 to 90 percent of their customers can get DSL service. The unlucky 10 to 20 percent are typically in rural areas or somehow geographically situated too far from their local phone company's *central office* to get DSL.

✔ **Networkability:** We just made this word up, but we like it. It refers to how amenable your broadband service is to serving a network of computers and devices. DSL is indeed well-suited to supplying a network with an Internet connection. The biggest issue is that many consumer-grade DSL connections require you to use PPPoE to establish a connection, meaning you'll need to make sure your router supports PPPoE. You can find premium DSL connections that eliminate the PPPoE and may offer fixed IP addresses.

If your DSL provider tries to give you a modem with a USB connection, avoid it like the plague. These are almost impossible to incorporate into a wireless network. Make sure your modem has an Ethernet connection (most do, and you can almost always get one if you ask).

When it comes down to actually getting DSL service, the picture gets a little muddy. That's because there are two entities involved in DSL:

  ✔ The DSL access provider who owns and operates the DSL equipment, and who owns or leases the copper phone lines over which the DSL runs.

  ✔ The ISP who uses this DSL equipment and who provides the actual connection to the Internet, as well as services like e-mail.

In many cases, these two entities are simply separate elements of the same company — the local incumbent telephone company. That's how most people get their DSL service, and it can work very well.

You can also get DSL directly from an independent ISP (like EarthLink or Speakeasy — find them at www.earthlink.net and www.speakeasy.net, respectively) and let them deal with the DSL access provider for you. Or you can find an independent DSL access provider (like Covad — www.covad.com), that leases lines from the local phone company and installs its own DSL equipment.

Using the tools we discussed earlier in the chapter (like Broadband Reports), you can find availability, pricing, and service information for any of these types of DSL providers.

Fiber comes home

For a really fast pipe into your wireless network, you can hope to be one of the lucky few to get your broadband connection over fiber optic cables. These connections use light beams to carry Internet traffic (and video and voice signals too!) at speeds potentially *hundreds* of times faster than cable or DSL.

FTTH (or Fiber to the Home) is a service that replaces copper phone lines with glass fiber optic cables that are capable of speeds of up to 1 Gigabit per second (Gbps) — a thousand Mbps! Most FTTH networks use a system called *PON,* or passive optical network, which shares this connection between 16 or even 32 users. That means the actual connection speed to any single user is less than 1 Gbps — but it's still fast

as can be, and can support not just high-speed Internet, but also multiple voice connections and digital TV services.

A lot of small developments, municipalities, and telephone companies throughout the U.S. and Canada are beginning to offer FTTH services. If yours is, well, don't wait on us tell you: Get signed up!

The really big news is that the two largest local telephone companies in the U.S. — Verizon and SBC — have both made commitments to begin deploying FTTH services in their territories. This is a truly big deal for anyone who lives in the Northeast or Southwest (these company's primary service areas), and who has a wireless network that they want to connect to the Internet.

If you're planning on doing some serious Internet stuff with your wireless LAN — like heavy-duty gaming, file sharing, hot spot operation, and so on — check out one of the independent DSL providers or ISPs. We like Covad and Speakeasy (they often work together). They are more likely to give you a fixed IP address and less likely to stop you from doing what you want to do (like run a server) on your network.

Cable moves with wireless

The other popular source of broadband connections comes via cable modem services offered by local cable *MSOs* (or Multiple Systems Operators). These MSOs (your friends at the cable company, in other words) have spent billions upon billions of dollars upgrading their networks to support new generations of services.

Specifically, they have upgraded their networks to something called a two-way *HFC* (Hybrid Fiber Coax) network. This means that cable networks are now designed to carry data in both directions, upstream and down (which is what "two-way" refers to), over a mixture (or hybrid) of fiber optic and coaxial cables. (These are the typical cable TV cables you have coming out of your walls.) With the addition of a cable modem somewhere in your home, you can get your network online via a high-speed cable connection.

The big advantage of this network architecture (for you as a customer) is that it can carry a lot of data across it — more than just plain phone wires, though not as much as an all-fiber network.

- ✔ **Speed:** For most folks (at least for the unlucky majority who haven't yet got FTTH), cable is the fastest broadband connection to the home. Typical cable modem connections offer speeds of 5 Mbps downstream, and somewhere between 128 Kbps and 1 Mbps upstream. If you're willing to pay more for a "business" connection, you can expect to double those speeds. Expect these speeds to increase over time as cable continually uses speed to maintain an advantage over DSL.

- ✔ **Price:** The added speed of cable modem services (compared to DSL) comes at a price — most cable modem services start at about $45 a month. The cable companies have made a conscious decision to not stake out the low price segment of the market, and instead are trying to offer a premium product (higher speeds, mainly) for a bit more money. Business-grade cable modem services cost about twice that amount.

- ✔ **Availability:** If you have cable TV service available at your home, chances are good that you can get cable modem service. According to the NCTA (National Cable & Telecommunications Association, the cable companies' trade group), 88 percent of homes passed by cable can get digital cable services such as cable modem high-speed Internet.

✔ **Networkability:** Most cable modem services offer users an Ethernet interface with a dynamic IP address — you'll typically not need to use PPPoE or any kind of login. With a business class connection, you can upgrade to a fixed IP address and also get support for hosting your own servers on your wireless network (something that many residential cable modem services do not allow).

For many folks, cable modems offer the best combination of price and performance, offering a good bit more speed than DSL for only ten bucks a month more. The DSL providers are not unaware of this situation, however, and are going forward with new technologies (as we described in the "Fiber comes home" sidebar) to catch up with and even push ahead of cable. It promises to be a fun few years as the cable companies and phone companies strive to one-up each other.

Getting the dish out on satellite and wireless

For some folks, particularly those who live "off the grid" — or at least outside of the cities and suburbs — cable modems and DSL simply are not options. Homes may be too far from central offices and cable company "headends," or simply too geographically dispersed to make broadband services profitable for telephone or cable companies. The number of people who fall into this category is shrinking every year, but will probably not get to zero for quite some time. (After all, a few tiny pockets of rural areas still haven't got telephones yet — after more than a hundred years of that service!)

For these folks, the best option is to look to the airwaves to find a wireless broadband source to feed their wireless networks! The most common and widely available wireless broadband service uses satellite dishes — the same basic kinds of dishes used for DIRECTV and Dish Network TV services. In this

UDP, UDP, what's UDP?

Remember the old song that goes, "You don't know what you've got 'til it's gone?" Danny thought of that first when his cable modem provider turned off UDP on his cable modem network. UDP (User Datagram Protocol) is a protocol that runs on your network; lots of programs use this protocol to do things, such as anti-virus software that uses UDP to check for upgrades. However, UDP is also used by some computer viruses to spread themselves, and that's why Danny's ISP turned it off. If you've ever used PING or TRACERT commands at a command prompt in Windows, you've used a UDP-based service. Without UDP, you can't do these services. So ask if UDP traffic is blocked on your intended broadband network. Not having this protocol available is a real pain.

section, we talk about satellite broadband — in the next section, we discuss some wireless options that are a bit closer to earth (using terrestrial antennas instead of satellites).

The folks at DIRECTV have put together a service called DIRECWAY (formerly known as DIRECPC) that can offer *(relatively)* high-speed Internet access over satellite dishes. Here's how DIRECWAY measures up:

- ✔ **Speed:** DIRECWAY service is considerably slower than DSL or cable modem, with a maximum downstream speed of 500 Kbps, and a maximum upstream speed of 50 Kbps. This pales in comparison to cable or DSL, but is considerably better than dial-up for many users. The biggest issue with DIRECWAY isn't the speed, but rather the *latency,* or delay, in the system. The trip up to the satellite and back down takes a long time, even at the speed of light, meaning that VoIP phone calls or online games won't work too well with this system.

- ✔ **Price:** DIRECWAY isn't cheap either — the service runs between $60 and $100 a month, depending on whether you buy the equipment up front (for about $600) or lease it (for the higher monthly fee).

- ✔ **Availability:** Maybe the previous two points didn't make you lean too much in favor of DIRECWAY, but here's the good part — you can get it pretty much anywhere in the continental U.S., Canada, or Puerto Rico. You just need a clear (unobstructed by trees or buildings) view of the southern sky and you're set. Doesn't matter how far you are from town, from your neighbors, and so on. That's a big deal!

- ✔ **Networkability:** Up until recently, DIRECWAY was *not* very network-friendly. Instead of connecting to a router or an access point, you needed to connect the satellite receiver directly to your PC, and only one PC could be connected. The latest versions of the satellite receivers used for DIRECWAY have taken away that limitation. They can be connected to your network and support both Macs and PCs on the network. You are, however, still limited in what you can do on that networked connection, both by bandwidth, and by limitations built into the service that essentially limit the connection to one simultaneous user on the network. For an additional $20 or $30, you can upgrade to the professional plan, which allows two simultaneous users — that helps, but still won't let you do a *lot* on your network. If you want to run servers or do videoconferencing, DIRECWAY is *not* for you.

Now we don't want to sound too down on DIRECWAY. If you live out in the boonies, it's as good a solution as you're going to find. Folks we know who use it say they're glad to have the option. But nobody we know who lives in DSL or cable territory has even considered it as an option — you get less for more money.

Tapping into metro wireless networks

A very limited number of folks have access to something that is very exciting to us (and probably to you, as a wireless network hacker and modder): *metro wireless networks.* These are simply wireless broadband access networks that cover part or all of a metro area — a town, city, or suburb. Some folks even call these networks something like "wireless DSL" to emphasize the true use of these networks — which is providing broadband connections to homes and businesses.

In Part III of the book, we talk about a variety of *mobile* wireless networks that you can tap into. These networks are designed to provide you high-speed network access when you're on the go. The networks we are talking about here are more *fixed* in nature, designed to provide access to your home wireless LAN.

These metro wireless networks differ from the DIRECWAY system we discussed earlier in that they use terrestrial antennas (mounted here on terra firma, or at least on towers and buildings, which touch the ground) and transmit over a limited area, rather than trying to blanket the entire continent from outer space.

Coming soon: WiMax

The incompatible and proprietary wireless technologies being used by wireless ISPs will soon converge onto a new standardized technology called WiMax. WiMax is simply a new set of several wireless technologies that are built around an IEEE standard called 802.16. If you have read Chapter 2 (we bet you did, we know you love reading about standards), you may recall that Wi-Fi is a set of technologies built around the IEEE standard 802.11. WiMax has the same relationship to 802.16 that Wi-Fi does with 802.11 — meaning that the WiMax Forum folks (www.wimaxforum.org) spend their time making sure that different models of WiMax-certified equipment from different vendors all work together seamlessly.

A couple of different variants of WiMax are coming out (just as there are different variants of Wi-Fi). The first WiMax products we expect to see will be used for fixed broadband wireless

access — in other words, for the metro wireless networks we discuss in this chapter. Further on down the road, WiMax will branch out to compete with Wi-Fi and even cellular networks for mobile wireless data applications.

As we write in mid-2005, WiMax is *almost* but not quite a reality. Vendors are shipping gear they call WiMax, but it's "pre-standards" gear that's not necessarily 100 percent fully compliant with WiMax — there's no actual certified WiMax gear available yet. A lot of really big companies are, however, investing a lot of time, brainpower, and money in WiMax (think Intel, for example), so we expect to see real WiMax gear, and a lot of it, hit the streets in 2006 and beyond. When it does, you'll be able to buy a "modem" to connect your wireless LAN to a metro wireless network "off the shelf" and get connected in no time!

Service providers use a variety of technologies to offer metro wireless net-works, ranging from variants of the 802.11 technologies described in Chapter 2 to a range of proprietary (meaning vendor-specific) wireless systems. Most *wireless ISPs* (which is what we call the folks who offer metro wireless broad-band) are using proprietary systems today — which means you can't just buy the wireless "modem" off the shelf at Circuit City, nor can you (most likely) use it with a different wireless ISP.

In the near future, we expect most wireless ISPs will adopt standards-based technologies — specifically a standard called WiMax, described later in this chapter in the sidebar "Coming soon: WiMax."

Broadband wireless has so many different variants that we can't put together a simple "speed, price, availability, networkability" set of criteria for you like we did for cable, DSL, and satellite.

What we can tell you is where to go for more information and to find out what wireless ISPs are available in your area: the site of our buddy Robert Hoskins. It's called Broadband Wireless Exchange (www.bbwexchange.com). Robert's got the best site that we know of for all things metro wireless. The site even offers a tool to drill down to your specific town and discover all of the avail-able broadband wireless options.

Just go to his locator at www.bbwexchange.com/wisps/ (the "wisps" stands for wireless ISPs), and you can search for wireless ISPs in your town. Happy hunting!

Part II
Boosting Performance on Your Wireless Network

The 5th Wave   By Rich Tennant

"We found where the security breach in the WLAN was originating. It was coming in through another rogue robot-vac. This is the third one this month. Must have gotten away from it's owner, like all the rest."

In this part . . .

This is where you'll really get your money's worth from *Wireless Network Hacks & Mods For Dummies*. We focus on taking your wireless network and making it better, faster, and stronger, just like the Bionic Man.

We start off with a discussion of a few of the biggest issues folks face when installing wireless networks: how to make them interoperate with their overall network. We talk about how to configure your routers and make your IP network work properly.

If you want to be able ensure that your network is doing what you want it to do, you need to be able to measure its performance. We tell you how to do that with a chapter on network monitoring.

Then we discuss how you can expand and extend your network by using antennas, signal boosters, repeaters, and more. You'll be able to reach all of the nooks and crannies in your house and even extend beyond it.

Finally, we give you some solid advice on how to keep all of this wireless networking secure from prying eyes.

Chapter 5

Combining Wired and Wireless Networks

*W*ireless networks fit into your home's overall network infrastructure. In some cases, a wireless network may be your *only* network — maybe you're in a studio apartment with a cable modem, a wireless router, two laptops, and nothing more. But as you do more and more with your networks, you find more uses for a whole-home network that includes wired (Ethernet), wireless (Wi-Fi or Bluetooth), and alternative network technologies (like technologies that allow you to send Ethernet data packets across phone lines, electrical power lines, or even over the coaxial cable used for your cable TV system).

All of these things are possible, and even probable. In particular, we suspect that you have some "wired" Ethernet gear on your network. Centralized devices such as media servers, NAS storage boxes, and printers sometimes just make better economic sense if they're connected with wires — you have no reason to spend extra money for wireless capabilities on devices that are going to live their entire lifespan three feet from your network's router.

Although we are wireless enthusiasts to the bitter end, we acknowledge that wired networks are cheaper, faster, and safer than wireless. That's why we are big proponents of building wired network infrastructure when you can, even if you plan on going wireless — if you're building or remodeling a house, take our advice and put in CAT-5e or CAT-6 cabling to enable Ethernet in every room. Trust us: Just do it.

Wired and alternative networks can also come in handy as a means of extending and improving your wireless network's coverage — sometimes the best way to get coverage in that remote room on the third floor is to just install a separate access point in that room, and the easiest way to do that is to run cabling to that location.

But don't despair if you *can't* run cable to remote rooms and build a wired backbone for your network. Some handy Wi-Fi devices like repeaters and bridges leverage the airwaves to extend your network further than it's ever gone before.

In this chapter, we talk about all of the technologies and devices that let you connect different networks together — wired to wireless or even just wireless to wireless. We will also spend some time discussing how to manage the network — how to configure routers and switches, how to ensure that IP addresses work, that devices can "talk" to each other, and even how to separate parts of your network to create "public" and "private" network segments. (This is really handy if you're creating a hot spot, as we discuss in Chapter 12.)

Connecting Your Networks Together

The most common network interconnection you make in your home is the intersection of a wired and wireless network. In fact, this is exactly what your wireless access point (AP) or router does by default — it provides an interconnection between a wired network (typically your broadband Internet connection) and a wireless one (your Wi-Fi network).

When you connect two different segments of a network together, you can use one of two primary pieces of gear:

✔ **A bridge:** A bridge does what its name implies — it creates a bridge or pathway between the two networks (Ethernet and Wi-Fi, for example). A bridge does *not* get involved in looking at the IP addresses and destinations of the packets flowing across it — it simply sends the data on its merry way and handles the translation between the different physical layers (the actual media carrying data).

An AP (as opposed to a wireless router) is a bridge between wired and wireless networks. Many people, however, use the term AP to generically refer to any kind of wireless base station, including wireless routers or gateways.

✔ **A router:** A router enhances the functionality of a bridge by examining the IP routing data attached to each packet and making decisions about how to best send that data on its way. Routers range from $30 commodity devices to million-dollar BFRs (big freaking routers) that sit inside the networks of the largest Internet and telecommunications service providers. In terms of the networks we're discussing, a router is the (relatively) inexpensive device that connects a home or small office network to an Internet connection. The wireless routers that we discuss in Chapter 4, in other words, fill our router bill.

Most wireless routers can be configured to act as either routers or as simple bridge-only APs. Many even include additional functionality that lets them work as wireless repeaters, using a system called WDS, which we discuss in the section titled "Bridging Wireless Networks Together."

Understanding IP networking

Before you can logically configure your networks (meaning, dealing with networking protocols rather than *physically* configuring them by connecting pieces and parts together), you should understand the nature of the TCP/IP protocol that underlies everything you do on a Wi-Fi or Ethernet home network.

After you understand TCP/IP, IP addresses, and, most importantly, a concept called *private subnets,* you are ready to dive into the configuration screens of your router(s) and access point(s) and do some fun stuff with your network.

Understanding TCP/IP

Transmission Control Protocol/Internet Protocol (TCP/IP) is the default protocol for communication on most networks. As the name signifies, this is really two protocols that work in conjunction with each other. For our purposes, we really only need to know that they work together and that it is the most widely-used protocol on the planet. The success of the Internet and networking in general can be directly attributed to TCP/IP's widespread and open nature. To maintain any type of network/computer connectivity, a good understanding of TCP/IP and how it works is essential. Some basic principles about the TCP/IP protocol include

✔ TCP/IP uses logical addressing to organize the network.

✔ IP addresses identify the network and the computers on it. Individual computers on a network are sometimes called hosts or nodes. *Host* is most often used when referring to the machine initiating the packet string to the network, and *node* is used as the default term for all devices or any receiving device.

✔ IP is fully routable and interoperates with almost everything because almost all vendors support TCP/IP. TCP/IP is built into every modern computer, networking device, and networked resources. Any Wi-Fi–enabled or capable device supports TCP/IP.

Every router and wireless gear vendor has their own system for configuring things like IP addresses and DHCP (which we explain shortly). Almost always, this configuration is performed by accessing a Web configuration page within the device. We can't tell you exactly how to do this on your gear, or even exactly what a particular setting is called on your router. We talk in general terms, using the common industry parlance. Keep in mind that the names of your specific settings may differ a bit — but through generous use of your user manual and help system, when required, you should be able to follow right along.

TCP/IP networking has four critical components, which are the basis of all communication and end-user interaction on a network:

- ✔ The *IP address* uniquely identifies each host on a network. The IP address also provides the logical networking structure used for routing.

- ✔ The *subnet mask* is used primary by routers to determine the originating network subnet of each packet so the correct routing of the packet can be established.

- ✔ The *default gateway* handles the routing of packets going to another network.

- ✔ A *Domain Name Servers server* (DNS server) is used to map the hierarchal host names to IP address so packets can be correctly addressed and routed.

TCP/IP addresses

An IPv4 address is composed of four bytes, each of which has 8 bits and is called an octet. An example address is 140.88.76.21.

The decimal value of a byte can range from 0 to 255, which is the range of the values an octet can represent. Each octet is separated with a period and, depending upon the subnet mask used, you can break an IP address into a network and a host ID.

The subnet mask

The subnet mask is required for all IP configurations. Unlike the IP address, the mask address ranges from the largest number first. A subnet mask is often composed of either values of 255 or 0, although other values such as 24, 36, 92, 240, or 224 can be used. An example is 255.255.255.0.

Its appearance is different than the IP address and other parameters because it really isn't an address. Instead, it's a way to interpret IP addresses. Technically, a subnet mask defines bits that are used to compare the local IP address with the address of a node the local host wants to communicate with. The purpose of this comparison is to determine whether the other host is on the same local network.

Gateway

The default gateway specifies the address of the router connected to the local network. This router provides a path for packets destined for other networks. Packets destined for hosts on the local network can be sent directly to the host through the local network switch. Packets for remote hosts have the remote address included, but are sent directly to the router so it can determine the proper path to deliver them.

DNS

The DNS address specifies the IP address of the DNS server. The DNS server has a database that indexes computer names and IP addresses. When a user specifies a computer name, such as a Web site in a browser like `www.digital dummies.com`, DNS automatically resolves that name to an IP address so that communications can continue.

Private subnets

Three IP network address ranges are reserved for private networks. The addresses are 10.0.0.0/8, 172.16.0.0/12, and 192.168.0.0/16. These addresses can be used by anyone setting up internal IP networks, such as a lab or home LAN behind a Network Address Translation (NAT) device, proxy server, or a router that provides NAT. Using these devices is always safe because routers on the Internet never forward packets coming from these addresses. This also means that these addresses cannot be used to access the Internet without some routable address attached to one of the devices listed above.

The 192.168.x.x address is by far the most common. As you spend more time playing around with home networking gear, you will find this reserved range of class C addresses used as the default for most home networking equipment.

Figure 5-1 shows a private subnet in action.

Subnetting an IP network can be done for a variety of reasons, including organization, use of different physical media (such as Ethernet, FDDI, WAN connection — like DSL or cable — and so on), preservation of address space, and security. The most common reason, from an ISP's perspective, is to control network traffic. From a corporation's perspective, the most common reason is to preserve address space.

In the end, it doesn't matter *why* your network has to be subnetted, just that it does.

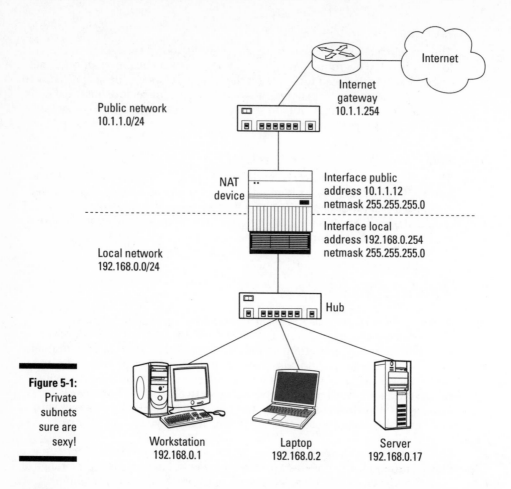

Internet

Internet
gateway
10.1.1.254

Public network
10.1.1.0/24

NAT
device

Interface public
address 10.1.1.12
netmask 255.255.255.0

Interface local
address 192.168.0.254
netmask 255.255.255.0

Local network
192.168.0.0/24

Hub

Figure 5-1:
Private
subnets
sure are
sexy!

Workstation
192.168.0.1

Laptop
192.168.0.2

Server
192.168.0.17

Someday in the not-so-distant future, ISPs will move from today's version of IP (IPv4) to a new version called IPv6. IPv6 supports more IP addresses than today's system does — orders-of-magnitude more — so that every network-able device in the world (even if every person had thousands of such devices) can have a unique IP address. When this happens (and it will be years from now when it does), NAT will be unnecessary — all of the devices on your home network will be full peers on the Internet.

One advantage of NAT is that it provides a bit of firewall-like protection. Because computers out on the Internet cannot directly connect to your 192.168.*xxx.xxx* IP-addressed devices, hacking your networked equipment is a bit harder for the people using those computers. The NAT router is a bit picky about which traffic it lets through the Internet connection and onto your network, so that helps reduce hacking. Considering a router that goes beyond just NAT and also includes an *SPI* (stateful packet inspection) firewall is still sensible, however: It actually digs into the data packets hitting your Internet connection to help filter out the bad guys doing bad things.

A firewall, whether it comes just from NAT or from an SPI firewall in a router (or even from firewall software on your PC or Mac) doesn't take care of the wireless-specific security that we talk about in Chapter 8 (and which is so vitally important). You need to both take care of securing your network from Internet-based attacks (with a firewall) and also secure it from over-the-air threats on the wireless connection.

Understanding Your Home Router

When you connect your wireless network to the Internet via a broadband connection, you are using the NAT functionality in your router (whether it's a stand-alone wired router, or a router built into a wireless broadband router product) to create a private network in your home.

In a NAT environment, you configure your network based upon two separate IP address spaces:

- **Your public IP address:** You've typically got only one of these assigned to your public-facing router by your Internet service provider (ISP).
- **Your private IP addresses:** These IP addresses are used within your private subnet.

Your public IP address is (in almost all cases) uniquely yours — no one else on the entire Internet should have the same public IP address that you do.

Managing your IP addresses

The first decision you need to make when dealing with IP addresses in your wireless network is whether you want to let your router take care of everything or manually assign the addresses yourself.

Most people just let the router handle the task — using a system called *Dynamic Host Configuration Protocol,* or DHCP, which is built in to all of the major operating systems and supported by just about every stand-alone Wi-Fi device we know of. The default state of just about any router we've laid our hands on in the past five years has had DHCP turned on, with the router automatically handling IP addresses.

This is a good setting for many folks — it's pretty much foolproof and it works right out of the box more than nine times out of ten. But in some cases, you might want to mess with the status quo. Some instances include

✔ You may have a device connected to your wireless network that needs a fixed IP address on the network to work properly. Some of the wireless gadgets discussed in Chapter 16 fit this rule.

✔ You may be doing a lot of file sharing or other computer-to-computer networking within your LAN and want to make permanent bookmarks or shortcuts to your shares on your desktop (or somewhere on your computer). This is a lot easier to do when you know that those shares aren't going to change IP addresses all the time.

If you're using just Windows or OS X, you can pretty much rely upon the file share *names* used by those operating systems (like the NetBIOS names used in Windows), which remain constant even when IP addresses change. But if you're mixing and matching other devices (like Linux-based NAS storage devices), it sometimes pays dividends to have fixed IP addresses that you can use.

✔ You may have multiple segments on your network that need to be configured manually. Perhaps you have more than one AP and you want to configure your network to allow network resource access from all wireless clients — or, conversely, you want to set up your network so that clients attached to some APs have *no* access to your networked resources.

The following scenarios provide some advice on how you may want to "mess with" your own IP addressing schemes on your routers and APs.

Cascading APs from a central router

Cascading APs from a central router works well if you have a really big home or office or a lot of users. In this scenario, you need, for reasons of coverage or capacity, to have multiple access points on your network — and you want them all to be on the same subnet.

Why would you want these wireless APs on the same subnet? Simply because you want to be able to do all of those fun (and common) networking things between and among the devices connected to the networks. For example, say you have two APs. Let's call them Opie and Cherry (not that either of your authors would name his AP ESSIDs after his dogs). You want a computer on Opie to be able to access network resources (like a printer server) connected to Cherry — the networks would have to be on the same subnet to do this.

To set up this kind of a network, you'd need to have a single router providing connectivity to the Internet connection, handling NAT and handing out IP addresses to client devices (via DHCP or manual configuration). How you make such a connection physically depends upon what kind of gear you've got on your network.

If you've got a wireless broadband router (that is, one of your APs is also your router), you would simply connect the second (and third, and so on) APs to one of the wired switch ports on your broadband router. If you are using a separate wired router with a built-in Ethernet switch, you would connect both APs to ports on that switch.

If you've got a really big network in your home that would exhaust the four or eight ports on most home routers, you'll probably have a router and a separate multiport (16 or more) Ethernet switch. (Danny's network is like this, with his 12 computers and countless other devices.) In this case, you can connect the APs to ports on this big switch.

Regardless of the physical layout (which varies depending on your unique situation), the logical layout is the same. The steps below explain (in general terms) how to set up a network of multiple APs, all controlled from a centralized router.

1. **Set up your main router to provide IP addresses to devices on your network.**

   If you're going to use DHCP for this (and you may want to), turn DHCP on. To do so, look for a setting called something like LAN DHCP Server or Distribute IP Addresses Automatically and select it.

   Your main router may be one of your wireless APs if you don't have a separate router. (Most people don't have a separate router!) If you don't, make sure DHCP is enabled in whichever wireless AP is connected directly to your Internet connection.

2. **Go into the configuration page or program for your other APs (or all of your APs, if you have a separate router) and turn off the setting that enables DHCP.**

   When turning this off, you may see text indicating that you are configuring the AP to work in "bridge" mode, or something along those lines.

3. **Restart your APs (use the configuration software or simply power them down and back up manually).**

In this scenario, all of your networked devices communicate through the AP with which they are associated (you control that with your device's drivers and operating system) and connect back to your router. All devices are on the same subnet.

One thing to keep in mind is that you may want to change the channels on each of the APs to separate nonblocking channels before you change them into bridge mode. If one AP is too close to another, they can interfere with each other and slow down the performance of your wireless network.

Separating your networks

Sometimes you want to make your network segments *not* talk to each other. Our favorite example of this is when you've set up one wireless (or wireless and wired) network for your own private use (with your personal PCs, file servers, and the like on that network) and another for public use.

Perhaps you want to set up an open "hot spot" AP (see Chapter 12 for more on this). Or maybe you want to create an AP in the lobby of your office to provide access to your visitors. You want users on this AP to be able to access your Internet connection, but not to get into your "private" LAN.

In such a scenario, you should configure your private router to be the farthest device from your Internet connection. This may require you to get another router if you need wired ports as well as wireless ones. Your shared network will be connected directly to your Internet connection and your private network will connect to the shared network, ideally through a cable to the AP at the Internet connection.

Take note of the IP address range used by the private router. As we've said several times, it will be something like 192.168.1.*xxx* (where *xxx* is a range from 0 to 150). You can find this setting somewhere on that screen where you enable DHCP and router functions, or turn them off to turn your AP into a non-routing AP-only bridging device.

For your "public" network AP, configure the AP so that its router functionality *is* turned on and so that the AP's DHCP server is active. Look at the IP address range for *this* network now. Make sure that it's different than the range being used by the private router (and your private network). If, for example, the private network is 192.168.1.*xxx*, set this network to be 192.168.0.*xxx*. Figure 5-2 shows a representation of such a network.

This keeps your networks separate — because private addresses are not *routable via the Internet.* That same simple logic is built in to most consumer APs so that a reserved IP range won't route to another reserved IP range inside of itself. This effectively means users on the public network can't connect directly to devices on the private network. At the same time, the NAT router within your secondary AP continues to allow devices connected to your public network to get access to your Internet connection and to get online.

If you really want to keep the public and private networks separate and secure from each other, you may want to establish some firewall protection between the two segments of your network. That's what the public/private gateway APs we discuss in Chapter 12 are all about — they have a built-in, preconfigured firewall that blocks unwanted segment-to-segment traffic. You can also use the firewall built into your router or even take a ready-for-retirement older PC and install it between your public and private APs and use some free firewall software on it to create this public/private blockade. See www.smoothwall.org for some free software that's easy to configure and will turn just about any old PC into a super powerful firewall.

This approach lets you access anything on that public network but it won't keep users on that public network from accessing *each other's* PCs if they have enabled file or printer sharing and have not otherwise locked down their own systems.

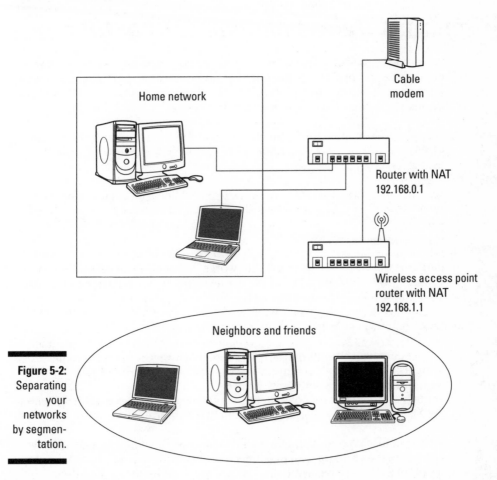

Figure 5-2:
Separating
your
networks
by segmen-
tation.

Here are a couple of things to keep in mind: You must make sure that your private network is inside of your public one to prevent the public from entering your network. It's easy to make the mistake and reverse this leaving your private network wide open to your customers, or friends using your publicly accessible network. Also, this approach won't really keep things very safe if you don't secure that private wireless network to keep folks from associating with your private APs. As we discuss in Chapter 8, we highly recommend that you set up and use WPA (preferably WPA-Enterprise) to keep that network secure.

Bridging Wireless Networks Together

Sometimes you want to establish a multi-access point wireless network in your home or office, but you don't have Ethernet cabling running to the locations where you want to add the extra AP. After all, you may be using wireless because you don't have wires in place already.

One way to overcome this problem is to use a system built into some brands of wireless APs and wireless routers that is known as Wireless Distribution System (WDS).

WDS basically creates a *mesh* network by providing a mechanism for access points to "talk" to each other as well as sending data to devices associated with them.

WDS *is* based on some standardized 802.11 protocols, but there is no standardized way of implementing it that works *across* different AP and router vendors. So if you have a D-Link AP in one location and you want to create a WDS link to a ZyXEL router in another location (just to pick two brands at random), you probably won't be able to get it to work. You have your best luck when you use equipment from the same manufacturer.

Some equipment that supports WDS does *not* support advanced security systems like WPA or WPA-Enterprise on a WDS network — only WEP. Think long and hard about your choice to use WDS in these cases — WEP is secure enough to keep your friends out, but should be considered essentially insecure if you've got anything that's seriously worth protecting on your network.

When you use WDS as a repeater system, as described below, it effectively *halves* the data rate for clients connected to your APs. That's because every bit of data needs to be sent twice (data is received by the AP and then retransmitted).

To configure WDS, you need to modify some settings on each AP within the network. Your exact steps (and the verbiage used) will vary from vendor to vendor. Generally, you'll see some settings like the following:

- **Main WDS station:** One of your WDS stations is the *main* base station for the WDS network. This AP is connected directly to your Internet connection, or connected to your router via a wired connection. The main station is the bridge to your Internet connection that all wireless traffic eventually flows through.

- **Repeater WDS stations:** In a simple, two-AP WDS network, the *other* "unwired" AP is a repeater. The repeater receives data from the main base station and relays the data to the wireless clients associated to the repeater station (and vice versa for data coming *from* the clients). If you have more than two APs, remote APs may be repeaters, or they may be *relays* that provide an intermediate stopping point for data if the repeater is too far away from the main station to communicate.

When you configure your main or base WDS station, take note of the channel you're set to and the ESSID or network name of your network. If your AP has any kind of channel auto configuration function that changes channels based on network conditions, be sure to disable this feature. If your main WDS station is also your network's router, make sure it's set up to distribute IP addresses in the network.

Write down or otherwise take note of the MAC addresses of all of your WDS stations — many configuration software systems require you to know these addresses to make the configuration settings work. Write down the *wireless* MAC address (it's often on a sticker) and not the Ethernet MAC address.

Turn on the WDS functionality in your main station (it's often labeled WDS, or may say something like Enable This Base Station As a WDS Main Base Station — that's the wording Apple uses for their AirPort Extreme products). When you turn on this functionality, the configuration software may ask you to identify the remote repeater(s). Have the MAC addresses of those repeaters handy in case you need them.

Depending upon how your software works, you may have to separately access the configuration software on the remote repeater APs to turn on WDS. Here are a few things to remember:

- You need to assign any other WDS stations to the *same* channel that your main base station is using. This is counterintuitive to many folks who have had the 802.11b/g "use channels 1, 6, and 11 and keep your APs on different channels" mantra driven into their heads for a long time!

✔ You set the ESSID of the remote location(s) using either a unique name or by using the *same* ESSID as you use for your main base station. (Whoa, our heads just exploded!) Using the same ESSID (a "roaming" network) is pretty cool. You associate with one AP one time and then your PC or Mac can associate with any AP on your WDS network without you having to do anything — it's more seamless this way. But remember, you don't *have* to do this — you can give each AP a unique ESSID and just configure your computer to associate with them according to your preference.

✔ Make sure you turn off any routing or DHCP functionality in the remote repeater stations. All of this functionality should be performed in the main base station or the network's main router.

We're discussing WDS in a repeater mode where the remote APs provide wireless access to PCs and other wireless clients. As we discuss in Chapter 3 (where we first bring up the concept of WDS), there can be "bridge" configurations of WDS where the APs talk only to each other and not to wireless clients. You can use this mode when you want to connect, for example, the wired networks in two buildings together without wires.

If you have Linksys wireless routers (or one of a few other supported brands), you can check out the Sveasoft firmware (www.sveasoft.com) discussed in Chapter 16. This software replaces your AP's existing software load and provides mechanisms for creating mesh networks that work in a way similar to WDS. You can get mesh without having to spend extra money on an AP that supports WDS.

If you need to create a big mesh network with multiple APs to cover some serious ground, check out the gear sold by Tropos Networks (www.tropos.com). Their equipment includes its own specialized operating system that controls the flow of traffic between and among access points — providing a specialized "mesh" traffic management system. These systems are used by many cities and municipalities when they create regional "hot zones" serving dozens of square miles of territory.

Bridging Other Networks to Your Wireless LAN

Your wireless LAN is your home's backbone over which a lot of traffic can pass, but it's likely not the only network in your house. You may have other wired networks that you wish to interconnect with your home's wireless LAN. Among these networks are

✔ **HomePlug (www.homeplug.org):** This is a standardized approach to communicating over a home's electrical wiring.

✔ **HPNA (Home Phone Networking Alliance, www.homepna.org):** This is a standardized approach to communicating over a home's telephone wiring.

✔ **MoCA (Multimedia over Coax Alliance, www.mocalliance.org):** This is a standardized approach to communicating over a home's coaxial wiring.

✔ **X10:** This is a standardized approach to communicating over a home's electrical wiring for short data burst for home automation applications.

✔ **Ethernet:** This is a standardized approach to communicating over CAT-5e four-pair wiring.

Interfacing with these networks is simple:

✔ **Use the network technologies' Wi-Fi adapter.** The networks may have an 802.11-integrated adapter unit as part of their offerings. A standard access point interfaces 802.11 wireless with Ethernet. For the other technologies, such as HomePlug for HPNA, you would use special units designed to have a co-presence on both networks. The Siemens SpeedStream 2521 Powerline 802.11b Wireless Access Point (www.siemens.com, $99), for instance, is an 802.11-outfitted "wall wart" access point module with HomePlug-compliant electrical prongs. Plug this unit into an electrical outlet, and your access point communicates with your HomePlug router over the electrical lines in your home — bridging between the two networks.

When these 802.11 integrated products came out from the various manufacturers, there was a lot of buzz, but not a corresponding spike in sales. That's because access points are so cheap and so fully functional that you are better off getting a simple Ethernet jack from HomePlug, HPNA, or other technology and plugging your access point into that. More recently, with the emergence of longer-range 802.11 in the home, like the Belkin Pre-N wireless devices (www.belkin.com), the need for the in-home wiring has been done away with altogether in many instances. As a result, most of these alternative devices are still just 802.11b-compliant and do not support advanced features like WPA. We can't say we really recommend them highly at this point.

✔ **Use your router.** If the networks do not support a direct bridge — or you do not want to use their direct interface for the reasons cited in the previous Warning — you can bridge via your router. Your access point is connected to your router, and your router routes your data to locations on the networks.

Wirelessly connect to your computer . . . in the other room!

Space is at a premium in all of our lives. Are we the only ones who have noticed that "desktop" PCs are anything but these days? They can get pretty big if you want to have expansion bays and lots of features.

So when it comes to putting your desktop computer in some aesthetically pleasing yet practical place on or under your desk, you sometimes simply have no room. Or, what if you want to access computer functionality in the garage or guesthouse? You may not want to devote a computer to that area full-time, or you may not have the temperature controls in place to protect a full computer. That's where *wireless KVM* gear comes in handy.

Don't feel bad if you don't know what *KVM* means. It stands for *keyboard, video, mouse* and refers to a class of devices that offer remote access to multiple computers using a single keyboard, video display, and mouse. (A KVM switch often also includes support for audio: a mini-phone stereo 3.5 mm interface in addition to the KVM.) It was developed for IT managers who had to manage a bank of 16 computers but only needed one keyboard and monitor since

they could only manage one computer at a time. Newer KVM units add support for USB peripherals, called KVMP devices, where the *P* stands for *peripherals*.

Unless you are like Danny, who has 12 computers in his house (no kidding), you don't need a KVM in your home to manage multiple PCs. However, KVM allows you some flexibility in where you locate your computer's base unit around your house. You could, for instance, place all your computers in one out-of-the-way location and use a wireless KVM extension to your working areas. Most wireless KVM devices are based on 802.11, so your computer and KVM extension can be up to 100 feet apart.

So ask yourself if you really need that PC on your desk, or can it be elsewhere? How often do you really access your CD or hardware features? It's something to consider. The wireless KVM products historically have been enterprise IT products and are just starting to hit the consumer markets as we write; check out the ATEN (www.aten-usa.com), Avocent (www.avocent.com), D-Link (www.dlink.com), and IOGEAR (www.iogear.com) sites to see what they have.

The decision of which approach to use, we think, is pretty clear — follow the paradigm of stereo gear, where "separates" win out over "all-in-one" gear. You are better off with a stand-alone access point and a stand-alone transport layer than mixing the two and compromising your future intentions. This being said, choose the "Use your router" option as your main way to interface between the networks.

If you have purchased a bundled package for one of the alternative network communications systems, have no fear — it's not that the adapter approach won't work; you're just more likely to have to make compromises in the way you approach your whole LAN, such as the WPA limitation noted earlier.

Chapter 6

Better Living Through Network Monitoring

*Y*ou've probably heard the saying, "You can't improve what you can't measure" before. This simply means that you need some way of gauging your efforts whenever you try to improve a process or system. You need to know where you are to figure out how to get where you're going!

Wireless networks are no different in this respect. As you grow your network — either in terms of the number of devices on the network, the area covered, or the overall speed of the network — you need some idea of how your network is working *now,* and how modifications affect it *later.* With some specific measurements of your wireless network's performance, you can make adjustments and modifications and immediately see the results in concrete terms, rather than flying by the seat of your pants.

In this chapter, we tell you how you can monitor your wireless network. With simple tools that are either free or cheap, you can use your existing computers and laptops (or even wireless handhelds, if you've got them) to monitor the airwaves and measure the performance of your wireless LANs. With these tools, you can see which parts of your home (or office, or entire property) are getting decent wireless signals, and which are not. You can also use these tools as real-time monitoring systems, so that when you add antennas or boosters, or simply reposition your APs, you can see the results as you make the changes. Feedback is important when you're making these kinds of changes.

Finally, you can use these tools to monitor for other wireless LANs nearby, to understand where and how they are impacting your own network. This can be an invaluable tool when you're trying to find a free channel, or trying to reduce interference. You can even monitor your network while operating non-LAN devices (like cordless phones) to see how they may be causing you network difficulties.

Understanding Network Monitoring

The first step to beginning a network monitoring project is to make sure that you understand the basics of network monitoring itself. It's worth a few minutes of our time and yours to define those network *metrics* (or measurable characteristics) that define the network's performance characteristics.

Figuring out the wireless ropes

All of the metrics we refer to here are specific to a particular point in space where the measurements are taken. If you move five or ten feet one way or another, all of these things will likely change. Don't measure signal strength, noise, SNR, or anything else in *just one place* and be done with it. Instead, use these metrics to examine the performance of your network in the locations where you want to use it. Take a laptop or handheld around your home to the places where you want to get online and take measurements there — then you can see where your network needs boosting.

These metrics are the common currency of any monitoring program. You are either presented with these metrics in a sort of "raw" format (for example, `The signal-to-noise ratio is 35 dBm`), or, if you're lucky, the program provides an easier-to-understand graphical presentation of the state of your network. Either way, here are a few of the basics that are being measured by a monitoring system:

- ✔ **Signal strength:** The most basic measurement taken by any monitoring system is the signal strength metric. Signal strength is simply the electrical energy of a wireless LAN radio signal, measured at a particular point in space. Every wireless LAN radio system (like an AP) transmits at a certain signal strength (this is affected by the power of the system as well as the antenna type). As you move farther away from the transmitting antenna, and also deal with *attenuation* (or decreasing strength) from things like walls, windows, and other objects, the signal strength decreases.

Signal strength can be measured in one of several ways, the most common being dBm or decibel milliwatts. See the sidebar titled "Decibels, milliwatts, dBm — what the heck?" for all the details. We use the term *dBm* throughout this chapter because it is the most common and convenient way of discussing signal strength.

✔ **Noise:** The signal coming out of your wireless LAN equipment's antenna is *not* the only RF energy that your wireless LAN gear is going to pick up. The airwaves are filled with RF energy from other radio systems (like cordless phones or Bluetooth devices) and from electronic systems that release RF energy unintentionally (like the microwave). This RF energy is referred to as *noise*. Basically, noise is the *background* RF environment that your signal must rise above to be distinguished by your wireless LAN gear.

Noise is measured in the same variety of ways as is signal strength, and we use the *dBm* terminology throughout this chapter.

✔ **Signal-to-noise ratio (SNR):** Perhaps more important than the absolute power and noise levels is how they relate to one another — the *signal-to-noise ratio* or SNR. The SNR tells you the *quality* of your wireless LAN signal — it defines how hard your wireless LAN system has to work to stay connected and send data back and forth. The bigger the SNR, the better. Because this ratio has two components (signal and noise), either one can affect your network's performance — you can have a high signal strength in a noisy area and still have a low SNR, or your signal can be relatively low, but because of little noise, your SNR is still fine.

You calculate SNR by simply subtracting the difference between signal strength and noise, when *both* are measured in dBm. (We told you dBm would come in handy!) The resulting SNR value is measured in dB (decibels).

We talk later in the chapter about how to understand SNR, but generally speaking, you want you SNR to be 20 dB or higher for the best network performance. If your ratio drops below that, you'll want to consider some means of boosting performance in that location. See Chapter 7 for details on how to do that.

✔ **Bit error rate (BER):** Another measure of wireless LAN quality that is less commonly used than SNR is the bit error rate (BER). This metric doesn't look at the wireless domain itself, but instead examines the data being sent across the wireless network. As the network quality degrades and SNR goes down, the number of data packets that get garbled and must be re-sent (the errors) goes up. A rising BER is a bad thing!

You won't run into BER nearly as much as SNR, but they are related — the lower the SNR, the higher the BER.

✔ **Receive sensitivity:** This isn't a measure of your network's performance, but it is an important factor in how the network works. The receive sensitivity of a wireless LAN device tells you the lowest signal level that can be picked up by the device at a particular *bit rate* or speed. A wireless LAN device can (and *will*) have more than one receive sensitivity — wireless LANs can knock back their speeds in certain situations to overcome poor signal strength or quality.

Decibels, milliwatts, *dBm* — what the heck?

One subject that makes us wish we'd paid more attention back in physics class in college is measuring the energy (or power) of electromagnetic radiation (radio waves, in other words). The overall concept isn't too difficult to grasp: A certain amount of power is emitted from a wireless system. As that energy spreads out across the airwaves, however, it reduces by the square of the distance it has traveled (this is called the *inverse square law*).

What are we bugging you with this old physics stuff for? Only to explain that there are multiple ways of measuring the signal strength (and of measuring noise) in an RF environment like a wireless network. The most basic measure is the strength of the radio signal in milliwatts (thousandths of watts). You can often find outputs of things like 802.11 radios listed in milliwatts.

Another common (probably the most common) system for measuring signal strength is the dBm, or decibel milliwatts. Decibels aren't used only for sound measurements, although that's probably the most familiar use of the decibel. They can also be used for any sort of measurement where a logarithmic scale makes sense. Because of that inverse square law, a logarithmic scale does indeed make sense for RF.

dBm measurements start off with a baseline of zero dBm, which is equal to 1 milliwatt of electrical RF energy. Amounts of energy less than 1 milliwatt are represented by negative dBm (like −50 dBm).

The rule of thumb essential to understanding the dBm (and to grasping why it's useful in wireless network monitoring) is that an increase of roughly 3 dBm means a doubling of power — a decrease of the same amount means a halving of this power. The ability to use the logarithmic scale lets you represent both very high and very low power levels without using scientific notation or tons and tons of zeros (no need to have a .0000000034 milliwatts power level — you can just say −84.69 dBm).

Energy levels are also sometimes measured by wireless LAN systems using a relative scale. This scale is known as the *RSSI*, or Received Signal Strength Indicator. RSSI can get kind of funky because different vendors implement this scale differently — based on a maximum number called the *RSSI Max*, which is an integer less than 255. Each vendor can implement its own RSSI Max value, which is what makes this RSSI scale relative — if one vendor's RSSI Max is 100 and another vendor's is 200, the signal strength received as 100 on one card is the same as 200 on the other vendor's card. This makes things quite confusing, and it's why the dBm scale is preferred — it's the same no matter whose equipment you are using.

We mention RSSI because if you use the software that comes along with many wireless network cards (the client software, in other words), you may see signal strength represented in terms of RSSI. Luckily, many vendors convert RSSI from a raw number to a percentage — which is relatively consistent from vendor to vendor. In other words, they *normalize* the RSSI by providing a percentage of RSSI Max indication — 50 percent of maximum power is 50 percent of maximum power, regardless of the RSSI scale used! (That's assuming maximum power is the same, which isn't *always* true, but is a safe enough assumption to make for these purposes.)

Deciphering the metrics

Understanding what the monitored characteristics of a wireless LAN are doesn't really do you a lot of good unless you understand what changes and trends in these various metrics mean in the real world. You're monitoring your network to make it better, not just for the fun of it! (Although it can be fun, too!)

To understand how network metrics affect you, you need to understand how wireless LANs (and in particular 802.11 networks) behave in different network conditions.

The easiest way to do this is to think subjectively about what happens to a wireless LAN connection as you move from a stronger, higher-quality signal to a weaker, lower-quality one:

- ✔ At the highest signal strength, with a high SNR and low noise levels, the client (your PC, for example) *associates* with (or connects to) the AP without any difficulty and maintains a steady connection. In this situation, the connection is made at the fastest possible nominal speed (11 Mbps for 802.11b, 54 Mbps (or faster) for 802.11a or g), and errors in data transmission are rare, so your effective throughput is very high (probably about half of the theoretical maximum speed).

- ✔ As you move away from the AP and begin to lose signal strength (or as the noise increases and causes a decreasing SNR), the first result is increased errors transmitting your data. More data needs to be retransmitted, and the overall network throughput (or actual speed for applications) begins to decrease.

- ✔ Make the situation a little bit worse by moving farther away from the AP or otherwise causing the SNR to decrease, and performance goes further downhill. As the SNR gets worse and worse and the BER (bit error rate) starts to rise, your AP and client hardware may not be able to maintain the nominal speed, and may step down to a lower speed (if so configured). You may even begin to occasionally lose your association with the AP — meaning there will be gaps in your connection.

- ✔ When things get really dire (you've walked clean out of the house or someone has cranked up that leaky microwave oven next to your PC), the SNR gets so bad that you start to reach the limits of your Wi-Fi hardware's receive sensitivity. The eventual result here is a completely lost connection — no association to the access point, and your Wi-Fi device's software begins to look for another AP to associate with.

To put a real-world and slightly more objective spin on this concept, consider some figures from Pat's home office and one of his APs:

- ✔ When he has his laptop in the docking station in the home office, about five feet from this particular access point, he's got an SNR of about 41 dBm. This is an excellent connection (Windows XP says so, anyway) and he can get the full throughput of about 6 Mbps using this particular (and ancient) 802.11b access point.

- ✔ Moving out to the family room, about 20 feet from that same access point, and with a wall between him and the omnidirectional antenna on this creaky old Apple AirPort AP, the signal-to-noise ratio is about 27 dBm. At this point, the connection is holding up fine, and Windows XP is still reporting a "very good" connection.

- ✔ Moving right out the sliding glass door to the table on the back patio, Pat's SNR drops to 24 dB.

- ✔ Way out in the back yard, beyond the hot tub and almost in the neighbor's yard (probably 65 feet from the AP, going through several interior walls and a stucco exterior wall), the SNR is 17 dB. At this point, Windows XP switches back and forth between "low" and "good" signal strength indications, and downloads and other network activities have noticeably slowed.

Pat would continue this exercise until he lost his signal, but he'd have to go over the fence. (He just spent a lot of money putting a new one up this winter after the storms, so he'd rather not damage it.) Hopefully you get the point now that we've put some signal numbers together with real-world situations.

When you get some network monitoring going in your own network, you can perform a similar *site survey.* Your results might be similar — or they could be like the results Pat had when he tried the same thing with the MIMO NETGEAR RangeMax router he just installed. With seven antennas and the MIMO functionality of this system, he never lost signal strength anywhere in the house or on his property. In fact, he can even get over to his neighbor Roy's house for a cold beer on Saturday afternoon (Roy is an excellent home brewer) without losing the signal.

Doing Basic Monitoring

The easiest way to monitor your home or office's wireless network is to use the tools built into the operating system. These are *not* the kinds of tools that enable you to get detailed information about a particular network, but they at least give you some of the basics and help you find the networks to connect to, along with some basic signal information. If you want to get fancier, you might use other tools to examine your network in more detail.

The cool thing about the tools built into Windows XP and Mac OS X (which is what we're focusing on in *WNH&M For Dummies*) is that you don't have to do *anything*. Just turn on your PC or Mac and the operating system and wireless networking subsystem do the work for you, searching out new networks and determining some basic facts about them for you. It's kinda cool when you think about it!

Using Windows XP

Windows XP uses a system called *Wireless Zero Configuration* (we usually shorten that to just "Zero Config") to find, evaluate, and associate with wireless networks. Anytime wireless networks are within range and can be "seen" by the wireless card(s) in your PC, Windows knows it — and you can see these available networks with just a few simple steps.

This section refers to Windows XP Service Pack 2. If you've not yet upgraded to SP2, you really should. SP2's support for wireless networking is almost incalculably better than older versions of XP.

To pull up a listing of available networks, simply right-click on the Wireless Network Connection icon in your Windows taskbar (the one that looks like a small computer with three concentric arcs radiating out from it) and select View Available Wireless Networks. A dialog box like the one shown in Figure 6-1 appears.

Figure 6-1: The networks available at Pat's house. (The unsecured network isn't his!)

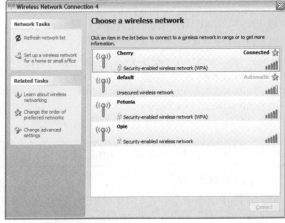

The Choose a Wireless Network dialog box lists all of the networks that Windows has detected in your area, and also provides some pertinent details about each of these networks, including

✔ **Network name (ESSID):** Opie, Cherry, and Petunia are the ESSIDs Pat has assigned to three of his access points. (The Default network belongs to a neighbor who hasn't read this book yet, or at least not Chapter 8, where we discuss security — that's a standard "out of the box" D-Link ESSID.)

Networks that have ESSID broadcast turned off do not show up on this list, but in the next section of this chapter, we describe some tools that allow you to see them anyway. Also, if you've previously associated with an access point and have added it to your preferred network listing, it shows up here even if the broadcast is turned off.

✔ **Security status:** If a network has a Wi-Fi security (encryption) system turned on, this is noted in the network's entry in the list of available networks. For example, in Figure 6-1, you can see that Opie has WEP encryption turned on, whereas Cherry and Petunia are locked down with the stronger WPA encryption scheme. Not to pick on the neighbor again, but you'll note that Default has no encryption turned on. That makes the neighbor's network a good backup should Pat's cable modem ever go down!

You'll note that there's no indication of which type of WPA encryption (Enterprise or Personal) is being used, or whether it's WPA or WPA 2 (see Chapter 8 for more on these terms). All you'll see in this dialog box is that a network is WPA (Security-enabled wireless network (WPA)), WEP (Security-enabled wireless network), or unsecured.

✔ **Signal strength:** Windows also provides a nice graphical representation of signal strength, using those five vertical bars you can see at the far right of Figure 6-1. (The bars are green, but because this is a black-and-white book, you'll have to trust us on that one.) The more green, the better — if all five bars are green, you have an excellent signal. These bars don't really tell you all that much info by themselves, but look at Table 6-1 for a translation of bars to SNRs.

If you mouse over the signal strength display and hover your pointer, Windows tells you in words how your signal strength is (we've included those words in the table as well). Excellent is best, poor is worst, and the rest are pretty much somewhere in between.

Table 6-1	Translating Windows Signal Strength Indicators	
Number of Bars	*Signal Strength*	*SNR*
5	Excellent	26 dBm or above
4	Very good	21 to 25 dBm
3	Good	16 to 20 dBm
2	Low	11 to 15 dBm
1	Very low	10 dBm or below

Using Mac OS X

Mac OS X doesn't have a single interface that shows available networks quite as completely as does Windows XP — the interface on the Mac is a bit less involved, but probably also a bit easier. To "sniff" out available networks using OS X, simply open Apple's Internet Connect application — it's in your Applications Folder, and may very well be located on the OS X dock.

When Internet Connect is open, click on the AirPort tab. You see a pulldown menu that displays each wireless network within range of your Mac (shown in Figure 6-2). Put another way, it displays each wireless network that has enough signal strength to reach your Mac. This display provides a green bar graph display of signal strength — simply choose another network from the pulldown menu.

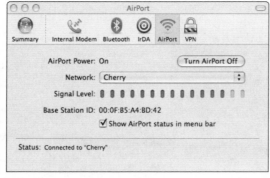

Figure 6-2:
Showing
signal
strength in
Mac OS X.

 You can streamline this process by putting your AirPort display in the OS X menu bar. Just go to System Preferences (in your Applications folder or on the Dock) and click on Network. In Network, click on the AirPort tab and make sure that the Show AirPort Status in Menu Bar checkbox is selected — if it's not, select it and click the Apply Now button.

When the AirPort status is in the menu bar, you always see a list of available networks in the menu bar, and you can open Internet Connect by simply using this pulldown menu.

Using wireless client software

Although Windows Zero Config is the easiest way for Windows users to find and examine wireless networks, it's not the only way. Most wireless network adapters include their own client software that handles network configuration, AP selection, and more.

These client software packages usually offer a network monitoring application that gives you more network information than the software clients that are built into the operating systems. For example, these clients may provide more elaborate signal strength and SNR meters and may even offer some raw data on the actual data throughput across your wireless network (for example, showing bit or packet rates and error rates).

For example, the client software included with NETGEAR's wireless network adapters, shown in Figure 6-3, shows transmit, receive, or both transmit and receive data rates graphically and numerically (in terms of packets of data per second). It also shows the packet error rate, which, although not identical, is proportional to the BER we discussed earlier in the chapter.

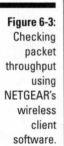

Figure 6-3:
Checking
packet
throughput
using
NETGEAR's
wireless
client
software.

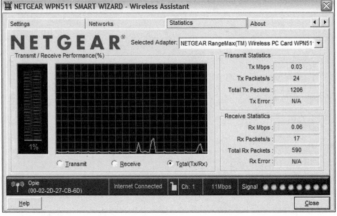

Using Free "Stumblers"

The Wi-Fi client software included with operating systems and network adapters can be very handy for tracking down available networks and for seeing really high-level representations of network performance, but they are *not* good tools for doing really precise measurements and monitoring of network performance.

If you're looking to really examine your wireless network environment, try this easy (and free!) solution: Download a wireless sniffer or monitoring program. The most popular (and famous) of these programs is an application known as NetStumbler — a Windows program — but there are other programs for Mac OS X, Linux, and even Pocket PC and Palm OS handheld computers.

Network Stumbler

The king of the network monitoring programs, at least for Windows users (which is to say, for most folks) is Network Stumbler (or NetStumbler), www.netstumbler.com. This freeware program (version 0.4.0 is current as we write) actively searches the airwaves for available wireless networks and displays a wealth of data about them, including

- ✔ SSID
- ✔ Channel
- ✔ Nominal speed (for example, 11 Mbps or 54 Mbps)
- ✔ Signal strength (in dBm)
- ✔ Noise (in dBm)
- ✔ SNR
- ✔ Encryption (NetStumbler doesn't differentiate between WEP and WPA; it simply says "WEP" when encryption is on, and is blank when it's not.)
- ✔ System vendor (helpful if you know you're looking for, say, an Apple AirPort)
- ✔ IP address

NetStumbler is easy to use — just download the software from the NetStumbler Web site and run the installer. A few seconds later, you're ready to try it out.

NetStumbler is an *active scanning* network monitoring tool. It finds and monitors networks by actively sending out *probe requests* on all the Wi-Fi channels supported by the card in your PC. Most networks respond to these probe requests, but not all do. A *passive scanning* monitoring tool (such as *Kismet* for Linux computers, or *KisMAC* for Mac OS X, which we discuss in the next section) sets your network adapter in a special "listening" mode (called *RFMON* mode) that can pick up *all* of the wireless traffic in your area. We mention this not because we think NetStumbler is a weak tool (we think it's a great tool, in fact), but to let you know that there may be some networks that it won't pick up.

NetStumbler doesn't support *all* wireless network adapters, but it supports many. You can find a list of supported cards in the Release Notes file on the NetStumbler site (www.netstumbler.com/downloads/netstumbler_v0.4.0_release_notes.pdf), but you may not know which chipset is inside your card. We recommend that you just download the program and try it out. It's free, it's not a big download, and it won't mess your system up at all, so try it!

The first time you run NetStumbler (to do so, just go to your Start menu and select All Programs⇨Network Stumbler), you'll want to set a few preferences. To set your NetStumbler prefs, do the following:

1. **Select Options in the View menu.**

   The Options dialog box opens, as shown in Figure 6-4.

Figure 6-4:
Configuring
NetStumbler
preferences.

2. **In the General tab, click and drag the Scan Speed slider all the way to the right to the Fast setting.**

3. **In this same tab, make sure that the Reconfigure Card Automatically check box is selected.**

   This allows NetStumbler to find all the networks in your area, instead of just the ones you're already associated with.

4. **If you like, you can click on the MIDI tab and select the Enable MIDI Output of the SNR check box.**

   Choosing this option causes NetStumbler to emit (through your MIDI-enabled sound card) "poor-sounding musical instrument noises." (We're quoting the NetStumbler help file here!) This is mostly annoying, but it can be useful in situations where you can't closely watch the screen while you're moving around trying to determine signal quality. The pitch of the musical instrument increases as the SNR increases. (The better the SNR, the more brain-rattling the pitch!)

5. **Click OK to save your settings and close the Options dialog box.**

When you run NetStumbler, it automatically turns off Windows Zero Config (as long as you checked that Reconfigure Card Automatically checkbox in the preferences) and begins to actively scan all channels in the 802.11a/b/g spectrum (depending upon the network adapter you're using) — as long as your wireless network adapter is supported.

Sometimes, NetStumbler does *not* see any available networks, even though they are there and "should" be seen. If this happens, your network adapter may not be supported. Before you give up hope, however, go into the NetStumbler Device menu and see if there's more than one driver for your wireless adapter. For example, for Pat's NETGEAR RangeMax 802.11g card, NetStumbler offers a choice of two drivers (Atheros and NDIS 5.1, as shown in Figure 6-5). For this particular card, the NDIS driver works with NetStumbler, and the Atheros driver does not. It should say `Unsupported` next to the driver if the driver won't work with NetStumbler, but occasionally it won't say that — NetStumbler just won't see all of your networks. Choose a different driver and see if that makes NetStumbler work for you! You can also check the following URL to see if your card is compatible: `www.stumbler.net/compat/`.

If you select the NDIS driver for your wireless network adapter, NetStumbler will receive RSSI data instead of signal and noise data (measured in dBm). In this case, the signal strength data in NetStumbler will be useful, but any noise or SNR data will not be.

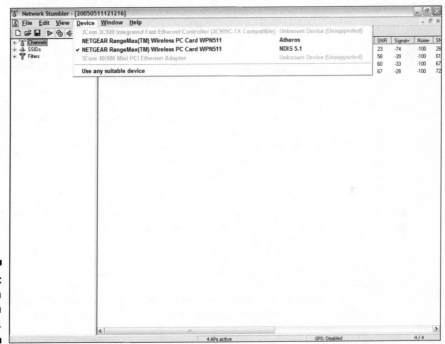

Figure 6-5:
Choosing a
driver in
NetStumbler.

After NetStumbler has begun monitoring the airwaves, you can find different ways to display (and therefore analyze) the data. In the left pane of the NetStumbler window (shown in Figure 6-6), you see several different display options, each with an expand/collapse plus/minus sign next to it (they're all expanded in the figure). You can sort through your networks using these controls by

- **Channel:** You can look at individual 802.11a/b/g channels to see which access points are on which channels. This can be handy when you're trying to figure out to which channel to assign your APs (you can figure out what the neighbors are using). Click on the plus signs next to individual channels to expand the listing of devices on each channel (listed by MAC address).

- **SSID:** You can also sort by SSID. This may seem unnecessary, but it actually can be a good tool to see if there are multiple APs using the same SSID. (Maybe your neighbors all bought identical routers during the last sale at Fry's!)

- **Filters:** NetStumbler also provides a range of filters that let you sort through available networks to find only those that meet certain criteria. A number of these filters are available, but some of the most interesting include

  - Encryption On or Encryption Off: You can quickly find "open" networks (or ensure that your APs have encryption enabled) by using these filters. This can be a handy tool when you're searching for that "free" AP at the hotel or café to check your e-mail.

  - ESS (AP) or IBSS (Peer): Use these filters to sort through the available networks by their status as access points and as peer-to-peer client networks. (You probably won't want to try to associate with peer-to-peer wireless networks unless you're absolutely sure who you're connecting to.)

  - Short Slot Time (11g): This filter tells you which 802.11g networks (if any are available) are set up for "802.11g only" mode. If you're looking for the fastest networks around, this is one way (along with signal strength) to find them.

When you sort NetStumbler using these navigation tools, you see a listing of each AP or network that fits into that particular category. From this view, you can read the text columns on the right side of the window (shown in Figure 6-7) to see important network data (like SNR) at a quick glance.

Figure 6-6:
Navigate
NetStumbler
by
expanding
or collapsing
the
navigation
tools on
the left.

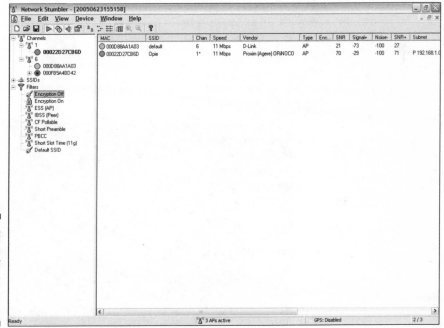

Figure 6-7:
Viewing
NetStumbler
data in
column
form.

To get a graphical representation of any particular network, simply click on the MAC Address of the device within the channels and SSID views and the right pane shifts to the display shown in Figure 6-8. From this view, you can see a running, time-based graphical representation of either signal strength (for the NSID drivers) or signal strength and noise (for other drivers).

This display can be very handy when you're changing your network in some way because you can watch the effects of changes unfold on your computer screen in real-time.

For example, if you're trying to find out how well your AP covers your home, you could use a laptop running NetStumbler and slowly move around the house (like the Verizon "Can you hear me now?" guy), and watch the signal strength or SNR dip and peak as you move in and out of good coverage.

If you find a room with poor coverage, have a helper adjust your AP or antenna placement while you watch the SNR and use NetStumbler as a tool for optimizing placement. You can also turn on the MIDI audio output we mentioned at the beginning of this section to add an aural dimension to this process.

We talk in more detail about how to do this kind of network optimization in Chapter 7, but we mention it here so you get an idea about how tools like NetStumbler can be used.

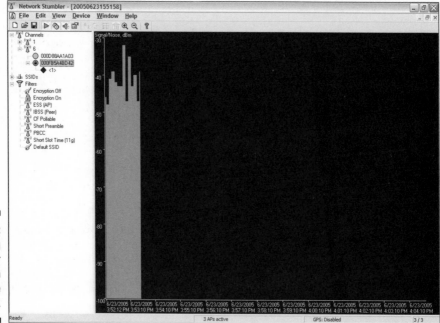

Figure 6-8:
Using
NetStumbler
to graph
performance
over time.

If you use a Windows Mobile/PocketPC handheld with wireless capabilities, check out the portable companion to NetStumbler, MiniStumbler. Currently compatible only with PocketPC 2002, PocketPC 3.0, and HPC2000 (until the next version comes out, anyway), this program gives you most of the functionality of NetStumbler in a truly portable platform, which is great for doing site surveys of your home or office.

Other stumblers and sniffers

A *ton* of network monitoring programs are available for download on the Internet. We talk about NetStumbler in detail because it's the most popular monitoring program and is the primary tool for Windows users, but it's not the only solution. Here are a few other programs we think you might want to try.

Check our www.digitaldummies.com site for links to the latest versions of these programs and for new additions as they become available:

- **MacStumbler:** Found at www.macstumbler.com, this Mac OS X utility is no longer being actively developed (which means that new versions are probably not on the way), but it remains a solid tool for detecting and monitoring 802.11b and g networks for Mac users. Although its name is similar to NetStumbler's (and so is the functionality — MacStumbler is also an active scanner), the program is not written by, or based on the code of NetStumbler. Sometimes imitation is the sincerest form of flattery!

- **Kismet:** This is probably the most powerful of all scanning programs — if you've got a Linux PC (which we're not covering here), get Kismet (www.kismetwireless.net). Kismet is a passive scanning program that can find any and all wireless networks within range, and scan all of the traffic going across the network. The real power of Kismet (beyond the passive scanning) is that the program can be used along with programs like Snort (www.snort.org) to become part of a wireless *IDS* or Intrusion Detection System.

- **KisMAC:** Because Mac OS X is a Unix-based OS, you can actually run a version of Kismet on Mac OS X computers (check out www.dopesquad. net/security/ for the drivers needed to do this), but only with the original 802.11b AirPort card — not with the current 802.11g AirPort Extreme cards. A similar application, built from the ground up for OS X, is KisMAC (kismac.binaervarianz.de). This program provides a passive scanning capability (like Kismet, which is its inspiration), and adds in support for AirPort Extreme cards and more — including functionality that can be used to "break" WEP encryption. Use it discreetly! Figure 6-9 shows KisMAC in action.

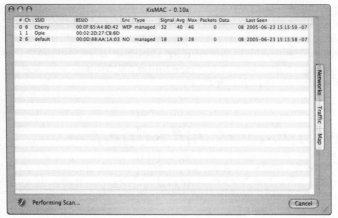

Figure 6-9:
Mac OS X
users can
be snoopy
with
KisMAC.

Getting Fancy

Freeware and open source tools such as NetStumbler, Kismet, KisMAC, and the like can be very powerful tools for monitoring and observing wireless LANs. If you've got a really big network to plan, build, and operate, however, you might want to consider investing in a system that goes beyond simple monitoring and offers some additional planning and security measures.

On the planning side of things, these programs allow you to enter the dimensions and characteristics of your building (or outdoor space) that you plan to cover — including details like building materials, room sizes and shapes, and so on — and they use some predictive software to recommend locations for AP installations.

Added to this predictive capability is a centralized monitoring software that works in conjunction with RF sensors (basically, "passive" access points that listen rather than transmit) to perform a supercharged version of the monitoring performed by your laptop using a NetStumbler-type program.

Some of these systems include

- ✔ **AirMagnet:** Found at www.airmagnet.com, this system is advertised as a wireless intrusion prevention system — using sensors and a centralized server, AirMagnet monitors the airwaves for unauthorized users, rogue access points, and more. You can also find laptop and handheld PC versions of the AirMagnet software for performing site surveys.

- ✔ **AirTight Networks:** The SpectraGuard system from AirTight Networks (www.airtightnetworks.net) is another monitoring system that combines hardware sensors and centralized server software to monitor and protect the airwaves.

✔ **Wireless Valley:** A leader in wireless network design for cellular and other wireless networks, Wireless Valley (www.wirelessvalley.com) has recently released some planning and monitoring tools for wireless LANs called LANPlanner and RF Manager to provide both up-front planning and ongoing maintenance and monitoring capabilities for large wireless LANs.

All of these products are designed (and priced!) for larger networks. The sensors, for example, are too expensive for home or small office networks. This is about to change because sensor prices are coming down rapidly. In fact, companies like AirMagnet are beginning to make partnerships with access point vendors to include sensors right in the AP (at a considerably lower price than standalone sensors). We think this trend will continue and that dedicated monitoring hardware (and the software that makes it work) will be reduced to prices that consumers can afford.

Chapter 7

Boosting Signal Strength Where You Need It

*W*ireless networking systems like Wi-Fi (or any wireless system, for that matter) sometimes need a boost. The power levels used to transmit Wi-Fi signals are miniscule compared to other radio systems, and there are plenty of items in homes and offices (walls, for instance) that can interfere with and reduce the strength of your signal. Distance itself is the enemy of a wireless LAN — every doubling of distance from a radio transmitter equates to a quartering of signal strength.

It doesn't take much to reduce a Wi-Fi signal's strength enough to reduce the speed of a network connection, or simply to cause some funkiness with your network's performance (like dropouts in audio signals to a media adapter or on a VoIP Wi-Fi phone call).

Fortunately, you can take steps to overcome signal strength issues and boost your network's signals as they travel around your home or office. In this chapter, we discuss some of these steps, beginning with a discussion of antennas and their effect on your network. We follow up with a discussion of signal booster products, which add amplifiers with higher power output levels to external antennas — providing an extra mechanism for improving signal strength. Finally, we discuss a new generation of Wi-Fi products — using a new antenna technology known as MIMO (Multiple Input/Multiple Output), which uses multiple antennas (and multiple signal paths) to increase range and speed across a wireless LAN.

Antennas for All

Most of us are familiar with what antennas do: provide a means for radiating radio waves to and from a transmitter onto the airwaves over which they eventually travel. There are a few basic concepts which define all antennas, including:

- ✔ **Gain:** The most important antenna characteristic is the antenna's *gain*. Gain is simply the measure of an antenna's ability to amplify a signal's strength in a particular direction (compared to an ideal antenna, which radiates its signal equally in all directions, three dimensionally. Antenna gain is typically measured in *dBi* (decibels gain over *isotropic* — that ideal 3-D radiating antenna). The higher the dBi gain of an antenna, the greater the signal boost the antenna can provide, at least in its optimal directions.

- ✔ **Radiation pattern:** An antenna's gain is usually greatly affected by its radiation pattern. For example, an antenna that is designed to focus its radio waves in a very tight sector usually has a higher gain than an *omni-directional* antenna, which sends equal signal strength in all directions. Most add-on antennas for Wi-Fi are directional — they have a greater gain in one or another specific directions or sectors. Typically, the narrower the optimal radiation pattern, the greater the gain of the antenna.

- ✔ **Resonant frequency and bandwidth:** These concepts define the optimal frequencies that an antenna operates in. The Wi-Fi antenna you buy is designed to operate best in a range of frequencies appropriate to the Wi-Fi system you're supporting (2.4 GHz for 802.11b and g, and 5 GHz for 802.11a). The key thing to remember here is that you can't just hook *any* antenna up to your Wi-Fi system and expect it to work. You need an antenna custom-built and designed for Wi-Fi frequencies.

So how does an antenna (and its gain) figure into your network's performance? Engineers use a complex formula to do radio frequency (RF) planning and optimization, but here's a simple reduction of it. To work properly, your Wi-Fi system needs to make sense of the following formula:

```
Received signal = transmission power - losses in the
          transmission path + transmitting antenna gain -
          over-the-air transmission losses + receiving
          antenna gain - losses in the receiving path.
```

What this means, in plain English, is that you have a certain amount of transmission power. You lose some of this power going through the cable and connectors in your transmission system, but you gain something via antenna gain. On the far end of the equation, you again gain something due to antenna gain, but lose something due to losses in the cables and connectors. The sum of all these gains and losses is the *received signal*.

To determine how a specific received signal will affect your Wi-Fi performance, you need only compare it to the *receiver sensitivity* ratings of your Wi-Fi system. Receiver sensitivity is basically a measure of how fast a Wi-Fi connection that a piece of equipment can support at a certain signal level and quality. As the received signal strength and quality drops, a Wi-Fi system drops down to a lower speed (for example, from 11 Mbps to 5.5 Mbps).

Quality *and* quantity both matter when it comes to your Wi-Fi signal. That's why signal-to-noise ratio (SNR) is such a great measure; it accounts for both the absolute strength of the signal and the quality of it (which relates to the amount of noise picked up by your antenna). A high-powered signal with a ton of noise might not be any better (in terms of your connection speed) than a lower power signal with almost no noise. Ultimately, you want relatively high power and relatively low noise.

To maximize your Wi-Fi system's performance, you want to ensure that your received signal is above the receiver sensitivity for the highest speed that your system supports. In Chapter 6, we talk about network monitoring software that can help you do just this.

Understanding Wi-Fi Antennas

Wi-Fi equipment (access points, network adapters, media adapters, bridges, and repeaters — any bit of Wi-Fi gear) comes standard with some sort of antenna. What kind of antenna your gear comes with — and more importantly, how it is mounted or connected to your system — makes a big difference in the performance and upgradeability of the equipment.

Counting your antennas

The first thing you might notice on many Wi-Fi systems (particularly on APs and Wi-Fi routers) is that they sport a *pair* of antennas. If you've skipped ahead to the end of this chapter and read about MIMO, you might think that there's something MIMO-ish going on here. In fact, there is *not*. Many systems use two antennas in what's known as an antenna *diversity* system. This means that both antennas receive a signal and the AP (or other device, although it's usually an AP) chooses the antenna with the strongest signal and uses it. Figure 7-1 shows the popular Linksys WRT54G Wi-Fi router with its pair of non-MIMO antennas.

Other types of Wi-Fi gear (like the Apple AirPort Extreme router) have *no* visible antennas — everything is hidden inside away from view (and prying fingers). Although such an approach is more aesthetically pleasing (and safer from accidental antenna snap-off incidents), it can sometimes reduce the performance of the system and also make upgrades a pain.

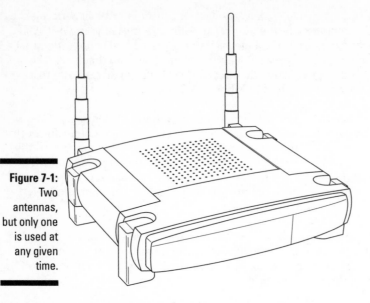

Figure 7-1:
Two antennas, but only one is used at any given time.

You can upgrade the antenna of most "internal" antenna system APs (as well as many laptops with internal antennas), but it often means getting inside your individual hardware and doing a bit of hardware modification. In many cases, you can find kits that include all the pieces and parts you need as well as very specific instructions on what and how to modify your hardware. An example is the QuickerTek 27 dBm transceiver for the Apple AirPort or AirPort Extreme (shown in Figure 7-2). This unit includes both an amplifier (discussed later in the section titled "Adding Amplification") and an external antenna connector for the AirPort. (The latest versions of AirPort Extreme already have an external antenna connector, but many existing AirPort Extreme base stations do not.)

Going external

You can really boost the signal of your Wi-Fi equipment when you connect an external antenna to the device. Despite a few glaring exceptions, most APs (and many other Wi-Fi devices like PCI card network adapters, bridges and repeaters, and media adapters) now come with external, removable antennas.

This is a great thing because a wealth of different antennas are now available on the market designed to supplement or replace the factory-installed antennas on your gear.

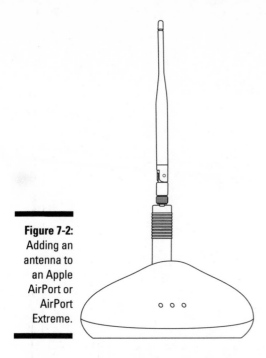

Figure 7-2:
Adding an
antenna to
an Apple
AirPort or
AirPort
Extreme.

Understanding the connectors

The following discussion may quite possibly turn your brain into jelly. Connectors are not fun, and they are obscure. Anything you learn about Wi-Fi connectors most likely will not ever help you again in your life.

Before you can add an antenna to your Wi-Fi equipment, you need to ascertain what type of antenna connection is available on that equipment. Dozens of different antenna connectors are used in the Wi-Fi world. (It's not simple like the connectors used for TV signals, where the F-connector is used for satellite, cable TV, and even most over-the-air antenna connections.)

A few of the most commonly used connectors are listed below (and shown in Figure 7-3):

- ✔ N-type
- ✔ SMA
- ✔ RP-SMA
- ✔ MC
- ✔ MC-X
- ✔ MMX

- TNC
- RP-TNC
- BNC
- APC-7

Male N connector

Female RP-TNC connector

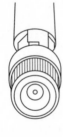

Male RP-SMA connector

Female MC (Lucent proprietary) connector

Figure 7-3:
A cornu-
copia of
Wi-Fi
antenna
connectors.

Some important facts to remember about Wi-Fi antenna connectors are

- RP stands for *reverse polarity.*
- The N connector is the most commonly found connector on the external antennas themselves.
- Almost all come in both male and female versions. The one big exception is the APC-7 connector, which is sexless.

> Pay attention to whether you need a male or female connector when you're buying an antenna or antenna cable. Nothing is more frustrating than getting your shiny new antenna and not being able to hook it up because you got the wrong type of connector.

- A few pieces of equipment go even further down the road to obscurity by offering standard connectors with reverse threads — making them even harder to find the proper cables to match!

Rather than spending a lot of time trying to figure out different connectors, we recommend that you just focus on those connectors that are installed on *your* equipment. A great online resource for determining connector types is www.radiolabs.com/products/cables/cable.php#connector.

Grabbing the pig's tail

If you have a fairly common antenna connection, you may very well be able to find external antennas that connect directly to your Wi-Fi device. This is especially true if you buy the antennas from the same manufacturer who made your AP or other device. If you've got an SMC AP and you buy a high gain antenna from SMC, the chances are good that it's got exactly the connection you need already.

But if you don't buy your antenna from the same vendor as your Wi-Fi gear, or if you've got a somewhat obscure connector to deal with, you will need a special cable called a *pigtail*.

A pigtail, shown in Figure 7-4, is simply a thin, short-range cable that connects a Wi-Fi device to an external antenna and that usually (but not always) converts between different types of connectors. Most pigtails have one of the many connectors described on one end, and an N connector on the other.

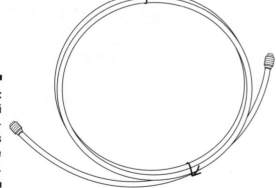

Figure 7-4: It's a Wi-Fi antenna-modifier's friend, the pigtail.

One key attribute of a pigtail is its small size. Because the pigtail uses thin cables without a bunch of shielding, it is designed for *short* runs between the Wi-Fi equipment and the antenna. A distance of 2 feet is a maximum, and 1 foot is even better. For longer runs, you can connect a length of LMR-400 cable between the pigtail and the antenna (this low-loss coaxial cable can withstand longer runs than can most pigtails).

Antenna types

After you've got your connectors and pigtails figured out, it's time to pick an antenna.

Looking at antenna types

Your most basic choice is to choose between directional or omnidirectional antennas:

- ✔ Omnidirectional antennas radiate their energy over 360 degrees, emitting a relatively even signal around the entire horizon, in a shape similar to a doughnut. Omnidirectional antennas are usually shaped like a simple pole or rod, and they transmit most of their energy (the dough-nut shape) outward from the pole itself — in other words, the energy "doughnut" is much like a ring around the pole in a game of ring toss.

  One interesting fact to note about the doughnut shape of this energy is that the weakest points are immediately above and below the AP's antenna. So don't expect to get a great signal if, for example, the AP is in the basement directly below the couch. It might be a short distance, but the signal isn't being propagated in that direction.

  The small pole antennas found on almost all APs with external antennas are omnidirectional.

- ✔ Directional antennas radiate their energy in some sort of a sector — be it narrow or wide — rather than in all directions. A wide variety of directional antennas are on the market, each with their own radiation patterns and uses. Some are quite specialized; some are good for almost all Wi-Fi users.

The directionality of an antenna affects not only its transmission characteristics but also its reception characteristics. So a directional antenna that transmits well in a certain sector also receives better in that same direction.

Going to the poles

All antennas have different radiation patterns in the horizontal and vertical planes as well. As we mentioned above, an omnidirectional antenna puts out most of its power in the horizontal plane (perpendicular to the antenna's axis) and very little vertically. Such an antenna's signal is said to be *vertically polarized.*

TIP

The key thing to remember about polarization is that you will get the best results when both antennas in a "connection" — your AP and PC's network adapter antennas, for example — use the same polarization. Some antennas can be either horizontal or vertical polarization, depending upon how they are mounted.

Looking at directional antennas

A large variety of directional antennas are on the market, built for a range of different functions. Some, for example, are highly directional, offer extremely high gain, and are well-suited for a point-to-point connection (for example, reaching another building with your Wi-Fi network). Others limit your best signal to a relatively wide sector, offering less gain but more flexibility for use in a home or office.

Making a move

Sometimes you don't need to go so far as to replace your antenna — you simply need to move it to avoid obstacles and to get a clear "shot" to the rest of your Wi-Fi network. You can try to do this by simply moving the Wi-Fi equipment itself (for example, raising your AP to a higher spot in the room), but such a move isn't always practical for infrastructure (cable placement, for example) or even just aesthetic reasons. (Have you *seen* some of these APs? Ugly!)

You may, however, be able to move just the antennas. For example, check out Linksys's AS1SMA Antenna Stand for SMA Antennas, shown in the following figure. (Check it out online at `www.linksys.com/products/product.asp?grid=33&scid=38&prid=647`.) This product, which you can buy online for about $20, provides you with a remote stand for a regular or high gain SMA antenna (Linksys also offers a model for TNC antennas). You do lose some of your signal strength by running the signal over a cable to this remote antenna, but in many cases you gain more in improved signal path (less path loss) than you lose in the transmission path.

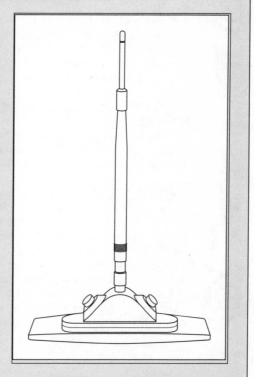

Some common types of directional antennas include

- **Patch or sector antennas:** These are the least "extreme" of the directional antennas, offering a sector that's as much as 180 degrees in a compact antenna that looks a lot like an omnidirectional that's been flattened out a bit. Patch or sector antennas can be helpful within a home or office when you just need a little extra help reaching the AP.

- **Yagi antennas:** We just love saying "Yagi." Yagi antennas are highly directional antennas that look sort of like the TV antenna you had in the attic as a kid (or at least like the one Pat had in his attic). They are hard to describe, so check out Figure 7-5 to see one in all its Yagi glory. Yagis are particularly good for outdoor, point-to-point applications, and not quite as good for general use indoors.

- **Parabolic antennas:** Even more directional are the parabolic antennas. These devices look like the "dishes" used to pick up satellite TV, and share similar design philosophies. You probably won't ever use a parabolic antenna in your network unless you're trying to shoot a signal across the country many miles.

- **Waveguide:** Have you heard of the Pringles can Wi-Fi antenna? This famous hack involves putting a waveguide antenna (an antenna that focuses the radio waves from your Wi-Fi system) inside a Pringles potato chip can. You can find a commercial version of this concept at `http://shop.netstumbler.com/detail.aspx?ID=288`.

When would you use a directional antenna if you're not building a point-to-point outdoor network? Typically, we recommend an omnidirectional antenna on your main AP (you may wish to upgrade your AP's antenna to a higher gain omnidirectional). Directional antennas come in handy on remote wireless stations in your home or office.

Can't reach the east wing of the house? Try a patch antenna or even a Yagi. Got trouble with the home office over the garage? See if a sector antenna helps. Our general rule of thumb is to stick with an omnidirectional for the AP and go with directionals where needed at the edge of your network.

Feel free to break this rule if the layout of your home or office dictates that your AP is not physically near the center of your space. If your AP is going in the home office in a corner of the house, feel free to try a sector or patch antenna that focuses your signal over 180 degrees and effectively covers the rest of the house better than an omnidirectional antenna would.

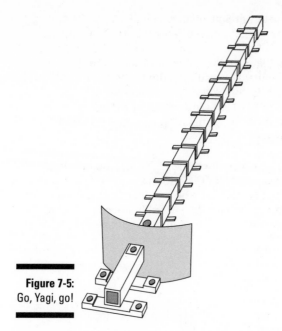

Figure 7-5:
Go, Yagi, go!

Adding Amplification

Recall the formula we mentioned earlier in the chapter for received signal strength, in the section called "Antennas for All"? One element of this formula was the transmit power. Antennas don't actually boost this power — at best, a high gain antenna directs more of this power in a particular direction, increasing the effective signal strength.

But in some situations, you need to start off with a little extra juice to begin with — meaning you want to increase the transmit power itself. To do this, you need to add a device known as a *signal amplifier* or *signal booster.*

These devices simply add an *amplifier* to the signal path between your Wi-Fi device and the antenna. This amplifier (like the amplifier in your home stereo, for example) simply increases the power level of a signal, hopefully with a minimum of increased noise and distortion.

A signal booster can have two components:

✔ **A transmit booster:** This increases the *outgoing* signal level by amplifying the signal *before* it hits the antenna.

✔ **A receive booster:** This increases the *incoming* signal level by amplifying it *after* it has been received by the antenna.

Most (legal) boosters transmit at about 500 mWatts (a half a Watt) of power, whereas the APs themselves transmit at one tenth (or less) of that amount.

Installation varies by unit, but most signal boosters are simple plug-in replacements for an existing antenna. For example, the RadioLabs 2.4Ghz Wireless Range Extender (www.radiolabs.com/products/wireless/wireless-range-extender.php, $119.95) plugs into any AP using an RP-SMA or RP-TMC connector and provides an instant power boost in both directions. Figure 7-6 shows this unit.

Boosters provide you with the most benefit on the transmit side of things — making it easier to pick up signals at greater distances. On the receive side of things, they do indeed "boost" the signal that's being picked up, but they don't improve the quality of the signal. If a signal is really noisy, the noise (as well as the signal itself) is also boosted — so you may not get a great increase in quality and speed.

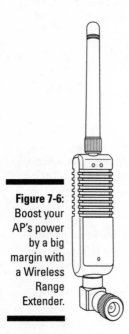

Figure 7-6:
Boost your
AP's power
by a big
margin with
a Wireless
Range
Extender.

Going with MIMO

The latest technological trend, however, is not to increase power, or even to increase the gain of antennas (although both of these techniques can work to boost your Wi-Fi network's range and throughput). Instead, you can boost your network's range by boosting the number of antennas (and signal paths) used to carry data across the network.

That's the promise of a new generation of technologies known as *MIMO* — Multiple Input/Multiple Output. MIMO technologies take a type of wireless interference known as *multipath* and turn it from a negative to a positive.

In simple terms, multipath occurs when a single radio signal arrives at an antenna more than once (and at different times) due to reflections and refractions (and other physics class phenomena that affect electromagnetic waves). In a normal system, multipath causes transmission errors and may slow down your network as it retransmits data.

MIMO, on the other hand, is inherently multipath and it likes it! MIMO systems add a *spatial* element to the mix. MIMO systems use multiple antennas on both the input and output side of things and use special algorithms and DSP (digital signal processing) to divide data up among these antennas and then send this data to a remote wireless device over separate physical paths through the airwaves.

The MIMO equipment on the far end receives these data streams and then reassembles them. The bottom line is that MIMO promises to be faster — perhaps a *lot* faster — than today's 802.11g and 802.11a systems.

The preceding description of MIMO is only *one* possible use of MIMO in a Wi-Fi system. Other MIMO systems use the multiple radios and antennas differently. For example, another system uses the multiple antennas to form a radio beam that is aimed at the remote receivers — sort of like an electronically-formed self-adjusting directional antenna.

MIMO will almost certainly be part of the future 802.11n specification (see Chapter 3). What is not clear today is exactly *which* MIMO system will take precedence. (As we write this, in mid-2005, two main technology "camps" are competing for dominance.)

You can buy MIMO-based Wi-Fi gear today, but it is *not* standards-based. Some vendors are calling this *Pre-N* gear, which is an understatement: Nobody knows exactly what 802.11n will require.

Don't buy any Pre-N gear with the anticipation that it will work with the standardized 802.11n gear in a year or two. Maybe it will, but odds are stronger that it won't. That doesn't mean your gear will stop working, but it does mean that you won't be able to easily expand your network without reverting back to 802.11g.

That said, you *can* buy MIMO gear today, and it really does work. We've used MIMO gear from a couple of different manufacturers and had some good results with them — greater range and faster throughput. You do need to have MIMO gear on both ends of the connection to gain full results, but some systems claim to offer increased range even with your old 802.11g network adapters on the far end of the connection.

Among the MIMO systems available today are

- **NETGEAR RangeMax:** With seven antennas, NETGEAR's "Smart MIMO" technology may be the early leader in the antenna arms race. But there's more to this router than just flashing blue lights. (Although there are plenty of them, too!) The RangeMax provides 108 Mbps speeds and promises 1000 percent increases in coverage over the previous generation of products. Figure 7-7 shows the RangeMax. Find out more at `www.netgear.com`.

- **Belkin Pre-N Router:** Belkin's Pre-N router uses MIMO technology from Airgo (`www.airgonetworks.com`) and promises an 800 percent increase in coverage and a 600 percent increase in speed compared to standard 802.11g products. The Pre-N router also is designed to continue to operate at its highest speeds (with Pre-N–equipped clients) even when 802.11b or 802.11g clients are connected to the network. Figure 7-8 shows the Pre-N router. Find Belkin online at `www.belkin.com`.

- **Linksys WRT54GX:** Linksys, the home and small office networking subsidiary of Cisco Systems (`www.linksys.com`), also uses Airgo's MIMO system in its new Wireless G Router with SRX (SRX is Linksys's own acronym for MIMO). Linksys claims three times the range and up to 800 percent speed improvements.

To put these performance numbers into perspective, here are a couple of things to keep in mind:

- "Coverage" refers to the area covered, not the range (that is, the radius of coverage). Remember that the area in a circle (and we can roughly assume that the coverage area is a circle) increases at the square of radius. Therefore, a 3x increase in range provides a 9x increase in coverage area.

- The speed claims are related to this increased coverage area. Remember that as received signal levels decrease below receive sensitivity levels, 802.11 systems degrade to lower speeds. An 802.11g signal at 250 feet might not be strong enough to maintain a full 54 Mbps connection, and may switch down to 27 Mbps or something even lower. The range of MIMO allows it to avoid this fate until much farther away from the access point — hence the huge percentage increases in speed.

If you were to measure speeds 20 or 30 feet from the router or AP, the MIMO advantage would be much less.

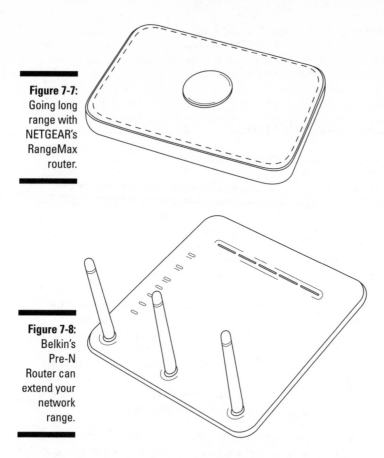

Figure 7-7:
Going long range with NETGEAR's RangeMax router.

Figure 7-8:
Belkin's Pre-N Router can extend your network range.

Boosting Cell Signals at Home

As mobile phones become *the* primary voice communications device for more and more of us, one of the dirty little secrets of the cellular world becomes apparent: Many cellphone services don't provide strong signals inside of buildings. In big buildings (like convention centers and huge office towers), the cellphone company often installs miniature cellphone base stations (called *picocells*) to improve coverage. Unless your plan is a heck of a lot bigger than ours though, we don't expect that you'll get one of these installed in your home.

What you can do, however, is install a cellular repeater. These devices are designed to be installed in a home or office (or even inside a boat or RV) and will provide a *regenerated* signal that basically takes what's available outside and makes it available inside. If your home office is in the basement (like our co-worker Ed's is), a repeater may be your cellphone answer!

Cellular repeaters always come with some form of very thick cable — usually what's called a *very low loss cable,* or *low impedance cable* — a powered box with a much smaller antenna on it, and a large pickup antenna that needs to be mounted as high in the air as possible.

Understanding cellular frequencies

Cellular repeaters are analog devices that simply retransmit the same signals their antennas pick up. This is different than Wi-Fi repeaters, where a repeater needs to know exactly what kind of signal it needs to work with — for example, 802.11b versus 802.11g and WPA versus WEP — an analog cellular repeater is only concerned with the frequency of the signals. A cellular repeater doesn't "look inside" the radio data it works with at all.

All that really matters is the frequency. In the U.S., cellphones use two primary frequency ranges: 824-849 MHz and 1850-1910 MHz.

Different cellular providers focus on different frequency ranges. Don't be fooled by the cellphone provider that says they are giving you a dual, tri, or quad band phone. They are talking about the type of signal that the phone can support and not what the provider's network will deliver to you. The 824-849 band is from the older TDMA and CDMA cellular networks that are owned by SBS, Verizon, and Cingular, while the 1850-1910 frequencies have been adopted by the newer providers in the cellular market, such as Sprint and T-Mobile.

Different cellular repeaters work with only specific frequencies. Some of the more high-end — otherwise known as expensive — repeaters support both frequency ranges. Before you buy, make sure that you've got the correct repeater for the cellphone service you are using.

Installing a repeater

If you're not comfortable with electrical wiring, grounding, or climbing up ladders, we recommend having someone knowledgeable (that is, a professional) help you set up your cellular repeater. With the repeaters that we have tested, the instructions are designed for installers and not end-users. There are also some daunting issues you need to account for — like lightning protection — when installing the pickup antenna that a cellular repeater requires.

We can share a few general tips with you about performing such an installation. First off, we can tell you that every location is different and you would do well to determine a few things about the environment into which you are installing one of these. Most importantly, you need to have a place — the roof of your house, back yard, a high tree — that can receive a reasonable amount of cell signal. If you happen to be in a place where the only cell signal you can receive on your cellphone is a mile down the road, a repeater on your roof is not going to do anything for you. The pickup antenna has to be in a place that has some reasonable level of signal for this to work at all. If your cellphone has four bars that represent the cell signal, you need a place that can get at least two of those bars lit at all times.

When installing one of these devices, keep these things in mind:

- ✔ **Distance:** The distance between the pickup antenna and the repeater is very important. If they are too close together, the pickup antenna picks up the signal from the repeater and creates a feedback loop that can damage the repeater.

  Vertical distance is always better than horizontal distance, so try to mount the pickup antenna as high as you possibly can. Most of these devices need between 45 and 50 feet of separation in a straight line from the pickup antenna to the repeater. In our experience, we found the best results came from mounting the pickup antenna at the top of the house and feeding the cable down the flue to the basement (which had no cell signal at all in it). That gave us the vertical separation we needed and we were able to make our basement cell-friendly so we could sit at the computer, type this paragraph, and order pizza with our cellphone instead of having to get up and go upstairs to use the kitchen phone.

- ✔ **Grounding:** Make sure that you or your installer follow the local and national electrical code recommendations for antenna grounding. After all, an improperly grounded antenna is nothing more than a big lightning rod with no place to send all that electricity except right down the antenna cable and into your house.

- ✔ **The power of the repeater:** Repeaters are transmitters, which means they flood the area they cover with RF (radio frequency) radiation. Most of us are already saturated with RF radiation, thanks to television, radio, cellphones, and other devices. The difference is that those RF transmissions are relatively weak. Most cellphones require less than half a watt of power to do what they need to do — such as to let you make a call from the middle of the soccer field while the kids are in a game. The FCC has set standards for cellphones that require all handheld phones be at no more than 1.5 watts. Only car-mounted, older style handsets with a separate base station can have a power up to 3 watts.

  Repeaters can range from less than a half watt to that full 3 watts of power. So you don't want to have the repeater sitting right next to your head. You need to size the repeater for the area you want to cover. If you live in an older building with a lot of wooded areas that can block the signal, a more powerful repeater is going to be required to cover the inside of that home. On the other hand, if your goal is merely to get cell signals in your workspace, you can use a much less powerful device.

We can't provide you with blanket recommendations on power levels, but we do recommend that you consult with the vendors of repeaters to get recommendations for your specific building (or boat, or RV). A couple of vendors to check out include

- **Wireless Extenders Inc.:** www.wirelessextenders.com

- **Digital Antenna Inc:** www.digitalantenna.com

Chapter 8

Staying Safe in the Wireless World

*I*f you believe everything you hear on the news, Wi-Fi and wireless networks are the greatest threat to computer security since — well, ever! Wardrivers, evil twins, guys in the parking lot of the local Lowe's — all of these topics have made the local and national news. (In case you've not heard, here's a recap: Wardrivers are folks who drive (or fly!) around town, looking for open access points and mapping them; evil twins are *fake* hot spots set up near real hot spots, designed to steal your personal information; and the guys at the Lowe's *did* sit in the parking lot, tap into an unsecured wireless LAN used for sales purposes, and steal customer info such as credit card numbers.)

Scary, huh? Well, we're here to tell you two things:

✔ You *should* be scared enough to take some security measures.

✔ You shouldn't be *too* scared — precautionary measures that'll make your network safe and secure are easy to take.

In this chapter, we talk about securing your network using the tools built into most access points and wireless routers, wireless network adapters, and within the Windows XP and Mac OS X operating systems. We take a practical approach here — telling you how to secure various parts of your network in different situations. We also tell you about some "gotchas" to keep in mind as you expand your network and add new equipment.

Network security of any kind is imperfect. Someone with enough time, skills, and motivation can break into just about any networked computer. This is even more true of a wirelessly networked system, simply because the physical aspect of security goes away in the wireless world. Anyone within range can physically pick up your wireless signals. Security measures, however, make it much more difficult to do anything with those signals, or to get anywhere within your network. The point to remember here is that "much more difficult" does not equal "impossible."

Avoiding WEP

The first thing we should get out of the way concerns the WEP (Wired Equivalent Privacy) system used on many older Wi-Fi networking systems. WEP-secured systems cannot be relied on as truly secure networks. That's because the encryption method used by WEP is not very *robust*. That's the polite way of saying that, in the face of a determined cracker attack, WEP simply stinks.

The *key* (the shared secret that locks and unlocks the encryption in WEP) is simply not secure enough. Data transmitted across the WEP-enabled network repeats itself too frequently — frequently enough that a hacker can "listen in" on a network (from a distance) to pick up these repeated elements and use some widely available programs to determine the network key.

With the key, these passive listeners can then decrypt anything being sent across your network. And there's nothing you can do about it — you can change your key (which means going to each device on the network and changing the key there), but it's only a matter of time (days, or on most busy networks, hours or even minutes) before the next key is broken.

Don't believe us? Check out programs like AirSnort (`airsnort.shmoo.com`) or WEPCrack (`wepcrack.sourceforge.net`). With one of these programs installed on a PC, you too can sit back quietly, gather WEP-encrypted Wi-Fi packets from the airwaves, and *break* WEP yourself.

There's a difference of opinion in the industry about the wisdom of using a compromised encryption system such as WEP. Although most folks agree that it's better than nothing, some security experts believe that you can get lulled into a false sense of security with a weak encryption system. Their thinking is that you'll get lazy about *other* security measures if you think you've got some measure of protection from WEP (or another weak security system).

Our take is that WEP *is indeed better* than nothing. Someone has to be making an effort to break into your WEP-encrypted network — an unsecured network takes considerably less effort. If you do use WEP (which we only recommend when your equipment doesn't support WPA), remember to take other precautions — like using SSL Web sites for activities like online banking.

Understanding WPA

As we discussed back in Chapter 3, the replacement for the insecure WEP system is a new security system called *WPA* (or Wi-Fi Protected Access) and the newer WPA2.

Unless we're pointing out a specific different function in WPA2, we'll refer to both WPA and WPA2 singularly as WPA because they are very similar — WPA2 differs from WPA primarily because it uses a stronger encryption system called *AES* or Advanced Encryption Standard. There's no practical difference between WPA and WPA2 from a user's perspective — except that WPA2 is even *more* secure.

WPA improves on WEP in several ways:

✔ It adds a strong user *authentication* system. Not only are the packets of data being sent over the airwaves encrypted (or scrambled), but users who connect to the network are also *authenticated* (or positively identified) using a system that's not easy to fool.

Not *all* implementations of WPA implement an authentication system. The simpler variant of WPA — WPA Personal — which we discuss in the section called "Figuring out a new 802 — .1X," later in this chapter — doesn't have an authentication system beyond the *pre-shared key* (PSK) that you give to users of your network.

✔ The encryption system is harder to break. WPA2, with the U.S. government-approved AES encryption system, is particularly hard to break, but even WPA's encryption is harder to "crack" than that used in WEP.

✔ The keys to the encryption system change constantly. Using a protocol called *TKIP* (or Temporal Key Integrity Protocol), WPA wireless systems change the keys used to encrypt data on an ongoing, packet-by-packet basis. So even if some miscreant trying to break your encryption system succeeds, it won't do him any good — you'll already have moved onto a new key by the time they "break" the one you *were* using.

WPA2 uses a system called *CCMP* (you *really* don't want to know what the acronym stands for — it's even got another obscure acronym inside it!). CCMP is the WPA2 equivalent of TKIP — someone "listening" to the wireless packets on your network has a very hard time spotting any kind of a pattern that helps them decrypt your data.

WPA and WPA2 are based on a new IEEE 802.11 standard — 802.11i. WPA2, with the inclusion of AES, is essentially exactly the same as 802.11i, whereas plain old WPA includes only part of the security offered by 802.11i. We talk about the IEEE and the 802.11 standards in Chapter 2.

Many pieces of Wi-Fi gear that were built before WPA hit the streets (in 2003) can be upgraded from WEP to WPA capabilities by simply performing a *firmware upgrade* (upgrading the system software in the system). Check your manufacturer's Web sites for information on this topic. Some really old gear is not upgradeable.

For WPA2 (802.11i), you'll probably need all new gear. The AES encryption cipher is computationally intensive — in other words, it chews up computer horsepower like crazy — so Wi-Fi equipment (access points, routers, client devices, and so on) needs an added *hardware accelerator* to perform the encryption. You can't retrofit this using firmware upgrades — you need new equipment. As we write in the spring of 2005, a few WPA2 devices are trickling onto the market, but most Wi-Fi gear supports the original WPA only.

You can't just mix and match older WEP and newer WPA gear in the same network — at least not if you want to use WPA. If you have old gear that doesn't support WPA, you won't be able to use WPA without replacing that gear. If you can't replace and can't live without your older gear, you might consider having *two* networks: Build a new secure WPA network for most activities, and keep your old WEP gear running on a different channel (with a separate access point) just for the old gear. An example of this non-WPA gear might be a wireless media server device (Chapter 13).

Sharing your keys with your friends

The easiest way to "turn on" WPA in a home or small office network (the kind we think you're most likely to be working on) is to use a pre-shared key or PSK. You can think of the PSK as a master password for your WPA network — you need to pass that password along to anyone whom you authorize to use your network.

WPA uses that master password to create the keys to the network encryption, and also to authorize users (they must know your PSK to connect to your access points).

A PSK isn't a foolproof means of authenticating users. If your network users blab the PSK to others, you lose your authentication. Or, if you choose a really stupid password (like "password"), strangers can launch a *dictionary attack* (using common words, in other words) and figure it out. For true user authentication, you need to use an authentication system like we discuss in the following section, "Figuring out a new 802 — .1X."

Typically, you won't give the actual PSK to your users: The PSK is a 64-digit hexadecimal string — which means that it's gobbledygook to the human eye and a real pain to type! Instead, you give them a *passphrase* (often called the *shared secret*) that's anything from 6 to 63 characters of letters and numbers. WPA systems automatically generate the PSK from the passphrase, and do so in a consistent way (so different computers, access points, and client devices all generate the same PSK from a given passphrase).

The big leap forward in WPA (compared to WEP) is that the PSK is used in combination with TKIP to change the encryption key with *every packet* of data that crosses your network (by using some random numbers and special mathematical functions). WEP, on the other hand, uses the same key with every packet, and that key is shorter in length and easier to guess.

As long as your PSK isn't given away by a user or guessed at (don't use your dog's name, in other words), you can consider WPA with a PSK *to be really secure* for whatever purposes you use your wireless network.

Figuring out a new 802 — .1X

An even better way of securing your network is to step up to the business class seats of WPA: *WPA Enterprise*. WPA Enterprise (and there are enterprise variants of both WPA and WPA2) adds an authentication element to WPA using a system known as 802.1X.

Stop shaking your head — we know how annoying all of these acronyms and 802-dot-whatevers are. If we could avoid them, we would! Note that 802.1X has only one "1" — it's a "dot one," not a "dot eleven" standard. In fact, 802.1X is a standard brought over from the wired networking world. Also, don't confuse 802.1X the standard with *802.11x* , the generic term often used for 802.11a/b/g.

As sharp readers will note (that means you!), 802.1X is another IEEE standard (see Chapter 2 for more on the IEEE), and it is designed to provide a few things in the context of WPA:

- ✔ **User authentication:** 802.1X uses cryptographic techniques to determine that users are exactly who they say they are (we talk about how this works in a moment).

- ✔ **Network/access point authentication:** 802.1X also uses cryptographic techniques to ensure that the access point and network that your users connect to is actually yours — and not some *rogue* access point that's trying to lure your users in to steal data or your passwords from them.

This double-ended authentication of both the user and the network is called *mutual authentication*. It's a big deal in corporate networks and also for hot spots where you're paying (or collecting money) for network access and exchanging data like credit card numbers.

✔ **Key management:** 802.1X offers a big jump forward in encryption secu-rity by managing the encryption keys for all users. Instead of creating a single PSK that all users get, 802.1X creates new keys on a per-user and per-session basis. This key management means that there's an even lower chance of some bad guy figuring out your network keys — because by the time a particular key gets figured out (already an unlikely event), it has been replaced by a new key.

To make 802.1X work in your network, you need a few things:

✔ **An access point or router that supports 802.1X:** This AP or router has certification from the Wi-Fi Alliance (www.wifialliance.org) that says *WPA-Enterprise.*

   If the device supports WPA2-Enterprise, it'll say that too! We refer to either certification as just WPA-Enterprise here.

✔ **Client devices and software that supports 802.1X:** This is called the 802.1X *supplicant.* Your client device also needs to have the WPA-Enterprise logo.

✔ **A server — in your network or remotely located (on the Internet, for example) — that provides the 802.1X authentication and key manage-ment:** These servers are usually called *RADIUS* (Remote Access Dial-In User Service) servers.

On the first count, we've got good news for you — any AP or router that sup-ports WPA-Enterprise by definition supports 802.1X. 802.1X is part of the standard. So you're set there.

Client devices that support WPA-Enterprise also support 802.1X, as do Windows XP and the latest (10.3 Panther and higher) versions of OS X. So the second bullet is also covered for most folks.

Some devices are certified by the Wi-Fi Alliance *only* for WPA (or WPA2) with-out any 802.1X support. These are labeled *WPA-Personal.*

The RADIUS server is the hard part for folks who are not IT professionals run-ning a corporate network. Instead of trying to set up your own RADIUS server within your home network (something that's just not worth the effort or expense, as far as we are concerned), we recommend that you take one of the following three approaches:

✔ You can use an access point with a built-in authentication server. These are much more expensive than your standard $70 AP/router device (by a factor of ten or more), and are usually designed for hot spots or heavy-duty enterprise usage. This approach is usually only useful if you're set-ting up a big "for-pay" hot spot like we describe in Chapter 12.

✔ You can set up a small RADIUS server on a PC in your network using some RADIUS software that replicates the big RADIUS servers used by telephone companies and ISPs. You can even do this with free software (check out www.freeradius.org).

✔ You can subscribe to an online *hosted* 802.1X authentication service. For a monthly fee, you can use a remote RADIUS server to authenticate users and manage keys.

As far as choosing between creating your own server and going with a hosted service, we're okay with both approaches. If you've got a PC that can handle it, running your own server is probably cheaper. But the prices for hosted services aren't really all that high, and they are fully supported and probably a bit easier to set up and maintain.

How 802.1X secures your network

802.1X follows a few steps to secure your network by authenticating devices connecting to the network:

1. **When a new *supplicant* (unauthenticated device) connects to your access point, the access point opens up a single *port*.**

2. **The open port allows the device to connect only to the authentication server (the RADIUS server) on your network or across the Internet.**

   All other traffic (like Web surfing, e-mail, or other network services) is blocked until the device is authorized.

3. **The 802.1X supplicant client software connects to the server using a protocol called *EAP* (or Extensible Authentication Protocol — see the section titled "EAP, PEAP, take a leap") and exchanges messages with the RADIUS server to confirm identities.**

   This authentication is two-way — the client confirms that it is, indeed, the client, and the wireless network does the same thing.

4. **After the authentication has taken place, the access point grants full access to the device that's connecting.**

   The authentication server also sets up an encryption key to secure the data flowing over the wireless LAN.

EAP, PEAP, take a leap

One very confusing angle to 802.1X is the EAP protocol that governs the actual authentication that happens within 802.1X. 802.1X defines the overall process of connecting to an access point and then to an authentication server, whereas EAP defines the actual messages sent back and forth and how they authenticate a device connecting to the network. Think of it as getting cash at an ATM — the overall process involves going to the ATM, putting your card into

the slot, getting your cash and receipt, and so on: That is comparable to
802.1X. The actual authentication process, comparable to EAP in this scenario,
happens when you type your secret PIN code into the keypad.

This "process within a process" approach makes 802.1X a very robust and
flexible system because different types of EAP authentication can take place
within an 802.1X system, depending upon a network administrator's needs
and wishes. EAP can evolve over time to include new and improved methods
of authentication without requiring any upgrade of Wi-Fi access points and
network infrastructure. Theoretically, a new EAP system could plug right into
the process without affecting everything else. To go back to our ATM example, the authentication process could be upgraded by replacing the PIN and
keypad with a fingerprint reader or an iris scanner. The rest of the process
would remain unchanged and (theoretically at least) the rest of the ATM
machine and infrastructure could remain the same.

What does this mean to you? Primarily, it means that you need to be aware of
what type of EAP process is being used by your authentication server. And
you need to make sure that the supplicant client software that you use to
authenticate your computer or devices on the network supports the same
EAP type used by the RADIUS server.

The EAP protocol has multiple variants, each using slightly differing methods
to govern how messages are sent back and forth between client devices on
the network and the authentication server. The Wi-Fi Alliance (the folks who
carry the most weight in these matters) currently defines the following types
of EAP for 802.1X and WPA-Enterprise certified products:

- ✔ EAP/TLS

- ✔ EAP-TTLS/MSCHAPv2

- ✔ PEAPv0/EAP-MSCHAPv2

- ✔ PEAPv1/EAP-GTC

- ✔ EAP-SIM

We're not going to bother defining all of the acronyms in the list above. Trust
us: You don't really need to know what they mean. What you do need to know
is which of those EAP methods is being used by your authentication server
so that you can make sure that your Wi-Fi equipment and supplicant software
can also support that EAP standard.

The most commonly used EAP standards are EAP/TLS — this was the original
EAP system tested and approved by the Wi-Fi Alliance. It uses digital certificates (encrypted documents on your computer or devices) similar to those
used by secure Web sites.

The other EAP standard often used in Wi-Fi networks is the PEAPv0/
EAP-MSCHAPv2 system. This standard uses a username and password combination for user authentication, instead of digital certificates. By the way, the
MS in MSCHAPv2 stands for Microsoft, so you won't be surprised to learn
that this EAP method is supported in Microsoft XP operating systems.

You can find the supplicant software needed for these different EAP types in
three different places:

✔ **In your operating system:** Macintosh OS X 10.3 (and later) and
Microsoft Windows XP (Service Pack 1 and later) both include support
for 802.1X and most common EAP types.

✔ **In your wireless adapter client software:** Although letting Windows
control your wireless networking hardware (with the Zero Config wireless networking system) is often the easiest approach — all Wi-Fi
adapters also come with their own drivers and client software that can
be used for connecting to networks, configuring the adapters, and such.
If the device supports 802.1X, you can also use this software as your
supplicant.

If you're connecting a non-PC device (like a media adapter or a wireless
Ethernet bridge), this is where you're going to find the EAP support —
usually in the Web-based interface to the device.

✔ **In some third-party software:** Many of the hosted 802.1X solutions we
talk about later in this chapter include special client software you can
install on your PC or Mac. This software includes the appropriate
802.1X supplicant, so you won't need to rely on one of the other two
sources. This is especially helpful if the EAP type you're using is a little
bit off the beaten path (in other words, not supported natively in
Windows or Mac OS X).

We give you some examples of how to use EAP and supplicant software to
connect to an 802.1X-authenticated AP in the next section.

Securing Your Own Network

Throughout the rest of this chapter, we step back from the boring (but
important) details about security standards and systems, and get into the
real meat of the matter — how to secure networks, computers, and data in
various situations.

We skip some of the very basic "click here and do this or that" steps here, for
two reasons:

✔ We figure that you already know how to do this, and that you're reading *WNH&M For Dummies* for more sophisticated information.

✔ The details vary depending on exactly which operating system and network adapter and access point you're using, and we've got limited space here.

You can always check out our other book, *Wireless Home Networking For Dummies,* for step-by-step details on things like turning on WPA encryption. Your equipment manuals (and vendor's Web pages) also likely have page after page of step-by-step tutorials for this process.

The first step to securing your own network is to take stock of what devices you've got connected to the network, and what capabilities each of those devices has. Each device's capabilities can be found on a label, on the original box, in the owner's manual, or on the manufacturer's Web site. You may also find a Wi-Fi Alliance certification (online or in the product's documentation) like the one shown in Figure 8-1. This certification explicitly lists which encryption and authentication systems have been approved for the product.

Figure 8-1: An interoperability certification identifies the security measures your device can handle.

Your wireless network is only as secure as the weakest link in the chain. If you've got some oddball device in the network that won't work in an encrypted, authenticated, secure Wi-Fi environment, you have only two choices:

✔ Shut down (or lower) the security of your network (not a good choice).

✔ Take that device off of the network (and replace it with something that supports your favored security system).

Sometimes you'll find older devices in your network (or even new devices that you're considering adding to the network) that don't meet the latest and greatest security standards. Table 8-1 shows what happens to your security if you try to mix and match between WPA, WEP, and unsecured devices.

You can't really mix and match security — your entire network will be capable of only the least common security denominator (for example, if you have five WPA devices and one WEP-only device, you're stuck with WEP for everything). Our point here is to simply let you know what happens if you own gear with differing capabilities, and how it affects your overall network security.

Table 8-1	Mixing and Matching Security	
Highest Security Type	**Lowest Security Type**	**Effective Security for Your Network**
WPA-Enterprise	WPA-Enterprise	WPA-Enterprise: highly secure including authentication
WPA-Enterprise	WPA-Home	WPA-Home: highly secure, no true authentication
WPA	WEP	WEP: marginally secure
WPA	None	None
WEP	WEP	WEP: marginally secure
WEP	None	None

A lot of the devices we discuss in Part IV of the book (relating to adding peripherals like printers, audio systems, and the like) do not yet support WPA. If you use these devices in your network, you can only use WEP encryption, which isn't very secure.

If you run into a situation where a "must have" device is not available with your preferred security system (WPA, in other words), you might consider setting up a separate network for it, with an inexpensive access point attached to one of the wired Ethernet ports on your primary access point or router. You can dedicate this network to the specialized purpose (gaming or music distribution, for example), and secure your entire network by setting up this network with a completely different range of IP addresses.

If you want to have a really secure wireless network, we recommend that you take as many of the following steps as your equipment allows:

✔ **Turn on your highest level of network encryption:** The most basic, and also the most important, step you can take is to enable encryption within your wireless network. WPA is what you want to use here — use WEP only if have no other choice.

If you *must* use WEP, do so, but remember that a determined person could begin reading your network traffic within a day or so with only minimal effort.

✔ **Enable and configure the firewall on your router:** This doesn't secure the wireless portion of your network, but you shouldn't overlook this step. Keeping Internet-based attacks and intrusion off of your network is just as important as securing the airwaves. And if your air security *is* compromised, having a firewall set up can help limit what the bad guy does with your network.

✔ **Use a personal firewall on each PC attached to your network:** Another step that won't make your airwaves more secure, but that will limit the damage if your wireless network is compromised, is the use of personal firewall security on each PC. Mac OS X and Windows XP both have fire-walls built-in, and you can also add a third-party firewall such as ZoneAlarm (www.zonelabs.com). The big benefit of a personal firewall is that it can reduce the chance that your networked PCs will be used for nefarious purposes like spam or virus dissemination because the fire-wall blocks unauthorized programs from accessing the Internet.

✔ **Use good password hygiene:** A lot of Wi-Fi (and network) security unfortunately relies upon passwords and passphrases. Don't choose a password or passphrase (like the one used to generate PSKs for WPA-Personal) that anybody just walking down the street could guess. The best passwords use a combination of numbers and letters, avoid sequential numbers, and don't use words from the dictionary. A random password generator, like the one found at www.winguides. com/security/password.php, can help you create a strong password without much effort.

Remember that no password is completely safe from a brute-force attack (in which a cracker goes through millions and millions of possible com-binations to get at your password). But if you mix letters and numbers, and upper- and lowercase letters, and stay away from easily-identifiable words, your password stands a better chance of remaining unbroken.

✔ **Keep open hot spots separate from your private network:** If you have your own hot spot access point and you're running it in "wide open" mode with no authentication or encryption, you should keep it sepa-rated from your own personal wireless and wired equipment. One of the best ways to do this is to properly configure your network topology and routing to use a completely different set of IP addresses for this public network. In Chapter 5, we show you how to do this.

✔ **If you can, use 802.1X authentication:** Just turning on encryption (with a PSK or passphrase) can help keep strangers from deciphering your wireless messages, but it doesn't do enough to truly lock down your network. If you work at home, have lots of confidential data flowing across the network, or simply want to have the most secure network you can have, you need to use an authentication system: 802.1X.

Most people will tell you that 802.1X is for the big guys — for corporate networks with highly trained (and paid) network admins, megabucks equipment, and the latest and greatest software and hardware upgrades. And until recently, that would have been true — most people can't afford RADIUS server-related equipment for a home or SOHO (small office/home office) network. But with the advent of some new inexpensive services and some consumer or SOHO-level authentication server products, you now can get the same kind of security that until only a year or two ago was the province of big corporations.

In the next two sections, we tell you how to set up 802.1X on your own network, and how to hook yourself up with a *hosted* authentication service that does all the heavy lifting for you (someone else owns and runs the RADIUS server).

Creating your own authentication server

The more difficult and expensive option is to set up your own RADIUS server on a computer *within* your network. Traditionally, RADIUS servers were built on big supersized server computers from companies like Sun Microsystems. You could build one of these, if you wanted, but the hardware, operating system, and RADIUS software would cost you many thousands of dollars.

Obviously, we don't think any *WNH&M For Dummies* readers are going to be putting together such a server for their home or small office networks — at least we hope not. For a smaller network with a limited number of users and access points, you can buy (or download for free!) software that runs on a Windows XP computer or even (if you've got one) a PC running Linux.

There are some pros and cons to running your own RADIUS server for 802.1X authentication. On the pro side:

✔ You run the server, so all aspects of the network's security are in your hands and under your control, and are not being trusted to a third party.

✔ You only have to pay one time (or never, if you use FreeRADIUS) for the software, rather than paying a monthly service fee in perpetuity for a hosted solution.

✔ Because the server is within your network, if your Internet connection goes down, your wireless network stays up. With some hosted services, you lose wireless connections if the DSL line or cable modem goes down.

On the other hand, hosting your own RADIUS server has drawbacks, as well:

- ✔ You need a computer that's attached to the wired part of your network and always turned on to run the RADIUS software. If you don't have a spare PC around to run this on, you might not be able to make an economic justification for a new one just for RADIUS.

- ✔ You have to give up some part of that computer's CPU time (and performance) to keep the software going. This isn't a huge problem, but don't expect to run the RADIUS software on the same computer you're using to render your gigantic Photoshop projects without seeing a performance hit. This isn't a really big deal, but if you're really limited on PC resources, keep it in mind.

- ✔ You have to buy the RADIUS software. We give you some suggestions for free or cheap-ish RADIUS software, but keep in mind that most options require more up-front cash than a hosted solution.

- ✔ You have to do all of the configuration and maintenance of the server and software. That means dealing with things like *certificates* (required by certain EAP types) and just the general upkeep of new users and other changes.

In the end, many folks find that getting rid of this headache and using a hosted service is worth the extra bucks. If you've got one or two APs in your network, and five or ten clients (PCs or other devices) on the authenticated network, going with a hosted service is probably worth the money. But you definitely might consider hosting your own authentication server if you've got a bigger network with dozens of devices, simply because the monthly fees for hosted services can really rack up.

If you do decide to host your own RADIUS server, here are a couple of options you might consider:

- ✔ **LucidLink:** If your network consists of Windows XP (or Windows 2000) computers, and you've got one that's always on and connected to your network, you might consider LucidLink from Interlink Networks, Inc. This product (available at www.lucidlink.com) provides an easy-to-configure (it takes only 15 minutes!) authentication server that you can administer yourself without breaking the bank. And it's simple enough to use that you won't feel like bonking your head on the nearest brick wall in frustration.

  LucidLink Home Office Edition can even cost you nothing (*nothing!*) in its simplest form, a three-user edition that could support a small network. Most folks probably have more than three computers or devices on their network, and for them, LucidLink offers a bunch of different software license options, supporting users in increments of ten or more. The LucidLink Web site has more details on the pricing, where to buy, and equipment compatibility and requirements. Figure 8-2 shows the LucidLink administration screen.

✔ **FreeRADIUS:** If you've got a Linux box in your network and you feel comfortable compiling software (if you're a Linux user, you know what this means — if you're a Windows user, and you don't know, don't worry about it), you can get into the RADIUS world for free. The aptly named FreeRADIUS project is designed to provide a full service, industrial-strength RADIUS server that can support even a large-scale Wi-Fi network.

Figure 8-2:
Running
your own
authenti-
cation with
LucidLink.

To find out more about FreeRADIUS, and to download the latest build of the software, check out the project's Web site at www.freeradius.org. You can also find a great online tutorial telling you how to get up and running with FreeRADIUS at the following URL: http://tldp.org/HOWTO/html_single/8021X-HOWTO/.

Another open source project for Linux users that might come in handy is the Xsupplicant project (www.open1x.org). This software project provides an 802.1X supplicant client software for Linux users, equivalent to those supplicants included in Mac OS X and Windows XP.

Using an 802.1X service

If you don't have the time and energy (or the spare computer) to run your own RADIUS server, tying your network into a hosted authentication service is a good alternative. These services require you to make just a few simple settings in your access point(s) (we'll let you know which settings), and then set up your PCs using either your own supplicant software (built-into the OS) or a piece of client software that makes it even easier to get up and running.

These hosted authentication products often have a "per-license" fee structure. In other words, you must pay more for each user or incremental bunch of users you add to the network. Users aren't just people using computers — they can also be devices on your network involved in machine-to-machine communications like storage devices, audio servers, or Xboxes. So although these hosted authentication products are often reasonably priced, if you add many users or connected devices to your network, you may end up finding a better bargain by configuring your own authentication server software.

Hosted authentication services are a relatively new thing on the marketplace. Tons of alternatives aren't available yet, but home and small office users do have a few choices. A couple of our favorites include

✔ **Wireless Security Corporation's WSC Guard:** Found at www.wireless securitycorp.com, this service provides a completely hosted and easy-to-use RADIUS authentication service for users ranging from a single AP and a few users up to bigger networks with dozens of APs and hundreds of users. WSC Guard uses the PEAP (Protected EAP) protocol for authentication, and can be used with a long list of Access Points (the WSC Web site has an ever-growing list of compatible models).

WSC Guard has a few unique features that make it particularly user-friendly:

  • Client software that takes care of both the supplicant client and all of the AP and client configuration. You don't need to spend any time in your AP's Web configuration page or in your PC's wireless config systems (like Windows XP Zero Config).

  • Free guest access for up to 48 hours at a time. You don't need to bump up your account to a higher number of users if you have occasional guests on your network. Guest users can download the free client software, or they can configure their computer's own supplicant programs (manually or using an Active X control on the WSC Web site) for access.

  • A Web-based management portal where you (as the "admin") can add users, delete users, control access levels, and more.

Figure 8-3 shows the WSC admin page. The service starts at $4.95 a month per client (less per month for larger networks, or if you pay for a year in advance).

✔ **WiTopia's SecureMyWiFi:** The closest competitor to WSC Guard is the SecureMyWiFi service offered by a company called WiTopia (part of a company called Full Mesh Networks). WiTopia's service offers many of the same service features as WSC Guard, including a Web-based management "admin" portal, and hosted PEAP-based 802.1X authentication services. You can find out more at www.witopia.net/aboutsecuremy.html.

The big difference between the two is philosophical. Whereas WSC Guard uses client software to configure APs and to control access from the PC (limiting the service to Windows XP and 2000 users — other operating systems can use it but are not officially supported), SecureMyWiFi relies upon the supplicants built into Windows XP/2000, Mac OS X, and some versions of Linux, and in doing so supports more users with mixed networks. You need to spend a few minutes configuring your equipment, but it's not difficult (we walk you through the general steps in the next two sections and WiTopia has specific instructions on their Web site). The big advantage is price — the service is just $29 a year for one AP and up to five clients (with additional fees for extra clients and APs). The one thing we think is missing is the free guest access found in WSC Guard — if a guest accesses your network and you're already at your limit of clients, you either have to pay more or not allow the access. Figure 8-4 shows the SecureMyWiFi admin console Web page.

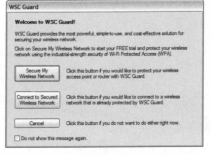

Figure 8-3:
Configuring
your users
with WSC
Guard.

One potential pitfall for hosted 802.1X services is that these services are directly reliant upon the reliability of your Internet connection. If your DSL or cable modem goes down, you lose your connection to the 802.1X server. And when this happens, your clients can't remain connected to the access point — they won't have a current key or authorization when the 802.1X authorization "times out" (usually in a matter of a few minutes).

WSC Guard provides a bit of software to protect against this — it reverts to the WPA PSK method of encryption if the Internet connection goes down. WiTopia's service doesn't provide this backup. If you're using your network primarily for Internet sharing (and not for computer-to-computer communications within the LAN), this really isn't a problem. If you do a lot of intra-LAN communicating, spending the extra money for WSC's service might be worthwhile, just because of this fallback position.

WiTopia
Supporting Your WiFi Security :: *Customer Portal*

| SecureMyWiFi | myServices | Forums | Docs | Logout |

AP Manufacturer	Model	Action		
Apple	AirPort Express	Info	Change	Delete
proxim	AP-600	Info	Change	Delete
LINKSYS A Division of Cisco Systems, Inc.	WRT54GS	Info	Change	Delete
CISCO SYSTEMS	AP 1200	Info	Change	Delete
D-Link	DI-624	Info	Change	Delete

Users	Password	Action	
steve@w0010020	XXXXXXX	Change	
tara@w0010020	XXXXXXX	Change	Delete
burak@w0010020	XXXXXXXX	Change	Delete
bill@w0010020	XXXXXXXX	Change	Delete
available	XXXXXXXX	Add	
available	XXXXXXXX	Add	
available	XXXXXXXX	Add	
available	XXXXXXXX	Add	
available	XXXXXXXX	Add	
available	XXXXXXXX	Add	
available	XXXXXXXX	Add	
available	XXXXXXXX	Add	
available	XXXXXXXX	Add	
available	XXXXXXXX	Add	
available	XXXXXXXX	Add	
available	XXXXXXXX	Add	
available	XXXXXXXX	Add	
available	XXXXXXXX	Add	
available	XXXXXXXX	Add	

Figure 8-4:
Controlling
your
network
access with
SecureMy
WiFi.

Setting up an AP

To get set up with a hosted authentication service, you'll need to take a few steps.

You need WPA-Enterprise/802.1X-compliant access points and client hardware/ software. Check the Web sites of your preferred service provider for their hardware and software recommendations.

1. **First, set up an account with your preferred service provider.**

   We talk about a few you might want to check out in the next section.

Keep in mind that you might need to set up your account a day or so in advance of actually using the authentication service — it can take that long for all of the certificates to get set up and issued.

2. **Print out the usernames, passwords/shared secrets, and certificates that you receive by e-mail from your hosted service provider and keep the hard copy someplace safe.**

   You may also receive a download link for *client* software that acts as the 802.1X supplicant and may also help you set up your access point.

3. **Select the Security tab within your AP's Web configuration page (you'll usually find this at 192.168.0.1 or at a similar IP address).**

4. **Turn on the encryption by selecting WPA RADIUS or WPA ENTER-PRISE or something similar (it varies by AP vendor).**

5. **Select TKIP for the encryption protocol.**

6. **Enter your service's RADIUS server *host name* (like radius.service name.com) or IP address, and *port number* (like 1812) in the RADIUS Server Address and Port boxes.**

7. **Cut and paste the shared secret or key from the e-mail you got from the service provider — this will usually be the public key for your authentication certificate of your service.**

8. **Save your setting and exit the configuration page.**

   Typically this reboots your AP and resets all connections.

The instructions above are purposely generic. Your own AP will have its own specific screens and steps to follow, but they should be similar to the ones we describe. Keep in mind that some services, like Wireless Security Corp's WSC Guard, include client software that not only sets up your computers, but also handles the AP configuration for you.

Setting up a client

After you've configured your AP, you need to go to each PC or device in your network and configure the supplicant software on each for your service's specific EAP type.

For example, for Windows XP computers, follow something similar to the following steps:

1. **Open Windows XP Wireless Zero Config by right-clicking its icon in the system tray and selecting View Available Networks.**

2. **Click the <u>Change Advanced Settings</u> link.**

   The Wireless Network Connection Properties window opens.

3. **Click Add.**

4. **In the window that opens, select the Association tab, type your network's SSID, and make the following selections:**

   • For the Network Authentication menu, select WPA.

   • For the Data Encryption menu, select TKIP.

5. **Select the Authentication tab and make sure that the Enable IEEE 802.1X Authentication for this Network checkbox is checked.**

6. **In the EAP Type drop-down menu, select the appropriate EAP type for your service provider.**

7. **Click Properties and, in the window that pops up, enter and select the certificate authorities and/or authentication methods according to the instructions you received from your service provider, as shown in Figure 8-5.**

Many services offer special client software that lets you avoid all or most of these steps — saving you time and effort.

Figure 8-5: Choosing an EAP type in Windows XP.

Part III
Wireless on the Go

The 5th Wave

By Rich Tennant

In this part . . .

*W*ireless networks don't end when you walk out the door. The whole world is wireless, and we're going to help you tap into the airwaves in this Part. First, we tell you how to jump onto the hot spot revolution — connecting to Wi-Fi networks wherever you are.

We continue by helping you figure out how to keep your data safe and sound when you're on the road at a hot spot (or hopping onto a wireless network at work, at a friend's, or elsewhere). We tell you about VPNs and other measures you can take to ensure that you'll always connect with confidence.

We also go mobile and tell you how to get your car outfitted with wireless gear. Between Bluetooth connections in the car, Wi-Fi connections in your garage, and mobile data services, your car can be about the most unwired thing you own.

Finally, we tell you how to create your own bit of the wireless world by showing you how to use your wireless gear to set up a hot spot at your home or business. Stop being a consumer; instead, be a provider!

Chapter 9

On the Road Again with 802.11

Showing you how to build and use your own wireless networks in your home or office is our primary focus here in *WNH&M For Dummies,* but we also want to make sure that you get the most out of your wirelessly-networked gear when you are away from home! We're like that — always looking out for you. Look how little you had to pay to get that kind of service!

In this chapter, we discuss the phenomenon of Wi-Fi *hot spots* — the public Wi-Fi networks that you can join (for free or for a fee — depending upon the wishes of the operator) to get your online fix wherever you are. If you live in the U.S., you can get onto one of tens of thousands of "known" hot spots, and that number doesn't include many unpublicized free hot spots or other networks to which you might have access on a temporary basis (like those at a convention center, or on a university campus).

In this chapter, we explain everything you need to know about hot spots, and how to get yourself connected to one when you're in range. We talk about both free hot spots (our favorite kind) and the "for pay" ones that we use when we're expensing it. We also tell you about how to search for hot spots — with sections on finding hot spots with prior planning (looking up hot spots online before you head out) and accessing hot spots on the spur-of-the-moment (searching for them wherever you are). We also discuss how to keep yourself (or at least your data) safe when connecting to a hot spot. Finally, we talk about some forthcoming technologies that are going to make hot spotting even more convenient and cool!

So what are you waiting for? Grab a laptop, head down to the local café, and read along!

Hot Spots for Everyone

If you've been involved in the high-tech world at all, you've probably read or at least heard quoted a book called *The Innovator's Dilemma* by Clayton Christensen, published by HarperBusiness. (He's a professor at Harvard Business School, but even more impressive to us, he's the father of former Duke Blue Devil hoopster Matt Christensen. Go Duke!)

In this book, Professor Christensen talks, among other things, about *disruptive technologies* — new products that totally change the competitive landscape of a market and push (or at least threaten to push) established, market-leading products behind. An example in the book is the Intel 8088 processor — which helped launch the PC revolution and moved the entire world from handfuls of big computers to billions of personal computers.

We think that Wi-Fi is a disruptive technology too (and we're not saying this to be clever or pat ourselves on the back — *everyone* thinks Wi-Fi is a disruptive technology). More specifically, we think that Wi-Fi hot spots themselves are, or at least can be, a disruptive technology too.

The concept is dead simple — hook a Wi-Fi access point or router up to an inexpensive "wired" broadband connection and offer free or low-priced Wi-Fi access to all passers-by. Why not? You can offer a public service, make a lot of folks happy, and perhaps even make a few bucks.

Up until recently, however, this dead simple equation hasn't been so dead simple in practice because the cost elements involved in creating a hot spot have been out of line with the benefits (social or economic). Buying the hot spot equipment and broadband access was a bit too expensive to allow most hot spot operators to break even.

This has changed, however, with a combination of an incredible plunge in Wi-Fi pricing (where Wi-Fi routers can be picked up for $30) and an increase in Wi-Fi users (everyone's got Wi-Fi in their laptops these days). These two developments mean that more folks can afford to offer free hot spots or can make a suitable return on their investment with for-pay hot spots.

But that's not the disruptive part. Wi-Fi hot spots are disruptive because they offer users a faster, easier, and cheaper means of getting online than anything currently being offered by mobile phone operators (at least in the U.S.). And with new *mesh* (networks where APs "talk" with each other to extend the network's range) and metro-wide Wi-Fi technologies hitting the streets, hot spots can become *hot zones* and compete directly (and effectively) with mobile 3G (third-generation, high-speed mobile) systems, in at least some areas. Add in the Wi-Fi VoIP (Voice over Internet Protocol) technologies we discuss in Chapter 15, and you've got something that will make any mobile phone/data operator stand up and take notice. (In fact, they have noticed, and many of them are playing the game of "If you can't beat 'em, join 'em," and starting their own hot spot operations!)

A matter of politics

A lot of cities, towns, counties, boroughs, villages, townships, and other forms of municipalities are getting involved in Wi-Fi hot spots. As we discuss in Chapter 1, these local governments are putting together their own Wi-Fi hot spots for a variety of reasons — including economic reasons (that is, attracting businesses and customers to town) — but mainly because high-speed Internet is a public service, like traffic lights, fire fighting, and parking regulation enforcement. (Okay, this last one isn't really a service we support.)

Many of the big telephone and cable service providers, however, don't like this idea at all. They say that they might someday install their own Wi-Fi networks, and if the city is already offering Wi-Fi, that's competition they don't need. The phone and cable companies are also afraid that the municipal Wi-Fi networks might keep people from ordering DSL or cable modem service in their own homes. So they have been spending many many millions of dollars lobbying politicians to pass state laws banning such networks.

To which we say (and we're quoting Col. Potter from *M*A*S*H* here): "Horse hockey!" Even if municipal Wi-Fi hot spots *were* competitive with services from the phone or cable company (and we're not sure we even concede that point), they are not *unfairly* competitive. In fact, these municipal services might be the only competitor that exists in many towns — and we believe, like the good capitalists we are (Danny went to business school, and Pat majored in economics, so we've got our capitalist street cred going here), that a little competition might be just the shot in the arm the incumbents need.

So what we're saying is this: If you agree with us, and you're feeling like entering into the political process, please do! If your state has such legislation on the docket, write a letter, send a fax, shoot off an e-mail. Make your voice heard. "We want our Wi-Fi and we're not going to take it any more!"

There, that felt good to say. As the bloggers often put it: `</rant>`.

Ultimately, we think that hot spots will both compete and cooperate with mobile wireless services. But even though Wi-Fi isn't going to "win" over 3G, it is going to have (and is already having) a significant, disruptive, effect on the market.

Finding Hot Spots

Maybe you already know about hot spots, or perhaps you've sort of heard of them before, but aren't sure what all the fuss is about. Or maybe, just maybe, you've missed all of the hype and have never heard of the whole crazy idea before you read this chapter. Whatever the case, we hope you're now psyched up, ready to take your laptop in hand and seek out your local hot spots.

Before you hit the road, may we recommend that you first do a little bit of research? You can, of course, just wing it and hope to find a hot spot wherever you are. And indeed, if you are in a big and densely populated city, like

New York or San Francisco (or London or Tokyo), you've got a good chance of just stumbling onto a hot spot.

Elsewhere, however, it pays to spend a few minutes doing some simple Web searching — particularly if you must get online (like when you've got to mail out that presentation that you're going to finish on the train — not that Danny ever does this!).

The majority of hot spots use the slower 802.11b Wi-Fi technology, although a few use 802.11g. This isn't a problem for those of you using 802.11g in your laptops or handheld computers because 802.11g is backwards-compatible with 802.11b. If, however, you're using an 802.11a solution (one that is *not* dual mode, with 802.11g also built-in), you will not be able to connect to any hot spots we've seen. Also, remember that advanced features like MIMO are not likely to be found in hot spots either.

Finding the freebies

For many of us, the best kind of hot spot is the one that doesn't cost us too much — so how about trying a free hot spot on for size? How can you beat that?

Free Wi-Fi hot spots abound, and if you play your cards right, and plan your trip accordingly, you can get online, send files, read your e-mails, and do your instant messaging (and even make VoIP calls!) without spending a penny.

Here are a few places you can get online without reaching into your bank account:

- ✔ **"Oops" hot spots:** Here's the dirty little (not so) secret of Wi-Fi: A lot of people want wireless LANs in their homes and offices for their personal use, so they hook a cheap access point into their cable or DSL modems. And they don't do anything else — like turn on security or do anything to "harden" their wireless networks (although access point vendors often now turn security on as default settings to fix this).

    That means that these hot spots are open for you to log into. We leave it to you to determine the ethical, legal, and moral elements involved in going online with one of these personal unsecured "hot spots." We think it's probably kinda okay to hop on to one of these hot spots for a quick e-mail check or other low-impact, short-term use. For anything beyond that, you might want to ask permission of the owner/operator. It's okay — plenty of folks are glad to share their broadband connection!

    Despite our brilliant rhetorical skills, neither of us are lawyers. If you get carted away to the pokey by local law enforcement for using an "unauthorized" hot spot, don't blame us. Blame the Patriot Act or whichever political party you didn't vote for!

As more people start using portable "travel routers," you'll probably find more of these "oops" access points in broadband-enabled hotels. Don't be surprised if the person three doors down has plugged in an access point just to be able to use his laptop while sitting on the bed or the patio. If the hotel charges for their in-room broadband, they would probably frown upon your logging into this open access point — although the folks we've spoken to who work in the hospitality broadband market say they don't specifically monitor for this situation.

✔ **"Open" hot spots:** Some folks are just generous. They install wireless access points in their homes, apartments, dorm rooms, or places of business and they leave them unprotected on purpose. Not only will they not get upset with you if you hop onto the Internet through their network connections, they welcome it.

The hard part here is determining the difference between "open" and "oops" hot spots. If you're unable to tell, you may wish to err on the side of caution. This issue explains why we're such big fans of the community networks that we discuss next — they make it easy to tell whether you're allowed to use the access points.

How do you tell if a particular hot spot is an "open" or an "oops"? Some folks make it easy for you by naming their networks — setting the ESSID, that is — with a name that expresses its openness. You may find, for example, the word `-open` or `-public` appended to the end of the network name. Other folks put a Web URL or e-mail address in the network name, so you can check in when you're online and see why they are offering free Internet access.

If you want to leave your access point open to the public, make sure that you name your ESSID something public and open-sounding, like "Sandy and Ron's Open Access" or "Holly and Danny's Public Wi-Fi," to let others know your intentions. Note that the ESSID is limited to 32 characters, so you can't write a treatise.

✔ **Community networks:** If you really want to go online for free without any moral, legal, or ethical qualms, try to find a *community network* in your area. These networks are put together by groups of volunteers who offer their time, money, or Internet connection to help provide free Wi-Fi access for neighbors. Literally hundreds of these community networks exist around the country and your best bet of finding one is to search through one of the Web sites devoted to tracking and aggregating such hot spots. A few of the best sources include the following:

• **FreeNetworks.org:** FreeNetworks.org is an overarching group that supports the development of free networks worldwide. Go to the Web site (`www.freenetworks.org`) to read the group's charter and peering policies. Basically, they ask affiliated networks (called, no surprise, FreeNetworks) to connect together (or peer) with open access to users and without modifying or interfering with data running across their networks. The site also helps you *find* free networks to connect to; just follow the links to any of the many affiliated FreeNetworks.

- **Personal Telco:** One of the FreeNetworks peered with FreeNetworks.org is the Portland, Oregon-based Personal Telco Project (`www.personaltelco.net`). The group has put together over 100 hot spots throughout the Portland metro area, and is aiming to blanket the entire city (already considered one of the most "unwired" in the country) with free Wi-Fi. If you live in Portland, or are just visiting, check out their site and map for more details.

- **NYCwireless:** If you're in the Big Apple, check out `www.nyc wireless.net`. This group promotes community networks in the New York City metro area, and has more than 700 hot spots up and running. Check out the site for a map of hot spots next time you head to NYC.

✔ **Municipal networks:** A large number of cities throughout the country have launched wireless hot zones. Although some offer their services for a nominal fee, many are providing Wi-Fi absolutely free. An example is the network built in the town of Hermosa Beach, California. Seriously, what could be better than hitting the beach and getting online for free? (Dare we say, "Surf's Up!") Check out `www.wifihermosabeach.com` for details.

✔ **"Free" commercial hot spots:** Although some commercial locations charge for Wi-Fi access (we discuss these hot spots in the next section, "Paying for your Wi-Fi"), many locations have made a business decision to offer free Wi-Fi to customers. They're not just being nice (well, maybe some of them are). Instead, they have discovered that the increased business they get from having Wi-Fi more than offsets the costs of providing such access. A few examples where you might find free commercially-operated hot spots include the following:

  - **Hotels:** Although most hotels started offering Wi-Fi as a profit center (meaning they profit, you pay), many chains have found the free WI-Fi religion, and have made Wi-Fi (as well as in-room "wired" Ethernet connections) a standard amenity. Surprisingly, it's not the big-dollar hotels who are doing this, but instead many of the lower and mid-priced chains who focus on frequent business travelers. In particular, many of the "Suites" chains are offering free Wi-Fi these days.

Some hotel chains offer free Wi-Fi and broadband to their "preferred" customers, but charge others. You usually don't have to pay any money to get "preferred" status; just sign up online or at the desk when you check in. For example, check out the Wyndham chain of hotels and their Wyndham ByRequest membership (`www.wyndham.com`).

  - **Retail:** Lots of retail locations are offering free Wi-Fi to customers. The most common, of course, are the coffee shops and cafes, but some national restaurant chains (like Panera Bread — `www.panerabread.com`) and even entire malls offer free Wi-Fi.

- **Airport lounges:** Most airport terminals have for-pay Wi-Fi networks in place for the great unwashed masses of air travelers. But if you're one of the super road warriors (or just a VIP) who belongs to one of the airline "lounge" clubs, you may just be in luck. Many of the airline lounges now offer free Wi-Fi along with their complimentary beverages and peanuts. Of course, you've gotta pay to get in the door, but if your business will buy you a membership, you're all set for using your airport time productively.

We think that most hospitality and retail hot spots — particularly those found in hotels — will eventually be free. Providing Wi-Fi to the casual user is becoming cheaper and easier nearly every day, and it's increasingly seen as a standard amenity, just like those little soaps in the bathroom.

Paying for your Wi-Fi

Sometimes you just can't find a free hot spot where you are (or where you are going). We know it hurts to admit it, but sometimes you just have to pay to play, and Wi-Fi is no different. The trend is towards more and more free Wi-Fi hot spots, but that doesn't take away from the fact that a number of businesses are built around for-pay Wi-Fi that can serve you very well (and reliably) when you're on the road.

The good thing about paying for your Wi-Fi is that you can expect something you won't get at any free hot spot: support. If you're paying good money, you should expect (and will usually find) an actual live, talking person who can help you out if you have trouble getting online.

Most for-pay Wi-Fi networks are designed around serving business travelers. That means that they have some additional features not found on your average free network, like the following:

✔ **High-speed backhaul:** *Backhaul* is just the fancy industry term for the broadband connection to the Internet that your hot spot uses to provide you with access to the Internet. In a free hot spot, you're usually relying on someone's cable modem or DSL connection, with a relatively slow upstream speed and absolutely no service quality guarantees. When you're paying, expect that the hot spot access points typically are connected to faster business broadband connections that offer equal speeds in both directions. These connections should have service quality guarantees and should not be oversubscribed like residential connections, so neighboring Internet connections should not slow down your throughput.

Oversubscription is a term that describes the situation where there is a larger requirement for bandwidth than is available. This is often defined as a ratio of the inbound demand to the outbound supply, such as 20:1. When applied to a hot spot, oversubscription refers to how many users are all contending for the same amount of bandwidth on the backhaul connection. An 802.11g connection to an access point that is connected to a mere 128K DSL connection shared by 40 other people at the same time does not yield a satisfactory online experience, particularly if you are trying to do VoIP. There's no industry standard for reporting over-subscription ratios and other items that would help you decide which hot spot is best for your needs. Unfortunately, you can't necessarily even claim that the for-pay options are always going to be better than those that are free (but they will be most of the time). Caveat emptor . . . you learn from your personal experience who has the best connectivity.

- ✔ **VPN support:** We talk more about VPNs in Chapter 10. A VPN (or *virtual private network*) is a secure "tunnel" through the Internet that allows you to connect to your office or corporate network just as if you were linked to that network through your own private line instead of a shared Internet connection. Most for-pay hot spots have routers that support VPN connections; many free hot spots do not. Many for-pay Wi-Fi services include a bit of *client* software that includes a VPN client so that every single bit of data you send over the airwaves is encrypted from the moment it leaves your computer until it gets to the provider's data center and goes onto the public Internet.

- ✔ **Airlink security and encryption:** Some for-pay networks are beginning to "turn on" encryption protocols like WPA, which secure your wireless connection from eavesdropping (we discuss WPA in Chapter 3). Today, this is still extremely rare, but we think that by 2006, you'll start seeing more hot spots using Wi-Fi security.

There are literally dozens and dozens of providers of for-pay wireless hot spots. For example, some hotel chains charge their guests for Wi-Fi access, as do many convention centers, meeting centers, and the like.

Identifying hot spot operators

Generally speaking, you can get paid hot spot access from one of three types of companies:

- ✔ **Retail and hospitality operators:** These are simply retail (restaurants, malls, cafés) and hospitality locations (like hotels and convention centers) that operate their own Wi-Fi hot spots. These companies own the business where the hot spot is located, and also operate the hot spot.

- ✔ **Hot spot operators:** Hot spot operators are companies who *don't* own the location (or run the business) where the hot spots are operated. Instead, they focus solely on the operation of lots of hot spots in lots of locations. Hot spot operators own and operate the access points and also provide the *backend* network that provides user authentication, billing, and more. A good example of a hot spot operator is Wayport (www.wayport.com).

Some hot spot operators are actually *WISPs* (wireless ISPs) who don't focus just on short-term access to users in a hot spot, but actually deploy Wi-Fi in a wider area and attempt to supplement or replace broadband ISP services like DSL and cable modem.

✔ **Aggregators/roaming services:** Some hot spot providers own neither the venue nor the Wi-Fi equipment, but they do own something just as valuable: a network that can connect hot spots to the Internet and to a security, billing, and access authentication system. These folks are called hot spot aggregators — the most famous being Boingo Wireless, who we discuss in the section later in this chapter entitled, "Putting on Your Roaming Shoes."

The lines between all of these categories are pretty blurry. Some companies operate their own hot spots and also aggregate, for example. Many hot spot operators join *peering* agreements with each other that let their customers *roam* between different networks without having to pay twice. We call them all *hot spot operators* generically, unless we're specifically talking about a function like roaming and aggregation.

Looking at the top hot spot operators

In the end, it really doesn't matter too much which type of company is operating a particular hot spot. The only real exceptions are the retail and hospitality operators who aren't using the services of a hot spot operator or aggregator, simply because these hot spots are less likely to have the more sophisticated and widely available security services.

Some of the most popular hot spot operators include the following:

✔ **T-Mobile:** These are the folks who've brought Wi-Fi to thousands of Starbucks coffee shops. They've also "unwired" Borders bookstores, FedEx Kinko's stores, and tons of hotels and airports. They have more than 5,400 locations as we write, and about 10,000 more *roaming* locations. Check out maps and listings of all of them, as well as account information, at www.tmobile.com/hotspot. If you've only heard of one hot spot provider, it's probably T-Mobile. You've probably also seen one of their ten million mobile phone service ads, and may already be a customer of that part of their business — if so, you can get a discount on their T-Mobile HotSpot service.

✔ **Boingo:** The *other* big and famous hot spot company is Boingo Wireless (www.boingo.com). Boingo was founded in the early 2000s (here we are halfway through the decade and we still don't know what to call it!) by a guy named Sky Dalton, who also founded another company you may have heard of called EarthLink. Boingo provides hot spot roaming services across more than 15,000 hot spots around the world. We talk a bit more about Boingo in the section called "Oingo Boingo" later in this chapter.

✔ **Wayport:** Wayport is probably the biggest independent operator of hot spots (*independent* meaning not owned by a telephone company). Wayport has more than 7,000 hot spots (along with wired broadband connections) in hotel rooms and Laptop Lane venues in airports. These hot spots are primarily focused on business travelers. Check out www. wayport.com for locations and pricing.

DSL broadband providers such as SBC and Verizon and mobile phone operators like Cingular and Verizon (who are the two biggest phone companies and cellphone operators in America, so they cover a lot of folks) are starting to get into the Wi-Fi hot spot business. One cool result of this is DSL companies offering Wi-Fi hot spot service as a very inexpensive add-on to DSL.

For example, Verizon has launched a service (called Verizon Broadband Anytime) in New York City that allows any DSL customer to use any of several hundred VZ (that's the insider lingo for Verizon) hot spots in Manhattan and the outer boroughs for free. As in no charge. Makes us wish we lived in Manhattan!

How to pay for your hot spot access

A basic truism of for-pay hot spots is that you've got to pay to get online. (Yep, we're not afraid to state the obvious.) How you pay varies from provider to provider, but there are three basic pricing structures:

✔ **Monthly:** The cheapest way to get hot spot access (besides using only free networks) is to sign up for a hot spot provider's monthly plan. Ranging between $20 and $40 a month — depending upon how long a term you sign up for and the number of hot spots the operator actually has — these plans give you unlimited access to all of the operator's hot spots. That includes both hot spots that the company may operate itself, and also any that are part of roaming agreements.

✔ **Day Pass:** If you're a truly infrequent user of for-pay hot spots (like an occasional business traveler), you can pay for access on the spot, so to speak. Most hot spots use a system called a *captive portal,* which means that your Web browser is directed to the hot spot provider's own Web site until you sign in with a monthly account or pay for a day pass. Most hot spot operators accept any major credit card, so you can sign up for the day pass without any human contact! The day pass typically lasts for 24 hours, and the price ranges from $6 to $10.

Many free hot spots in locations such as hotels also use a captive portal, where you might be required to enter your name and room number to authenticate yourself as an authorized user.

A few providers (like T-Mobile) offer "pay as you go" plans where you pay a per-hour or per-minute fee. These plans enable you to go online for a 20-minute e-mail check without spending as much as a day pass. If you're going to be online for more than an hour or so, the day pass is usually the better bargain (in the case of T-Mobile, after an hour and a half, you're spending more on a pay-as-you-go session than you would have spent if you'd just paid for the whole day).

✔ **Prepaid:** Staking out the middle ground is the *prepaid account*. Just like prepaid cellular phones, you spend some amount of cash up front and then you burn off the "minutes" in your account. The biggest proponent of this approach is Wayport, who offers prepaid cards for between 3 and 20 "connections" — a connection being the equivalent of a day pass. Depending on how many you buy, you'll pay between $5 and $8 per connection.

Which is the best approach? It depends upon two big factors: how often you need access, and how often you frequent locations served by the hot spot operator. If you always go to Starbucks or Borders, or always stay in a Wayport-served hotel chain, a monthly plan makes the most economic sense. If you're an infrequent user, you may decide to just pay as you go.

If you travel a lot and you don't always end up in locations served by a single hot spot operator, you might want to consider one of the roaming accounts we discuss next. They sometimes cost a bit more, but they provide a wide variety of mobile access solutions, including not only Wi-Fi but also hotel "wired" broadband and even dial-up Internet.

Putting on Your Roaming Shoes

If you're a real road warrior, you probably won't be able to stick to just one hot spot operator. We know some folks who are both road warriors and coffee hounds, and they basically work by traveling from Starbucks to Starbucks, ordering up quadruple lattes and T-Mobile hot spot access everywhere they go.

We're going to use Starbucks/T-Mobile as an example here, but you can insert your own favorite hot spot operator.

Unfortunately, your ability to avoid the caffeine jitters may not equal that of our road warrior buddies (and friends don't let friends drink decaf!). Or you simply may travel someplace where there is no Starbucks (yes, there are still a few places left!). If so, you may need the services of a hot spot roaming service provider.

For the most part, these roaming services are offered by some of the aggregators we discuss above. For example, Boingo — who partners with hundreds of hot spot operators of all sizes — provides roaming services on networks worldwide.

What these roaming providers all have in common is a series of roaming arrangements with the companies who own hot spots combined with a piece of client software that makes it easy for mobile users and travelers to find access wherever they are. This client software usually also includes security elements like *two-way authentication* (which ensures that you are who you say you are, and also that the hot spot is indeed the legitimate hot spot), VPN support, and encryption.

Oingo Boingo

For $21.95 a month, you can sign up for Boingo's unlimited plan and connect to any of 16,000 hot spots worldwide. The best part about the Boingo experience, in our opinion, is the Boingo client software. This software is available for free download for Windows, Mac OS X, and even for Pocket PC handheld PCs and can be used for *all* of your Wi-Fi connection management. Figure 9-1 shows the Boingo interface in Windows XP.

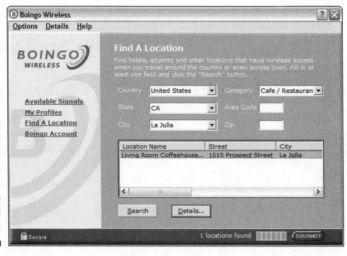

Figure 9-1:
The client not only gets you on Boingo's network, but can control all your Wi-Fi.

Here comes the evil twin

We've all seen it before (on *Melrose Place,* at least). The trusted character starts acting in an unexpected and entirely inappropriate way. Too late, everyone discovers it wasn't the trusted character after all — it was his or her mysterious evil twin. (For you *Doonesbury* fans, it's George Bush's evil twin, Skippy!)

Well, that can happen at Wi-Fi hot spots too! You show up at a location where you expect to find your favorite hot spot provider, you turn on your computer, and up pops the old familiar "Acme hot spots" on the list of available networks. So you sign on to the captive portal Web page, enter your account password and username (or even your credit card), and go online. Except you aren't connected to Acme hot spots at all. You didn't give your confidential account information to the authentication system of Acme hot spots — you gave it to a bad guy!

The evil twin of the hot spot world is a cracker who uses her laptop to "mimic" the real hot spot by broadcasting an identical or deceptively similar SSID near the real hot spot. If you log on, the bad guy uses fake Web pages that look deceptively like the real thing to steal your login information. He may even steal more of your personal information by serving up other fake Web sites (or simply copying everything you send and receive over the network).

The evil twin, by the way, is a variant of those annoying *phishing* e-mails that probably fill your inbox with fake (but realistic) bank and credit card Web pages.

Your best way of avoiding the evil twin is to use an authentication system like those built into many hot spot roaming clients whenever you log into an unfamiliar hot spot. Authentication systems use digital certificates and keys to ensure that every participant in the hot spot is who they say they are. And always remember to use SSL (secure Web sites, in other words) when you're doing any kind of confidential transactions online at a hot spot.

The Boingo client allows you to connect to your home Wi-Fi network, free hot spots, and any Boingo network hot spot, all from the same interface. When you're on the Boingo network as a paying customer, all of your Internet traffic is encrypted and carried through Boingo's own VPN network, so no one can *sniff* your packets and intercept your Internet traffic.

Sniffing packets refers to the act of listening in on a network connection and reading the data as it goes over the network. People with the right equipment can sit next to you while you work and read information as you transmit it from your machine. It's not very nice, we agree, but a good reason to limit credit card use on the Internet when surfing at a public location.

The Boingo client can also protect you against the "Evil Twin" security attack (for more information, see the sidebar titled "Here comes the evil twin"). That's because the Boingo client uses a strong authentication system to ensure that a hot spot with a Boingo SSID will actually be on Boingo's network.

Check out Chapters 8 and 10 for the bottom line on all the things you should be doing to secure your Wi-Fi connections (and your Wi-Fi network).

Finally, Boingo's client (which we discuss in the section later titled "Using the Boingo client") has a built-in hot spot database. This database functions sort of like the location-based databases used in many dial-up Internet dialer programs. You can plug in a country, state, city, area code, or ZIP code, press a button, and the client program spits out a list of hot spots nearby. In many cases, this hot spot display even includes a map of the hot spot and a picture.

Boingo's network and client software aren't used only for Boingo customers. The company "white labels" — provides a customizable generic version — its software for other companies like MCI, EarthLink, and BT Infonet. If you use one of these services to get onto hot spots, you're actually using Boingo!

Going with corporate remote access

Boingo's not the only game in town when it comes to hot spot roaming. A whole category of companies out there is dedicated to providing *remote access* services for businesses. These services are designed to do a few different things, including

- **Provide multiple modes of remote access.** Subscribers to these services can get connected to the Internet (and their corporate networks) via Wi-Fi hot spots, dial-up connections, wired broadband connections, and even wireless data services like 3G.

- **Provide secure connections to corporate networks.** Remote access services offer not only VPN connections over the wireless portion of the network (like Boingo offers), but also provide a way of connecting all the way through the Internet into corporate VPNs. This allows road warriors to securely access file servers, e-mail, intranets, and other network assets just as if they were in the office, no matter where they are.

- **Provide *policy management*.** This makes the network administrators at your business really happy. Because the remote access service controls and monitors the end-to-end network connection, it can ensure that users follow all of the corporate policies regarding network and Internet access. No checking the ESPN.com college basketball scoreboard from that expensive hot spot in Timbuktu!

A lot of companies specialize in remote access solutions. For the most part, these companies are a lot different than Boingo (or T-Mobile or Wayport) in that they really do specialize in the enterprise market. So the average person can't sign up for an account — the focus here is on bigger businesses.

If your business is in need of something more sophisticated than a simple Wi-Fi roaming service, consider one of these services. They're a great way to keep connected (via Wi-Fi or otherwise), and they can provide all of your employees with a secure solution without a lot of sophisticated set-up (using their own client software, which includes the VPN).

We don't talk about them too much here, but if you're looking for a remote access provider, you might want to check out these two companies:

✔ **iPASS:** www.ipass.com

✔ **GoRemote:** www.goremote.com

Getting Online at a Hot Spot

Connecting to a hot spot network is usually as easy as (and in many cases, even easier than) connecting at your home or office.

Using Windows XP Wireless Zero Config

If you're using Windows XP, the easiest way to get online at a hot spot is to just use XP's built-in Wireless Zero Configuration system.

1. **In the system tray in the lower-right corner of your screen, right-click your wireless network adapter's icon.**

2. **Select View Available Wireless Networks.**

   A window like the one shown in Figure 9-2 appears.

3. **Search through the list of available networks until you find the network to which you would like to connect.**

   Note that security-enabled networks (those using WPA or WEP, and which require a password) are identified by a lock icon and the words Security-Enabled Wireless Network.

4. **To select the network you want to connect to, click it to select it, and then click Connect.**

   Your computer connects to the hot spot.

5. **Open your Web browser and try to load a Web site.**

   It doesn't matter what site you load — you can load our site www.digitaldummies.com if you'd like!

If the hot spot is free, you should get onto the Web site right away — if it's a hot spot that requires you to log in, you'll probably see the captive portal site instead. If you get the captive portal, just fill out the required information and log yourself in!

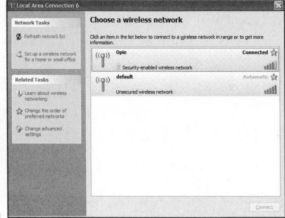

Figure 9-2:
Finding
a hot spot
in Win-
dows XP.

Using the Boingo client

Boingo customers can use the company's software *client* — the program that anyone can download at www.boingo.com — to connect to any hot spot. You don't have to connect to a Boingo hot spot with this client — anyone can download it and use it to help them find and connect to hot spots.

You can also log into many Boingo hot spots just by using a Web browser and going to the captive portal site. The big advantage of using the Boingo client is that the client has a built-in VPN software system that encrypts all of the data you send out over the wireless network. No one sitting nearby your in the airport can surreptitiously "sniff" your data packets and read your email, steal your files, or intercept your downloads of that *American Idol* recap on TWOP (www.televisionwithoutpity.com).

On the Mac

Like Windows XP, the Mac OS X operating system is designed for easy connections to wireless networks. The steps for connecting to a hot spot are similarly short and sweet:

1. **In the Dock, click and hold on the Applications folder and select Internet Connect.**

2. **In the Internet Connect window that opens (Figure 9-3), click on the AirPort icon.**

3. **In the Internet Connect window, use the pull-down menu to select the hot spot network to which you would like to connect.**

4. **If the network requires an encryption key, use the pull-down menu to select the key type and then type the key itself in the text box, as shown in Figure 9-4.**

Boingo also has a client for the Mac OS — it can be used with Mac OS 10.2.8 or above. It works really well, but it doesn't have all of the security features found in the Windows client (although the folks we know at Boingo tell us that the Mac client will be equal to the Windows client in this regard by the end of 2005). It's already a prettier- and more elegant-looking piece of software because Apple has allowed Boingo to very tightly integrate it with the Airport software and the Safari Web browser.

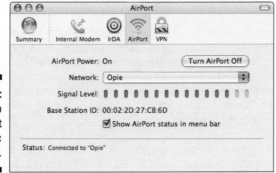

Figure 9-3: Getting onto a hot spot with Mac OS X.

Figure 9-4: Entering an encryption key.

Help, I Need Wireless Access in Paris!

Searching for hot spots on the Web pages of any one hot spot network — be it a free network, a metro or community network, or a pay network — always limits you to a subset of the total number of hot spots available for public use. After all, hot spot company A isn't going to tell you about hot spot company B's network unless they are working together as partners.

So if you want to really find *all* of the access points available to you, you need to cast a wide net.

One way to do this is to simply use some software on your computer to thoroughly search the "airwaves" around you looking for access points. The NetStumbler software we discuss in Chapter 6, for example, does a bloodhound-like job of sniffing out APs nearby.

You don't *need* NetStumbler to do this. The Wireless Zero Config software in Windows XP and the AirPort software on Mac OS X both do a pretty good job of finding any available access points — they just don't give you quite as much detailed information as NetStumbler does.

What NetStumbler and other similar programs (like MacStumbler for Mac OS X) *can't* tell you is whether an open access point is truly a hot spot, or is just one of those unprotected "oops" hot spots we discussed earlier in the chapter.

You can also use a Wi-Fi Finder, which we discuss in Chapter 16, to try to find nearby access points. These devices let you search the airwaves without having to start up your computer.

If you want to err on the side of caution and stick with APs that you know are legitimately available for public use, you can either use a roaming client, or use a Web database to search for them.

Using a roaming client

If you are some place unfamiliar and you unexpectedly have the time or need to go online — meaning you didn't have time to do your homework up front — you can rely upon a roaming service software client.

Roaming software like Boingo's lets you drill down by city and state, ZIP code, or area code and also by location type (like hotel or café). Just enter the basics about where you are and what you're looking for, and the software digs through its database and finds you the nearest hot spots.

You're not just limited to hot spots on Boingo's for-pay network either. The company has added thousands of free hot spots to the database to help you find a connection. You don't even have to pay to download the software — and it assists you in finding available signals too.

The folks at GoRemote, another of the big Wi-Fi roaming providers, have similarly added thousands of free hot spots to their roaming client software. You do need to be a customer to get a hold of this software, but if your business is using it, you have access to over 10,000 hot spots.

Using a Web database

The best way to find hot spots is, of course, to plan ahead. If you're not heading out on a *Family Circle*–esque adventure and you can map out your route to some degree, you can find hot spots ahead of time.

A ton of online hot spot directories enable you to search for both for-pay and free hot spots. Listed below are two of our favorites:

✔ **JiWire:** With more than 61,000 hot spots (and growing), JiWire (www. Jiwire.com) has one of the biggest free directories of hot spots that we know about. You can browse countries, states, and cities, or enter specific addresses or airport codes, and JiWire helps you track down hot spots. You can even specify 802.11g to search for those few hot spots using this higher speed technology.

Although it's not available as we write, and we haven't seen it yet, JiWire is working on its own roaming client software that integrates the JiWire database with software on your PC, so you won't need to be actively online to search for hot spots. We're really looking forward to seeing this when it comes out.

✔ **NodeDB:** JiWire is a commercial effort — it's a company, in other words, and we expect that at least part of their offering will therefore eventually cost money (probably the forthcoming software). An alternative grassroots effort is NodeDB. Found at www.nodedb.org, NodeDB is a free and collaborative effort to map out hot spots worldwide. Any hot spot owner or operator can include their hot spots, both free and for-pay, although the focus so far is more on free and community networks.

Chapter 10

Staying Safe on *Any* Wireless Network

. . . .

. . . .

*E*lsewhere throughout *WNH&M For Dummies,* we tell you how to secure your wireless network and keep your PCs, servers, and Internet connection safe and sound when you're at home or in the office. But one of the real beauties of wireless networks is that you can access them *wherever* you go. Some of these "wherevers" are known locations with a relatively high degree of security, but most are not.

In fact, most "public" Wi-Fi access points, whether they're an "official" hot spot, a community network, a "guest" network at a business, or just a plain old "open" access point, do not offer *any* security for you the user. At best, these access points have been configured to provide some measure of security for the owner of the network — to keep bad guys out of the rest of the network and to limit use of the wireless network to just Internet access. But usually *nothing* is done to make your connection to these networks secure.

In this chapter, we give you some strategies for dealing with this issue and for keeping safe away from home. First, we tell you how to deal with security in a hot spot environment — using the tools that some hot spot providers offer to encrypt communications and provide authentication on their networks. Then we discuss simple steps you can take (such as accessing secure versions of Web pages) that can help make your life more secure. Finally, we give you some step-by-step instructions for connecting to a VPN (virtual private network) to ensure that *all* of your communications take place inside a secure tunnel that can't be easily intercepted even if someone can monitor all of your over-the-air communications.

Securing Hot Spots

Security isn't a big deal just within your own home network: It's important on the road, too. Unfortunately, one area where people tend to neglect their wireless security (through no fault of their own, most of the time) is when they're out using the wireless hot spots we discuss in Chapter 9.

That's because most hot spots don't have any Wi-Fi security turned on. In fact, most hot spot operators purposely keep WEP and WPA turned off because it's difficult for their users to configure quickly (almost not worth the effort to some folks for a five-minute online session to check e-mail) — and if users think it's too much bother to get online, the hot spot won't make any money.

If hot spot operators don't take security seriously, don't worry: Take matters into your own hands. You can take some steps when accessing hot spots to keep yourself safe and sound and your data out of the hands of the bad guys, even if the hot spot you're using is not secure.

Using Wi-Fi security when you can

One of the very best ways to stay secure on hot spots is to use the same security measures that you'd use in your own home wireless network. That means using WPA and 802.1X authentication to encrypt all the data crossing the airwaves and to perform mutual authentication (of yourself and of the AP you're connecting to).

Such an approach can keep your data secure and also prevent you from logging onto an "evil twin" AP (we discuss these in Chapter 9 — it's an AP that's masquerading as the one you're trying to log onto, in an attempt to steal your personal information).

Unfortunately, not many hot spots are yet using such methods — simply because they feel it's just too difficult for their customers to bother with. Some networks that do use WPA and 802.1X include

✔ **T-Mobile:** The hot spot (and cellphone) company that's unwiring Starbucks coffee shops (and thousands of other locations) has begun to roll out 802.1X authentication throughout all of its hot spots. To use it, you simply need a T-Mobile account and the T-Mobile client software (find out about both at www.tmobile.com/hotspot). Folks who sign onto T-Mobile hot spots *without* the T-Mobile client software (using the Web site instead) are *not* protected by WPA and 802.1X.

✔ **Radiuz:** This community network (which we discuss in Chapter 12) is designed to help users share their wireless networks securely while also taking advantage of other users' networks as a roaming service. As the company's name implies, RADIUS is a big part of this, and users must authenticate themselves and join a secure network using WPA and 802.1X. Find out more at www.radiuz.net.

Connecting to a VPN

If you're like the vast majority of hot spot users, you can't rely on connecting to the hot spot via a secure connection. When this happens to you — when you're forced to connect to a hot spot "in the clear" — your best bet for security is to use a *VPN* (virtual private network).

VPNs take everything you send across the wireless network (and even across parts of the wired network) and *encapsulate* the data into a secure *tunnel*. This means that even though your data is passing across a bunch of unsecured public networks (like the wireless LAN and the Internet), it is scrambled and encrypted and therefore secure until it reaches its final destination.

You can get a VPN on your connection in one of three ways:

✔ **Corporate VPN:** If you're connecting back to your own corporate network, you may already have a VPN set up (and VPN software on your computer). A corporate VPN sets up a tunnel from your laptop (or handheld computer, for that matter) all the way back to the VPN *concentrator* within your corporate network. Many teleworkers and telecommuters already have VPN connections set up from their home office back to the headquarters.

Depending on what type of VPN connection your company has set up, you may have secure VPN tunnels only for certain applications (like your e-mail and access to the corporate file server) and *not* for other applications (like your personal e-mail or Web browsing). Check with your network admin before you assume that your corporate VPN secures *all* of your online communications at a hot spot.

✔ **VPN built-in to hot spot client software:** Many hot spot providers (like Boingo or iPass) provide their customers with special hot spot client software. This software provides users with a directory of hot spots, and also configures computers to access the network. But the really big advantage of using these clients is that they have built-in VPN capabilities. All the data leaving your computer is encapsulated in a secure tunnel until it gets to the hot spot provider's own network, where it is decrypted and sent to its final destination on the Internet. If you're using one of these clients, you can feel safe that your data is secure on the wireless network.

  ✔ **Wi-Fi VPN service:** Even if you add up all of the hot spots that use WPA/802.1X and all those that can be accessed with a hot spot client software like Boingo, you still find a lot of hot spots that *don't* offer any security. For example, you may be getting online in a small coffee shop that just put together their own hot spot without any security; or you may be accessing a wireless AP in a client's conference room where you don't have any idea how secure things are. For these types of situations, you can get your own hot spot–ready VPN account with a specialized VPN provider. These companies host their own VPN services and sell them to all takers for a monthly or annual fee. The VPN is *terminated* in their own network, which means you have security from your laptop into the provider's data center. Beyond that, your data goes across the Internet just like it would with any Internet connection — no more or less safe than a connection from your home's DSL or cable modem.

One thing to keep in mind about VPNs is that the secure, encrypted tunnels that they create must end (or be terminated) somewhere. With a corporate VPN, that termination point is within your corporate LAN; with the other services, it's somewhere in that service provider's data center. The point to remember here is that the VPN provides security over the airwaves and over the wired part of the network *up until* the tunnel is terminated. After that, there are no special security measures in place. So if you're accessing a Web site or sending an e-mail, use the same security measures that you'd use for any type of connection — just because the airwaves have been secured doesn't mean that the VPN has secured *everything*.

If you're interested in checking out a VPN service that you can use at *any* hot spot (or even from wired connections when you're on the road — like hotel Ethernet broadband services and dial-up modem connections), you might want to check out one of the following:

  ✔ **WiTopia's personalVPN:** The folks at WiTopia (we discussed their SecureMyWiFi service in Chapter 8) have come out with a VPN service that is tailor-made for hot spot users and other road warrior–type folks. For $79 a year, you can set up an SSL (secure sockets layer) connection using WiTopia's VPN client software that tunnels communications from *all* applications on your computer and sends them to WiTopia's secure Internet gateway. With a 128-bit Blowfish cipher (a really tough bit of encryption to crack), your communications are secured from any and all prying eyes on the network. You can check out the details at www.witopia.net/aboutpersonal.html — Windows XP/2000 operating systems are supported now, and Mac OS X and PocketPC are both slated to be available by the time you read this. In the section later in this chapter titled "Making a VPN Connection," we give you some step-by-step details on using this service.

✔ **JiWire Spotlock:** The folks at JiWire (you might know them for their hot spot "finder" services) have just launched a VPN and security service for hot spot users called Spotlock (www.jiwire.com/spotlock.htm). Spotlock combines IPSec VPN connectivity with JiWire's hot spot database, making it easy for you to both find and securely connect to a hot spot. Other features for your $4.95 a month (or $49.95 a year) include a connection manager that saves and manages your hot spot connections for you, and an SMTP relay service that makes it easier to send e-mail messages when you're away from home (that is, if your ISP doesn't allow outgoing e-mail when you're not connected to the ISP's own network).

✔ **HotSpotVPN.com:** Another company focusing on the wireless security of mobile workers and hot spot aficionados is HotSpotVPN. The company offers a slightly broader menu of services than personalVPN — with both a software client-based SSL service (HotSpotVPN2) or a service that uses the VPN client software built into Windows 2000/XP, Palm OS, Mac OS X, or PocketPC (HotSpotVPN1). The range of choices also includes the strength of the encryption used — ranging from very strong (128-bit Blowfish) to super-duper-pretty-much-unbreakable-by-even-the-government (256-bit AES).

The pricing of HotSpotVPN varies depending upon the service taken (1 or 2) and the strength of the encryption. You pay less money for weaker encryption, which isn't quite as secure, but which makes for a faster connection! Costs range between $8.88 and $13.88 a month. You can also buy short-term one-, three-, or seven-day contracts for less than the monthly amount, if you get on the road only infrequently.

Using SSL to connect to Web sites

Whether you're using a secure or insecure hot spot, or whether you're using a VPN, you should take some basic security precautions when doing sensitive things on the Internet. For example: Don't send your credit card number in an unencrypted e-mail, be sure to turn on your PC's firewall, and so on.

One active step that you should always take when you're in a hot spot environment, even if you're taking other precautions, is to always use secure Web sites whenever you can.

For basic Web surfing, you don't have this option. You can't check the news on CNN.com at a secure version of the site — they simply don't offer this option. But you can *(and should)* always make sure that you're using an SSL Web site when you're doing things like checking your Web mail, accessing a personal banking site, doing some online shopping, or any other activity where you share confidential information such as passwords or credit card numbers.

You know you're on a secure Web site because of two things:

- ✔ The site's URL starts with an `https://` instead of a plain `http://`.
- ✔ Your browser displays a yellow padlock icon (in most browsers, this appears on the status bar at the bottom-right of the window).

If you're connected to a secure Web site, even if all of your other hot spot traffic is being intercepted, you can feel confident that the data you send back and forth with the secured Web site is *not* being read by the guy sitting across the room with his laptop out — at least not in any legible form.

Some Web sites have secure log-in using SSL, but they hide that fact from you. For example, Google's Gmail service (`gmail.google.com`) has a secure login inside a *frame* within the overall window. Even though you don't see the `https://` or the yellow padlock, your log-in information is indeed secured. Unfortunately, the only way to know if your favorite Web site does this is to check out their FAQs or to ask them!

It's very rare, but potentially you could connect to a hot spot that *isn't* the one you wanted to connect to (the evil twin we mentioned earlier in the chapter) or that was set up by someone who is up to no good. On these rare occasions, a person could set up a fake Web site that looks like an online banking or other secure site and lure you into giving out your personal login data. You can avoid this by using authenticated hot spots or a VPN connection — but if you can't do this, you can at least examine the security certificate of the Web site you're visiting by double-clicking on the yellow padlock in your browser. Check to make sure that it's actually the site you intend to visit. If you've got some really confidential information, and you're not sure that you're securely connected to the legitimate site you're looking for, consider waiting until you're back home!

Some ISPs (not most, but many) let you set up your e-mail client software to connect to your e-mail servers using SSL. This is a simple checkbox setting within your favorite e-mail client. (Outlook Express, Eudora, and Apple Mail all support SSL connections to the POP and SMTP mail servers.) Check with your ISP to see if they offer this option — if they do, get instructions from them to set up your e-mail client software for SSL. This keeps the e-mails you send back and forth from a hot spot secure. If you can't use SSL for checking your ISP's e-mail, you might consider switching to a Web mail service like Gmail, which *is* secure, at least while you're on the road. Figure 10-1 shows these settings in Microsoft Outlook Express using Windows XP.

Figure 10-1:
Setting up
secure mail
checking.

Making a VPN Connection

Connecting to a VPN requires a few different things, both on your PC and in the location that you're connecting to "privately." Specifically, you need

✔ **A VPN server or *appliance* at the remote location to terminate your connection.** This is simply the device that your computer connects to on the remote end of the VPN connection. Most of the time, the VPN functionality is built into a company's *firewall* or network security appliance. If you're connecting to your corporate network, this may be a server or appliance that you own (like the NETGEAR ProSafe VPN Firewall (http://netgear.com/products/details/FVX538.php), which retails for about $550, but you may be able to find it for a couple hundred less). If you're connecting to a service (like WiTopia or HotSpotVPN.com), the VPN server or appliance is owned and operated by the service provider. You simply need the IP address (and a few other bits of data) for this networked device.

If you're using a VPN firewall to support more than a few users, look for a device that has been equipped with *hardware accelerated encryption,* which can help keep the throughput of your network from bogging down when multiple users access it.

✔ **VPN client software on your PC, which establishes the secure connection to the server and encrypts the communications, leaving the PC to**

ensure that they can't be intercepted. A client can be as simple as your Web browser (for some more limited VPNs, your Web browser can connect via SSL and establish the VPN); it can be built into your operating system (both Windows and Mac OS X have support for VPN built-in); or it can be a separate piece of software that you install on your computer.

✔ **A VPN protocol.** The VPN client and server "talk" to each other using standardized protocols — your client and the server must support the same protocol in order to communicate securely. Three primary protocols are used in VPNs:

- **SSL:** This is the same protocol (secure sockets layer) used for making secure Web page connections. For very simple VPNs, you can simply use a Web browser to make the connection and access mail, files, and servers. For more complex VPN uses (where you need to use a variety of applications), you can use a client like OpenVPN (www.openvpn.net).

- **IPSec:** This is the most common protocol for corporate VPN services and is widely supported right in operating systems. Mac OS X, Windows 2000, and XP, and most UNIX variants (like OpenBSD and Solaris) support IPSec connections right in the OS.

- **PPTP:** Point-to-point tunneling protocol is an older but still widely supported VPN protocol developed by Microsoft. Most security experts think that it's less secure than IPSec (and it's often less widely supported and used these days).

✔ **An Internet connection between the two points.** Finally, you need an Internet connection to make this all work. When the VPN client and server "find" each other and make a connection, they create a secure "tunnel" across the public Internet, which uses encryption to keep prying eyes out.

Setting up an IPSec connection with Windows XP

The most common way to connect to a corporate VPN connection (or to many VPN services that use IPSec) is to use the IPSec VPN client built into Windows XP. This client allows you to establish the secure tunnel for *all* applications on your computer — so you can set up a wireless hot spot connection, turn on the VPN connection, and surf (or e-mail, IM, and transfer files) without worry.

When you connect to your "work" VPN, you are secure, but you may not be free to do what you want on the Internet. Many businesses have strict policies on Web surfing and Internet usage, and may restrict what you can do (or even log what sites you visit — which could cause you grief later on).

Some corporate VPNs may be set up to allow *split tunneling*. In such a case, all of your corporate-specific traffic (like e-mail and access to the intranet) goes through a VPN tunnel, but all of your other Internet traffic (like Web surfing and your personal e-mail) does not. If you are using a corporate VPN, talk to your IT folks about how things are set up; if you've got this kind of split arrangement, take other precautions (as we discuss throughout the chapter) when you're online on the road.

To get set up, you simply need some basic information about your VPN server (obtained from your IT manager or from your service provider) and then follow the steps below:

1. **Open Network Connections and click Create a New Connection. When the New Connection Wizard window opens, click Next.**

2. **Select the Connect to the Network at My Workplace radio button and click Next as shown in Figure 10-2.**

Figure 10-2:
Starting
to create
a VPN
connection
in Win-
dows XP.

3. **Select the Virtual Private Network Connection radio button and click Next as shown in Figure 10-3.**

4. In the text box in the Connection Name window that appears (shown in Figure 10-4), type a name for the network (it can be anything that you can easily remember later). Click Next.

Lots of *Nexts* to click in a wizard!

5. In the Public Network window that appears (show in Figure 10-5), select the Do Not Dial the Initial Connection radio button and click Next.

This button is used only when you're using a dial-up connection to connect to the VPN — we're skipping the wires!

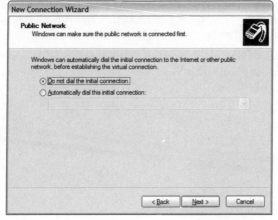

Figure 10-5:
For Wi-Fi connections, turn off the automatic dialing.

6. **When the VPN server selection window opens (as shown in Figure 10-6), type the IP address or host name of your VPN server and click Next.**

   Your service provider or network administrator gives this data to you.

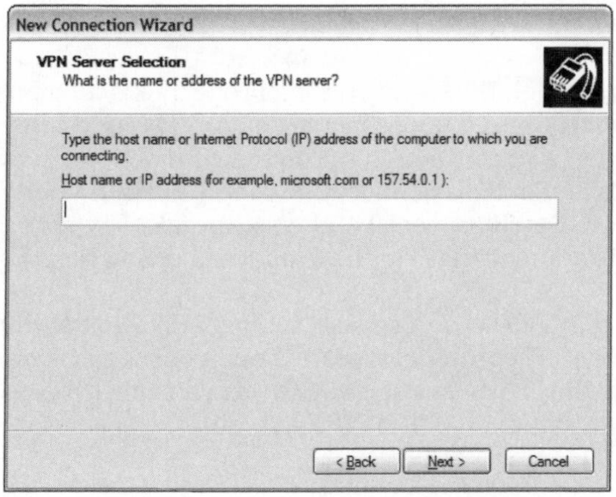

Figure 10-6:
Your network admin or VPN hosting company gives you the server address.

7. **In the final window, select the Add a Shortcut to This Connection to My Desktop check box and click the Finish button.**

   A new dialog box appears on your desktop, as shown in Figure 10-7.

8. **You can connect to the VPN immediately if you have a username and password provided to you, or you can click the Properties button to configure advanced properties of the VPN connection.**

To invoke your VPN connection later and connect securely, simply establish your Wi-Fi (or other) Internet connection and then right-click on the VPN connection icon you created on your desktop and select Connect.

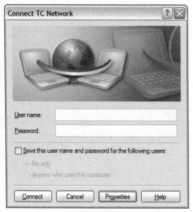

Figure 10-7: Use this Windows dialog box to begin a VPN session or to set advanced properties.

We don't walk you through the setting on the Properties dialog box because the settings vary widely based upon the particular VPN to which you are connecting. The steps we walked through set up the connection to automatically negotiate protocols and make a connection to *most* VPNs. If your VPN requires specific settings (like special authentication *EAP* types), you can make these configuration changes in the Properties dialog box.

As we mentioned, this VPN wizard sets up a connection that automatically negotiates things like VPN protocol type. Although our focus is on IPSec VPNS here because they're most common, the exact same process sets you up (generically) to connect to a PPTP VPN as well.

Using OpenVPN client and WiTopia's SSL VPN service

An alternative to IPSec VPNs are those that use the SSL encryption protocol. As we mention earlier in this section, the simplest SSL VPNs exist simply in the domain of a Web browser: You log into a secure `https:` Web portal and perform your VPN activities from within the Web browser.

This approach is great if your VPN needs are relatively simple: Web browsing, file access, chat — applications that can be built into a Web browser, in other words. If, however, you wish to use non-browser applications on your PC, these simple SSL VPNs won't provide you the security you need.

To make *all* of your applications secure on an SSL VPN, you need some client software on your computer that basically acts as an intermediary between applications and the Wi-Fi or Internet connection that your computer is using. (This is what the built-in IPSec VPN client in Windows does.) One good (and free!) client for this purpose is the OpenVPN client, an open source (GPL-licensed, if you're interested in such things) client that provides cross-platform (Windows, Linux, Mac OS X, and so on) SSL VPN connectivity.

You can download an appropriate build of OpenVPN at the project's main site: `www.openvpn.net`. For a version specifically designed for Windows operating systems, with a full *GUI* (graphical user interface), check out the OpenVPN GUI for Windows version at `http://openvpn.se/`.

The cool thing about OpenVPN is that companies can build upon the basic OpenVPN framework to create their own variants of the software. For example, the folks at WiTopia (we discuss their service a little earlier in this chapter) have built their own WiTopia VPN service around a variant of the Windows GUI version of OpenVPN.

Installing the WiTopia personalVPN client

As soon as you subscribe to WiTopia's personalVPN service (`www.witopia.net/aboutpersonal.html`), you receive an e-mail with some details about your order and about the service. You must take two steps to get your service up and running:

- ✔ **Download the client software:** Included in this e-mail is a link to download WiTopia's version of the Windows GUI OpenVPN client software. It's a simple installation process — just double-click on the downloaded .exe file and follow the onscreen instructions. The e-mail you receive has explicit instructions — basically, you just need to accept all of the default settings in the installer program and click Next until you're done!

  This software runs on Windows 2000 and XP computers.

- ✔ **Register for a certificate:** This is the real key to the service. The certificate identifies you as the authorized user, and in turn identifies WiTopia's VPN server as the legitimate end point for your VPN connection. The certificate provides *mutual authentication* so that you can rest assured that you and only you can use your account, and that you'll not be connected to a bogus VPN server somewhere along the line. We talk about how to get your certificate in the remainder of this section.

In order to create your certificate, you need to access both a Web browser and the WiTopia.net Certificate Wizard program, which opens when you complete the installation of the VPN software.

1. **Follow the onscreen instructions within the Certificate Wizard program, as shown in Figure 10-8.**

   You fill out some details about yourself (name, e-mail address, country, and state) and provide the system a ten-digit (or more) password.

Figure 10-8:
Using the
Certificate
Wizard to
generate a
unique
certificate
for your
VPN.

Don't forget your password — this is used every time you log onto the VPN.

2. **The results of Step 1 include a *private key* (which is created in your C:\Program Files\WiTopia.Net\config folder, and a certificate request key (which is a bunch of gobbledygook on your screen beginning with the words ----BEGIN CERTIFICATE REQUEST ----). Select this text and press Ctrl+C to copy it onto your clipboard.**

Don't close this window just yet — you may need to come back and re-copy the certificate request text, just in case you accidentally clear your clipboard.

3. **Switch to your e-mail program and click the link that says <u>To activate personalVPN service from WiTopia, click the following link:</u> in your e-mail from WiTopia.Net (the exact URL is different for every customer).**

   The link opens in your Web browser (if it doesn't, cut and paste the link into a new browser window).

4. **Follow the steps onscreen, including the pasting of the certificate request text.**

   When you're done, close any remaining open WiTopia programs and go about your business. You need to wait for up to a day for your certificate to be generated and e-mailed back to you.

   You soon get an e-mail from WiTopia containing two files: your certificate (named *FirstName_LastName*.crt — substitute your actual name as you registered yourself), and a .zip file containing that certificate (.crt) file. You get both because some e-mail programs don't handle .crt files very well — for example, with Lotus Notes and Gmail (the two mail systems we use), you can't open a .crt file at all — the .zip file helps you get around this. Open this e-mail and see which of the two files you can access. Depending on what you see, follow these steps:

   a. If you can access the .crt file, simply save it in the c:\Program Files\WiTopia.Net\config directory on your computer using your e-mail client's standard Save process.

   b. If you can't see the .crt file, but you can see the .zip file, simply open the .zip file with your favorite .zip decompression utility (we like WinZip — www.winzip.com — but any .zip utility can handle this task), and save it to that same directory.

   c. If you can't see either file, your e-mail program isn't handling the certificate files in a friendly way at all (Gmail does this, unfortunately). Reply to the e-mail you've received with a *different* e-mail address, and the certificates are forwarded to you again.

After you've installed that certificate file, you're ready to go. The OpenVPN GUI client is installed in the Windows taskbar on your computer. To make your VPN connection, simply right-click the icon and select Connect. Enter your password (the one you created in Step 1) in the OpenVPN Connection window that pops up (shown in Figure 10-9).

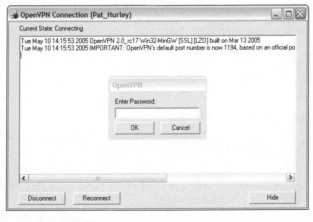

Figure 10-9:
Connecting to WiTopia's personal VPN service.

You are connected to the WiTopia.Net VPN server and your connection is secure. You see a notification (shown in Figure 10-10) above your taskbar showing the new public IP address of your VPN connection. (Your computer will no longer use the public IP address of the Wi-Fi network you are connected to, but instead will appearto be located in WiTopia's data center.)

Figure 10-10:
Pat's
connected
securely
through
personal-
VPN.

Chapter 11

Outfitting Your Car with Wireless

*W*ireless technologies have been creeping into the car ever since Paul Galvin, the head of Galvin Manufacturing Corporation, invented the first car radio back in 1929. Not unlike many new technologies for cars today, the first car radios back then were not available from carmakers; instead, you bought a retrofit kit from Galvin's company. Galvin coined the name *Motorola* for the company's new products. The rest is, as we say, history.

Today, you can still add neat new wireless gizmos to your car, but you're still likely to have to do so via some sort of third-party device. Only a few high-end cars even offer any sort of wireless integration into the car, and even then it's usually limited to putting a cellphone into the dashboard.

We've got better ideas than that, and this chapter tells you how to add Bluetooth, Wi-Fi, and even satellite TV to your car. And as a bonus, we also tell you how to seamlessly integrate your cellphone into the equation. If you love cars as much as Pat does, this will simply be an irresistible set of first projects for you to tackle!

In this chapter, we don't spend a lot of time talking about cellular phone or related data services themselves, but instead focus on how to link your cellphone to your car to take advantage of that mobile data stream.

Bluetooth for In-Car Communications

When it comes to adding wireless capabilities for audio, video, and computing purposes to cars, automakers have changed their minds about a zillion times. They've explored proprietary wireless services, building wireless-enabled consumer devices into the cars, linking car components to commercial wireless services, and all sorts of combinations and in-betweens of the above.

Although it's still early in the wireless-enablement game, automakers finally appear to be heading down some consistent paths regarding deployment of specific wireless technologies in automobiles — and the first major commitment, at least for the near-to-mid-term, is to the Bluetooth standard for communications between the car and consumer devices like cellphones and iPods. (Check out the official Bluetooth Web site — www.bluetooth.com — for details about the technology itself.)

Automakers found out that it was rather a pain to try to outfit cars with cellphones built in. See, even the fastest new improvements to cars take 18–24 months from concept to car lot; in the cellular industry, 18–24 months can represent three cellphone generations and a whole lot of technical advancement. So by the time a car outfitted with a cellphone made it to your town, the cellphone technology would likely be obsolete — usually *very* obsolete.

So the carmakers abandoned that approach and have focused on using Bluetooth as a wireless technology to "talk" to cellphones to enable integrated, hands-free communications in the car, and support access to the Internet and other data locations via the cellphone's data services. With this approach, which phone or which carrier you use is unimportant: As long as it has Bluetooth on board, the car can talk to the world. (Makes you wonder what Chitty Chitty Bang Bang would have ordered from Amazon.com, doesn't it?)

Bluetooth in action

Here's a practical usage scenario: You climb into your car and turn it on. Next to your speedometer is a liquid crystal display of your telephone's address book — complete with your most recently dialed numbers, missed calls, scheduled calls, and so on. You scroll through the list, find who you want to call, press the Call button, and you hear the call being placed through the car's sound speakers.

It gets better: If your phone rings when you are in your car, your sound system lowers the volume on the music and replaces it with your caller's voice. Caller ID is displayed on the dashboard, naturally. Some cars even use voice recognition: You can simply call out a string of numbers, and they are recognized by your phone, which places the call. Most of these systems support speed-dial phrases: Just say "Home," and that phrase is matched to a phone number, which saves you the trouble of remembering a number. Your signal strength and battery level can also be displayed on the dashboard readouts, depending on the specific phone you own.

But wait, there's more! You can use your cellphone to enable your car to send diagnostic info to your car dealership as well. Way cool.

All this is possible today, starting with select 2005 model cars, and all of it happens with the phone still in your pocket — the car is talking to your phone via Bluetooth, accessing its phone records and speed-dial numbers, and extending the speaker system and microphone pickup to the domain of the car itself. You can control your car's phone functionality from buttons usually located on your car's steering wheel. Now that's seamless interconnectivity.

Although you can pair (or network) more than one phone with your car, you can only use one phone at a time to place calls using the car's functionality.

Although more than 20 carmakers offer factory-installed Bluetooth options on more than 30 2005 models, you can expect this number to explode to near-ubiquity within a few model years. Bluetooth costs have plummeted and the demand for integration — spurred by devices like the iPod — is booming. Where there's demand, there's usually supply within a reasonable timeframe.

Car-based Bluetooth modules and your Bluetooth phones are loaded with Bluetooth profiles. A *Bluetooth profile* is a specification that defines the minimum requirements that the Bluetooth device must support to do specific things, like to place phone calls or to display signal strength. These requirements define the end-user services and the features and procedures that the Bluetooth device must support to enable interoperability with peer devices. Devices with similar profile support should be able to support similar features. Most Bluetooth car kits sport the *Bluetooth Hands Free Profile*. More and more, you also see the *Bluetooth SIM Access Profile* for Bluetooth-enabled GSM mobile phones that incorporate the SIM Access Profile.

Wanna see this in action? Check out the video on the Acura Web site at www.acura.com/models/handsfreelink_index.asp?referrer=acura to see someone using their Bluetooth-enabled phone with their Acura car.

Now for the disclaimers. Not all Bluetooth-enabled phones work with all Bluetooth-enabled cars. Before you buy that $45,000 accessory (a new car, in other words) for your Bluetooth phone, ask if the car supports your specific phone and service plan — and ask them to "pair up" the phone to make sure it works in the car you want. For instance, at the time of this writing, Bluetooth was only partially implemented on some cellular provider's phones. We found one user on the Audi technical support forums with this to say: "I am unable to download my address book, the car's signal strength meter does not work, the car can not recall the last numbered dialed. I am able to make calls through the car's multi-media interface. The rumor is that [my carrier] is considering fully supporting Bluetooth in the near future." So try before you buy.

You can find a lot out about your car's Bluetooth integration — and other wireless tidbits from actual users — at Inside Line (www.edmunds.com/insideline/do/ForumsLanding), by car expert Edmunds.com. In the Maintenance and Repair Forums for each car type, you'll find the lowdown on your car's wireless capabilities.

Bluetooth aftermarket options

If you are like us, you don't have a Bluetooth-enabled car and you don't have a Bluetooth-enabled phone. That doesn't mean you are left out of this revolution! You can get Bluetooth adapters for your phone (or get a new phone), and you can buy and install a Bluetooth aftermarket kit to enable your car.

Like anything else in life, the more functionality you want, the more it costs. The easy answer is to buy a new Bluetooth phone (as we write, we crave a Treo 650 from Handspring — www.handspring.com). You are probably on a cellphone term plan with your cellular provider — check out their site for information on Bluetooth-enabled phones. Here are some URLs for the major U.S. carriers:

- **Cingular:** http://onlinestorez.cingular.com/cell-phone-service/cell-phones/cell-phones.jsp?CategoryId=1717200037&CategoryId=1717200027
- **Sprint:** www1.sprintpcs.com/explore/PhonesAccessories/AllPhones.jsp
- **T-Mobile:** www.t-mobile.com/products/default.asp?class=phone
- **Verizon:** www.verizonwireless.com/b2c/splash/bluetooth.jsp

If your phone or PDA has an SDIO (Secure Digital Input/Output) card slot, you can add an SD Bluetooth Card that adds a Bluetooth radio to the device.

Just because a device has an SDIO card slot doesn't mean that it can take an SDIO Bluetooth card. SD cards are used for lots of things and you need to make sure that your device has software drivers for Bluetooth functionality before it will work. Case in point: The fabulous Treo 600 unit from PalmOne has an SDIO card slot, but does not support a Bluetooth SDIO card. Do your research to be positive that a device offers driver support before you order anything for your phone or PDA. The best source for info is the device manufacturer's own Web site; search for *Bluetooth* to find information fast.

Want to find out more about SDIO cards? There are lots of neat applications, including TV tuner SDIO cards. Check out the SD Card Association's summary of SDIO cards at www.sdcard.com/usa/TextPage.asp?Page=5.

For your car, there are a range of aftermarket kits to transform your car into wireless central. The most common aftermarket kits on the market today come from Motorola, Nokia, Parrot, and Sony Ericsson — and they range from professionally installed units to small portable ones that clip on your visor or plug into your cigarette lighter. Here's a sample of the growing number of kits on the market:

- ✔ Motorola (www.hellomoto.com) has three units. The top of the line is the Motorola BLNC Bluetooth Car Kit IHF1000 ($240). The IHF1000 supports voice activation in four languages. The mid-range product is the HF850 ($150), which has many of the same features of the IHF1000 but has less sophisticated voice recognition capability. Both the IHF1000 and HF850 have a backlit controller that is mounted to the dashboard. At the low end is the HF820 ($100), which is a portable product that requires no installation and can be carried into, and out of, any car you drive. For more on Motorola Bluetooth products, go here: http://promo.motorola.com/bluetooth/index.html.

- ✔ Parrot (www.driveblue.com) has three aftermarket kits — the Evolution 3000 ($114.99), 3100 ($199.99), and 3300 ($349.99) — which are installed units that offer either no LCD, LCD, or LCD plus GPS, respectively.

- ✔ Parrot also has two plug-and-play units. The Parrot EasyDrive is designed to plug into your cigarette lighter and provides hands-free operation (using a tethered control unit; see Figure 11-1) when paired to the Bluetooth phone ($99). The DriveBlue Plus ($79) is a similar but slightly older model that has a clip-on capability.

- ✔ On the ultra-simple side, you can also get Bluetooth speakerphones for your car, which is nice because not many of the Bluetooth-enabled phones also have speakerphones on board. The Motorola HF800/98595 Bluetooth Portable Wireless Speaker ($75, www.motorola.com) is a nice little unit that you can use as a hands-free speaker in the car (it clips to the visor) or on your desk or table for conference calls with business associates or friends.

Nokia and Ericsson have similar add-on kits. Models change fairly frequently, so check the manufacturer sites for the latest versions. New gear is coming out all the time. There's no limit to how much you can Bluetooth-enable your car. LG Electronics has demonstrated a rearview mirror that displays caller identification information as calls come into your Bluetooth mobile phone; the driver just pushes a button on the rearview mirror to answer the call. "Pretty handy!" we say.

Figure 11-1:
The Parrot
EasyDrive
just plugs
into your
cigarette
lighter.

Remember our discussion earlier in the chapter about profiles? Profiles are very important with aftermarket gear because some gear can be quite specific in what it does and does not do. Be sure to buy wisely. Look for profiles such as HFR (Hands Free), HSP (Headset Profile), and DUN (Dial-up Networking) — these are profiles commonly available in many current production cellphones. Other Bluetooth profiles you might see include IP (Intercom Profile), FTP (File Transfer Protocol), FP (Fax Profile), SAP (SIM Access Profile), LAN (Local Area Network), PAN (Personal Area Network), SP (Synchronization Profile), and so on. A lot of Bluetooth products only support a single profile. Car kits generally support only the hands-free profile, and a few (notably the Parrot car kits) support hands-free, headset, and DUN profiles. If you want to know more about some of this techie stuff, check out Microsoft's site on the topic at `http://msdn.microsoft.com/library/default.asp?url=/library/en-us/wcecomm5/html/wce50conBluetoothProfiles.asp`.

If you use a system with a car radio mute feature, remember that this is usually not a user-selectable feature that you turn on and off — it's either installed or not. Be sure to make that decision before you install your unit. Also, if you have a lot of other aftermarket stereo gear in your car, the car mute option might not work. Unfortunately, we can't give you a lot of guidance here because there's no real guide to incompatibilities among aftermarket manufacturers. Just know it can be an issue and check out any manufacturer Web sites beforehand if you can to snoop around for any potential problems.

For more Bluetooth for your car, check out the Bluetooth Special Interest Group's site at www.bluetooth.com. Not only can they update you on wireless options, but they have a listing of Bluetooth-certified products as well.

Setting up a Bluetooth aftermarket kit

There's not much to installing a Bluetooth aftermarket kit. If you have ever installed any sort of electronics in your car, you have a good idea of what's involved. And even if you haven't ever done this before, it's really not that hard.

There's a great reference site for some of the details about how to remove your car stereo and how to install new aftermarket items. It's run by a small stereo install shop in Florida called Factory Car Stereo Repair, Inc., and has great info on a per car, per model basis. Most of their info costs a couple of bucks to look at — insanely reasonable, we think — and it helped us get Danny's stereo out of his car and back in without his wife knowing about it — very nice! (If you are married, you know exactly why that was important!) Check out www.carstereohelp.com/stereoremoval.htm, as shown in Figure 11-2.

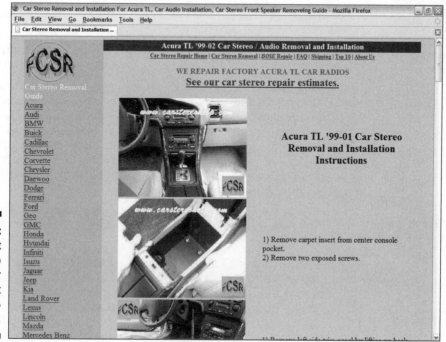

Figure 11-2: Finding out how to remove your stereo at **carstereo help.com.**

To give you an idea of what you're in for, here's a high-level view of the steps required to install a system, using the Parrot CK 3300 Kit as our example:

1. **Always check to make sure that your battery has been disconnected.**

   Some car alarms, radios, and other electronic gear require you to enter a code for reconnection of the battery. If you don't know these codes, be forewarned that you may be digging out some manuals at the end of this process.

   Carstereohelp.com explains how to find the stereo codes: "Look through the glove box for what looks like a white credit card, the 'Code card.' The code can be four or five digits depending on the automobile and stereo. Many times, dealerships write the code on a piece of tape or label and may place it in one of several areas — on one of the sides of the glove box, on the bottom of the ash tray, in the trunk on the trunk lid, in the trunk on the bottom of the package shelf, or in one of the door jambs. Check the owner's manual; the code may be written in one of the stereo pages, one of the covers, or other pages by the previous owner. On rare occasions, the code may be written on the stereo."

2. **The 3300 has five major components that we recommend you install first before hooking up everything to the control box. You'll be running a cable for the microphone unit, the LCD screen, the power cable, the GPS antenna, and the in-car radio input.**

   Parrot does a nice job of labeling all the wires for you, so hopefully you won't get confused. See Figure 11-3.

   How you connect your car radio depends on what sort of connectors it has on the backside of the radio. Here are three possible options:

   a. **Line-in connectors:** Take the green ("positive") and brown ("negative") wires and attach them to the corresponding +/- inputs of your radio; plug the end of the yellow mute cable into the mute interface. Do not connect the yellow mute wire; this also mutes the Parrot. Because most line inputs are auxiliary lines, most radios switch sources automatically when input is detected. If it does not switch automatically, the user will have to switch manually when a phone call is made or received.

   Line-in connectors are more common on aftermarket radios. Most stock radios make use of the car kit's ISO connectors. (See Figure 11-4.)

   b. **ISO connectors:** Take the factory harness out of the radio and plug it into the female ISO connector of the car kit. Take the male ISO connector from the car kit and plug it into the radio. The yellow mute wire is only needed in vehicles that have more than four speakers. Because the ISO connector has support for up to four speakers, any speakers connected to the car kit will automatically be muted by the relay (the smaller black box). If you do need to connect the yellow mute wire, connect it to the mute input at the back of the radio. If the radio does not have a mute input, the ground signal from the mute wire can be used in a power relay (which you can buy at Radio Shack) to shut off the ignition connection at the radio. This in effect mutes all the speakers in the vehicle.

c. **Other connectors:** You'll need to get an ISO adapter cable for that particular radio's audio input connector. Try www.carstereo help.com.

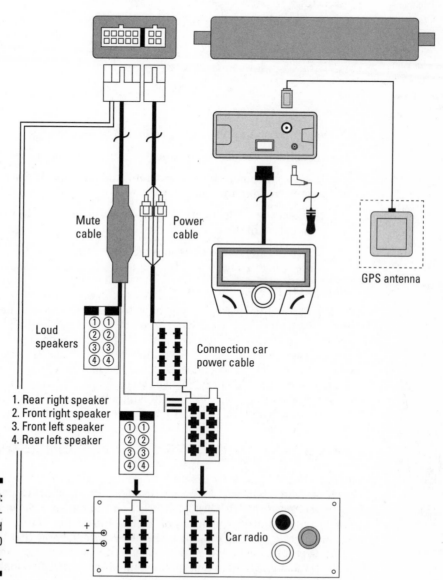

Figure 11-3:
Your GPS-
outfitted
CK3300
components.

Mute cable

Power cable

GPS antenna

Loud speakers

① ①
② ②
③ ③
④ ④

Connection car power cable

1. Rear right speaker
2. Front right speaker
3. Front left speaker
4. Rear left speaker

① ①
② ②
③ ③
④ ④

Car radio

+

−

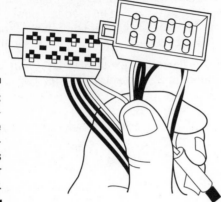

3. **Now you can hook up the cables as shown in Figure 11-3:**

   a. Disconnect the car radio's speaker and power harnesses.

   b. Connect the male connectors of the audio cable and the power supply cable to the car radio.

   c. Connect the vehicle's audio and power supply leads to the female connectors of the electronic box.

   d. If the car radio has a Mute input, connect the yellow wire on the Mute cable to one of the Mute inputs.

4. **Connect the power supply cable.**

   It's fairly straightforward, but you have to ignore the manual here. If your vehicle does not use the ISO connectors, cut off the gray ISO connectors — be sure to cut the red and orange wires after the white plastic fuses in the power supply cable so that they are still in the wiring path. If your car does have ISO connections, use them. Attach the red wire of the power cable to the permanent 12V connection (also called the *12V constant*); the orange wire to the 12V ignition connection (also called the *12V accessory*); and the black wire to the ground connection (amusingly called the *earth* connection in the manual).

   That's it! You've installed the CK3300. That wasn't hard, was it?

You do not want to leave your orange wire connected to the permanent 12V circuit — you might find your batteries dead after a short while. Take a second to verify the electric wiring of the power bundle. In some vehicles, it is necessary to reverse the positions of the red and orange wires. This operation is simply done by reversing the fuse holders. You'll know that you have it right when you turn off the car and see a goodbye message on the LCD screen. If you don't see that, your ignition and permanent 12V connections need to be reversed.

Understanding your powered connections

In most aftermarket device manuals, you'll hear references to wires like *+12V run* or *+12V constant* wires. What does this all mean? Many of these wires are actually the same thing called by different names. Most connections have two main power wires:

✔ **Ignition:** The *ignition* wire is so-called because it is only powered when the ignition key is turned to its "accessory" or "run" position. Accordingly, some people call it the *accessory* wire or, less commonly, the *run* wire.

✔ **Constant:** The *constant* wire is so-called because it is always powered, even when the car is turned off and not running. This is used to provide power for retaining memory on user-programmed functions, like keeping the clock set to the right time or your security codes intact. That's why if you have to totally disconnect the power during an installation, you have to reset all the system codes to restart all your electronic security and radio functions. Note that compared to the capacity of your battery, the current drawn by these devices is minimal, so having them run your car battery to zero power is unlikely unless a wire is crossed or misconnected.

If your car came with, or you have installed, an extra amplifier/booster in your stereo system, you will probably need to call technical support for help figuring out the wiring — it's not the same, but we can't really tell you exactly how to adjust these directions because we don't know what you've got. (Hey, we're smart, but not clairvoyant.) If the vehicle has an external amplifier, the car kit can be installed in the same fashion, except after the amplifier. The car kit already outputs an amplified signal. Feeding that to the amplifier would amplify the signal twice causing the volume to come out dangerously loud. This can also damage the amplifier. The setup would be radio⇨amplifier⇨male ISO of car kit⇨female ISO of car kit⇨speakers.

After it's installed, you have to "pair" your phone to the CK3300. To do this, simply activate Bluetooth on the phone and search for any available peripheral devices. You should see the Parrot CK3300 displayed on your phone. Enter the link code **1234** to validate the connection. You will see the phrase `Pairing Underway` displayed on your 3300 screen. When you see `Pairing Complete` on the Parrot screen display, you are all set up. Your CK3300 then connects to the phone, and once connected, it displays a Bluetooth logo on the screen.

If you have a phone with only a headset profile, the Bluetooth logo does not display.

Coming soon: The Love Bug's evil twin

Wireless capability in cars is, in many ways, an accident waiting to happen. Increasingly, cars are controlled by electronics and, as more and more subsystems become interlinked, forming a true car LAN, the opportunity exists for someone to sneak in via a wireless link and wreak havoc. Some fool will think that it would be funny to build a virus to slam on your brakes when you are cruising down the highway, or to lock the steering wheel. We don't even want to imagine driving such a possessed car.

Although no one has documented an intrusion into an automotive electronics systems, via wireless or otherwise, many are anticipating the day when it occurs. Depending on how you outfit your car with voice, data, and video functionality, you

may be making this easier for a would-be hacker. Given this is still theoretical at this time, we can only advise you to treat your car as you would your PC. If you installed a car PC, for example, add virus protection and limit sharing to shared folders. Limit connectivity to known interfaces such as into your speaker system and stereo head unit (where the most damage someone could do is play Pat Boone over and over). If you know enough to hack into your car's maintenance and control systems, it would be ridiculous of us to say, "We don't advise this and if you do, be careful doing it," so we won't.

When the appropriate security measures for your car come of age, don't hesitate to install them. You don't want to be the first car hack statistic.

You can now access your cellphone's address book and other features via the LCD screen, as shown in Figure 11-5. You can also make use of the GPS software loaded on your PDA or phone. Figure 11-6 shows the Parrot CK3300 installed in a console.

Figure 11-5:
The LCD
screen of
the Parrot
CK3300.

Here comes HSDPA mobile broadband!

The forthcoming WiMax wireless broadband protocol (check out www.wimaxforum.org) has the potential to really reinvent your broadband access, but it's not the only high-speed game in town — HSDPA (high-speed downlink packet access) is on the horizon.

HSDPA is the next step for GSM cellphone technology, improving upon the 384 Kbps speeds of UMTS with a promise of 3 Mbps to your mobile phone. Although it's not as fast as WiMax, it's expected to be much more portable. HSDPA uses cellular infrastructure, so supporting it

simply requires downloading new software. On the other hand, WiMax involves deployment of new technology.

The world will start seeing the first HSDPA in Asia in 2005/2006, in phones, handhelds, and PC cards. HSDPA will arrive in the U.S. soon thereafter.

With speeds up to 3 Mbps to your car, all the major applications for voice, data, and video are possible. It will be like you plugged your cable modem into your exhaust pipe. Vroom, vroom!

Figure 11-6:
The Parrot CK3300 LCD unit installed in a car.

Wi-Fi–Enabling Your Car

Bluetooth is nice if you just want to have hands-free dialing in your car. And to be fair, other Bluetooth applications are being developed to build out your car's local area network.

But a wireless local area network is usually more the domain of Wi-Fi, and wouldn't you know it — Wi-Fi is making a play here as well. (Savoir Faire, Wi-Fi is everywhere!)

Wi-Fi is making its in-roads into the car as a mechanism for synchronizing with sources outside the car — such as "docking" with your home's LAN when it comes into the garage. Wi-Fi can also provide a link between cellular data services and the car, much like Bluetooth does. After you have an access point in your car, any compatible Wi-Fi–enabled device can hop on and have fun.

Getting your car on the wireless grid

You can install a Wi-Fi access point in the car by merely plugging it into a power converter plugged into your cigarette lighter. Voilá! An in-car wireless access point.

Is an in-car AP necessary? For instance, if you wanted to communicate among laptops, you could just launch your wireless client and look for other devices to establish an ad-hoc connection with them. You don't need an access-point for that.

An access point *is* nice, however, for a hardwired booster to get those hard-to-reach signals to your laptop. Install an access point and link it to a permanently installed omni-directional antenna, and you can use your car to hone in on those signals so definitively needed by your in-car systems. Such an arrangement makes linking to the Internet easier as well.

If you want to take on a fun project, consider creating a *Stompbox* — an EV-DO/Wi-Fi router that uses your cellular data connection to give you a permanent Wi-Fi link to the Internet. Check out how to make one at moro.fbrtech.com/~tora/EVDO/index.html. (See Figure 11-7.) Be forewarned: If you leave your EV-DO/Wi-Fi router on with no security enabled, make sure you've got an unlimited data plan *and* you are not roaming, or you could get a huge bill if a lot of people choose to camp onto your AP. Ouch.

At the time of this writing, the few commercial EV-DO Wi-Fi routers on the market are pretty expensive — $700–$1,300. Although we expect the cellular data service providers to come out with some sort of EV-DO Wi-Fi router over the next few years, they are still likely to cost a lot more than building one yourself. If you want the shrink-wrapped approach, Junxion (www.junxion.com) and TopGlobal (www.chinatopglobal.com/products.asp) have market-ready units. Check out the special area devoted to this topic at EV-DOInfo.com (www.evdoinfo.com/EVDO_Products/EVDO_Routers/).

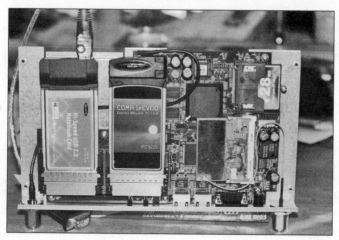

Figure 11-7:
The insides
of a
completed
Stompbox
EV-DO/Wi-Fi
router.

In Chapter 9, we discuss how to set up roaming accounts for Wi-Fi access on the road. Your roaming access point can hop onto a T-Mobile hot spot using your T-Mobile account, for instance. Drive up to a Starbucks, stop by a FedEx/Kinko's, or check out a Borders bookstore — and log in without leaving your car.

We don't know of any access points that have been developed just for your car, but you can add any access point to your car: Just select a unit with a detachable antenna interface. The rest is a standard matter of power — connecting the AP to your car's systems is as simple as installing any power inverter system. Done.

Come on, feel the (Wi-Fi) noise

If you are looking to be able to play your MP3 and other digital audio while in your car, you can certainly load it onto your iPod or other music player, slap on an FM transmitter, get in your car, and turn on your radio and listen. Pretty simple.

But for those of us with large music collections and a propensity to lose our cellphones, not to mention our iPods, there's a much better and fabulously cost-effective solution on the market — the Rockford Omnifi DMP1 (www.omnifimedia.com, $199, as shown in Figure 11-8). You get all the benefits of an iPod with the reliability and ease-of-use of an installed car radio. It's the best of both possible worlds.

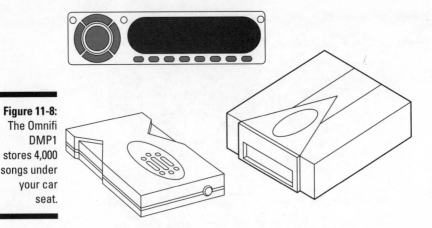

Figure 11-8:
The Omnifi DMP1 stores 4,000 songs under your car seat.

With the Omnifi system, you can store more than 4,000 songs in your car to listen to at any time. What's more, via a wireless connection, you can automatically synchronize with your home network's music store — ensuring that all your music is at your fingertips while driving. The Rockford DMP1 supports WMA and MP3 formats, and also supports Internet-based services like audio books from Audible.com (`www.audible.com`). An extended service that gives access to Internet radio stations, online content, and other media is $49.95 annually. To us, the Omnifi DMP1 is not just a great way to listen to music in your car; it's the only way to do it.

The Rockford Omnifi DMP1 consists of a controller and a removable 20G hard drive with housing. You mount the drive housing anywhere you would put a CD changer in your car — preferably in the center console somewhere — and it links to your car audio system via either FM modulation or RCA cabling. It also has USB 2.0 and 802.11b connections, along with a synchronization program for your PC called *SimpleCenter* for downloading information to the device. SimpleCenter works like most media organizers: It scans your network for audio files and builds a library of files from which you can select what to load to your car's DMP1 hard drive.

Use the USB direct connection for the initial download of all your songs to the DMP1 hard drive because the USB is faster than the 802.11b connection. Thereafter, you can use the 802.11b Wi-Fi for the ongoing updates (synchronizations) as you come into range. By the way, Rockford's Wi-Fi adapter is a custom-branded DWL-121 D-Link adapter, as shown in Figure 11-9, so you know it's high-quality.

Figure 11-9:
The D-Link
DWL-121
for your
Rockford
DMP1.

The Rockford DMP1 wirelessly synchronizes in four ways:

✔ Automatically synchronizes at 3 a.m. (default sync time).

✔ Automatically synchronizes at time set by user at SimpleCenter.

✔ Automatically synchronizes when vehicle ignition is turned off.

✔ Started manually by the user via the Settings menu on the Controller: Settings➪Synchronization➪Synchronize Now.

The 20GB hard drive stores an equivalent of roughly 4,000 songs, depending on the size of the files — determined by the encoding algorithm you used when creating the MP3 or WMA files.

The Rockford mobile digital media player and SimpleCenter software support UPnP (Universal Plug'n'Play) — a standardized architecture that supports zero-configuration networking and automatic discovery. Under UPnP, a device can dynamically join a network, obtain an IP address, announce its name, convey its capabilities upon request, and discover the presence and capabilities of other devices. That makes quickly hopping on your Wi-Fi network easy. Check your Wi-Fi gear for the UPnP logo — if your gear has this logo, your setup will be, well, plug-and-play!

Another unit on the market that gets a lot of press is the KHD-CX910 Kenwood Excelon Music Keg (www.kenwoodusa.com, $700), which has a transportable 20G hard drive that you carry back and forth to your house to synchronize. The Kenwood supports direct-to-head unit integration with a line of Kenwood stereo units, in addition to supporting the use of an FM modulator (which simply retransmits the signal over an unused FM band) to any radio. It also supports WAV and FLAC in addition to MP3 and WMA encoding. Still, aside from these differences, it is incredibly more expensive than the Rockford Omnifi and, without the wireless synchronization capability, it's worthless to us.

Setting up your Rockford DMP1 kit

Installing your Rockford DMP1 will take a little time and some bending over and around. Be prepared for some spousal comments about losing some weight if you don't fit into your car easily.

Do yourself a *big* favor and preload your music on the DMP1 hard drive before installing it in the car. The USB transfer rate is much faster than the wireless transfer rate, so if you have as much music as Danny (he's already filled up his DMP1), you don't have to wait a long time while your music loads to take a drive. To do this, install SimpleCenter on your PC and catalog your music collection. Then grab your hard drive cartridge. Plug in the AC adapter into the back of the hard drive and attach the USB 2.0 cable to the hard drive and to your PC as well. Use the manual USB synchronization capability of SimpleCenter (it's the Synchronize Now! button) to load all your music onto your hard disk. Now, you're all set to hit the road when the installation is complete!

Because this is a wireless hacks and mods book, and not the *Car Hacks and Mods For Dummies* book by David Vespremi, Wiley (which we highly recommend if you like souping up your car), we focus more on the steps to set up your wireless network than how to mount your hard disk housing in your car. The Rockford installation manual is pretty clear-cut about the dos and don'ts of installing your system.

In general, to install your Rockford system, mount the hard disk housing someplace out of the way, preferably inside the passenger compartment (as opposed to in the trunk) if you are in an environment with extreme temperatures. (See Figure 11-10.) Then mount the controller, and then link the cables to power, the radio, and the hard drive. You'll add your Wi-Fi adapter last, and then experience mobile Wi-Fi, probably very loudly if you are like us (have to let the neighbors know what you've got now!).

Mount the hard drive vertically with the removable drive facing skywards — it was designed to absorb vibrations that way. Also, stay away from mounting it near any speakers: The magnetic fields are not suitable neighbors for your hard disk. Finally, make sure the hard drive has at least one inch of space around it to allow for good airflow — this is an electronic unit and does get warm.

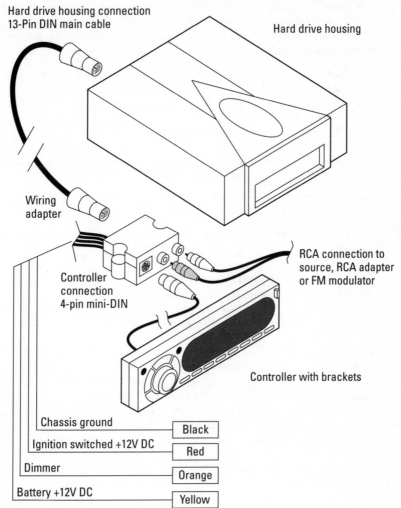

Hard drive housing connection
13-Pin DIN main cable

Hard drive housing

Wiring
adapter

Controller
connection
4-pin mini-DIN

RCA connection to
source, RCA adapter
or FM modulator

Controller with brackets

Chassis ground — Black

Ignition switched +12V DC — Red

Dimmer — Orange

Battery +12V DC — Yellow

Figure 11-10:
Your DMP1
components
are straight-
forward to
install.

Here are some good location options for the hard drive unit:

- ✔ **Center console:** By far, the best location is the center console if you can get room.

- ✔ **Passenger firewall:** This is the barrier between the passenger and engine compartments of any vehicle. Your feet are usually resting on it when in the front seat. Mounted high on the firewall (out of the range of your feet) or to the sides is okay.

✔ **Rear cargo space:** In an SUV or minivan, a vertical mounting in the back, tucked up against a seat, can be an optimal place as long as it is out of the way of your true cargo area and folding seats. Take into account the new removable and storable seats when picking your spot.

✔ **Under seat:** Although you probably can't position a hard drive vertically here, an under-the-seat location has the advantage of being out of the way and having good air flow.

The following are almost always bad locations:

✔ **Glove box:** Usually not firm enough to provide stability to the unit and not very good airflow.

✔ **Passenger door:** Too many opportunities for people to kick it getting in and out of the car.

✔ **Under the hood:** Vulnerable to temperature variances and lots of vibrations.

You need at least the length of the hard disk cartridge plus 2 inches to remove the cartridge from the unit, so don't cram this into a corner where you can't get at it. Although you probably only occasionally will need to get at this unit, you do have to have access to it.

Actually mounting the hard drive unit is a matter of mounting the housing cover to the car with screws and then sliding the unit into it. Pretty simple.

Mounting the controller is a little easier: You'll want to put it near the right of the instrument panel or on the center console so it is easily accessible to the driver and front passenger alike. Avoid the glove compartment or compartments like the center hideaway storage area because you'll be driving when you access this. Plan smartly. If you have an available ISO-DIN slot in your center console, the Omnifi SMP-1 has a bracket designed for it that comes with the system.

Wiring the system is very straightforward. The primary wires are connected at the same location as any aftermarket source unit, or at the fuse panel.

Make sure that you are making the connections on the correct side of the fuse panel — that is, on the *load* side of the fuse.

To install the wiring adapter, follow these steps:

1. **Strip the black wire, which is your ground wire, and attach a ring connector.**

If you have an available ground for the wire — either from another after-market device you have installed or for any other gear in the area — attach the ring connector to the grounding post. Otherwise, find a place on the chassis where you want to attach your grounding screw, clean it of any paint, grease, and so on, and then screw the ring connector to the chassis with a non-anodized screw and star washer.

2. **Attach the red wire (your 12V ignition wire or accessory wire connection) to your switched accessory position (ACC) on your ignition.**

   If your ignition does not have an ACC position, use the ON position of the ignition.

3. **Attach the yellow wire (your 12V constant wire) to a source of 12V constant power; your radio should have a constant connection running to it, for instance.**

4. **Attach the orange wire (the dimmer wire) to the lighting switch terminal in your car.**

   This dims the main display of the controller when your headlights are on (so it is not blaringly bright at night).

 Professionals use heat-shrink tubing to stabilize all twisted and soldered connections where possible. Heat-shrink tubing is exactly what it sounds like — tubing that you cut and slide over the connection until no bare wire is showing, and then use a heat source like a blow drier to form-fit the tubing with the connection. This makes sure that your connections stay intact even with all the vibrations of your car. Check out www.heatshrink.com; you can find this gear at most auto stores.

Note that you'll have three options for connecting wiring adapter to your car's radio:

✔ Use RCA cables to connect directly to the AUX inputs on your radio. This is the highest quality connection because it inserts the audio before the volume control of the source unit.

✔ If your source device does not have RCA connections, obtain an RCA adapter for your radio, connect it, and then connect the RCA cables to the adapter.

✔ Use RCA cables to connect to the inputs of an FM modulator, which sends the signal to a preset FM station on your radio.

Finally, connect your hard disk unit to the wiring adapter via its 13-pin DIN cable, and the controller via its 4-pin mini-DIN cable. Your main unit is installed.

Your Wi-Fi caravan

So say you put an access point in your car, and so does everyone else. You're driving down I-95 heading for sunny weather, and you've got four cars following you going to the same place. Given Wi-Fi's range is well within the distance between cars, does this mean you can set up a CAN (car area network)?

The short answer is yes — you can very easily set up intercar communications using Wi-Fi, subject to all the other distance and interference limitations of the particular flavor of Wi-Fi you are using. The longer answer is that everyone needs to be homed on the same SSID, and you need to support the same security, and so on. New standards for mesh and roaming coming down the pike — like 802.11r and 802.11s — will help find and maintain such signals as you move in and out of traffic. But the idea of a self-creating, daisy-chained, 100-car-long Wi-Fi system is not publicly available yet. That will probably come sooner or later from the car manufacturers.

The concept of intercar communications on the road is being hotly debated now among car manufacturers. The manufacturers are more interested in having cars talk to one another than people in the cars communicating with each other. There are many benefits to having cars talk to one another. Have you ever been stuck in a traffic jam and wondered if there was a way to get everyone to just start moving faster all at once? Wireless networking can help there. Or, think about those fog-bound pile-ups we read about all the time — if cars could talk to one another, warnings could be sent out. It's not a given that the Wi-Fi will be the mechanism for intercar communications, or for talking with other vehicle-oriented devices like tollbooths. In fact, the car industry has been looking at a new standard called *Dedicated Short Range Communications (DSRC)* for some applications between cars and other devices, like toll-taking. Look for a new wireless standard, 802.11p, to serve as the foundation for DSRC. (You can find out more about DSRC at http://grouper.ieee.org/groups/scc32/dsrc/#.)

For the wireless component, you just need to install your D-Link DWL-121 Wi-Fi adapter via the USB 2.0 connection on the back of the hard drive housing. You need to find a firm out-of-the-way place to locate your Wi-Fi adapter.

Some words of caution about situating your Wi-Fi adapter:

- ✔ Do not place the Wi-Fi adapter inside the trunk of the car — the metal of the trunk kills your signal.

- ✔ Do not place the adapter in the glove compartment for the same reasons.

- ✔ If you have windows with any metal tinting, keep the adapter at a good distance from that window as the metal interferes with the radio waves.

- ✔ If you have roll bars or other heavy metallic bars in the car, these are also not great places to tuck your adapter.

Where is a good place for your Wi-Fi adapter? The dashboard, the rear deck, tucked in the headrest . . . anywhere that you can ensure that the antenna stays in a vertical position. Wherever you end up putting your adapter, use some adhesive-backed or sewable Velcro to attach it firmly.

After you've installed the wireless adapter, the physical installation of the DMP1 is complete.

Setting up your DMP1 wireless connection

Configuring your wireless connection options in the DMP1 is pretty straightforward. Before you get started, make sure you are in range of your wireless network and that your Wi-Fi adapter is plugged into the unit.

You use your controller to configure your device. Turn your car on, and your controller should be powered up. You will see the Omnifi logo when the controller is starting up.

The default settings for the DWL-121 are

- SSID = Default
- Channel = 6
- Network mode = Infrastructure
- Encryption = No WEP

To set up your wireless connection:

1. **Access the Settings mode by pressing the HOME button and the LEFT NAVIGATE button.**

   You care about three areas in this Setting mode:

   > Network settings: This is where you can view or modify your static IP address, subnet (mask), and gateway IP addresses.

   > Wireless settings: This is where you view or modify your SSID and mode, as well as change your WEP key. (You won't configure your channel here — your channel is not configurable and is set by your AP.)

   > Synchronization: This is where you set up your synching options.

   The DMP1 is preset to automatically acquire an IP address from your wireless network — you don't have to do anything else unless you wish to assign a static IP address to your car's unit.

If you want to stick with an automatic IP setting, skip to Step 7. If not, proceed.

2. **If you do want a static IP address, use the SCROLL knob to get to the Network Settings area and press the SELECT button or the RIGHT ARROW button.**

   You will see the Auto (Manual) Configure option.

3. **Press SELECT to toggle between Auto Configure and Manual Configure. Choose Manual Configure to input an IP address. Press the SELECT button when you are finished, or press STOP if you want to exit the function without saving any changes.**

   You also have to input your subnet mask and gateway address, so have those handy. Use the SCROLL KNOB to move through numbers until you reach the desired value. Use the NAVIGATE RIGHT or NAVIGATE LEFT button to move between IP address values.

4. **When you are done inputting an IP address, press the NAVIGATE LEFT button and you are asked if you want to save your changes. Select Yes or No.**

   Your Rockford Omnifi may restart after you make changes.

5. **Use the SCROLL knob to get to the Wireless Settings area and select the SSID function that appears at the top of the Wireless Settings list using the SELECT button.**

   This causes your Rockford Omnifi to search for available networks. It displays a list of available networks (SSIDs). If your home network is the only network available, you see only the SSID of your home network. Select this SSID using the SCROLL knob to highlight the SSID and the SELECT button to choose it.

6. **If you do not see your SSID, you can manually enter it. The display shows an option for entering an SSID using the SCROLL knob.**

   We advise you to move the unit closer to your network and let it find the SSID automatically because merely entering an SSID does not mean the unit will find that network. You are better off finding the network first.

   Next set your Mode. If you chose to have an automatic IP address, this is autoconfigured for you and you can skip to Step 11.

7. **Select the Mode option.**

   If your home network includes an access point, choose Infrastructure mode, using the SELECT button. If your wireless network does not include an access point and you are connecting directly to a PC with a wireless adapter, choose Ad-hoc mode.

8. **If you have the wireless encryption protocol installed on your network, set your WEP key (see Chapter 8).**

   If you use a WEP key with your home network, you must input that same WEP key on your Omnifi DMP1 or you won't be able to log onto your home network. To input a WEP key, select WEP using the SELECT key.

   If you use WPA or WPA Enterprise on your LAN, you won't be able to connect the DMP1 to your network. You may consider attaching an older 802.11b AP to your network and enabling WEP on it for attaching devices like the DMP1 (or most audio and video networking devices).

   You have the following choices:

   - Disable WEP
   - 64-bit alpha
   - 128-bit alpha
   - 64-bit hex
   - 128-bit hex

9. **Select one of the WEP key options shown above.**

   If you select one of the WEP formats, the display shows a line of character boxes with 0s in them. Use the SCROLL knob to change the values. Use the NAVIGATE RIGHT or NAVIGATE LEFT buttons to move between the entry areas. Press SELECT to save, or the STOP button to cancel out of this input mode.

10. **When you are done entering the WEP key information, press the NAVIGATE LEFT button, and you will be asked if you want to save your changes. Select Yes or No.**

    Your Omnifi may restart after you make changes.

11. **In the last area, the Synchronization area, select the first option, Sync, and then select Yes, Auto Synch Daily if you wish to have the wireless network automatically synchronize with your car (we suggest this option).**

    Press SELECT to save.

12. **Scroll down to Synchronize Now and select Synchronization using the SELECT button.**

    Note: You cannot skip this step — you must manually synchronize at least once in order to establish a connection to your wireless network. Selecting Synchronization triggers a wireless synchronization with SimpleCenter on your PC. The display shows a percentage completed value for the current synchronization process. You can verify the last successful synchronization process by scrolling to the Last Sync option in the Synchronization area.

13. **When the synchronization is done, press the NAVIGATE LEFT button and you are asked if you want to save your changes. Select Yes or No.**

    Your Omnifi may restart after you make changes.

That's it: You're wirelessly connected. If you have any problems, check out the Rockford support FAQ at `www.omnifimedia.com/scripts/omnifi tech.cfg/php.exe/enduser/std_alp.php`.

Note that you can drive your car away from your home wireless network while the Omnifi is performing a synchronization without damaging your Omnifi data. However, some portion of the new media that was scheduled to be synchronized may not be available. If you drive away from your home network while synchronization is in progress, the Omnifi display reverts to the top level of the media playback mode.

Introducing the Carputer

Now that we've whet your whistle by showing you how to outfit your car with a fantastical auto-synching audio server, you may be thinking about something more. Like video. Like games. Like worksheets. Hey, scratch that last one, you're on vacation!

Now you're ready to step up to a *carputer* — a computer designed to be installed in the car. What's special about a carputer? They are designed to be smaller and less expandable than regular computers, use less power, and are simply more purpose-built for a rugged car experience — all while meeting users' fairly demanding application performance needs. Figure 11-11 shows the Xenarc Small Footprint, which measures just 5.8" × 9.8" × 2.79".

Figure 11-11:
A Xenarc
Small
Footprint
Fanless PC.

We don't go into a lot of detail on carputers here for the following reasons:

✔ From a wireless perspective, these are just like installing wireless clients on your desktop PC. Many people use USB to add on Bluetooth and Wi-Fi, like the D-Link AirPlus G DWL-G120 USB Adapter (www.dlink.com, $50), or a USB GSM GPRS Modem, like the Laipac M2M-3310 (www.laipac.com, $230).

✔ From an installation perspective, it's a lot like the process we just described for putting in the Rockford Omnifi unit. That was pretty simple to install — so are these products. Some carputer models are small enough — single DIN-sized — to fit in most factory radio slots. Most can fit where you'd put any CD changer (in fact, they are often smaller than changers). Power requirements are controlled by DC/DC 12V mainboards, so no power supply needs to convert the power from AC to DC. Decent power management shuts off the PC when your car is off for a little while, waking up only to perform synchronization, so you largely do not need to worry about your PC draining your car battery. All-in-all, installing a car PC is a pretty painless experience.

If you want to get decent Wi-Fi range from your carputer, get a Wi-Fi card for your PC that can handle an external antenna attachment. PCI is preferable — most of these cards use standard connectors that let you add a stronger antenna. You want an omnidirectional — not directional — antenna, as we discuss earlier in the chapter and in Chapter 7. For best results, the minimum you should get is a 5dBi antenna. (See Figure 11-12.) For great ideas — and full kits — for adding an optimal Wi-Fi antenna to your carputer (or laptop if you want to as well), check out the complete *wardriving* kits at the NetStumbler shop at shop.netstumbler.com.

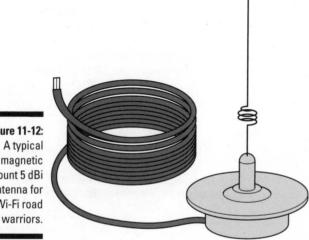

Figure 11-12:
A typical magnetic mount 5 dBi antenna for Wi-Fi road warriors.

Synching your carputer to home databases

If you want to keep your car's on-board systems synchronized with specific folders on your wireless LAN, Natalie and the folks at Carcpu.com suggest you consider using Microsoft Windows 2000/XP's built-in synchronization capabilities. Open up Windows Explorer, go to My Network Places⇨Entire Network⇨and so on until you find the network drive, folder, or file you wish to synch with, right-click it, and select Make Available Offline. This sets up synchronization between a local hidden folder on the carputer and the folder on your wireless LAN. When you are outside of your wireless LAN's area, you can still access the files by navigating in the same way in the car OS. Lo and behold, the files will be there, updated as of the last synchronization.

When you do this for the first time, a wizard asks you a few configuration questions. Using this option enables you to access network-originated files even when there is no network present.

Windows automatically replaces them with files stored in a hidden cached folder and updates them when you synchronize with the network.

One problem you may encounter is that offline folders are slow to synchronize and won't work on many specific file types, such as Visio, Access, Filemaker, Notes NSF, and certain integrated Excel/Access files that use Visual Basic code. Also, synching is a manual process and needs to be done on a regular basis.

Finally, this works only if the folder you are selecting to sync with is *shared* and you will see the file as available only when this is the case. Also, the target to be synchronized has to be a folder inside a shared folder object. As an example, if you see Sharedata on your home's server, you can sync a folder under Sharedata but not the Sharedata itself.

If you want to talk carputers, our two favorite places are

- ✔ MP3Car.com (www.mp3car.com): You've got a store to buy parts in, and a forum to ask what to do with them.
- ✔ CarCPU.com (www.carcpu.com): This is a higher end store for solid carputers as well as the advice it takes to really make them work.

Also, check out the Mini ITX site, which is a site for people who find the strangest places to put computers — a car is one of the more normal locales. It's at www.mini-itx.com.

Watching Satellite TV on the Go

Some people just don't want to miss their *American Idol* live. And if you are on the road, what do you do? You bring the TV with you, that's what.

What about satellite radio?

We won't talk too long about satellite radio because it is just broadcast radio and does not really entail much networking. Satellite radio is just as easy as video — you can buy specific stereo headend units that go in your dash, or small units that have a built-in FM modulator so you can stream XM to your car stereo via an empty FM station slot.

The two major providers are XM radio (`www.xmradio.com`) and Sirius (`www.sirius.com`). Monthly fees apply, usually about $12.95 per month per radio; extra radios can be added at $6.99 per month.

To display TV signals in your car, you'll need an in-car entertainment system of some sort. We won't go into all the options for in-car entertainment systems — if you want to know more about that, you can find out about the zillion aftermarket products at JC Whitney, Inc. (`www.jcwhitney.com`). Most entertainment systems come with an option for receiving over-the-air (OTA) signals for VHF 1-13/UHF 14-62, via an OTA antenna mounted in the car.

What's neat is adding satellite to this equation. You can add a receiver in your car to your existing satellite service for only $5 extra a month. However, expect to shell out at least $2,300 or so for a full roof-mounted satellite antenna and receiver, and this is a *huge* roof antenna. It's 5 inches tall and 32 inches in diameter and subsumes your rack space on your car or van. That's the only complex part — the antenna merely connects to the receiver, which you can mount under a seat anywhere in the vehicle's interior. You just connect the receiver to your vehicle's existing mobile video system via a set of RCA audio/video outputs. Pretty simple.

KVH Industries (`www.kvh.com`) markets its video-only solution called TracVision A5 that works with DirectTV. RaySat (`www.raysat.us`) has a more expensive ($3,500) option that also includes Internet data access; the company, new in 2005, expects to announce service agreements that offer download speeds up to 4 Mbps, with a maximum of 128 Kbps upstream. Winegard (`www.winegard.com`) also has a range of products for mobile satellite.

The satellite antenna requires an unimpeded view of the southern sky for satellite TV reception, and if you are driving around Manhattan with its tall buildings, don't expect a signal. Reception can be blocked temporarily by very large obstacles, such as bridges, mountains, and so on, as well. This technology is optimal for stationary use.

Coming soon to a phone near you is streaming TV. You can get small versions of TV shows now, but soon you'll be able to have the data rates required for a decent quality live video stream over the Internet to your car. Your Bluetooth-enabled phone will surely enable you to stream video data to your entertainment system and onto that backseat screen. The individual parts are there, but you won't be able to really make it happen with an off-the-shelf kit for a while yet. If you install a car PC, you can link your cellular data service to your PC, and use your browser to launch your TV service on your screens. Lacking a PC in the car today, your only real cost-effective options are over-the-air and satellite signals.

Follow That Taxi (with GPS)!

Old movies are so much fun to watch, particularly when it comes to the chase scenes. (Danny's favorite is the taxi cab chase scene in *What's Up, Doc?* where they all end up in San Francisco Bay.)

But alas, times have changed, and with new technologies, today we're more likely to be stuck with an *Alias* episode where they are tracking someone's car from a satellite in space. The wide availability of GPS devices allows you to track anyone anywhere — when that GPS signal receiving technology is tied with an outbound data messaging technology to tell people where you are.

GPS stands for *Global Positioning System,* which is funded and controlled by the U.S. Department of Defense (DOD). GPS provides specially-coded satellite signals that can be processed in a GPS receiver, enabling the receiver to compute position, velocity, and time. The GPS system is enabled by signals from 24 satellites above the earth — signals from any four or more of these are used to compute positions in three dimensions and the time offset in the receiver clock. Consumer products using the GPS are not as precise as military and other authorized government products because they are not allowed access to the restricted *Precise Positioning System* signaling system used by the government; consumer applications have to settle for the *Standard Positioning System* which pinpoints locations within about 100 meters horizontally and 156 meters vertically. That's probably close enough for us casual users.

In shopping for GPS, you'll also hear about the Wide Area Augmentation System (WAAS), which monitors the GPS satellite data through a field of 25 ground stations to make signal corrections and provide even more accurate positioning information to WAAS-receiving units. You'll want to check out WAAS channel support when comparing potential devices.

The Parrot 3300 unit we discuss earlier in the chapter comes with an onboard GPS receiver to track where you are — it communicates with your smartphone or PDA running any GPS software (like the Tom Tom Navigator (www.tomtom.com, $150) to deliver your personal tracking application when you are in the car.

Other in-car mounted GPS systems include portable devices, such as the StreetPilot units from Garmin (www.garmin.com, ranging from $750 to $1,200) and the RoadMate GPS units from Magellan (www.magellangps.com, ranging from $450 to $1,000), as well as add-on devices for your PDA or laptop, such as the Pharos iGPS Portable Navigator system (www.pharosGPS.com, $250). A truly huge lineup of products is available — if you are interested in these units, check out CNET's coverage of GPS auto systems in the Car Tech section of CNET Reviews (reviews.cnet.com).

The predominant application for all of these GPS units is navigation — helping you find your way out of Dodge in a hurry. They vary substantially based on where they can be used (that is, what maps the units support), how many maps are loaded on the systems (or whether you have to load maps onto the units from your PC), and how portable and feature-rich they are (with extra features like voice commands and memory card support).

Another category of GPS-enabled auto gear is GPS tracking devices. These are minicomputers that track all sorts of vehicle data, like speed, location, and so on, as well as control various car functions, like lock/unlock doors, disable ignition, and so on.

There are two major applications for tracking vehicles with GPS — so-called *fleet applications* for businesses who want to know where their trucks are, and personal tracking applications for parents who want to see if their kids are at Lovers' Lookout or in the wrong part of town.

GPS is a one-way technology — your GPS receiver tells you where you are. If you want to know where your car is when you are not in it, you need to use some sort of wireless communications service, typically a cellular service, to tell you what the GPS receiver is reading real-time. GPS units from which you download data in non-real-time are called *passive* units.

Consumer tracking units generally start at around $300 and can run more than $1,500 for the most feature-rich units. However, a wealth of products at the low end of this price range are quite functional. A good example is the Alltrack USA service (www.alltrackusa.com/index.html), which is a real-time product that costs $389, and passive products ranging from $338 to $1,730 at the time of this writing.

Real-time products incur usage fees. In Alltrack's case, each time you request the location of the car, you're "polling" it to determine its location. Each time the car contacts the Web site, it's "polling." The fees for each poll start at about $.50 per poll and go down to $.25 per poll, based on volume. Their monthly fee starts at $8.50 for 15 polls.

What do you get for your money? Quite a lot, actually. You can use any phone or Internet browser to find out where your car is right now, what speed it is traveling, and in what direction. A typical response from your phone? "Danny is located at 1244 Storrs Rd., Mansfield Center, Connecticut, and is traveling 0 miles per hour." (Now it won't say that Danny is at a Starbucks, getting much-needed caffeine — that must be coming in a future version.)

But wait, there's more! You can get extras like these:

- **Speed threshold alert:** Alerts you when, where, and by how much a vehicle speeds. So you will know if your teen is driving over that 60 mph speed limit you gave him or her.

- **Electronic fencing alert:** Alerts you when any of up to ten predefined boundaries have been crossed. You can create up to ten rectangular or circular regions; you're notified immediately if your car goes into or out of any of these regions. The system can send you e-mails (be sent an e-mail at work if you car arrives at the mall during school time), text messages (get a text message when your teen arrives safely at school in the morning), or automated phone messages (be told that your son has gone to "that kid's" house again).

- **GeoFence alert:** Alerts you when your car goes outside of a circular region with a predefined radius that's centered on the car's current location. (You can tell your kid not to drive more than 10 miles away from home.)

- **Car alarm alert:** Alerts you when the car alarm goes off. (If it is stolen, you can tell the police exactly where it is.)

- **Low battery alert:** Alerts you when the vehicle battery falls below a predetermined voltage of 9.5 or 10.5 volts. (Also known as the "You left your lights on, fool" alert.)

- **Towing/flatbed alert:** Alerts you if your car is being towed away. (This is done by seeing if the car is moving with the ignition off.)

In addition to these alerts, you can take action too, like unlocking your doors and disabling/enabling the starter.

Higher end models can do more things. Alltrack's high-end tracking product, Shadow Tracker Premier ($1,700), has a wireless download option on one of its passive systems that allows you to capture your data via a 900 MHz download when the vehicle returns to your home.

What about OnStar?

You may have heard commercials on the radio about OnStar (www.onstar.com) and how it can help stranded or injured motorists in the middle of nowhere get help when they need it. Think of OnStar as a combination of AAA (American Automobile Association) services, an in-dash voice-activated cellphone, and GPS. The car manufacturers have figured out that they too can provide emergency car services, but with a better twist — they build it into the car's electronics so it can detect when an airbag has deployed, track your car if stolen, or unlock your car if you locked your keys in it. Oh, and you can use it to make hands-free phone calls too.

OnStar has been offered since the 1997 Cadillac models, and is now on a growing number of GM and other vehicles. It is a factory option and cannot be installed by a dealer or retailer. There are monthly service fees that start at $16.95 per month/$199 per year.

Note that OnStar is getting some traction and the attention of other players in the market, so new bundled plans are starting to emerge. For instance, Verizon offers its America's Choice Plan with OnStar that bundles OnStar with your cellular bill and applies Verizon cell minutes when you use your OnStar system for in-car personal phone calling. If you have an OnStar car and a cellphone service plan, call your service provider and see if there is a better bundled option.

Other car manufacturers are following suit, by the way. BMW offers the similar BMW Assist, for instance. Look for this to be a real baseline offering on most cars within a few years.

If you're a sucker for sappy commercials, you can check out the movies on their Web site, www.onstar.com/us_english/jsp/idemo/index.jsp.

There's a trade-off of sorts between the data-rich storage of a hard drive and the cost considerations of cellular data transmission. Most real-time tracking systems do not provide you with the wealth of datapoints that you get with the hard disk–based systems. These are the most expensive units, however. So you might be able to see where a car is in real-time, but you cannot tell everywhere the car has been for the last 24 hours — you can with the passive systems. Ideally, you have the best of both worlds with a large hard disk system that also can be controlled in real-time.

Alltrack USA is merely one of several tracking services on the market. More and more commercial wireless tracking companies are launching consumer versions as well. You can find the range of products on the market at sites such as GPS On Sale (www.gpsonsale.com/vehicletrackingdevices/index.htm).

Chapter 12

Operating Your Own Hot Spot

*T*hroughout this book, we talk about how to extend your wireless world by accessing the tens of thousands of hot spots available worldwide. All of those hot spots were built to solve a problem — namely, the problem of finding Internet access while on the road. So why not be part of the solution by creating your own hot spot for public use?

You can be part of the solution and, while doing so, bring more customers to your business, or even make a few extra bucks every month for your home budget by operating your own hot spot. In this chapter, we tell you how to do it.

It's really not all that hard, although things get a wee bit more complicated if you're trying to get very fancy with a for-pay hot spot. We help you decide whether you want to charge for your hot spot, and then we help you figure out what kind of equipment you need, how to choose a hot spot–friendly ISP, how to promote your hot spot, and how to join a community or roaming network. Finally, we give you some good tips on keeping your hot spot secure and keeping the rest of your network safe while strangers are using your hot spot.

The Big Question: Free or Pay?

If you're going to create a hot spot, the very first decision you need to make — before you do *anything* else — is to figure out whether you're going to charge users anything to get onto your wireless network.

This is the most fundamental decision you face, as it drives everything else you do, such as what kind of access point and other equipment to use, what kind of software to use to control access to and monetize the hot spot, what kind of ISP connection you require, and more.

This decision isn't, strictly speaking, a binary one either. You can create a free network that's wide open to everyone, or one that's restricted in some ways. Your for-pay hot spot can be part of a full-fledged business (if you're feeling entrepreneurial), or just a way to earn a few extra bucks. You decide what you want — and we help you make the right choices that flow from that decision.

Both the free and for-pay hot spots have pros and cons — trying to make money in the hot spot game isn't for everyone. Many folks might even find some middle ground between the two — setting up some of the aspects of a pay network, but not actually exchanging cash money for hot spot service. For example, a coffee shop may make access free, but only to folks who've actually bought something. Double espresso and Yahoo! News, anyone?

From the operator perspective, we like to divide hot spots into five categories:

✔ **Free, unsecured hot spots:** These are the hot spots where the owner just plugs in an unsecured access point and lets anybody have at it. We don't recommend that you do this, but the choice is ultimately yours.

✔ **Free access, secured hot spots:** These hot spots don't use encryption or require users to log in or register, but they are secured from the *rest* of your network, so that you have a much lower chance of someone out in the parking lot or street using your hot spot to get onto your file server or into your Quicken files on your networked laptop.

These free access, secured hot spots are the *minimum* we think you should shoot for. Setting up a hot spot this way isn't hard, and it keeps your own personal network safe from intruders.

✔ **Free, registration-required hot spots:** These hot spots are available to users without charge, but you put some restrictions on access to them — you don't want to let just *anybody* get on the network. Many "free" commercial or municipal hot spots fit into this category. You can use this registration/login process with a WPA encryption system using a user-name and password or certificates, or you can use a Web-based system (we talk about some hot spot–specific access points later in the chapter that have a built-in Web server for exactly this purpose).

This free, registration-required hot spot is what we were referring to with our earlier example of the café that provides free hot spot access with a purchase. These are also common in places like hotels, restaurants, and even in the lobby of an office building — anywhere you want to let some people onto the network, but not everyone.

✔ **Stand-alone for-pay hot spots:** These are the kinds of hot spots you might establish in your business (particularly if you're in the retail business). You own and operate the hot spot, you pay all the bills, and you get to keep all of the money. Simple as that.

✔ **Networked for-pay hot spots:** You may not want to get too deeply involved in the day-to-day running of your hot spot(s). You may simply have the right location for a hot spot, but not the inclination to do it all yourself. You're in luck: There are companies out there that will provide the equipment you need, help you get set up, and then remotely manage users' accounts and support. These companies keep some of the money — you typically get paid a few bucks for each user's session — but they also take away a lot of the headache and risk for you.

The system used to track and authenticate users on a for-pay or a free, registration-required hot spot is known as an *AAA* (Authentication, Authorization, and Accounting) system — most folks call this *triple A*. The three functions of AAA, as it relates to hot spots (AAA is also used for a lot of other forms of networks, including mobile phone networks), are pretty simple to understand:

✔ **Authentication:** This function simply verifies that a user (or potential user) is who they say they are. This can be done by means of a username and password combination, or it can be done with a set of encrypted certificates, as discussed in Chapter 9. Either way, the authentication function establishes the identity of every party involved in the hot spot.

✔ **Authorization:** After a user is identified, he can be *authorized* to do certain things. For example, a user at our prototypical coffee shop might authenticate with a onetime password provided at the checkout — sort of like the password you get at some gas stations to use their car wash if you fill up your tank with gas. This password authorizes this user to connect to the access point and access the Internet for, say, one hour. More sophisticated hot spots have a larger set of *policies* for authorization, so different users get access to different sets of services.

✔ **Accounting:** If money is involved in your hot spot, you have to have a way to keep track of what users are doing so that they can be billed accordingly — that's what the accounting function of AAA accomplishes. Basically, the system keeps track of each user's logins, the amount of time they spend online, and so on, to provide the hot spot owner or operator a way of billing (or deducting prepaid time, if that's the billing model being used).

All three of these systems work together in a very intertwined and interlocked fashion — authentication and authorization work together to give a user "rights" on the network; authorization and accounting work together to make sure the user gets billed for the services she actually uses; and so on.

If you're building a big network of hot spots to establish yourself as a Wireless ISP (WISP) and you plan to run dozens of hot spots for hundreds (or thousands) of customers, the AAA solutions we talk about in this chapter aren't for you. You need to spend some serious money and implement a professional "telco grade" AAA system from a company like Bridgewater Systems (www.bridgewatersystems.com). For the kinds of hot spots we discuss here (small single to several AP networks, not big commercial networks with dozens of APs), you can get by with the AAA built into a hot spot–ready AP, or you can use an external service to provide you with your AAA. We talk about both of these options later in this section as we discuss your for-pay hot spot options.

Setting up a free hot spot

The easiest kind of hot spot to set up and run is a free access point. In its most basic form, you create a hot spot whenever you turn off WPA or WEP encryption on your access point and let passers-by hop onto your Internet connection.

Although that is indeed the easiest way to set up a hot spot, we wouldn't exactly recommend that you do it that way. At the very least, if you're setting up a free hot spot that way, take some minimal security measures, such as those we discuss in the section titled, "Securing Your Hot Spot," later in this chapter.

So although you can create a free hot spot by just "unlocking" your access point, a better approach is to create one of the "free access, secured" hot spots we mentioned in the beginning of this section. This isn't rocket science — nor does it cost you a lot of money.

The real trick here is finding a way to keep the access point open and available to potential "customers" while keeping the rest of your network safe and sound. The basic functions you need to support for this hot spot include the following:

- ✔ A router to provide DHCP functionality for users — to give them IP addresses and properly route their Internet traffic to their computers (providing Internet sharing, in other words).

- ✔ An access point (or several) to provide the wireless link. This is usually (but doesn't have to be) integrated into the same device as the router.

- ✔ A firewall to keep hot spot traffic off of your own local area network and private computers and servers. This is usually built into the router. You can also consider donating an old PC to the task (use two Ethernet NICs in the PC and connect it between your main router and the hot spot AP). Check out www.smoothwall.org for some free firewall software that runs even on a very old PC and keeps the rest of your network safe from hot spot users.

- ✔ A broadband Internet connection like cable or DSL. You can't use just *any* broadband connection, however — as we discuss in the section titled, "Dealing with Your ISP," later in this chapter. Some forbid you from operating a hot spot without paying more for your monthly broadband connection.

These are the basic elements of *any* hot spot (or any wireless network at all, for that matter). As you get more sophisticated, you simply need to add some additional elements (like an AAA system), either by upgrading your hardware or by subscribing to a service provided over the Internet.

To securely create an open hot spot, you can take one of several approaches (listed in descending order of security and flexibility):

- ✔ Use two access points — one for your own network, one for the hot spot. This is the safest approach — it allows you to have a safe yet flexible personal network along with your hot spot. To take this approach, you can

  - • Use a separate wired router to control your network, and connect both a "private" AP and a "public" hot spot AP to the router. Secure the network by placing the public hot spot in a different IP address range and behind a firewall as described in the "Securing Your Hot Spot" section later in this chapter.

  - • Use a wireless gateway/router device that is set up to provide hot spot access, and then add a second "private" AP (with WPA enabled) to one of the wired Ethernet switch ports on that gateway device. We discuss such a gateway device in the section titled "Getting Your Hot Spot out of the Box," later in this chapter.

In both of these two AP scenarios, you'll want to assign each AP to a different channel.

✔ Use a single AP for both your hot spot and your own "internal" network traffic. In this situation, you are sharing the AP with friends and strangers connected to your AP, so you won't be able to use any encryption to secure your network. In this case, we highly (very highly!) recommend that you turn off any file sharing, printer sharing, or other similar functions on your network. Use SSL (secure socket layer) for Web transactions and VPN (virtual private networking) for any important network activities.

We think that using only one AP is just not the right way to set up a hot spot unless you fit into one of the following categories:

✔ You're not using the network for any personal networking use — the entire network is entirely dedicated to Internet access only, and not being used for local area networking, file servers, music servers, and so on.

✔ You use an authentication system and encryption and create a hot spot that allows only trusted users onto the network. This is described in the section, "Letting only your friends (or customers) in," later in this chapter.

✔ You've got a special *public/private wireless gateway* access point (these run about $500) that handles network security for you. We talk about these in the section titled, "Getting Your Hot Spot out of the Box," later in this chapter.

✔ You just don't care if someone gets on your network and accesses your files, music, photos, and the like. We suspect you don't fit into this category, but some folks do.

The other reason we think a second AP really is worth the effort and expense is that the cost is so darn low. You can buy an AP for a free community-style hot spot for $50, and often far less if you shop around. When you consider the added security that you get for the relatively small expense, we think you'll agree that adding a dedicated AP for your hot spot is worthwhile.

If you have a free and "open" hot spot running on your wireless network — and you let anybody and everybody use it to access the Internet — you may be responsible for what folks do when they're online. You won't necessarily be legally responsible — we doubt you'll get carted off to jail if someone uses your network to launch a *DDOS* (distributed denial of service) attack, for example — but we can pretty much guarantee you that you'll be liable for any

ISP rules and regulations that get broken by your hot spot users. Now we're not paranoid, and the bad apples who use your network are way outnumbered by friendly folks, but we do feel we need to tell you that this risk exists.

Letting only your friends (or customers) in

Because you do take on at least some liability when you create an absolutely open hot spot, many people try to create a hot spot for a smaller *closed user community*. In other words, they pick and choose who they let and don't let onto their network. Here are several reasons why you might want to do this:

- ✔ **You're worried about liability.** As we mentioned earlier in this chapter, you could find yourself in a bit of hot water if some stranger uses your hot spot to launch a virus, download illegal material, harass or threaten someone, and so on. Some folks are willing to take this risk; others are not. We leave it up to you.

- ✔ **You're worried about network performance.** The bandwidth on both your wireless network itself and on the critical bottleneck of your Internet connection is limited. The more users that are on the network, the more ways these smallish slices of pie need to be divided. Some folks limit users on their network simply to keep from having everyone's Internet speeds slowed to a crawl by a bandwidth hog BitTorrenting the latest episode of *Deadwood*.

- ✔ **You're using the hot spot as an incentive, not a public service.** Perhaps you own the café we've talked about so much in this chapter, or a bed and breakfast. Or you manage a small apartment building. The list is almost endless here, but the point is that you might want to let certain users onto your network simply as a means of attracting or rewarding customers, clients, or partners. You don't want the Wild Wild West, but you do want relatively simple access for, as they say in the military, "friendlies."

Regardless of your motivation, if you're building a free hot spot with a user registration/login requirement, you need to deploy or "turn on" some sort of user authentication and login function on your hot spot AP or within your network. Read on to find out how!

Using Wi-Fi encryption

The easiest to implement (and most elegant) solution for such an authentication system is to simply use the security systems built into any modern Wi-Fi access point — namely, WPA and 802.1X (also known as WPA Enterprise). Using these standards (which we suggest you use to secure your own private Wi-Fi network — we tell you how to set this up in Chapter 9), you can ensure that every user is legitimate and wanted. WPA and 802.1X require all users to have either an identifying encrypted certificate on their PC or a username and password combination.

Unfortunately, in a hot spot environment, you can't always rely upon all users having equipment — Wi-Fi adapters, client software, and PC operating systems — that supports WPA. If you've got pretty tight control over the users within your hot spot community, WPA is the way to go.

The easiest way to set up an 802.1X/WPA server in your hot spot network is to use one of the *hosted* solutions we discuss in Chapter 8. (We also tell you about one solution in the sidebar titled, "Getting some help with your free hot spot.") These solutions let you send all authentication requests over the Internet, without having any extra equipment installed on your network.

You could always use the weaker *WEP* (Wired Equivalent Privacy) encryption protocol instead of WPA. WEP is so weak a protocol that it's essentially not secure at all, but all Wi-Fi clients (even the ancient ones) support it.

Setting up a captive portal

The other option for securing who gets into your hot spot is to use what many commercial for-pay hot spots opt for — a *captive portal*. With a captive portal system, users can connect to your wireless network, but they cannot connect to the Internet or other computers on your network until they have authenticated themselves using a username and password or *shared secret* (this is roughly equivalent to a password).

The *captive* part of captive portal comes into play when the user opens his Web browser and tries to load a Web site. Until the user has been authenticated, all Web page requests are directed to the authentication page (the portal to which the user is held captive). If you've ever used a wired broadband connection in a hotel and gotten the hotel's Web page when you launched your browser, that's a captive portal.

The big advantage of a captive portal system is that anyone who has a Wi-Fi card and a Web browser can authenticate themselves and get onto your network.

There are two ways of setting up a captive portal system:

- ✔ **Using a Wi-Fi hot spot gateway with a built-in captive portal.** This can be a hot spot–enabled AP or a separate Wi-Fi appliance (we discuss these in the section later in this chapter titled, "Getting Your Hot Spot out of the Box"). In either case, this is the easiest (although not cheapest) way to set up a captive portal solution — you don't need to set up a separate server PC in your network. You do, however, have to pay $500 or more for the hardware you need.

- ✔ **Using a software-based captive portal.** If you've got a Windows or Linux server on your network (or simply an extra PC that's connected to the wired portion of your network and is always running), you can skip the extra hardware and simply run a bit of software that provides the captive portal for your hot spot users. Two of the most popular solutions are the following:

  - **NoCatAuth:** An absolutely free solution for Linux-based servers, NoCatAuth is an offshoot of a wireless community network in Sonoma County, CA (the NoCatNet — visit their Web site at www.nocat.net to find out where the name comes from!). When installed on a Linux server, NoCatAuth provides an SSL-encrypted login Web page that authenticates (the "Auth" part of the name) users as one of three groups (public, co-op, and owner) with different permissions (bandwidth limiting, local network access, and so on) granted to each.

  - **FirstSpot:** If you've got a Windows server (2000, XP, or 2003), you might consider FirstSpot, from Hong Kong–based software company PatronSoft (www.patronsoft.com). This program provides a captive portal and a host of related functionality (like user time tracking and automatic logout when a user's out of time). The software offers a wide range of options, and pricing reflects those options — you can spend $95 for a basic free hot spot, or $1,000 or more for a very sophisticated version supporting a for-pay hot spot.

If you take this latter option (using software instead of a hot spot appliance), you need to install the server with your captive portal software as a *proxy server* within your network. That means that the server you use needs two Ethernet *NICs* or network cards and should be installed in your network between the access point and the main router or broadband modem you use to connect to the Internet. Figure 12-1 shows this setup.

Getting some help with your free hot spot

If you *do* want to control who gets onto your free network, but you *don't* want to have to spend a lot of time and effort (and money for that matter) setting up 802.1X or a captive portal (or another AAA solution), you might want to try out a hosted authentication service like that offered by the folks at Radiuz (`www.radiuz.net`).

Radiuz is a remotely hosted service that offers WPA Enterprise (802.1X) user authentication services for hot spots within the Radiuz network. All you need to sign up for a free account is your own WPA-enabled access point (which is basically any recent 802.11g access point or wireless router/gateway device) and a broadband Internet connection like a cable modem or DSL.

To get started, just go to `www.radiuz.net`, sign up for a free account (make up your own username and password), and then follow the online instructions for configuring your router. Basically, all you need to do is change the ESSID used by your router to `www.radiuz.net`, turn on TKIP encryption, and point your router to Radiuz's Radius server. After that's done, you simply need to give Radiuz some simple data (like the MAC address of your wireless router) via their Web site, and you're all set.

When you use this service, your hot spot is set up to be available to other Radius.net users — and you'll be able to use theirs. That's the only price you pay for free roaming and for security. You'll also be able to sign up friends, coworkers, and others with their own Radius.net accounts so that they'll be given permission to use your hot spot. They won't, however, be able to roam to other Radiuz user's hot spots unless they too add a hot spot to the network.

As we write, Radiuz is still a new company, in beta, but we are impressed by their idea — it seems like a great way to spread the community network bug without making anyone sacrifice the security of their private network.

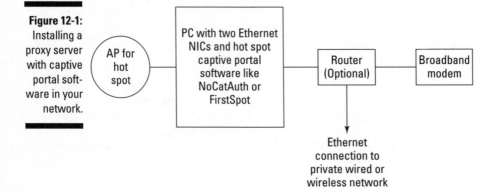

Figure 12-1:
Installing a proxy server with captive portal software in your network.

Sharing the wealth

If you want to make some money directly from your hot spot (as opposed to just using it as a free service to drive revenues in your primary business), you need to get a little bit deeper into the AAA realm than just authenticating and authorizing users — you need to tack the *accounting* part of triple A onto your network.

The easiest way to do this is to not do it! Let someone else worry about user authentication, authorization, and accounting. Let somebody else do the heavy lifting of account management, billing, and reconciliation. Heck, let somebody else create your advertising, promotions, and even the "look and feel" of your hot spot portal page.

If this sounds good, and you don't mind sharing your revenues, consider putting your hot spot under the umbrella of a hot spot aggregator service. These services work with hundreds (or even thousands) of hot spot operators of all sizes and provide the pieces and parts that make a for-pay hot spot feasible for both the owner and the users. Specifically, they provide you with

✔ **Hardware recommendations/kits:** Most aggregators make it really easy for you to get the equipment you need to set up a for-pay hot spot and to get yourself up and running. Typically they provide a list of approved or recommended equipment. You'll usually also find prepackaged solutions that you can buy directly from retailers or the aggregator themselves. The biggest aggregators also have deals with the leading Wi-Fi equipment vendors, such as NETGEAR or Linksys, so you can buy, for example, a Boingo-ready wireless router for your hot spot.

✔ **User authentication services:** When you connect to an aggregator's network using their approved equipment, you set up your access point to automatically route wireless users directly to the aggregator's online captive portal. How you do this varies from aggregator to aggregator, but typically it involves just a simple configuration step using the access point's Web configuration page. The aggregator handles all the AAA functions back in the network — you have to do nothing but the initial setup of the router.

✔ **Billing and credit card processing:** You also don't have to mess around with the occasionally pain-in-the-rear process of gathering money from your Wi-Fi users. With an aggregator, all of this payment is done online via a secure Web portal (or a monthly account with the aggregator), so you don't have to get involved.

A number of hot spot aggregators are on the market. All of the big "roaming" providers are in the business of aggregating hot spots for their customers, and they are all constantly looking to expand their network footprints by adding new hot spots.

You have to give a little to get a little with an aggregator. In other words, to get listed on their networks and to start bringing in revenues from their roaming customers, you must meet specific equipment, business practice, and technical requirements.

The biggest aggregator of hot spots is Boingo Wireless. We talked a lot about their services to end-users in Chapter 9. To create their network of more than 16,000 hot spots, Boingo has obviously partnered with a *lot* of hot spot operators — and they'll gladly partner with you too. You can either deploy one of Boingo's "Hot Spot in a Box" solutions — where you buy a specially-certified wireless router and connect it to your broadband Internet connection — or you can partner with one of Boingo's network provider partners to have your hot spot designed or installed for you. Either way, you pay for some hardware up front, and for your Internet connection, and then Boingo gives you a cut of all revenues for Boingo customers on your network. Check out `boingo.com/hso/` for all the details.

In addition to the aggregators, some companies specialize in setting up and running hot spots for hot spot location owners — these companies don't have their own "network of hot spots" and don't sell services to end-users, but they do have all of the back-end AAA and billing networks that the aggregators provide. Their business model is to make money getting your network up and running — they collect from you rather than from the end-users.

One of these *hot spot network providers* is a company called Sputnik. Sputnik focuses on helping hot spot operators of all types — from free and community networks up to hot zones consisting of dozens of access points. Sputnik's business model is different than Boingo's — instead of an ongoing chunk of your hot spot revenues, Sputnik gets paid up front (for their own Sputnik-branded access points, and for a service initiation fee), and then collects a monthly service fee (which varies based on the number of access points you have up and running — between $10 and $20 per AP). All the revenues you earn from your hot spot are yours to keep — so there's a bigger risk with Sputnik, but also potentially a bigger return. Find out more at `www.sputnik.com` (check out the SputnikNet section).

Sputnik isn't the only player in this game. A whole bunch of smaller companies will help you set up, operate, and manage a hot spot. Many of them — like NetNearU (`www.netnearu.com`), Surf and Sip (`www.surfandsip.com`), and FatPort (`www.fatport.com` — focused on the Canadian market) — are partners with Boingo. This is an ever-growing and -changing list of providers, so check out our own Web site — www.digitaldummies.com — for a current list.

Show me the money: Building your own for-pay hot spot

If you don't want to deal with an aggregator, or just aren't sure that you're ready to be part of a bigger network, and you don't want to pay a hot spot network operator to help you out, you can go it on your own and build a for-pay hot spot of your own.

If you want to do this, your best bet is to pick out a wireless router/accesss point specifically built for hot spot use. These routers have built-in authentication servers and captive portals and even connect to hot spot aggregators (when you decide to take that route later on — after you're all set up and established). Check out the discussion of hot spot gateways in the section titled, "Getting Your Hot Spot out of the Box," later in this chapter.

Dealing with Your ISP

The basic underlying purpose of the hot spot is to provide users a way to connect to the Internet (and Internet-based services) without wires. To make this work, the access points in a hot spot need to be connected to an Internet service provider's (ISP's) network via a high-speed connection (like the ones we discuss in Chapter 4). Pretty simple, huh?

Unfortunately, it's often anything but simple. That's because the ISP connections most of us use for our homes and apartments, and even for many businesses, are not suited for hot spot use. The connections themselves will do the job — most DSL and cable modem connections are fast enough, at least in the downstream (to the home or office) direction, to handle most hot spot traffic. But the agreements we all sign when we get service (knowingly or not) often forbid things like hot spots, either explicitly (that is, language that says "No hot spots") or implicitly (with restrictions on usage that effectively make a hot spot a non-starter).

Understanding terms of service

These service agreements are usually called *Terms of Service* (TOS) or *Acceptable Use Policy* (AUP). Whatever this document is called, it's a long, drawn-out, and usually relatively undecipherable bit of legalese that's either

✔ Hard to understand

✔ Boring

✔ Or . . . both

It's also an important document to find (usually on your provider's Web site — send them an e-mail or make a phone call if you can't find your provider's agreement). Somewhere deep down in the arcana of the TOS or AUP, you can find your provider's opinions on sharing your connection with people outside your household via Wi-Fi.

Typically, you find one of three TOS situations regarding hot spots:

✔ **No restrictions:** This is rare on "consumer-grade" (read that as cheaper) broadband connections, but not unheard of. If you want to open a for-pay hot spot, this is what you want.

✔ **No restrictions on free sharing:** You don't run into this too often, but some providers may not prevent you from running an open Wi-Fi hot spot, but they have specific language keeping you from reselling their bandwidth. If you want to join a community network, or just operate a freebie hot spot, this kind of connection should work.

Watch out for hidden "gotchas" like bandwidth caps or "excessive usage" clauses in the TOS. Even so-called *unlimited* service plans sometimes aren't actually unlimited, and if you drive your usage up too much with the hot spot, you might find that you get billed extra or even have your service terminated. Ask your provider if there are any limits on so-called unlimited service.

✔ **No hot spots, period:** This is common for residential ISP services from the local telephone company or cable MSO. These providers want you to bump up to a higher-priced *business class* connection if you're running a hot spot.

Some ISP recommendations

If you are building an unadvertised, informal hot spot that you're making available just as a nicety for a few friends and neighbors, you can probably get away with just connecting with your normal residential broadband connection.

Share the burden with Speakeasy

Some broadband ISPs don't mind if you share your connection via Wi-Fi — a few even specifically allow it in their TOS or AUP. But only one that we know of actually *encourages* Wi-Fi sharing of broadband and helps you use a hot spot to defray the monthly expenses of your DSL or T1 line. We're talking about Speakeasy (www.speakeasy.net), a Seattle-based nationwide ISP who we think is one of the most innovative out there.

Speakeasy's NetShare service (netshare.speakeasy.net) is built around the proposition that sharing your broadband with your friends and neighbors is a good thing. (We agree!) With this service, you can add a secure (WPA- or WEP-enabled) access point to your

Speakeasy broadband connection and sign your neighbors up as customers of *your* broadband service. You pay Speakeasy a monthly fee for your broadband service, and your hot spot customers also pay a small fee to Speakeasy (starting at around $20 a month) to get onto your network. At the end of every month, Speakeasy credits 80 percent of the fees generated by your customers back to your account.

NetShare isn't a way to make money from your hot spot, but it is a great way to defray the costs of broadband among a group of people — legally and without any hassle from your service provider. Try getting *that* from one of the big ISPs — trust us, you won't.

We've seen stories about a cable company in New York City going after some of their own customers for hot spot activity, but this rarely happens. If you create a hot spot on a residential connection, however, you're doing so at your own risk.

A better approach for any type of hot spot is to use one of these connections:

✔ **A business connection from your local phone or cable company:** For an extra $20 or so a month, you can upgrade to a business class connection for your DSL or cable modem service. These connections typically drop the hot spot restrictions from the TOS, and often add extra speed and even a *fixed* IP address, which can come in handy if you're hosting any servers on your network.

✔ **A DSL or T1 connection from a CLEC:** A competitive phone company (or *CLEC* — competitive local exchange carrier) typically offers DSL or T1 connections that are designed for SOHO (small office, home office) and SMB (small and medium businesses). Most of these connections don't restrict you from operating a hot spot. The largest DSL CLEC is Covad Communications (www.covad.com). We checked with our friends at Covad just for you, our beloved readers, and they say hot spots are A-OK on their network.

✔ **DSL service from an independent ISP:** You don't have to get DSL service directly from the telephone company who offers DSL (local or CLEC); you can also get DSL through third-party ISPs. Many of these ISPs offer services that allow hot spot activities. Check out the sidebar titled, "Share the burden with Speakeasy," for our favorite example of this.

Getting Your Hot Spot out of the Box

Although you can set up a hot spot with any Wi-Fi access point, using an access point specifically designed for use in the hot spot environment offers many advantages. These access points (often custom-designed for specific hot spot networks) combine standard access point and router functionality with security and AAA functionality that you might otherwise need to install a separate gateway device, hosted service, or proxy server to get.

Generically, these access points are called "hot-spot-in-a-box" — a term that Boingo has trademarked for their own pre-fab hot spot access point partnership with Linksys. Many vendors are selling these solutions; here are a few of the most common devices:

✔ **Linksys WRV54G Wireless G VPN Broadband Router:** This device is specifically designed for the Boingo network. With a street price of around $150 to $170, the WRV54G is a powerful router for any home or small business Wi-Fi network, with support for 802.1X authentication, multiple VPN tunnels (for corporate VPN users), and more. The real difference between the WRV54G and other more generic 802.11g wireless routers is in the *firmware* (basically, the router's operating system) of Linksys's router.

By downloading a firmware upgrade from Linksys's site (www.linksys.com/splash/hotspotinabox_splash.asp), you can activate a special configuration page within the router's Web configuration page that lets you connect to Boingo's hot spot network. You can be up and running in about five minutes, after doing a simple registration with Boingo.

For your own personal wireless networking, we recommend that you add another inexpensive wireless router to one of the wired Ethernet ports of the WRV54G. It's best to completely segregate your traffic from the hot spots, and the WRV54G does *not* support WPA — get yourself a cheap WPA-enabled router for your own networking.

✔ **SMC EliteConnect Hotspot Gateway Kit:** With a list price of $899, SMC's EliteConnect Hotspot Gateway Kit is designed to provide all the elements you would need to create your own hot spot — without relying on a network aggregator or service provider. All of the AAA functionality you need is built right into the EliteConnect gateway, including an authentication database that can support up to 2,000 users, and built-in Web redirection (captive portal) pages for advertising and log-in.

If your hot spot gets bigger, the EliteConnect system can grow to support additional access points (connected via Ethernet — including POE, power over Ethernet — or wirelessly using Wireless Distribution System, WDS). A partner *POS* (point-of-sale) ticket printer can be attached to the router, so you can print out tickets or receipts for your customers with their log-in information. You can also connect the EliteConnect system to an external 802.1X/Radiuz server, if you need to support more than 2,000 users (that's quite a hot spot you've got going there!). Figure 12-2 shows the EliteConnect system — you can find more on SMC's Web site, www.smc.com.

Figure 12-2:
SMC's Elite Connect Hotspot Gateway Kit lets you create your own hot spot.

✔ **D-Link Wireless G Public/Private Hot Spot Gateway:** D-Link's entrant into the pre-fab hot spot arena is similar in many ways to the SMC product and can be bought for a street price of about $550. The Public/Private gateway has a "public" Wi-Fi access point built in for hot spot customers, and a pair of wired Ethernet ports that are also on the "public" side of the gateway. An additional pair of Ethernet ports make up the "private" side of the network — you can connect your wired personal networking gear or even your own second access point. The key point here is that the public and private networks don't intercommunicate — so customers on your hot spot network can't snoop around on your private network.

Like the SMC gateway, the D-Link gateway supports internal AAA and can also connect to an external 802.1X server for large-scale user bases. You can also add in D-Link's own POS ticket printer, which can be handy for hot spots in a retail environment. You can see the D-Link gateway in Figure 12-3.

Figure 12-3:
D-Link
wants to
keep your
network
private
while giving
you a hot
spot.

If you start moving into high volume, large area hot spots — the kinds of hot spots where you might have thousands of users and require dozens of access points — you can find a variety of vendors who offer access points, routers, and gateways with even greater capabilities and scalability.

This "high-end" hot spot is beyond the scope of our book, but if you're interested, we'll whet your appetite with a few vendor descriptions:

- **Colubris Networks:** Colubris makes a range of high-capacity access points and gateway devices specifically for larger scale hot spots (as well as a few stand-alone APs that work well for a smaller hot spot). You can find out more about Colubris at www.colubris.com.

- **Cisco Networks:** The parent company of Linksys, Cisco is of course the biggest and baddest (in the good sense) networking company in the world, selling billions of dollars worth of equipment to enterprises and service providers every year. So it should probably come as no surprise that they've got Wi-Fi gear for the serious hot spot. In fact, Cisco's Aironet product line is the best-selling set of access points for commercial deployments. You can learn more about Aironet at www.cisco.com/en/US/products/hw/wireless/index.html.

- **Vivato:** If you want to get really fancy with a hot spot, check out the solutions offered by Vivato (www.vivato.com). These access points use a special military-developed technology called *flat planar array antennas* (like those used on Navy Aegis cruisers), which can electronically "aim" the Wi-Fi beam to very specific areas. A Vivato "base station" can provide a hot spot to an entire building or an outdoor area that is many times larger than what a normal hot spot can provide. Expect to pay thousands of dollars for the privilege, however, which is why most Vivato deployments have been funded by cities doing municipal hot zones, and not by individuals!

Securing Your Hot Spot

We talk about security in detail in Chapter 8, including how to keep your network safe from intruders, and how to keep your PC secure when you're using a hot spot. In this section, we just give you a few tips that apply *only* to your hot spot configuration and security. We don't like to waste your money by repeating ourselves throughout the book, so we concentrated all the important security stuff in that chapter.

The one bad thing about hot spots is that they can really wreak havoc with your network security — simply because most hot spots don't have the traditional WEP or WPA activated (just to make it easier for casual users to connect).

You can, of course, make your wireless hot spot safe and secure by ignoring this convenience factor and turning on WPA encryption. If you make all of your hot spot "customers" use WPA encryption, and have them authenticate themselves on your network using a PSK (preshared key) or 802.1X, you're pretty much safe from wireless mayhem.

Even in this situation, however, you need to take some steps to keep your own private network secure from your users. Even in a closed hot spot community like Radiuz, you probably don't want your fellow hot spot users having access to your file servers and other networked equipment.

Regardless of what authentication methods you are using or what wireless encryption techniques you have turned on, you can take a few steps to keep yourself secure when you've got a hot spot on your network:

- ✔ **Keep your own private wired or wireless networks separate from the hot spot.** Use a second access point for your own private use if you're doing something other than just accessing the Internet. Configure your routers to provide a separate subnet of IP addresses for personal networks (see Chapter 5 for more on this topic).

- ✔ **Use the firewalls on your routers/gateways.** When you set up the wireless access point/router for your "private" network, be sure to turn on any firewall features. You want to keep traffic that's outside of that private network (people on your hot spot, in other words) outside that firewall. Alternately, you can connect a firewall between the hot spot AP and the rest of your network, and use that to secure your network.

- ✔ **Use personal firewall software on your PCs.** Both Windows XP and Mac OS X have built-in firewalls that work pretty well, or you can try a third-party firewall, like ZoneAlarm (www.zonelabs.com). This software helps prevent sneaky folks in the hot spot from sneaking into your hard drive.

✔ **Don't forget to use WPA encryption and authentication for your own private wireless LAN.** Don't let anyone you haven't authorized get onto your private wireless LAN, and don't let anyone who's in range of your private network sniff your packets and steal your data.

✔ **If you can set up a hot spot captive portal system to do authentication, do so.** You can use a hot spot router with a built-in AAA system, or use a proxy server. Either way, the goal is to know who (or at least what type of user) is on your hot spot, and to keep anyone who isn't you or yours off of the private part of your network.

✔ **Encrypt your important files.** Both OS X and Windows XP have built-in file encryption systems that let you encrypt files on your hard drive with super-tough encryption methods like AES. Think of this as a last line of defense for your really important files — even if the bad guys get onto your private network, get past your firewalls, and gain access to your computer, they won't be able to read or do anything with your encrypted files. Check out `support.microsoft.com/kb/307877/EN-US/` to find out how to do this in Windows XP, and `www.apple.com/macosx/features/filevault/` for information about Apple's FileVault encryption system for OS X.

Promoting Your Hot Spot

Whatever your motivation for building your hot spot is — whether you're trying to make a buck or just serving your fellow man (or woman) — we're pretty sure that you want to get people using it. Why else go to all the trouble, right?

Some folks out there know how to sniff out a hot spot — check out the Wi-Fi "finders" we discuss in Chapter 16, for example. But not everyone knows how to search the airwaves for a hot spot. And even if they do, they won't always know if it's a legitimate hot spot they can use, or if they're potentially breaking some law and causing a national security violation by jumping onto a network. Help them (and yourself) out by promoting your hot spot.

The simplest thing you can do — and we do mean simple — is to "name" your hot spot (when assigning its ESSID) properly. Come up with some language that tells people that this is a hot spot. You've got 32 characters; use them well. Something like "Pat's free hot spot," or "Danny's lobster shack freenet" should help people understand what they're getting into.

If your hot spot is part of some network of hot spots (like Boingo or Radiuz), you'll be given specific instructions on what to call your network.

If your hot spot is not free-for-all and it's not part of a recognizable network like Boingo, we recommend that you put an e-mail address or Web site URL in the ESSID field that has more information about the hot spot. It might not help someone get on right at that moment, but it will give them a chance to figure things out later.

If you've got a free hot spot, you may want to list it in one of the community networks that are popping up all over the world. The best place to look for nearby community networks is at www.freenetworks.org.

You can advertise and promote a for-pay hot spot just as you would any service you might be offering — signs and posters, Web sites, advertisements, and so on. Joining a roaming aggregator network like Boingo, iPass, or GoRemote can help get your hot spot listed in more places.

Finally, no matter what type of hot spot you've got, getting it listed in a directory like JiWire (www.jiwire.com) is an essential step. Just go to the main JiWire page and follow the List your hotspots in our directory link.

Part IV
Cool Wireless Toys

The 5th Wave — By Rich Tennant

"Frankly, the idea of an entirely wireless future scares me to death."

In this part . . .

*I*f you're a gadget geek or a gizmo junkie, this is the Part of the book for you! In Part IV, we talk about all of the cool stuff you can add to your wireless network to extend its capabilities beyond just computer-to-computer communications.

We begin with a discussion of wireless audio networking products, and tell you how to get your MP3 and other digital music files from your PC or Mac to your home audio system and around the house without wires.

We also tell you how to use your wireless network as a security and surveillance tool — you'll be able to see who's at your home's front door while you're at the office!

If you're into making phone calls, check out the chapter on wireless Voice over IP (VoIP). We tell you how to get your wireless network enabled for making inexpensive phone calls. Soon you'll be able to throw away those old-fashioned cordless phones.

Finally, we devote an entire chapter to those little gizmos and gadgets that warm our hearts. If you're interested in things like wireless print servers, Wi-Fi finders, Wi-Fi travel routers and more, be sure to read on!

Chapter 13

Building a Wireless Audio Network

*I*f you haven't gone digital with your music, we can say only this to you: C'mon in, the water's fine! Moving your music collection to digital (using MP3 and other file formats) is a great way to enjoy your music wherever you are. We think digital music formats are worth their weight in gold just for the ability to throw a few thousand of our favorite songs onto our iPods whenever we're working out or on the road.

But digital music can go beyond just the PC or Mac and iPod. When combined with a wireless LAN, your digital music can easily extend throughout the home. Instead of schlepping CDs from room to room, you can put your CDs in storage — move all of your music to a hard drive and listen to it from anywhere in the house.

In this chapter, we give you a quick rundown of digital music, so you know your MP3s from WMAs. We make sure that you know how to get digital music onto your computer, both from your own CDs and from sources on the Internet. Then we get the wireless LAN into the action, giving you some strategies for getting audio around your home. We also spend some time discussing the devices that you need to make the connection between your computer-based music files and the final listening device — your ears.

Digital Music 101

For most folks, music has been digital for about 20 years — since the compact disc (CD) replaced vinyl LP records and cassette tapes as the primary source of prerecorded music. At its most basic, digital sound has had its analog acoustic waveforms of music (or any sound, for that matter) converted to a digital "zeros and ones, bits and bytes" format through a process called *sampling*.

This process simply uses an electronic/computer system to record the amplitude of a bit of music at an instant in time, and then to store that amplitude as a chunk of digital data. This process has two key elements:

- **Sampling rate:** The number of samples that are taken in a given period of time
- **Sample size:** The size of those chunks of data (the samples) measured in bits

All other things being equal, digital music with more frequent samples (higher sample rates) and bigger samples (more bits) sounds better and more like the original analog music. CDs, for example, have a 44.1 kHz sample rate (44,100 samples per second) and use 16-bit sampling. Some newer digital music formats have sample rates in the millions of samples per second, or have samples that are as large as 24 bits.

Understanding compression

The full digital music files found on CDs are *uncompressed,* which results in some very large file sizes. The digital files that store CD music on a disc take up 16 bits of space 44,100 times per second for each of the two stereo channels. Another way of looking at this is that a music CD with approximately 70 minutes of music on it takes up 650MB of storage space. That's a lot of space — imagine trying to fit 650MB CDs onto your 10 or 20GB iPod. You might be able to fit only 25 CDs (say 250 songs) on 20GB of space. That's far from the advertised 8,000-song capacity of an iPod!

The secret is that most digital music files used on computers or other computer-like devices (and therefore suitable for use on your wireless network) are *compressed*. Compression performs various mathematical techniques on music files to reduce the number of bits needed to digitally "describe" the music. These are the two primary categories of compression:

- **Lossless codecs:** Compression *algorithms* or *codecs* (encoder/*dec*oder) that reduce the storage (and network bandwidth) requirements of digital music files without throwing away any of the data describing the music are known as *lossless* codecs. When you play back music that has been encoded with a lossless codec, it is an exact duplicate of the uncompressed file that you began with. Examples of lossless codecs include

- **Windows Media Lossless:** Part of Microsoft Windows Media 9 and 10, this codec is built into the Windows Media Player software, and is supported by some of the wireless systems we discuss in this chapter.

- **Apple Lossless:** Included with Apple's iTunes software, Apple's Lossless Encoder is supported by the Apple AirPort Express system.

- **FLAC:** *Free Lossless Audio Codec,* or FLAC, is, as its name implies, a lossless codec that is free. It's part of an open source initiative, and you can find out more at `http://flac.sourceforge.net`. A few Wi-Fi audio players are beginning to support the FLAC codec, including the Sonos Digital Music System and the Slim Devices Squeezebox.

✔ **Lossy codecs:** Most audio compression codecs used in digital music systems are *lossy* codecs. These codecs use a scientific technique called *psychoacoustics* to figure out which parts of an audio signal can safely be thrown away without audibly "hurting" the music. Examples of lossy audio codecs include

- **MP3:** MPEG (Motion Picture Experts Group) 1 Audio Layer 3 is the full name of the most common digital music format. MP3 audio files are the ones commonly traded (usually illegally) on the Net, and they are the most common digital music codec used on PCs and digital music systems in a wireless network.

A limited number of systems and software applications also support the more advanced mp3PRO codec, which adds a technology called SBR (or Spectral Band Replication) to improve the sound quality over standard MP3-encoded music files.

- **WMA:** *Windows Media Audio* (WMA) is the standard audio format used by the Windows Media Player and compatible hardware. A lossless version of WMA (discussed above) does exist, but most WMA files use a lossy compression system.

- **AAC:** *Advanced Audio Codec,* or AAC, is the format used by Apple Computer's popular iTunes Music Store and is the default codec used for music encoded using the iTunes application. Like WMA, there's also a lossless variant of this codec, but most AAC files are lossy.

- **Ogg Vorbis:** Another free codec is Ogg Vorbis (`www.vorbis.com`). Ogg Vorbis (which we discuss in greater detail in the sidebar titled "MP3 is dead; long live Ogg Vorbis" later in this chapter) is designed to be free from the licensing fees that software and hardware companies must pay for other codecs like MP3, while providing improved sound quality compared to other lossy codecs.

The key takeaway here is that a lot of different codecs are out there, and any digital music being sent over a wireless network should use *one* of them: You have no good reason to send uncompressed audio across your network, or to store uncompressed audio on your networked PCs, Macs, and audio servers. Lossless codecs provide the promise of unaltered and unadulterated digital sound, but take up more storage space and network bandwidth — lossy codecs, on the other hand, are easier on your infrastructure, but may not measure up to your expectations if you're a golden-eared audiophile. You have to decide between the two, but either way, uncompressed digital audio is just a waste of network resources!

Being constant, being variable, being bitsy

The codec itself isn't the only determinant of the sound quality of a digital music file — how you use it also makes a difference. Lossy codecs can be configured to encode digital music files in a variety of ways, using different encoding techniques to change the quality and size of the music file.

When an uncompressed audio file is converted to a compressed format like MP3, AAC, WMA, or Ogg Vorbis, a piece of software known as the *encoder* performs the compression. The encoder (and encoding process itself) can affect the sound quality of a compressed music file in one of several ways:

- **Bit rate:** The *bit rate* of an encoded music file is simply the number of bits of data used to represent a second of music. For example, many MP3 files are encoded at 128 Kbps (128,000 bits per second). Generally speaking, the bit rate is a rough measurement of the amount of compression applied to a digital music file. The higher the bit rate, the less compressed the file is — and with lossy compression algorithms like MP3 or WMA, less compression means less of the original music is "thrown away," and more of the sound quality remains.

The bit rate refers to the amount of bits per second used for *both* of the channels of a stereo audio recording together. So 128 Kbps encoding means that there are two channels (left and right), each encoded at 64 Kbps. Occasionally, your encoding software refers to the single channel rate when you're setting your bit rate, rather than the stereo bit rate. Make sure you check this before you try to do an apples-to-apples comparison between two different codecs.

- **Constant versus variable bit rate:** When music is encoded, the bit rate can be varied according to the complexity of the music itself. Simple passages, for example, may require fewer bits to encode than a full orchestra playing something complex. Music encoded this way is known as *VBR* or variable bit rate. VBR is the most space-efficient way to encode digital music because you use high bit rates only when you need them for complex recordings. Constant bit rate (CBR), on the other hand, uses the same amount of bits no matter what the requirements of the music.

Some audio codecs, like Ogg Vorbis, are inherently VBR, whereas many others, like MP3 or WMA, can be configured as either CBR or VBR. Critical listeners tend to prefer VBR encoding because it not only saves space (or bandwidth), but also can allow additional peak bandwidth for the most complex musical passages. The big benefit of CBR encoding, particularly in a wireless or other networked environment where the music is being streamed across a network, is that the bit rate is always the same, and you don't have to worry about supporting sudden peaks — if you've got enough bandwidth for the simple parts, you've got enough for the entire piece of music.

For the most part, we feel that you don't really need to worry about VBR versus CBR when it comes to your wireless network. Even a high bit rate VBR audio stream shouldn't have peaks that exceed your wireless network's capabilities. To put it another way, if you have issues sending audio across your wireless network, using VBR instead of CBR encoding is probably not the problem!

✔ **Encoding technique:** Finally, the encoding technique used by the encoder software can vary from application to application, even when using the same codec for the compression. For some codecs, like WMA, you don't really have a lot of choices when it comes to the encoder you use, but other codecs — particularly MP3 — have several encoder options available, each with their own impacts on the sound (and their own proponents).

For example, many MP3-using music buffs prefer the LAME encoder for creating their own homemade MP3 files. LAME (find it at `lame.sourceforge.net`) provides a new and improved encoding method for creating MP3 files, using its own custom algorithms to create the MP3 from an uncompressed digital audio source (like a music CD). You can find links on the LAME Web site for stand-alone software that encodes MP3s using LAME and also for software modules that plug into your existing software — for example, if you use iTunes on your OS X Macintosh, check out iTunes-LAME (`http://blacktree.com/apps/iTunes-LAME/`). This software works with iTunes to allow LAME encoding for any CDs that you "rip" on your Mac. Figure 13-1 shows iTunes-LAME in action.

As we talk about the hardware and software you need to get digital audio around your wireless network, these codecs, bit rates, and encoders will come up again. Specifically, you need to make sure that all of the hardware and software you use in your wireless network supports the codecs, bit rates, and encoders that you choose when you create or purchase your digital music!

Figure 13-1:
Using
iTunes-
LAME to
encode an
MP3 file in
Mac OS X.

MP3 is dead; long live Ogg Vorbis

If you are not up to speed on the latest open source software trends, you'd probably think *Ogg Vorbis* is some Tolkein character that you missed in *The Return of the King*. But it's not — Ogg Vorbis (sometimes called just *Vorbis*) is a rather popular open-source audio format similar to MP3. Ogg Vorbis was created as a license-free, lossy audio format after Fraunhofer's 1998 claim for licensing fees for use of its MP3 format. Ogg Vorbis is an efficient encoding format that sounds every bit as good as (or better than) MP3, can be played back on a lot of portable devices, and is actively being enhanced by the strong open source developer community. Make no mistake about it: MP3 is entrenched, but Ogg Vorbis is steadily growing in support. Ogg Vorbis

is supported by many major music playing destinations, such as software like Winamp, the Xbox, and even D-Link's streaming media player. If you have a choice, buy a device with Ogg Vorbis on board — if nothing else, wondering where the name *Ogg Vorbis* came from will give you something to talk about at parties.

From WhatIs.com: "The Ogg part of the name came from the network game Netrek. In Netrek, an Ogg is a tactical maneuver, and the word has entered broader usage to mean "doing something forcefully, perhaps without due consideration of possible consequences." The Vorbis part of the name came from a character in the book Small Gods by Terry Pratchett."

How to Get the Music

We've already mentioned that *most* music that people buy these days is already digital — simply because the dominant form of physical music distribution is the CD. But CDs need some work before they're ready to be part of a wireless music distribution system — the songs on them need to be *ripped* (or encoded) to an appropriate format before you use them in your network.

Of course, not *all* music needs such a step. Unless you've had your head under a big music-blocking rock for the past few years, you've probably heard of Napster (or of LimeWire, or Kazaa, or any of the other dozen or so peer-to-peer file sharing programs) and you're probably aware of the online MP3 phenomenon. You're probably also familiar with the move of radio stations to the Internet — both established big-transmitter-owning brick-and-mortar broadcasters and small do-it-yourself Internet-only broadcasters. They provide even more digital music for your wireless network!

In this section, we discuss these three primary ways of getting digital music into your network: growing your own (from CDs), acquiring (legally!) digital music files online, and tuning into Internet radio.

Ripping your own

If you're like us (old? spendthrifts? music lovers?), you've probably got a *ton* of CDs lying around your house. Actually, if you're like us, you also have tons of LP records too, but that's a different story entirely. (Check out the sidebar "Got vinyl? No problem!" for more on this.)

If you own CDs, creating digital music for your network is a snap. Simply use a digital music/media player software application to rip those CDs into compressed digital music files on your PC. Dozens and maybe even hundreds of these programs are available. A few of the most popular (and most capable) include

✔ **Windows Media Player:** Found at www.windowsmedia.com and already installed on most Windows XP (and 2000, ME, and even Windows 98 PCs), Windows Media Player (version 10 is current as we write) is simply Microsoft's media platform. It supports all sorts of media — both audio and video — and isn't just a player, but is also a *library management* tool that helps you organize and display all the media on your PC. Windows Media player, by default, rips music CDs in the WMA format, but the player can support additional formats (like MP3) by using additional software modules. Check out the aforementioned site for more info.

- ✔ **iTunes:** Apple's music player is designed to work with the insanely popular iPod digital music player, but it can be an excellent music encoder/player and library manager all on its own. iTunes supports the AAC and Apple Lossless codecs, as well as MP3 files, and can be extended to support other formats (recall the iTunes-LAME software mentioned earlier in the chapter). The really cool thing about iTunes (shown below in Figure 13-2) is that it provides you with access to the iTunes Music Store — the most popular online digital music store. (We talk more about these stores in the next section.) It's also the only program (and store) designed to work expressly with the iPod. Find iTunes (for Windows 2000/XP and Mac OS 9.X) at www.apple.com/itunes.

iTunes does *not* support the WMA file format at this time. You can convert your WMA files to the AAC format to use them with iTunes, but only if the files are not copy-protected. If you poke around inside the "package" of the iTunes application (right-click the iTunes application icon and select View Package), you notice "placeholder" icons for WMA, Ogg Vorbis, and other codecs. Don't be surprised to see more support for these formats in the future.

- ✔ **RealPlayer:** Real Networks is probably the leading nonoperating system vendor of media player software (meaning not Apple or Microsoft). The RealPlayer software (www.real.com) is a free encoder/player/library management software program that supports just about every digital music format, for playback, anyway. (For encoding or ripping your own discs, you have to pay for the RealPlayer Plus version to get support for some encoding formats.) The coolest thing about Real Networks and RealPlayer is its support of the company's Rhapsody Music Service (check out the discussion below in the section called "Getting your radio from the Internet").

- ✔ **Winamp:** The granddaddy of media player/encoder programs is Nullsoft's Winamp (www.winamp.com). Nullsoft offers a free version of this program that offers player and library management only, and a Pro version for $14.95 that includes an MP3 encoder. Winamp isn't quite as fancy as some of the other programs, but it works very effectively and supports just about any kind of file type.

We don't really have any favorites amongst these (and the many, many other media player/encoder) programs. We think that what you use is often very much a situational decision. Do you use an iPod or maybe Apple's AirPort Express and AirTunes? Well, you have to use iTunes. Do you have a Windows XP Media Center Edition PC, or just love everything that Bill Gates has ever done? Go for Windows Media Player. Or, go for broke and find some open source Ogg Vorbis player that 99.99 percent of the world has never heard of!

Media players are a pretty mature bit of software these days. They all basically work well. In the end, it comes down to what features you want and what works with the rest of your wireless and music equipment. Some wireless media adapter devices include their own proprietary software (usually based on Windows Media Player) and don't offer you any other choices.

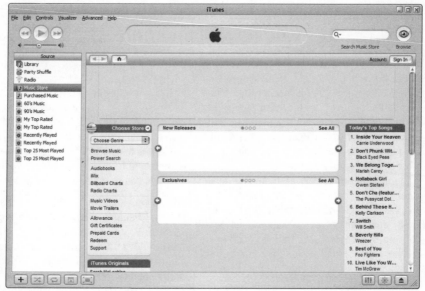

Figure 13-2:
Got iTunes?
You should!

Buying your music online

You don't have to rip your own music from CDs (or records and tapes). You can just skip the whole physical media thing and get digital music files from the Internet. Earlier in the chapter, we mention Napster (the original Napster that is — the file sharing program) and its many successors. Many people (every college student we know, for example) obtain and share music with these programs. The problem is, most of these people, for better or worse, are breaking the law by downloading copyrighted material without paying for it.

Peer-to-peer file sharing programs have *many* legitimate uses, and plenty of music out there is legal to download and share. But be careful: Cadres of record industry lawyers are running around suing the pants off of music downloaders. Be careful and be legal!

Fortunately, there are an increasing number of legal, legitimate, and actually pretty cool online music stores that let you download music for a price, while ensuring that the musicians actually get paid. (We know some musicians, and they deserve to get paid too!)

Got vinyl? No problem!

Got a ton of old vinyl in your collection that you want to put on your wireless music distribution network? This is a vexing problem for some folks: You can't just plug a record player into your PC and start creating digital music. Instead, you need to deal with something known as the *RIAA equalization curve* — which is basically a special set of equalizer settings (adjusting the volume or intensity of an analog music signal differently at different frequencies) that makes the music coming off a vinyl record sound "right" when it comes out of a stereo. If you plug a record player into a receiver or amplifier in your home audio or theater system, you use a special set of inputs labeled *phono* that run through some circuitry that accounts for the RIAA equalization curve.

If you look at your turntable, you also notice that in addition to the standard pair of left and right stereo audio cables (the RCA plugs), your turntable has an additional ground wire attached. This wire connects to a special grounding terminal on a receiver or amplifier and is designed to eliminate an audible hum that often gets picked up and played along with the music.

PC and Mac audio inputs don't have this equalization nor this ground wire built in, so you need some special software and hardware to make the turntable connection.

One inexpensive solution is from Griffin Technology (`www.griffintechnology.com`). Griffin offers a special Turntable Connection Cable for less than $13 that plugs into a miniplug audio input on your PC (or to one of Griffin's iMic USB audio interface boxes, which runs $39.99). Add to the mix some free Macintosh OS X software called Final Vinyl (available on the Griffin site) and you're ready to go to town.

If you've got a PC, you might consider a solution like the XPsound XP201 Audio Interface (`www.xpsound.com/xp201.htm`). Listed at $99.99, this box does it all — connecting both vinyl and standard line level audio sources (like cassettes or the audio output from other devices like VCRs) — and also includes software (Diamond Cut 32) that allows you to apply RIAA equalization and also edit your vinyl music.

After you've got a solution like one of these in place, you can use your operating system's built-in sound recording software (like Sound Recorder on Windows XP) to create an uncompressed digital audio file (.wav) of your discs, and then run them through your favorite encoder to rip a compressed version for your network. Alternatively, or you can get some third-party software (like Blaze Audio's Rip-Edit-Burn — `www.blazeaudio.com`) that does it all in one fell swoop!

There are two primary types of online music stores:

- ✔ **Download stores:** Some music stores, like the iTunes Music Store, let you purchase and download individual songs or whole albums — for about a buck a song or ten bucks an album. You download 'em, you own 'em, and, within some limits, you can do what you want with 'em (for example, burn a CD, copy to portable music players, and so on).

- ✔ **The celestial jukebox:** Other music stores let you access *any* of the music within the store's catalog (often a million or more songs) to play with an approved device (like your PC with the music store's software) any time you want, all for a monthly fee. It's like paying a flat rate to be able to punch the buttons on the biggest jukebox ever — and no one else gets a turn! You can't, however, "keep" the songs; you just get to access them on demand. Rhapsody and Yahoo! Music are examples of this kind of store.

A few stores combine these approaches. In other words, you get the "celestial jukebox" access for a certain monthly fee, and then can download and "keep" music for an additional a la carte fee.

Some of the most popular music stores include the following:

- ✔ **Apple iTunes Music Store:** The most popular music store around is the Apple iTunes Music Store (ITMS). For $.99 a song (or $9.99 for most albums), you can download 128 Kbps AAC versions of just about any song. The ITMS has no "jukebox" element, just downloads, but the store is very slickly incorporated into iTunes (there's nothing else to download) and is *the* solution for iPod users.

- ✔ **Rhapsody:** The originator of the "celestial jukebox" is Rhapsody, now part of Real Network. This service offers access to millions of songs, with different service levels (it's about $8.33 a month for full access to the million songs). Rhapsody also offers downloadable music and supports some portable media players. Find out more or download the player at www.rhapsody.com.

- ✔ **Napster:** The *new* Napster isn't a file sharing service. After Napster got bankrupted by the record industry, the name was bought up and applied to a music service. Napster (www.napster.com) is a combination of a "celestial jukebox" and download service and costs $8.95 a month for the service (plus $.99 a piece for downloads).

- ✔ **eMusic:** eMusic (www.emusic.com) is a traditional (if we can use that word to describe digital music) download service aimed at the independent music market. (Want to find that Pavement remaster? Go on eMusic!) There are different tiers of service, offering varying numbers of monthly MP3 downloads. One cool thing about eMusic is that the music is often of higher quality than most other download sites (higher bit rates, VBR encoding) and has no copy protection (so you can burn as many CDs or make as many copies as you'd like).

- ✔ **Yahoo! Music:** The new entrant to this market is Yahoo!'s music service, Yahoo! Music (or simply Y! Music) (http://music.yahoo.com). Yahoo's service is still in beta as we write in mid-2005, but it should be great competition to some of the other services out there like Rhapsody. Y! Music offers that same celestial jukebox model, with access to more than a million songs for only $4.99 a month. We haven't had a chance to test this one out, but it's worth watching!

High resolution audio and your network

Back in the 1980s, when CDs were brand-spankin' new, marketing folks hyped them as "Perfect sound, forever." The forever part (meaning that a CD wouldn't wear out with repeated playings, as did LP records and cassette tapes) pretty much came true. (Okay, some CDs do have problems with internal oxidation that renders them unplayable over time, but we've never personally experienced that problem, even with CDs we've owned for nearly 20 years.) But the perfect sound part? Eh . . . not so true. CDs can sound very good — exceptional in fact — but there's long been a core group of listeners who felt that that CD sound was harsh and "missing something" compared to the best of analog recording mechanisms.

So, in response to this "market need" — or, as some would argue, a cynical marketing ploy to get you to buy the same album for the third or fourth time (LP, cassette, CD, and now again) — the record companies and consumer electronics manufacturers have come up with some new digital audio disc formats — the SACD (Super Audio CD) and the DVD-A (DVD-Audio) — that use larger samples and higher sampling rates to create better-sounding digital audio.

We've spent some time listening to both formats and they both really do sound great. But — and this is a big "but" — both formats have very strong copy protection systems that effectively keep you from creating your own digital MP3/WMA/Ogg Vorbis/AAC music files from these discs. Yeah, it's perfectly legal for you to do so, but the record companies have decided they'd rather try to make you buy a *fifth* copy specifically for your PC or digital music player.

Some folks might have some workarounds to this issue, but keep in mind that they might not be legal to use (we leave you to make your own decisions). One option that *is* legal and also practical is to look for *hybrid discs*. These are most common with SACDs, and consist of a single disc that has both SACD and DVD on separate *layers* on the disc. With one of these discs, you can enjoy the highest quality playback when the disc is physically in your SACD player, and still have a CD version to play in the car or (more importantly) rip onto your hard drive for your wireless digital music distribution system. Hybrid DVD-A discs (both formats on a single disc) are also beginning to appear and should offer the same convenience.

Each of these online music stores offers pros and cons. We're particularly partial to iTunes Music Store (we have iPods) and eMusic. We love that we can find some really awesome independent music on eMusic and that the files are not heavily copy-protected, so we can do with them as we please — within the law. Finally, the "any music at any time for a fixed rate" approach of Rhapsody just blows us away.

In the end, however, they all work well. Just as with media player/encoder software, what's really important is what works with your whole network. If you have an Apple AirPort Express, use iTunes Music Store. If you want to use Rhapsody, use a media adapter (like NETGEAR's adapters, discussed in the next section) that supports that service.

Getting your radio from the Internet

You don't have to pay to get music from the Internet — plenty of Internet radio stations out there broadcast free streams of music for your listening pleasure.

Internet radio stations fall into two categories: Internet-only stations (our favorite is Radio Paradise — www.radioparadise.com) and traditional broadcasters who simulcast online.

You can find online radio stations by simply doing an Internet search on Google, Yahoo!, or your favorite search engine. You can also look online at some Internet radio hosting or search sites like the following:

- ✔ SHOUTcast: www.shoutcast.com
- ✔ Live365: www.live365.com
- ✔ Radio-Locator: www.radio-locator.com

Any of the media player programs we discuss earlier in this section (like iTunes and Windows Media Player), and most of the software for online music services (like Rhapsody and Y! Music), also offer online radio guides and services, either for free or for a small monthly fee.

At the risk of sounding like a broken MP3 here, we say it again: Match service to hardware to software to make Internet radio work over your wireless network. If you want to listen to Internet radio that uses MP3 encoding, make sure all of your wireless gear supports MP3. Or if you want to listen to Rhapsody's Internet Radio, make sure your media adapter supports Rhapsody.

Getting the Music Around Your Network

Now that you know where digital music comes from and how to get it into your house and onto your computers, you're ready to extend it across your wireless network and around your home (or office).

There's one really simple (but not inexpensive) way of doing this: simply put a wirelessly-enabled PC near where you want to listen to music. Use the PC's speakers or connect its audio outputs to a stereo or other device.

This approach works, but it isn't particularly elegant: Unless your PC is a Media Center Edition PC or a home theater PC that includes a remote control, you must use a mouse and keyboard to control your music playback.

A better approach, in our opinion, is to use a *wireless media adapter* product. These devices are simply small, Wi-Fi–enabled audio components that include a Wi-Fi radio, specialized DSP chips that can decode a variety of digital music formats, connectors for hooking into a home theater or stereo system, and, finally, an interface that glues it all together. The media adapter is simply a remote extension to your PC's music library, providing access to digital music files in remote locations.

If your media adapter is near a TV, look for one that's got a video connector and an onscreen display that lets you use the TV to browse through your PC's music collection. This is a heck of a lot more efficient than using a small LCD display, especially when you're comfortably parked on the couch.

The most important thing to look for in a media adapter is support for your favored digital music file formats. If all of your music is encoded in AAC format, the best MP3-only media adapter in the world won't be worth a hill of beans to you.

If you're a subscriber to an online music service like Rhapsody or Y! Music, you need to worry not only about file formats but also *DRM* (digital rights management). DRM is the software that protects the music on these services from unauthorized copying — and which authorizes you to listen to the music you pay for. With these services, you can only use a media extender that has been specifically designed and authorized to support the service's DRM. For example, the NETGEAR MP101 Media player supports Rhapsody's service (it says so right on the box) — but the Slim Devices Squeezebox 2 (which we love) doesn't. So if you're a Rhapsody nut, you've got a simple decision to make. If you want to extend a music service's files around your home wirelessly, double-check compatibility before you buy *any* media adapter.

Dozens of media adapters are on the market (we list a bunch of them on our Web site: www.digitaldummies.com). A few that we find interesting include the following:

✔ **NETGEAR MP101:** NETGEAR's digital audio media adapter (www.netgear.com/products/details/MP101.php) supports Rhapsody's music service (in fact, it comes with a 30-day trial). That alone makes it worth checking out in our opinion: We're big fans of Rhapsody. The player works on 802.11b or g networks (the unit itself is 802.11b) and supports both MP3 and WMA music files (including VBR MP3 files and bit rates of up to 320 Kbps on MP3s and 192 Kbps for WMA files). It also comes with a remote control and a bright four-line LCD display (to tell you what you're listening to). What's missing is support for WPA encryption (see the Warning at the end of this section for more on this). Figure 13-3 shows the MP101.

✔ **Squeezebox2:** Slim Devices makes what may be our favorite media adapter: the Squeezebox2. This is a truly "high end" appliance with all of the buzzwords supported: 802.11g, WPA, lossless codecs (this unit supports Apple Lossless, WMA Lossless, and FLAC), and even fancy audiophile features like Burr Brown DACs (digital-to-analog converters) and digital audio connections (for hooking up to a home theater receiver). The price is a bit higher than some competitors ($249 at www.slimdevices.com/), but you get a lot for your money. Our only real complaint is that the Squeezebox2 doesn't support a lot of the big-name online music stores like ITMS, Rhapsody, and the like.

✔ **Apple AirPort Express:** The smallest and least fancy of the media adapters is Apple's AirPort Express. This is a funky little multipurpose device that's part media adapter, part travel router, and part print server. Oh yeah, and it can also be used as a Wi-Fi repeater to extend your network's reach using the WDS system. It's the size of most people's power adapters (the whole thing plugs into the wall like a "wall wart"). All for $129! Most importantly, the AirPort Express is the only media adapter that can play music purchased from the Apple iTunes Music Store.

The big drawback of the AirPort Express is that it is a much simpler device than most other media adapters. It's got no remote control, no LCD, no onscreen display — no interface at all, for that matter. You use iTunes on your remote Mac or PC to control your music. We expect that Apple will launch some kind of remote or even a tablet-like device for controlling devices like the AirPort Express, but right now, you've got to walk back to your computer, which defeats the purpose for many folks.

You can buy a remote control from Keyspan (www.keyspan.com) called the Express Remote ($59.99) that lets you control iTunes on a remote PC or Mac. This doesn't solve the "no display" problem, but does make the AirPort Express a lot easier to handle.

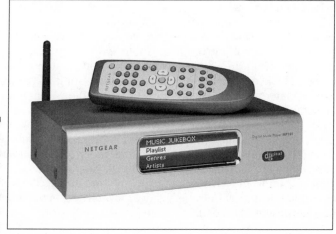

Figure 13-3:
Listen to Rhapsody wirelessly with the MP101.

Go wireless the old-fashioned way

Why not just skip all of this fancy Wi-Fi stuff and just send audio to your FM radio? That's what you can do with the Griffin RocketFM (www.griffintechnology.com/products/rocketfm/index.php).

For $39, the RocketFM connects to a powered USB port of your desktop or laptop computer (Mac or Windows) and includes software that controls the system. Conceptually, the RocketFM is a computer version of the iTrip radio devices that Griffin has been selling for years for iPod

users — converting computer or iPod audio to a short-range FM radio transmission that you can pick up with any FM radio.

Like an iTrip, the RocketFM is software-controlled, which means you use the software on your PC to adjust the transmit frequency to an open frequency in your area (in other words, a frequency without any nearby stations). Simply tune the RocketFM to an open frequency, tune your radio to the same frequency, and play away!

Most media adapters (we mention two all-too-rare exceptions above — the Squeezebox2 and the AirPort Express) support only WEP encryption. This is a real problem if you use WPA in your network. If you are stuck with WEP for your music device, you have two choices: You can degrade your entire network to WEP (because you can't mix and match WPA and WEP), or you can use a second access point on a nonblocking channel (for example, use Channel 6 if your main AP is on Channel 1 or 11) just for your music and other WEP-only devices, like many print servers.

Moving off the PC

Media adapters are a handy way to extend your PC's music collection to another location in your home or office. You may wish, however, to move your digital music off of the PC entirely and put it onto a stand-alone *music server* system. These devices include all of the computing horsepower and storage space that your PC normally brings to the table — using specialized systems optimized for music.

The biggest advantage of using a music server system is that you don't need a PC running at all times to have wireless digital music. So if you have laptops only, for example, you don't have to leave one of them running and plugged in at all times if you want to listen to music. And you don't have to worry about rebooting the "music PC" every day or few days — most music server systems run a version of Linux that's pretty much bulletproof and can go weeks, months, or longer without a reboot!

A lot of music servers are on the market, but many of them are not configured for wireless use. Instead, they are designed to sit right next to the stereo or home theater system, holding all the music locally and connecting via short lengths of standard audio cables. Or they can be networked, but they connect via Ethernet cables and don't have built-in wireless capabilities.

If you've got a wired Ethernet music server that you want to get on your network, you can always use a Wi-Fi to Ethernet bridge.

What we're focused on in this section is music servers that are inherently wireless — that have Wi-Fi or another wireless networking technology built-in.

One of our favorite digital music systems — this is a real technogeek fetish item — is the Sonos Music System (www.sonos.com, about $1,100 for a two-room system). This slick-looking (and slickly designed) system was debuted in late 2004 to a flurry (and we mean a *flurry*) of glowing press reviews, online buzz, and general lust.

- ✔ **The Sonos Zone Player:** This is the heart of the system, with all of the audio analog-to-digital and digital-to-analog converters to handle the audio signals, the wireless networking gear (based on the 802.11g standard, but with a twist, which we describe in a minute), and all of the inputs and outputs you'd expect in an audio system. The Zone Player has some extras too, like a built-in audio amplifier so you can hook speakers directly to the system, and even a four-port Ethernet switch so you can use the Zone Player to hook up computers and other Ethernet-enabled devices.

  The Zone Player supports a wide range of digital music file types, including the major lossless formats. Figure 13-4 shows the Zone Player.

- ✔ **The Sonos Controller:** The controller is the brains of the system: a handheld, wireless pad with a built-in LCD screen and an interface that gives its props to the interface king, the iPod. The screen and touchpad of the controller let you *control* your system — both in terms of day-to-day operation and also for configuring and customizing your system.

- ✔ **The Sonos Loudspeaker:** The folks at Sonos don't want to leave you hanging when it comes to setting up a system, so they also offer a slick-looking pair of speakers that match up well with the Zone Player and come in the box with all the wires you need to hook things up. (That's a nice touch, believe us — we wrote *Home Theater For Dummies* and we've dealt with cable envy before!)

There's a not-so-optional component that we didn't list above because it doesn't come from Sonos: a computer or *NAS* (network attached storage) device to hold all of your digital music files. The Sonos Zone Players themselves don't have hard drives to hold all of your music. Instead, they access the music stored elsewhere.

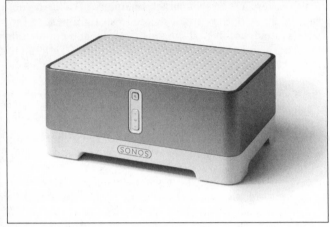

Figure 13-4:
The Sonos
Music
System is
hot stuff!

You *can* use the Sonos system with the music files on a PC or Macintosh instead of using NAS. We prefer the NAS approach, but you can always start off using a PC or Mac and then add in a NAS box later as you grow your network. We prefer the NAS for a couple of reasons:

✔ It "offloads" your music file storage from your PC. NAS devices are pretty much "set it and forget it" devices; they won't need as much maintenance or rebooting as a PC, and crash less often too.

✔ Having a NAS device on your network opens up all sorts of other possibilities, like using it as a shared photo file server, or as a backup server for all the PCs on your network.

Our advice for something like the Sonos system is to save a few bucks and buy a wired Ethernet NAS device to connect to your Sonos. Using a wireless NAS device with your Sonos Zone Player offers no real advantage, and you can save some money by going wired here. Just connect the wired NAS unit to your main router's switch ports or directly to one of your Zone Players.

The really cool thing about the Sonos system is how it departs a bit from a standard 802.11 network when you have more than one Sonos Zone Player. Sonos has fiddled a bit with its wireless networking system to provide a *mesh* network (sort of like WDS, but more sophisticated) that connects each Zone Player to the network. The Zone Players talk to each other and extend the network so that if Zone Player 3 is out of range of Zone Player 1, the signal can be routed through Zone Player 2.

There's more to it than just mesh, however: Sonos's "secret sauce" is software that provides synchronization across this mesh network so that if you're playing the same music on two different Zone Players at the same time, the sound is perfectly synchronized. And you don't have to play the same thing either — you can play different music on each Zone Player.

Getting (Blue)toothy

Wi-Fi isn't the only game in town when it comes to getting your audio on a wireless network. Some Bluetooth systems out there are also designed to provide music distribution without wires.

Bluetooth is a PAN (personal area networking) technology with a considerably shorter range than Wi-Fi (most Bluetooth equipment can theoretically reach only 30 yards at most, and effectively much less). So Bluetooth is not typically used for whole-home wireless music distribution. Instead, you can find Bluetooth being used for music as it is for many other applications — as a replacement for local interconnection cables.

An example is the Bluetake Hi-Phono BT460EX system. This system (www.bluetake.com/products/BT460EX.htm) is specifically designed to allow you to skip the wires when hooking remote speakers up to an audio system. Simply connect the outputs of the audio source to the transceiver and the speakers to the amplifier and receiver devices. Pair them together (press a button on both the transceiver and receiver units at the same time) and you've got a connection.

We expect to see a lot more Bluetooth in applications like this, particularly for home theater applications. (It's a really big pain in the rear to get those back speakers wired up in a surround sound system.)

Even though Sonos deviates from the 802.11g standard with this mesh networking, it *does* use standard 802.11g radios and channels. Part of the Sonos setup system is an option to select your channel, so you can configure your Sonos to be on a different, noninterfering channel from your 802.11g or b computer network.

Another popular wireless music server comes from Yamaha, the huge musical instrument and consumer electronics maker. Yamaha has its own 802.11-based system called the MusicCAST. MusicCAST is not a peer, mesh-based system like Sonos. Instead, it includes a centralized server (the MCX-1000) and client hardware (MCX-A10) devices. One server can support five wireless MCX-A10 clients plus two more wired clients. You can find out more about the MusicCAST system at www.yamaha.com/yec/products/musiccast/index.htm. Figure 13-5 shows the MusicCAST system.

MusicCAST is different than some other systems in that it is relatively closed. It supports MP3 only and isn't designed to work with any music services. The server has a built-in CD player/burner and can both import music from your CDs and create new CDs from your music collection on the server's internal hard drive.

Figure 13-5:
Yamaha's
MusicCAST.

Wi-Fi and Audio: Network Impacts

Theoretically, any Wi-Fi network — 802.11b and up — can support audio distribution. Even lossless compression methods use up less than a megabit per second of bandwidth, whereas the throughput of even 802.11b is several times higher than that.

That's not to say that some things can't make a difference in your musical performance. Here are some suggestions:

✔ **Go with a faster standard:** 802.11b *should* support music streams, but it doesn't always do so without breakups and other issues. If you can find equipment that supports 802.11g (some media adapters now do, but not all of them), go for it. 802.11a can also be a good choice for media adapters, but it's pretty rare to find such devices.

✔ **Boost your signal:** If your network isn't operating at its highest possible speed due to poor signal strength, consider finding a way to boost the signal. Some choices include

  • **Use an external antenna on your media adapter.** Many media adapters let you upgrade to an antenna that's directional or has more gain. You can also consider adding a higher gain antenna to your AP.

Whither WMM?

A new Wi-Fi Alliance standard known as WMM (Wireless Multimedia) is coming on the scene. WMM is a subset of the forthcoming 802.11e standard, which defines QoS (Quality of Service) mechanisms for Wi-Fi networks. Plain Jane Wi-Fi is based upon Ethernet — which means that there's not really any mechanism to give priority to one type of traffic over another. WMM (and eventually 802.11e) provides that mechanism and allows delay-sensitive traffic like music streams to go first on the network, ahead of things like e-mail checks.

A lot of access points and a few network adapters on the market today support WMM. Unfortunately, as we write, no media adapters yet support this standard. Keep an eye on the Wi-Fi Alliance Web site (www.wi-fi.org) to see when gear hits the market. Keep in mind that *everything* in the audio chain — the AP, the media adapter, the network adapter on a source PC — must be WMM-certified for the system to provide any benefit.

- **Add a booster to your AP.** Some APs accept a signal booster that can bump up the power output to increase signal level at your media adapter.

- **Try MIMO.** Although MIMO (Multiple Input/Multiple Output) and Pre-N routers need matching radio systems on the far end for their full performance boost, many also offer improved performance for any client on the network (like your media adapter).

We talk about all of these techniques in Chapter 7.

✔ **Use a second network:** If your performance issues are caused by congestion on your Wi-Fi network (maybe you've just got too much traffic to provide adequate bandwidth and low delays for music streams), add a second network. We're big proponents of adding a second network dedicated to things like media adapters if your home needs it. You can pick up an 802.11g or an AP for $40 or less and connect it to a switch port on your main router. Use a different, noninterfering channel and set up a network *only* for functions like music distribution. This may not be an elegant solution, but until there's a QoS mechanism in Wi-Fi networks, it's a cheap and functional one.

Getting into Video

Although most media adapters support only music files, a growing number add in support for video files. These devices add in additional hardware (video decoding hardware) and software (enhanced codec support) to support the display of video files and still picture images on a remote TV.

Here are a few important codecs to look for in a video-enabled media player:

- ✔ **MPEG-2:** This is the standard MPEG codec used for things like DVDs and digital cable. Most video files found on the Internet (those with an .mpg file extension) are encoded with MPEG-2.

- ✔ **MPEG-4:** A new codec (part of some forthcoming HDTV DVD systems), MPEG-4 is a more efficient codec than MPEG-2, using less bits for the same picture quality.

- ✔ **DivX:** A popular codec for Internet distribution. More information can be found on the DivX site (`www.divx.com`).

- ✔ **WMV:** Windows Media Video, WMV, is the video equivalent of the WMA files Windows Media Player uses for audio.

Media players that support video come in two main forms:

- ✔ **Stand-alone media adapters:** These devices, like D-Link's MediaLounge (go to `www.dlink.com/products/category.asp` and click on the Multimedia category to find) and NETGEAR's MP115 (`www.netgear.com/products/details/MP115.php`), are simple single-purpose components that add some video support to the functionality found in audio-only media adapters.

- ✔ **"Connected" DVD players:** These products, like D-Link's MediaLounge with DVD or Buffalo Technology's Wireless Media Player with Progressive Scan DVD (`www.buffalotech.com/products/product-detail.php?productid=96&categoryid=18`), combine a DVD player with the media adapter functionality. This approach can save space and also save you some money if you are in the market for a new DVD player.

You can also find a few flat panel TVs (like Philips' Streamium TV — `www.streamium.com/products/streamiumtv/`) that have built-in Wi-Fi and media adapter functions. This is a category that we expect to see grow over time, particularly with smaller flat panels that fit in the kitchen, den, or bedroom, away from source devices like DVD players and home theaters.

We give relatively little attention to the video side of wireless media adapters because we think it's a product set that's not really ready for prime time yet. A lot of work is yet to be done in the areas of QoS and video content provisioning before we spend too much of our own money on a video media adapter. But if you have a specific need and a source of Internet video that you want to display on a remote TV, by all means, check out a video media adapter.

Chapter 14

Wirelessly Securing, Monitoring, and Automating Your Home

*W*ireless has played a huge role in cutting the costs of deploying state-of-the-art security, monitoring, and automation technologies in private homes. If you can avoid snaking wires in existing walls and structures, everyone is better off. Wireless has also opened up a whole new world to do-it-yourselfers; before wireless technologies became mature, not many people would try to install their own alarm systems and home automation from scratch simply because of the difficulty of running all that wiring. But with wireless technology, installation is almost "Take it out of the box and turn it on" simple.

However, those in the security, monitoring, and home automation space have not yet been fully assimilated by the wireless Borg that is Wi-Fi. Most of those systems are still powered by proprietary wireless technologies. Of the parts of these systems, only the network-based cameras have really found their way into the 802.11 mainstream.

This chapter focuses mostly on the network cameras for this reason. We discuss proprietary security, monitoring, and home automation devices towards the end of the chapter, but our focus initially is on network camera technologies, key decision points about what to buy and how much, and how to link it with your Wi-Fi backbone. We firmly believe that over the next few years, devices in the home will move towards both Wi-Fi and Bluetooth for these applications, so that's why we continually stress the importance of sharing these standardized wireless networks in your home.

Introducing the Network Camera

Security and surveillance have really become part of the mainstream these days. We see camera footage from car washes, malls, traffic intersections, and so on as part of reported news every day on TV. What's changed on the consumer end of the equation is that previously expensive security cameras are now extremely affordable, and wireless connectivity makes it possible to put cameras anywhere you want.

Every home should have a wireless camera in it. Case closed. If you'd like, we can go into all the bad things that can happen, from someone breaking into your house to your child disappearing, but we won't. It's a real downer, and we like to be positive! So read about network cameras and install one. You can get some peace of mind *and* be able to rewind that camera to prove to your spouse that you really did take out the trash last Thursday before leaving for work! Now that's a winning idea in any household.

You've heard of Web cameras — cameras that enable you to send images of yourself over the Internet. These cameras have to be attached to a computer to operate. A network camera, as we discuss in this chapter, does not need a computer to send images directly over the Internet or to other devices — network cameras are network-enabled on their own and can act as full peers on an IP network.

Applications with your network camera

You are probably aware of *closed-circuit television (CCTV)*. Almost any movie that involves breaking into some totally secure, not-even-Batman-could-get-in-here facility features a scene of guards asleep in a guard room with lots of televisions showing camera shots of hallways, loading docks, and of course, any would-be thieves.

Those cameras historically have been linked to a physically-private communications network ("closed-circuit" as opposed to "broadcast") viewable by only those on the network.

The Internet has made the concept of a closed network less of a physical definition and more of a logical one — you can create a closed network with secure passwords and other network checks to ensure that only you have access to the images. So-called *network cameras* can be attached to your home's wired or wireless network and send images to any device running a display program, to any media storage device, or, with Web-enabled versions, to any browser.

A network camera is fairly easy to define — it's a camera that can be attached to a network. Having said this, the network camera can play a lot of different roles on a network, and as such, you encounter them in all sorts of applications:

- ✔ **Home monitoring:** Network cameras are part of home monitoring kits that also include the ability to detect temperature drops and water in the basement.

- ✔ **Home security:** Network cameras are part of home security kits that provide the ability to detect doors opening, windows breaking, and motion.

- ✔ **Home automation/control:** Network cameras are part of home automation kits that allow you to see who is at your front door to let them in when you are away from home, or to check on the baby in the nursery.

That a network camera can play any of these roles shows you how fundamental a piece of your home wireless network a camera can be. Your camera can play several roles at once, just like your computer can be used to order products from Amazon.com or to write a book.

All sorts of surveillance cameras are for sale. Many of these are part of the age-old security and surveillance industry and are not network cameras — they are merely cameras that can be connected to units that can then make them accessible to the Internet. A network camera has either a wireless IP or a wired Ethernet connection to the network. Don't be fooled by cameras that are merely Internet accessible but require a bunch of extra hardware or computers to make that work. A true network camera is fully self-contained.

Evaluating network cameras

Of the major consumer wireless vendors, D-Link has the largest selection of network-cameras. At the time of this writing, Linksys (www.linksys.com) had just one camera, Netgear (www.netgear.com) had none, but D-Link (www.dlink.com) had almost 20 products, most under its Securicam product line. So if you are shopping for a network camera, D-Link is your first stop.

D-Link and others refer to network cameras as *Internet cameras,* to underscore their accessibility by anyone on the Internet. For our purposes here, network cameras and Internet cameras are one and the same.

Today's network cameras reflect a growing trend towards increasingly smart cameras. Earlier surveillance cameras and CCTV systems store their images to special VCRs or processing units that would digitize, compress, and store images. Image recording could be turned on and off based on *triggers* sent by sensors (such as motion detectors) attached to the recording unit. As hard disk systems popularized by TiVo hit the stores, these surveillance VCRs grew into DVRs as well.

The network camera is a step beyond this — driven by the increasing sophistication of processing capability in the cameras themselves. The typical network camera is a very self-contained unit, having its own built-in Web server and network connectivity. Digitization functions previously centralized in the VCR/DVR/control unit have now moved to these "smart" cameras, and compression is now done in the camera. Adjunct items like motion detectors and audio recording microphones are likewise built into the camera itself.

The rest is handled by software that is located elsewhere, on a remote system. Network-enabled cameras all have some sort of management software that helps you configure options, establish access rights, reposition the camera, determine motion detector alerts, and so on. More advanced software enables you to do this for multiple cameras from one piece of software, enabling you to create tiled or sequential views of each of the cameras in your system. All of this comes over your home's LAN. Add in stackable network storage units (some of these are even wireless, we discuss them in Chapter 16), and you've got a very scalable model for multicamera surveillance of your property.

Buying a network camera brings in a whole host of new acronyms and features that you don't normally find on other wireless devices. Terms like *pan* and *tilt* are gibberish to those used to looking at wireless access points, routers, and A/V units.

We've got you covered! Here's a handy list of the key things to look for when buying a wireless camera:

- **Speed of connection:** For wireless, the cameras available are almost all exclusively 802.11b or g. You just have to decide between fast and faster. You know our stance on this one: Go for the gusto with 802.11g!

- **Motorized pan/tilt/zoom:** This is one of those "You're going to pay more for it" features that you ought to just splurge for because not having it is noticeably . . . well . . . less cool. The ability to remotely move your camera around (pan) and zoom in on different areas is not only cool and fun, but incredibly practical too. Nothing's worse than trying to view your camera image only to find that someone accidentally moved it while dusting. Argh.

   You'll find two types of zoom — optical and digital. *Optical zoom* actually moves the lens back and forth to zoom in and out. *Digital zoom* approximates this by blowing up the image based on the pixels it has available. So where digital zoom can get fuzzy the closer you get, a good auto-focus/auto-iris optical zoom lens allows you to see with really good detail. Also, when evaluating pan and tilt, look at the degree of motion quoted. It looks something like this: Pan 270° ± 135° Tilt: 90° ± 45°. This tells you the range of left/right, up/down motion of the camera. Obviously, the greater the range of motion, the better.

✔ **User-selectable compression codec:** Most cameras support MPEG or MPEG-4, depending on whether you want clearer images (MPEG) or smaller file sizes (MPEG-4). If you are just checking in on the baby, MPEG-4 is great because the smaller file sizes move faster over your broadband connections. If you want to read license plates in your driveway, MPEG may be the better way to go, recognizing that it will take longer to download the files to view.

✔ **Frame rate and resolution:** Video quality is determined (in large measure) by two things. First is *frame rate,* measured in *frames per second (fps).* A rate of 30 fps is required to mimic full motion; 10 fps is a little jerky but viewable. You'll often see frame rates quoted alongside the second element, image resolution. For example, you'll see video quality described by metrics like "Up to 30 fps at 352x240, up to 10 fps at 704x480," where 352x240 represents the number of horizontal and vertical pixels in the image. Maximize your frame rate and resolution sizes as much as possible.

✔ **Motion detection:** No one has an infinite supply of video storage space, so if you are using this to monitor your home when away, for instance, a motion detector ensures that you only capture action when it's happening. Make sure the system has alerts to your e-mail or cellphone messaging.

✔ **Security:** You don't want someone snooping in on your camera. Make sure your camera has WEP on board.

If you can find a camera that supports WPA (or even better, WPA-2), go for it! These systems offer a big leap in security, as we discuss in Chapter 9. One model (or set of models) that we know supports WPA is D-Link's DCS-6600 series.

✔ **UPnP:** UPnP is short for Universal Plug'n'Play, which is a networking architecture that provides compatibility among networking equipment, software, and peripherals. A UPnP-enabled network camera is easier to configure if your operating system is UPnP-enabled, which Windows XP is by default. Look for equipment that has UPnP support: It'll save you a lot of hassle.

✔ **Compatibility:** Although a network camera can operate on any network, not all software supports all browsers, so check the fine print. For instance, at the time of this writing, the Linksys camera doesn't work with Internet Explorer on Macs or with Mozilla Firefox on any computer.

✔ **Detachable antenna:** You want to maintain the option of adding a larger antenna if you need to put your video camera far away from your wireless network. A nice directional antenna helps here, but only if you have a means to attach it to your camera.

✔ **Simultaneous cameras:** Some systems allow you to have more than one camera active at one time. The D-Link IP surveillance software provided with the DCS-6620G Internet camera allows you to monitor and manage up to 16 cameras. You can set recording schedules, configure motion detection settings, and change settings to multiple cameras from one software interface.

✔ **Simultaneous viewers:** Some systems have limits on the number of viewers who can be looking at your images at one time. Limits of ten simultaneous viewers are common on most network camera units.

✔ **Two-way audio:** Not everyone uses two-way audio — the one-way audio supported by most built-in camera microphones is sufficient — but some cameras allow you to hook up external speakers via 2.5 mm mini-plug connectors so that you can talk back to those you can see. "Smile, you're on Internet camera!"

✔ **IP address display:** Linksys has pioneered the display of the IP address of the unit on an LCD screen on the face of the camera. Way cool! We wish that all devices had this; it's so helpful in connecting to devices. We hope other vendors follow suit and put similar displays on their networked units.

For the most part, your network cameras interface with your existing wireless network infrastructure — you won't need to add a new base station or special video router to your network to make this work. However, Panasonic has designed an integrated 802.11b/g access point, broadband router, and camera management software into one bundled package, the BB-HGW700 Camera Management System with Wireless Concourse Home Gateway Router (www.panasonic.com, $499).

We don't recommend buying into this bundled approach. Your access point coordinates far more than just cameras, and we prefer the "best of breed" approach, rather than just choosing a product because it was all bundled together. Some of these bundled systems still use 802.11b, while 802.11g cameras are available, and soon we bet 802.11n cameras will arrive on the market. You can manage most of this with software on a PC; you don't need a hardware device for that.

We do, however, provide a partial exception to the rule we just stated. If your primary wireless network uses WPA (which we recommend) and you choose cameras that support only WEP, you may consider picking up an inexpensive AP (or using an older one that might otherwise be retired to the old electronics graveyard in the "junk closet") and using it as the AP for your camera network. Just set this network on a different, nonblocking channel. Use WEP for the cams and use WPA for your important (and private) data on your PC network.

Installing Your Network Camera

Adding a network camera to your home network used to be a really complex operation that involved special settings throughout your network. It's gotten a lot easier to install a network camera, but you still need to fiddle with your router to make it work outside your home.

When installing your home network camera, here are some things to keep in mind when deciding on camera placement and its resulting *field of view* — that is, the view the camera sees:

- **Height matters.** In general, you want to mount your camera as high as possible, preferably above 6 feet, 6 inches. This improves your wireless performance because it has less mass to travel through, on average, to get to its receiving unit. If your camera has a motion-detection feature, a high mounting position increases its range of motion detection. Finally, it typically brings in a broader background, which generally provides better backlighting for what you are filming in the foreground.

- **Light matters.** Your image is highly affected by the lighting in the area. You want a well-lit field of view, but you don't want the camera pointed at the sun under any circumstances. (This ruins the camera.) Watch out for a field of view that has high contrast — that is, where a portion of the field is dark and a portion is light. This often happens in areas with a lot of shade or with roof overhangs. Your camera washes out the well-lit area trying to make the darker area more viewable; the result is simply a bad picture.

- **Mass matters.** Think about what is between your camera and its receiving base unit. Microwave ovens — which operate in the 2.4GHz frequency — affect transmission signals when turned on for cooking, so try not to have one in between your sending and receiving units. Other masses (even people!) affects signals, so lots of people in a particular area, like a lobby or elevator waiting area, degrade the signal too. In general, lots of walls and building materials between the two units also degrade the signal.

- **Positioning matters.** If you have a motion detector in the camera, you want to anticipate the angle of motion in your field of view. You want as much motion across the field of view as possible; motions directly towards and away from the camera are less desirable.

- **Antennas matter.** If your camera has a detachable antenna, remember that you can install a higher grade antenna if you have issues. Keep your antenna in a vertical position for best results.

The general installation process for a network camera is much like setting up any wireless device on your network. You start with a wired connection to the camera, install the software that comes with the camera, configure settings like SSID, name of the unit, DHCP, or static IP address, and so on. Then the software configures the camera, and you're ready to detach it from your wired connection and start viewing images. Customize a few more settings in your software and then you can access it from the Internet too. Add on some audio speakers, set your motion detector options, and you have a really souped-up system that you can access from anywhere on the planet. Isn't life grand?

Getting your camera on the wireless LAN

In this section, we walk through the installation process for a D-Link DCS-5300G. The 5300G is an 802.11g network camera with pan, tilt, and 4x digital zoom features. The DCS-5300G has an internal microphone; however, you also have the option of using an external microphone by plugging it into the microphone port on the rear of the camera base. It also has a terminal block with two pairs of connectors situated on the back panel — these are called I/O connectors because, not surprisingly, one pair is for input and the other is for output. The I/O connectors provide a physical interface through which you can send and receive digital signals to and from a variety of external alarm devices. All in all, it's a very nicely designed device that is a great example of all the things you would want to do with a network camera. Figure 14-1 shows the DCS-5300G.

Figure 14-1:
Watch your home from anywhere with the DCS-5300G.

Here's how to get your DCS-5300G up and operational:

1. **Remove the unit from its box and assemble it by attaching the antennas, base, and power cable.**

2. **Load the CD into your PC. The Installation Wizard starts.**

   If it does not start automatically, launch Windows Explorer, navigate to the CD drive, and launch autorun.exe on the CD.

3. **Select Install Software on the main menu and then select Installation Wizard on the next menu. Click through each step of the installation process until it is finished.**

4. **Click on the Installation Wizard icon on your desktop to launch that program.**

   The opening screen shows a fair amount of information that reflects the status of your camera. You see the MAC address and IP address that have been assigned to your camera by your router's DHCP service. (See Chapter 3 for info on DHCP.) A Yes in the Assigned column indicates that your camera has successfully found your router and established its presence on your wireless network.

   If you do not see a Yes in the Assigned column, you may need to perform a hardware reset of the camera. Gently insert a straightened-out paper clip into the reset hole on the back of the camera. Watch the LED on the front of the camera — it will begin blinking red and green. Wait until it stops blinking, and then continue to hold in the reset button until a second cycle of blinking red and green lights indicates a second reset cycle has completed. This should take about 5–7 seconds.

   If you have bought a lot of wireless gear in the past, you probably recall the headaches of configuring your new wireless device — namely, trying to get the IP address range to match your existing network (for example, getting a camera with a default IP address of 192.168.1.xxx on a network that's in the range 192.168.0.xxx). The great news is that D-Link has resolved all of those headaches, and the network configuration is self-discovering, as noted above. The bad news is that not all vendors have been as smart and some still drag you through those hassles. Some vendors ask you to connect your camera to your PC with a wired Ethernet cable and then go through a configuration process in a connected fashion first. So read your quick-start guide and see which process applies to you. Personally, we found the D-Link setup so easy, we feel it's a great reason to forego other options just to avoid all those hassles.

5. **Select the check box next to your device, and then click Link to Selected Device(s).**

   The software automatically launches a browser showing the images being captured live by your camera. Wow, it's that simple to set up!

Jot down the IP address from your browser's window on a piece of paper (or in a text document on your PC) so you know where to find your camera on your wireless network.

Accessing your camera from the Internet

After you've installed a camera on your wireless LAN, you can load a second program from the CD — the IP surveillance software for the DCS-5300G Internet camera. This provides you with

✔ Real-time monitoring

✔ Video and audio recording to hard disk

✔ Maximum of 16 cameras with different display layouts

✔ Configurable automated alarms

✔ Scheduled recording for each camera

✔ E-mail/FTP video snapshots

✔ Motion detection for each camera, as well as other features

Here's how to install and configure the IP surveillance software:

1. **Put the CD into the CD-ROM drive. Select Install Software on the first screen that appears and IP Surveillance on the second screen.**

2. **Click through the Installation Wizard for the program until the process is finished.**

3. **Launch your Internet browser and enter the IP address of your camera, which you hopefully wrote down earlier.**

   You should see your camera image in the center of the window and hear sounds coming from the camera to your computer speakers.

   The first thing you need to do is secure your camera from outside snoops. The default settings for security is Null, meaning there are no outside limits on accessing your camera if it is open to the Internet. Because we're about to go through the process of opening up your camera to the Internet now, you need to establish your security levels first.

4. **To configure security, click the Configuration button. In the dialog box that appears, select the Tools tab.**

   This brings up the Administrator's screen, where you can assign all viewing privileges for the camera. You can enter an Administrator's password and create accounts for outside users. You definitely want to create a new admin username and password for yourself (don't stick with the defaults — anyone can look them up on the Web and get into your camera). Use the Add User section to, well, add users (you can provide limited access to friends or relatives this way). You can also remove

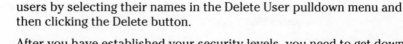

users by selecting their names in the Delete User pulldown menu and then clicking the Delete button.

After you have established your security levels, you need to get down to the nitty-gritty of the camera's configuration relative to your LAN's router and Internet connection so that the images can be viewed from the Internet. (If you are not familiar with routers, check out Chapters 3 and 5 for more info before proceeding.) Recall that your router has a built-in *firewall,* which protects your LAN from all the bad guys roaming the Internet looking for networks to break into. (If your router doesn't have a firewall, get a new one that does ASAP.) Routers talk to the Internet over a series of ports, sort of like how you talk to tellers in a bank — through special windows for different tasks. By default, most of these ports are closed for your network's protection; to offer video over the Internet through your router, you need to open up (or enable *port forwarding* on) some of these ports. For each camera that resides on your network behind a router, four ports must be forwarded by the router to obtain both audio and video. If audio is not desired, only the HTTP port needs to be forwarded. The four default ports are as follows:

- **80 HTTP port:** This allows access to Web configuration and transmits video if other ports are not forwarded.

- **5001 control channel port:** This is used to synchronize audio and video.

- **5002 audio channel port:** This is used to transmit synchronized audio.

- **5003 video channel port:** This is used to transmit synchronized video.

To change your router's port settings, you need to know your router's IP address (your gateway address) on your LAN, your passwords for accessing your router's innards, and where to open virtual server ports on your router. We help you figure out how to discover your router's IP address and how to open ports in the following steps, if you don't know how to do so already.

 5. Click the Advanced tab of the IP Surveillance software window.

This tab shows the default settings for your IP camera for the HTTP and streaming audio/video ports. These are the ports that you need to open on your router in order to enable your camera to send images over the Internet. If you plan on having just one camera on the Internet, don't make any changes; just write them down so you have the proper port numbers for your router's configuration area.

If you intend on having multiple cameras on the Internet, you need to change these settings. You are going to create a one-to-one match between your router's ports and your settings here, so that any traffic bound for or sent from this camera is routed through those specific ports. So for two cameras, bump HTTP Port 80 to Port 81, and the streaming ports to 5004, 5005, and 5006.

You may find that these ports are being used on your router by other inbound wireless applications, like your security system or a music server being remotely synchronized over the Internet. If that is the case, come back here and adjust these to new ports as well.

We use a standard Linksys router for our example, a model BEFSR11. The same generic steps can be used for any router. We assume that you have a router that is accessible via a browser interface. (If not, you should spring for a new router: Your router is probably more than five years old, and important security and functional improvements have been made since then.)

6. **Type your router's IP address into the browser to access it; enter your user ID and password to gain entry.**

If you don't know your router's IP address, you can find it by going to a command prompt and checking your current IP address settings for your computer. In Windows XP, click the Start button, select Run, enter **CMD** (which stands for "command line") in the box that appears, and click OK. A black and white screen appears from deep within the bowels of your pre-Windows computer system, where only geeks like us go now. You should see a line that reads something like:

```
C:\documents and settings\dbriere>
```

presumably with your username where Danny's is. At this command line, enter the following:

```
ipconfig
```

This returns your computer's IP address, subnet mask, and, most importantly for our discussion, the IP address of your Internet gateway router. It looks something like 192.168.1.1, as shown in Figure 14-2. This is your router's address on your LAN. Type this into your browser as directed in Step 6 to access your router's administrative area.

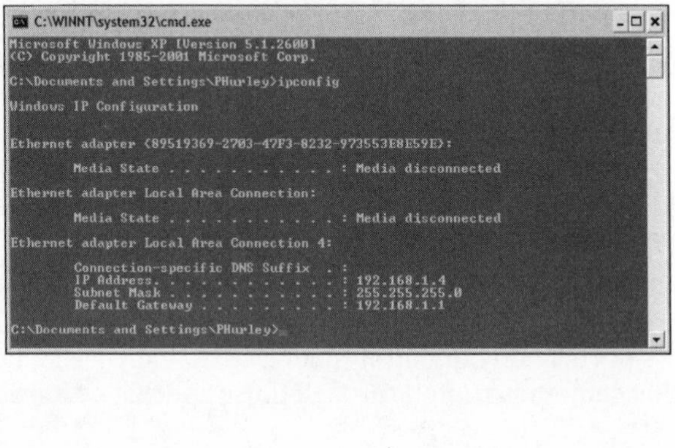

Figure 14-2: Checking your router's IP address with IPCONFIG.

We now enter a clouded, murky world called *NAT traversal*. A lot of people are working to make sure you never, ever have to know what this means. But we're going to tell you because you need to know what's going on in your router. *NAT* — short for Network Address Translation — is used in routers to create the boundary between the public Internet and your home's LAN. As IP packets from your home's LAN traverse the router, NAT translates a private IP address and port number to a public IP address and port number, tracking those translations to keep individual sessions intact. As information flows to and from your router, from many different IP devices and servers, NAT traversal keeps these "conversations" private to the communicating devices. An insanely cool and practical feature called *UPnP (Universal Plug'n'Play) NAT traversal* is available to UPnP-conversant devices; it allows them to talk to each other and assign unique ports as required, without you having to go into your router and muck around. (See, we told you that you wanted a network camera with UPnP!)

For UPnP NAT traversal to work, three stars must be aligned: your router, operating system, and camera must all support UPnP and have it enabled. You can check a couple of places (besides the box) to see if your router is UPnP-enabled: Microsoft's Xbox Live site has a listing of routers that work with their service, which uses UPnP (`www.xbox.com/en-US/live/connect/routerlanding.htm`). You can also check your vendor's site, usually under Internet gaming support (NETGEAR's gaming info page is at `kbserver.netgear.com/kb_web_files/N100725.asp`), or the UPnP Forum's certification page (`www.upnp-ic.org/certification/default.asp#devices`). Your Windows XP PC is configured for UPnP unless you disabled it; click on the Start button, go to Control Panel, click on Add/Remove Programs, on the left click on Add/Remove Windows Components, select the Networking Services option, and click on the Details button. If the UPnP User Interface check box is selected, as shown in Figure 14-3, UPnP is enabled.

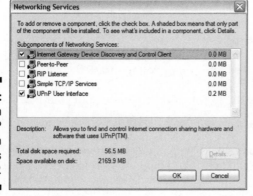

Figure 14-3:
Turning on
UPnP
support in
Windows
XP.

7. If you don't have UPnP (or even if you do and just want to verify that the settings are correct), go into your router's admin area and look for a tab called Forwarding, Port Forwarding, Port Range Forwarding, or something like that.

With the Linksys BEFSR11, click on the Advanced tab. When you click on the Forwarding tab, the Port Range Forwarding dialog box appears.

8. For each port you need to open, create an entry in the table. You want to select both TCP and UDP protocols. Set the external (public) port and internal (private) port to the same value (for example, 5001) when entering that value into the table. Enter the LAN's IP address for the camera, and click to enable the entry.

Do this for each of the HTTP and streaming video port assignments you require, and repeat again for each camera in your system.

Some ISPs block access to port 80 and other commonly used Internet ports. If you have problems making this work with port 80, try changing the settings in your router and on your camera to port 81 or another number.

Now you should be ready to view your camera from the Internet. You're going to need to find out the public or Internet IP address for your router. You can find this on the main Status page of your router's browser interface, under the WAN (Wide Area Network, or Public Network) heading. It should look something like 68.118.191.12.

9. To view your camera image (cue drum roll), enter this address and your HTTP port into the browser's address window in this format: *68.118.191.12:80*, **where port 80 is the HTTP port and 68.118.191.12 is the WAN IP address.**

You should see your camera's image.

If you have Windows XP Service Pack 2 installed, you must activate the D-Link plug-in in Internet Explorer before you can view the live video from the Internet camera. You will see a yellow bar appear across the top of your Internet Explorer browser that says, `This site might require the following ActiveX Control: 'Name of ActiveX control here' from 'D-Link Corporation'. Click here to install`. Click to install the ActiveX Control, and you will see successive pop-up windows that prompt you to install the software (MPEG3 SP (Audio) Control from D-Link Corporation). You should install these as prompted. The live video will now be streamed to your PC.

A couple of random notes to complete this process:

✔ If you have problems saving your camera settings, try disabling your antivirus program and possibly the Windows XP Service Pack 2 firewall. Both may interfere with configuration. You may also have to turn off your firewall and antivirus software to view images. Review your antivirus software's documentation to see how to approve your camera as a valid device on your network.

✔ Use of audio or video equipment for recording the image or voice of a person without their knowledge and consent is prohibited in certain states or jurisdictions. Don't be sneaky!

✔ Never record someone and upload it to the Internet on any sort of file swapping service or other movie posting service. You might think it is funny, but scores of people have been humiliated beyond belief by this. Witness the now infamous *Numa Numa* video that ruined this kid's life: www.newgrounds.com/portal/view/206373. (Turn on subtitles for the best experience.)

Setting up dynamic DNS

Your broadband connection has a WAN IP address associated with it. This IP address is provided by your broadband provider. Most WAN IP addresses are dynamic — they change from time to time. Thus, the WAN IP address you used above to find your camera most likely will not be valid over time. This not only makes letting people view your video images difficult, but also makes it tough to control the camera itself.

To resolve this situation, you can take two approaches:

✔ **Obtain a static IP address from your ISP.** A static IP address is a fixed IP address that does not change over time. Not many ISPs provide inexpensive static IP addresses — these tend to be the domain of business-class Internet access services. At the very least, you can expect to pay more per month for this service, and the next option below is probably a cheaper approach to take.

✔ **Use a dynamic DNS service.** A *dynamic DNS service* (DDNS) allows you to assign a permanent Web address to the camera that is easier to remember than an IP address and is static.

Setting up a DDNS service with your camera is vendor-specific. For instance, D-Link has a list of preapproved partner DDNS providers that you can select from within the administration interface. The DCS-5300G automatically updates your DDNS server every time it receives a different IP address.

Linksys offers an optional dynamic DNS provider service called SoloLink. The service is free for the first 90 days and costs $19.95 a year thereafter. You can get two years for $34.99. This fee covers unlimited devices per account. To register for the service, just click on the SoloLink DDNS tab on the camera's Setup page.

If you want to use another DDNS vendor (and there are hundreds), buy a domain name and assign it to them to provide DNS services; download a client to a computer on your network that keeps the DDNS servers notified of changes to your DNS. We don't think this is really worth the effort — go with one of the integrated services offered by your network camera provider.

Be sure to find out in advance how many simultaneous viewers can be on a link at any particular time. For instance, the SoloLink service allows a maximum of only four viewers at one time.

What else can you do with your camera?

After you have your camera up and working, here are some of the other things you can do:

- ✔ **Add motion detection:** Some cameras have built-in motion detection, such as the D-Link-2100G. Others, such as the DCS-5300G, have an I/O interface for attaching external motion detector units and alarms. You can get these at any Radio Shack or at `www.smarthome.com`.

- ✔ **Add pictures to your Web site:** You can set up your camera to take pictures on a scheduled or event-triggered basis and send pictures to your file server. These pictures can then be accessed by your Web site for display on any page. As pictures are updated on your file server, they are updated on your Web site automatically.

- ✔ **Set up e-mail alerts:** You can have images sent to your e-mail on a scheduled or event-driven basis so that you can be assured that things are okay at home. You need your SMTP e-mail account information for setting this up (you can get this from your ISP directly — just look in the support section on their Web site).

- ✔ **Add two-way audio to your camera:** Grab some small speakers, plug them into your camera, and start talking back.

- ✔ **Refine your image settings:** After you've installed your camera, you need to focus it. This takes some running back and forth, or at least some loud, obnoxious screaming to someone standing by the camera. (Better yet, get a set of walkie talkies!) You can also manipulate the color makeup, size of image, quality setting, and more within your software configuration tool. You can even put a time stamp or text on the image.

- ✔ **Check your wireless settings:** You can change your SSID, WEP security settings, and all other standard wireless options to make sure your connection is optimized for your home's network.

D-Link's IP Surveillance software is truly amazing. You can program all sorts of automated and triggered events in some very sophisticated ways. You can create a range of notification options and can manage all your files for up to 16 cameras. If you are looking at a surveillance application for your home, D-Link is the way to go.

Evaluating Non–Wi-Fi Camera Kits

As we mention earlier in the chapter, you can also get network cameras that are part of overall monitoring, automation, or security kits that are not Wi-Fi–compatible.

The pros of these units are

- ✔ **Self-contained:** Everything you need for this application is bundled together into a kit.

- ✔ **No wireless network needed:** You can plug in these units and not worry about having to install an underlying Wi-Fi network as well. Just install the base unit and your system is working.

- ✔ **Low cost:** Generally, if you try to buy up all the parts included in these kits and create your own kit, it would cost a lot more. These kits are purpose-built to solve a specific need, and priced to match.

The cons of these units are

- ✔ **One vendor:** You are tied to this vendor's proprietary scheme, so if you want to expand or upgrade, you can only do so within the vendor's product line. If that vendor discontinues the product line, you are stuck with an obsolete system that cannot be added to or enhanced.

- ✔ **Nonstandardized system:** These products aren't Wi-Fi, so you cannot use it on your Wi-Fi network for anything else.

- ✔ **Interference:** Depending on frequency used and the manner in which the signals are sent within the frequency, these products can interfere with your home's Wi-Fi network.

Many "kits" that include home wireless cameras have proprietary wireless network approaches and do not use the 802.11 standard. This means that although they may state that they use the 2.4 GHz and 5.8 GHz frequencies, the camera is not Wi-Fi–compatible. This really limits that camera to that one application. By now, you know that we are big fans of a home Wi-Fi backbone that uses the 802.11 standard. If you install a camera that uses the same frequencies but not in a standardized fashion, it will likely cause interference for your other Wi-Fi applications. If you want to buy a proprietary camera because you really like the overall kit that it's part of, do so, but realize that you probably won't be able to use that same camera for other uses and it might cause some performance issues with the rest of your network. If you want a camera that uses the 802.11a/b/g standard, you need to specifically look for the Wi-Fi certification or other evidence that it is indeed Wi-Fi–compatible.

In addition to these kits, you can find a whole host of proprietary wireless products that are designed to alert you to specific events, like someone driving up your driveway, the garage door opening, or water in the basement. These are niche products that do a specific thing, and usually pretty well for little money. You can find a bunch of these at SmartHome (www.smarthome.com).

The lines between the three major applications — home monitoring, home security, and home automation — are rapidly blurring. In the next sections, we tell you about some kits available on the market — recognize that some of these kits play dual roles in light of these three core applications.

Home monitoring

Motorola has one of the easiest systems to install in your house for home monitoring applications, called the Motorola Home Monitor and Control System (http://broadband.motorola.com/consumers/home_monitoring.asp). The system supports a pretty broad line of products that include wireless sensors for windows and door entry, water presence, and temperature measurement.

The core of the system is the Motorola Home Monitor and Control USB Gateway that attaches to your computer's USB port. This serves as your wireless base station and allows you to manage your system settings. You can attach the following components to this system:

- **Wireless/wired camera:** Allows you to capture color still images and video with sound; a built-in motion detector can trigger the camera to start recording. Comes in wired and wireless models.

- **Wireless door/window sensor:** Allows you to monitor entry points for movement and to trigger a nearby camera to record data when activity is detected. The system alerts you either via cellphone or by sending you an e-mail that something is amiss.

- **Wireless temperature sensor:** Allows you to monitor temperature levels the same way you'd do in your wine cellar.

- **Wireless water sensor:** Allows you to detect the presence of water in water-prone areas like basements.

The system supports up to three wired cameras, six wireless cameras, and eight sensors.

The notification options are pretty neat: If you have a cellphone, you can receive either text messages or text messages with color still images. For e-mail via computers, you can get text messages including color video with sound. You need an always-on broadband connection, however, to send out these alerts. You can also output video to a VCR through an RCA A/V interface cable.

The company sells a starter kit for $250 — Easy Start Kit HMEZ1000 — that includes the base unit and a wireless camera. The sensor units run about $35. Figure 14-4 shows the Motorola system.

The Motorola USB Gateway has the built-in ability to work around the channels used by your Wi-Fi network so that it doesn't interfere with your Wi-Fi wireless network and vice versa, but you have to manually set this in the Motorola system. In the provided Motorola software, you select the channel that your Wi-Fi network uses. The Motorola software then uses another channel for its communications. Note, however, that as your Wi-Fi network becomes more dynamic and changes channels based on outside Wi-Fi interference (say, from your neighbor's Wi-Fi), static definitions like in this Motorola unit become less viable. (Didn't we say you should use a Wi-Fi–based system?)

Shell had a fairly well-publicized product called *HomeGenie* that was similar to this product — in fact, it had many of the same Motorola components — but it has been discontinued.

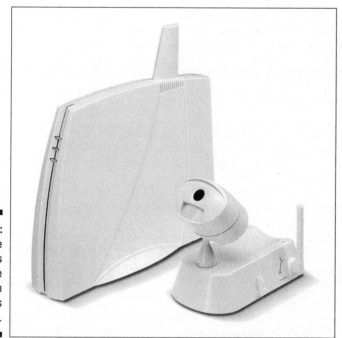

Figure 14-4:
Going the wireless cam route with Motorola's system.

X10 or not X10 — you make the call!

It sounds very Shakespearean: "To be X10 or not to be X10." That's a fundamental decision you encounter when you try to build home automation on your own.

X10 has long been the primary means of controlling devices in an "automated" home — X10 has been around for a long time and lots of products based on X10 are available through many outlets. The X10 protocol uses your home's power lines to provide communication between devices. Contrast that with new up-and-coming technologies (see the sidebar entitled, "Who's going to beat X10 for home automation?") that are faster, more secure, and more reliable, but often not available yet or in limited models. The more you like tinkering, the more you want flexibility to mix and match items, and people like that tend to like X10 simply because it is a standardized system supported by a number of vendors. You may find that X10, even though it's an old technology, can still fit well into your home's networks, as a primary automation network, or coexisting with your other wireless or wired automation networks.

Home security

Quite similar to the home monitoring kits are home security kits that are designed to secure your premises and report to central monitoring stations when someone breaks into your home. Wireless has had a huge impact on the security area, where the installation of wired systems can cost a lot of money. Wireless systems are installable out of the box; a whole home could be secured in an afternoon by even the least experienced DIYer, and the systems start at about $200.

Most systems have wireless devices for passive infrared motion detectors, door/window magnetic contact sensors, temperature/water sensors, and a wealth of other devices. In general, if it is available as a wired sensor, you can pretty much get a wireless version as well.

Dozens of such systems are on the market — you can get a good sampling of them at online security outlets like homesecuritystore.com. Wireless home security systems work well — and meet most people's needs for protecting the home — but again, they aren't 802.11-based. The recurring theme of this book is integration of such systems onto your wireless LAN so that security cameras can also serve other needs too. Wireless security systems are self-contained but functional.

Home automation

Who says you can't get comfort, safety, convenience, and energy savings from one place? If you have an integrated home automation system, you can do all of this and more. A good example of this is HAI Systems's Omni Automation Controller Systems (www.homeauto.com, prices start at about $1,500 for an installed system). The Omni automation system helps you save money by managing your HVAC and lighting, makes you more secure with integrated security, and gives you greater control through telephone, Internet, and PC access. Figure 14-5 shows the HAI Omni System.

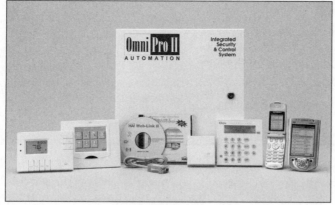

Figure 14-5: It's not HAL, it's HAI — the Omni, to be precise.

You can also create all sorts of automated and manual environments to match your lifestyle — a home theater mode when you are watching a movie, or a welcome mode when you drive up the driveway. The Omni comes with several standard modes, such as Day, Night, Away, and Vacation, and can accept customized *scenes* such as "Good night," "Good morning," or "Entertainment" that automatically set temperatures, lights, and security around the house with one touch of a button.

Wired and wireless security and temperature sensors can be used to adjust lights, appliances, and thermostats and monitor activity and track events. Touchscreen LCD consoles show status and allow control and scheduling of lighting, security, temperatures, and accessories.

You can talk to the system via voice recognition, and it can talk back to you — a built-in digital communicator can report alarm events to a central station and can dial additional phone numbers chosen by the home owner for voice notification. It can even be controlled from your TV set via integration with Microsoft's Windows XP Media Center Edition operating system for PCs.

Getting into broadband security services

One of the most interesting wireless home security products is NextAlarm's Abbra Professional Series system (www.nextalarm.com). The hardware has the usual wireless PIRs (*passive infrared sensors*, which pick up body heat), sensors, and keypad you expect from a security system, plus a few nice accessories like wrist and pendant transmitters that are integrated with the system for emergency personal assistance applications.

But what is more interesting is their use of the home's broadband connection for central station monitoring. A broadband adapter allows you to redirect phone line alarm traffic to your broadband Internet connection, resulting in dramatically reduced rates. It can sit behind your firewall and works with all types of broadband connections and with wired and wireless local area networks.

NextAlarm also has created extensive links to e-mail and cellphone messaging, with its E-Notify service. E-Notify can alert you when your children arrive home from school or when your security system needs maintenance. You can even use the E-Notify service to alert you when certain events don't happen — like your child not disarming the system by 3 p.m. Very cool.

We think broadband and wireless LAN integration into security systems is a logical step for anyone. You can see if the NextAlarm monitoring service is compatible with your existing installed alarm service by checking nextalarm.com/abn_compatibility.jsp.

So as great as the HAI system is, you might be asking yourself (as we are), "Where's the wireless?" Well, wireless applications for home automation are just moving out of the nascent stages and into the mainstream (see the sidebar later in this chapter called, "Who's going to beat X10 for home automation?"). Up to now, most of the wireless applications for home automation have been limited to providing a radio frequency link to X10 products — things like wireless handheld remote controls and wireless motion detectors. A plug-in X10 unit outfitted with an antenna is required to catch the radio signal from the wireless unit and put the X10 signal onto the electrical lines where it can interface with all the X10 devices.

X10 (www.x10.com), the company as opposed to the technology, has a very inexpensive system called Active Home Professional (www.activehomepro.com) that supports wireless connectivity for its cameras and some sensors. You can set lighting scenes, monitor security, check temperature, and other such basic items around the house, using a combination of X10 and RF devices.

However, X10 wireless as a category is very limited and proprietary — which by now you have guessed we're not big fans of. There is no quality of service monitoring, no standardized link to your home 802.11 wireless LAN, and as a result, the quality is simply not business-class.

Companies such as Z-Wave, ZigBee, and INSTEON have a vision to transcend this and create a more whole-home wireless infrastructure that intercommunicates and functions more like a wireless LAN, focused on these home automation applications, but they're not there yet. When these features are routinely available, we expect vendors like HAI to support these wireless interfaces.

Who's going to beat X10 for home automation?

The X10 standard for home automation has been around for a long time, serving as a glitchy means to automate your light switches, thermostats, security devices, sprinklers . . . heck, even your Christmas tree. But major efforts are underway to replace the aging X10 standard — the ZigBee Alliance (www.zigbee.org), Z-Wave (Zensys, www.zen-sys.com), INSTEON (Smarthome, www.insteon.com), and Universal Powerline Bus (Powerline Control Systems, www.pcslighting.com). Each of these approaches promise two-way, low-power, narrowband mesh networking that will enable all consumer electronics and other devices in the home to communicate with each other and with sources outside the home via Internet gateways.

The ZigBee Alliance has an IEEE open standard (IEEE 802.15.4) at the core of its technology. Although it has not shipped any product yet, it does have several big companies as members and expectations of products sometime in 2006 if not sooner.

Zensys's Z-Wave technology has had chips on the market for more than three years and now is into its second generation chip. Consumer products based on Z-Wave first hit the market in 2005.

INSTEON is the most compatible with the X10 customer base: It is the only one of these products that is backwards-compatible with X10. Consumers with X10 devices installed don't have to rip them out — they can just add on INSTEON units to complement them. Where ZigBee and Z-Wave are both wireless only, INSTEON also uses a home's existing wiring or powerline together with wireless. Products are already on the market at www.smarthome.com.

Powerline Control Systems has also set out to top X10 and has lighting control-focused products on the market using its Universal Powerline Bus (UPB) technology. The firm has lined up some players in the home automation space to support UPB in their products, but the other three mentioned initiatives appear to have more industry backing at this time.

There's no telling who the ultimate winner in this race will be, if there is a single winner. However, all these products will likely be on the market for a while before any clear winners and losers appear. For now, know that each of these companies are rapidly expanding their product lines in the home automation space, and you can expect to hear more about them in the major magazines and online stores.

Chapter 15

It's Your Dime: IP Calls and Your Wireless Network

*W*e've long been proponents of *Voice over Internet Protocol* (or VoIP, as it's more commonly known). In fact, the first *For Dummies* book we ever wrote, ten (long) years ago, was *Internet Telephony For Dummies*, which explained how to make free PC-to-PC phone calls over the Internet.

In those intervening ten years, a *lot* has changed. For one thing, you don't need a computer to make a phone call over the Internet (or over networks running Internet Protocol — many "IP phone calls" run partially or totally over private IP networks owned by the VoIP service providers). All you really need is a broadband connection (cable modem or DSL), an Analog Telephone Adapter *(ATA),* and a phone service that uses IP (like Vonage).

In fact, VoIP has become so mainstream (at last count, more than 600,000 homes were using Vonage, and there are *hundreds* more companies offering similar services) that it's almost not worth writing about. But VoIP has begun to move into the wireless networking world, and it has brought with it an entirely new way of thinking about telephone calls.

In this chapter, we tell you what you need to know about VoIP-ing your wireless network. We start off by giving you an understanding of how VoIP phone calls work, and what kind of infrastructure equipment and services you need to make them work. We then talk about the hardware and software you use for the calls themselves: Wi-Fi VoIP handsets (think of cordless phones on steroids) and *softphones,* which use software on wirelessly-equipped laptops or handheld computers. Then, we spend a little time dealing with the security and performance issues that VoIP brings to the Wi-Fi network. We conclude by talking about how Wi-Fi and VoIP can work together not only in your home or business, but also when you're on the road, to give you cheap (or free) calls from anywhere you happen to be.

There's a lot to VoIP, and much of it is entirely independent of network type — wireless or wired, it doesn't really matter. In this chapter, we cover some VoIP basics that apply across all network types and then spend our time looking at the intersection of VoIP and Wi-Fi. You could write a whole book on VoIP alone (check out *VoIP For Dummies* by Timothy V. Kelly, published by Wiley, for example). We just want to hit the highlights here as they relate to wireless.

Many VoIP services and systems do *not* provide a full replacement for a traditional phone's Enhanced 911 (E 911) service. If you call 911, it may not be routed to the appropriate local emergency services department, and your location information may not be sent to whomever *does* answer the call. Some services (like Vonage) let you configure your 911 calling so that it does go to the right place and send the right information. But in these cases, if you use your VoIP system on the road, as we discuss in this chapter, you will not have the correct 911 connections. Of course, 99.99 percent of the time, this isn't a big deal, but you should be aware of it, just in case. Unless you're sure that things are properly configured in your VoIP system, when an emergency strikes, use a conventional landline first, a cellphone second, and a VoIP only as a last resort.

Grasping the VoIP Basics

The first thing to understand about VoIP (pronounced *voyp,* which rhymes with no word we know of in the English language) is that there isn't a single "kind" of VoIP. Instead, as with most things Internet-related, a variety of *standards* and *protocols* define VoIP, and these standards and protocols are important when you're choosing VoIP equipment and services. Simply put, the equipment you choose must support the standards and protocols used by your VoIP *service provider* or network — or, if you're doing a peer-to-peer call to another user across the Internet, you need to make sure that the standards and protocols that you both use match up.

The same thing is true on the *PSTN* (public switched telephone network) for *POTS* (Plain Old Telephone Service — that's an actual industry acronym), and for mobile networks. For POTS, these standards are about 100 years old, so no one thinks about it: Every POTS phone works without a hitch.

Mobile networks, however, are a good comparison to VoIP, as there are still differences between different providers. Just as you choose a cellular phone built for, say, Verizon's network, you choose a VoIP phone built for a specific network (like Vonage's). And like mobile networks, if two networks share the same standards (for example, Cingular and T-Mobile both use GSM networks), it's relatively easy to switch from one to the other with your existing equipment.

Take a long SIP

The most common standard used for VoIP calls is known as *Session Initiation Protocol* or SIP (pronounced like what you do with a drink of water). SIP is a standardized protocol that can be used to initiate all sorts of communications sessions on the Internet and IP networks, ranging from voice calls (VoIP phone calls, in other words) to videoconferencing or even multimedia collaboration (for things like online meetings, presentations, and Webcasts).

SIP's big function in the network is to provide the mechanism for establishing calls, terminating them when they're through, and maintaining the connection in the interim. Basically, SIP makes the phone on the other end ring when you dial out on your VoIP phone, and makes yours ring when someone dials *in* to you.

SIP doesn't define *all* of the characteristics of VoIP phone calls — there are other important protocols such as the *codecs* (encoder/decoder algorithms used to compress analog voice into signals that can be sent digitally). And not every VoIP phone call uses SIP for call setup and initiation. Indeed, some services (like the very popular Skype service that we discuss later in this chapter) use their own proprietary protocols for call control (though Skype's protocol is at least based on SIP).

The great thing about SIP is that it *is* a widely accepted protocol (Skype notwithstanding), and that makes it easier to mix and match equipment and services.

Although a bit of tweaking and configuration may be necessary, if a VoIP phone supports SIP, it theoretically works with any VoIP service that supports SIP. It's sort of like Wi-Fi, where different vendors get along. Unfortunately, VoIP doesn't have an organization like the Wi-Fi Alliance (we discuss them in Chapter 2) who spend time and money making sure this is true. Do a bit of double-checking before you make any purchases.

The precise name of the SIP protocol we're discussing here is SIP v2 (version 2), compliant with the RFC 3261 protocol (just in case you ever have to take a test on the subject!).

Compressing your voice

Another important protocol in any VoIP system is the compression codec used to turn your digitized voice into a signal that can easily be carried over the Wi-Fi network and through a broadband Internet connection.

When you speak into the headset or handset while making an IP phone call, two things happen:

- ✔ Your voice is converted from analog to digital signals that can be carried as bits of data. This process (called *digital-to-analog* conversion) creates a relatively large (or high bit rate) digital file of your voice.

    Bit rate simply refers to the degree of compression of a codec. Lower bit rate codecs require less bits per second of network bandwidth and are therefore more highly compressed.

- ✔ This digitized voice file is *compressed* to a lower bit rate format using the compression codec. This makes the voice data more suitable for transmission across networks of unknown bandwidth or quality of service.

Depending upon what kind of VoIP call you're making (for example, from a PC, from a Wi-Fi handset, and so on), these two steps may be performed by the same device and be relatively indistinguishable. We mention them as separate tasks just so you'll understand what's happening.

Here are two important things to keep in mind about the codec you are using in a VoIP phone call:

- ✔ You need to use a codec that is "understood" on both ends of the call. Particularly if you're making some sort of peer-to-peer call (making a call between two SIP phones, for example), you need to have equipment terminating your call on the far end that supports the same codec you're using to make a call.

    This isn't usually a problem, but can come into play if you're getting fancy and trying to call directly to another VoIP user without going through a service. For the vast majority of calls, you never need to worry about "matching up" codecs.

- ✔ The lower the bit rate of the codec, the lower the perceived sound quality. To put this another way, higher bit rate codecs usually sound like someone's natural speaking voice — low bit rate codecs tend to sound sort of artificial. Relatively high bit rate calls (using codecs that require about 64 Kbps or higher in most cases) are often referred to as "toll quality" (equivalent to a standard telephone call), whereas relatively lower bit rate calls sound more like a cellphone call.

There isn't an absolute and linear relationship between bit rate and voice quality on a call. All of the codecs used for VoIP phone calls are *lossy* — which means that some of the digital information captured when your voice is converted to digital signals is thrown away in the process of compressing those digital signals. The science behind compression systems improves every day, and some relatively low bit rate codecs sound subjectively better than other older and higher bit rate codecs.

The impact of your VoIP codec is on your local (wireless) and access (DSL or cable modem, for example) network bandwidth requirements. Many VoIP software programs (if you're using a PC to make calls) and hardware systems (if you're using a dedicated VoIP device) use codecs of 64 Kbps or higher *per call* — actually, it will always be higher due to some *protocol overhead,* so expect a 64 Kbps codec to actually need about 90 Kbps of bandwidth in each direction. Although this shouldn't overtax your Wi-Fi network (even with a very conservative throughput assumption, 802.11b can handle many such calls, and 802.11g and a even more), the real bottleneck comes into play with your broadband access connection.

Most residential and small business users have relatively slow *upstream* connections — 128, 256, or maybe 384 Kbps. (Folks outside of North America do much better — like the folks in Hong Kong who can buy a *gigabit per second* connection into their homes over fiber optic cabling!) In a perfect world, with no *overhead* (extra bits required for underlying network protocols), you might be able to support only two calls (or a single *three-way* call) before you ran out of all of your bandwidth for other applications.

Luckily, most VoIP systems provide a range of codecs, starting at very low bit rates (as low as 24 Kbps), to support a wider range of users. In many cases, you don't have to do anything — the system autoconfigures itself with the best codec based upon network conditions. For example, Skype (which we discuss in the section titled "Skype-ing Your Way Around the World") auto-configures a codec between 24 and 128 Kbps based upon your connection speed, the connection speed of the party you're speaking with, and the connection between you and across the Internet.

Some VoIP systems allow you to manually select a codec. The higher bit rate codecs (those above 64 Kbps) can actually sound *better* than a conventional POTS phone call. In fact, some of the VoIP providers we know use this as marketing differentiator — trying to move VoIP from "cheaper" to "better than traditional" phone services.

Peer-to-peering versus calling regular phones

Besides the underlying call control protocols and codecs — which are the technological underpinnings of VoIP calling — the big distinction among different types of VoIP phone calls is how the calls themselves are routed across the Internet or other IP networks.

There are two main methods of routing VoIP calls:

✔ **Peer-to-peer:** Some VoIP calls are routed directly between the two users (although the initial connection may involve a separate *directory server* that tells users how to find each other on the Internet). The most commonly used peer-to-peer VoIP solution is Skype, which we mention earlier and which we discuss in more detail shortly. Skype has millions of users making phone calls from PC to PC across the Internet.

Most peer-to-peer VoIP systems use software on PCs (or on handheld computers) to place calls. You can, however, use a special VoIP phone (a *SIP phone*) to place calls peer-to-peer as well by using the IP addresses or SIP address of each phone to place the call.

The great thing about peer-to-peer calls is that they are usually free. You can use a peer-to-peer system to call anyone in the world for nothing, as long as you both have compatible VoIP systems and adequate (high speed) Internet connections.

We're using the term *peer-to-peer* somewhat loosely here. A server of some sort is often involved in the process (usually as a means of finding the people you're calling on the Internet), but the calls themselves usually travel directly from party to party across the Internet, and do not route through a centralized server.

✔ **Through a service provider:** Other VoIP calls travel across your Internet connection and into the network of VoIP service provider. Having this service provider in the middle of your call opens up the possibilities greatly because it expands the number of people you can place calls to (or receive calls from). In fact, with most service providers, you can make or receive calls from just about anyone in the world with a phone — just as you can with your non-VoIP phones.

You get more flexibility going through a service provider, but you do have to pay for it. Whereas most peer-to-peer VoIP phone systems are free, you have to pay a monthly service charge (and often per-minute rates for at least international calls) with a VoIP service. The good news is that most VoIP services are considerably cheaper than traditional phone services.

Hardware? Software? Both?

As we've already alluded to throughout the chapter, VoIP phone calls can be made using either general-purpose hardware (a PC or handheld, in other words) or using specialized hardware (like purpose-built VoIP phones). Generally speaking, you're likely to see three options:

- ✔ **Softphones:** Software that runs on a PC or other computer (Mac, hand-held, Palm, and so on) and that uses the audio and networking sub-systems of that computer. Skype is an example of a softphone, as is Windows Messenger (included with XP) or iChat AV on the Mac. Some VoIP service providers (like Vonage) are now offering softphones as an adjunct to their phone-to-phone service.

  Although many softphones are used primarily for PC-to-PC calling, you can use some softphones with a service provider to make PC-to-telephone calls or to receive telephone-to-PC calls.

- ✔ **ATAs:** ATAs, or *Analog Telephone Adapters,* are hardware devices designed to connect to your local area network and broadband Internet connection. They provide a connection between traditional POTS phones and a VoIP service provider. Essentially, an ATA is a network device that converts POTS into VoIP (and back).

  We won't focus on ATAs too extensively in this chapter because they are *not* wireless devices. However, keep in mind that ATAs are very common (and increasingly inexpensive) devices that are used by many VoIP ser-vice providers. We focus on Wi-Fi VoIP in this chapter, but you can always hook up a conventional cordless phone system to a VoIP ATA for a quick wireless connection to VoIP in your home or office.

  You can find ATAs that are built into a wireless router from companies like Linksys. The phone connection remains wired (there are a couple of phone jacks on the back of the router), and the Wi-Fi part of the system is meant for data only. These devices don't have wireless VoIP, but they can be a good way to reduce clutter in your office or wherever you are placing the AP. Check out Linksys's WRT54GP2 (designed for the Vonage network) for an example of these devices (www.linksys.com/products/product.asp?prid=657&scid=35).

- ✔ **Dedicated VoIP phones:** Many manufacturers build VoIP handsets that can communicate using SIP and have all of the pieces and parts (like *DSP* — digital signal processing — hardware to handle analog-to-digital and digital-to-analog conversions and codec work) to initiate and termi-nate VoIP phone calls on their own. These phones (usually called *SIP phones*) don't need an ATA or a conventional phone — you just give them a network connection and the configuration data appropriate for your VoIP service, and you're set.

In the forthcoming section titled, "Taking your VoIP service wireless," we dis-cuss a few of the more interesting dedicated VoIP phones. Staying true to our *WNH&M For Dummies* theme, we focus on Wi-Fi VoIP phones that leverage your wireless network for VoIP calling.

Skype-ing Your Way Around the World

The easiest way to bring VoIP to your wireless network is to try out Skype (www.skype.com). It's really painless: It's absolutely free and it works really well, a combination that we're particularly fond of. Skype is available for the following platforms:

✔ Windows XP or Windows 2000 PCs

✔ Mac OS X 10.3 (Panther) or later

✔ Linux (Skype provides builds for several distributions of Linux; check www.skype.com/products/skype/linux/ for the latest details.)

✔ PocketPC handheld computers using Windows Mobile 2003 for Pocket PC or newer

Figure 15-1 shows the main Skype window in Windows XP (the other operating systems look relatively similar). As we mention earlier in the chapter, Skype is a softphone client that uses a proprietary SIP-based system for establishing and receiving calls. Skype also includes a range of codecs that are automatically configured during the call, ranging from 24 to 128 Kbps (the codec used is based upon the quality of your end-to-end connection).

Figure 15-1:
Getting
into Skype.

Skype provides several options for calling over your wireless network (or over any broadband-connected LAN):

✔ **Peer-to-peer calls:** This is where Skype got its start, earned its reputation, and became the most popular VoIP system in the world. Peer-to-peer calls to the millions of other Skype users are free, regardless of where the users are physically located.

✔ **SkypeOut calls:** Skype doesn't just provide free VoIP peer-to-peer software. In fact, the company (like most) wants to make some money. One way it does this is by offering a PC-to-phone VoIP service called SkypeOut.

✔ **SkypeIn calls:** The newest feature (still in beta) of Skype is a local telephone number that is associated with your Skype account — a SkypeIn number. When a friend or business associate calls your SkypeIn number, the call is routed through Skype's network and then to your Skype client. SkypeIn even includes a voicemail service that answers your calls when you can't.

Calling peer-to-peer

Placing a peer-to-peer Skype call is quite easy. First, you need to find the person you're calling in the Skype directory. You can search for a user by any one of a number of criteria like Skype name (username), actual name, city and state, country, language spoken, and more. Figure 15-2 shows a directory search in progress.

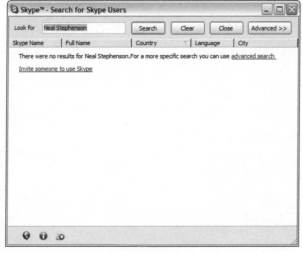

Figure 15-2: Looking for a Skype user.

When you find the person you're looking for, simply right-click on their name and select Call from the context menu that appears to place a call. You can add users to your contact list — just as you would add someone to an IM program. Placing calls is as simple as double-clicking a name in your contact list.

Reaching out and calling someone

Although there are millions of Skype users worldwide, that's just a small fraction of the billions of people you can reach with a traditional telephone call. That's where SkypeOut comes into play.

The first step to using SkypeOut is to buy some SkypeOut credits — SkypeOut is a prepaid service, similar to some cellular plans. You buy a certain amount of SkypeOut credit (denominated in Euros) and then use them for outgoing calls. The standard ten Euro "chunk" of SkypeOut credits buys you about ten hours of calls to the main Skype calling locations — these Skype Global Rate areas (mainly in North America and Western Europe) are 1.7 Euro cents per minute. Other areas are more, depending upon how expensive network connectivity to that region is; SkypeOut to tiny little islands in the middle of the ocean is more expensive than it is to, say, Japan.

Using SkypeOut is dead simple. Just click the Dial tab in the Skype interface and use your keyboard or mouse to dial a number, just as you would with a regular phone. Figure 15-3 shows the SkypeOut dialer in action.

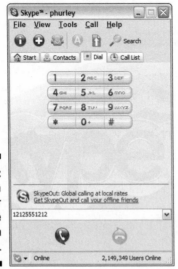

Figure 15-3:
Calling a
regular
phone
line with
SkypeOut.

What's special about Skype?

The directory is really Skype's "secret sauce" — the one thing that they do better than all of the myriad peer-to-peer VoIP programs we've been using and writing about for more than ten years. When you experience Skype and use the directory service (and have it quickly sort through millions of potential users), you won't be surprised that the folks who created Skype also created the peer-to-peer file sharing program Kazaa. Like Kazaa, Skype uses a decentralized model to distribute the processing and "user finding" process — meaning you can quickly and accurately search for users. At the same time, directory services are cheap and scalable for the folks at Skype to set up.

In the days before Skype, users of VoIP softphone clients would need to know the other party's IP address, or log into a special directory server to find other folks to talk to — neither of which were convenient.

The really cool thing about SkypeOut for mobile users is that the rates have nothing to do with where you are calling *from* and everything to do with where you are calling *to*. So if you're from California and you're on a trip to Korea, you can make SkypeOut calls to home from one of the tens of thousands of hot spots in Korea for the same rate as if you were just calling across town.

Even more peer-to-peer

Skype is by no means the only game in town when it comes to peer-to-peer VoIP phone calling. A few other players include

- ✔ **SIPphone (www.sipphone.com):** This peer-to-peer service is based upon the SIP standard (as you no doubt inferred from the name) and uses either softphone software (several downloads are available on the site) or a hardware ATA (compatible models are listed on the site as well). Like Skype, SIPphone offers a for-pay service to call non-SIP phones, and a *Virtual Number* service similar to SkypeIn.

- ✔ **Teleo (www.teleo.com):** Another popular peer-to-peer service is offered by the folks at Teleo. For about $5 a month, you get a phone number that supports both inbound and outbound calls to regular telephones (the outbound calls are charged on a per-minute basis), voicemail, and more. Teleo is totally SIP-based, so you can place free SIP-to-SIP calls to other Teleo users or to anyone who's got a standards-based SIP phone.

- ✔ **TelTel (www.teltel.com):** Another standards-based service, TelTel is a combination of a free SIP softphone client and a directory service for peer-to-peer calls. TelTel also offers some PC-to-telephone calling, but as we write, the long-term model for this service is unclear.

Do your calls Yahoo!?

As we go to press, Yahoo! (www.yahoo.com) has just launched a new VoIP-enabled beta version of their popular Yahoo! Messenger IM program. Yahoo! Messenger 7.0 beta includes a true, full-duplex (meaning both parties can speak at the same time) VoIP capability built into the Messenger client. So any two Yahoo! users can make PC-to-PC calls from within Messenger, and for a charge, any user can make calls to a regular phone using the Net2Phone service. Yahoo! isn't yet trying to be an all-things-to-all-people VoIP telephone service provider (at least not officially), but this service certainly is worth keeping an eye on. And if you already use Yahoo! Messenger for IM, well, now you've got an extra reason to keep using it!

Using a Phone-to-Phone VoIP Service

Although Skype has expanded with the additions of SkypeOut and SkypeIn (which is still in beta and not generally available as we write), the main focus for most Skype users is peer-to-peer calling, and their platform of choice is a PC (or handheld PC) running softphone software.

This can be great — when we're working, we often use Skype or other softphone products, and they work really well. But we don't like to be tethered to our computers at all times. (Hey, we're not always working!) So we also like to use VoIP services that are more like traditional POTS phone services. These services usually take away the spontaneous (and free) peer-to-peer call option, but make up for it by offering an easier-to-use, more familiar, and more widely available phone service.

Looking at the services

The biggest of these services is Vonage (www.vonage.com), which is available anywhere in the U.S. and offers unlimited local and long distance calls in the U.S. and Canada for about $25 a month. (Vonage also offers small business plans and cheaper home plans.) All you need is a broadband connection and a few bucks to pay for your service. Your service provider furnishes the ATA and any other hardware or software needed for your service.

The really cool thing about Vonage (and many of its competitors, we list a few below) is that, for all intents and purposes, it is indistinguishable from a more expensive POTS service. The voice quality is as good as (if not better than) POTS, and you can use your existing POTS phones (connected to the Vonage

ATA). You get all of the calling features and services that you might expect; you just pay less for the privilege. Plus, you get a whole new level of control over your calls through a Web interface that lets you control aspects of your phone service (like call forwarding, "follow me" services, do not disturb, and more) that you would have to pay a service modification charge for in the POTS world.

Vonage has the lion's share of the VoIP service market, but it is far from alone in the market. A few of the other popular services include

- ✔ **ATT CallVantage:** www.callvantage.att.com
- ✔ **Broadvoice:** www.broadvoice.com
- ✔ **Packet8:** www.packet8.net
- ✔ **Lingo:** www.lingo.com

In the tradition of "If you can't beat 'em, join 'em," you can now even find VoIP services from traditional telephone companies. Both Verizon and SBC, the two biggest telephone companies in America, have launched VoIP service offerings for their broadband customers.

Taking your VoIP service wireless

By default, the standard method for connecting to a VoIP service like Vonage or Lingo is anything but wireless. Take one broadband "modem," add a router (wired or wireless), an Analog Telephone Adapter (ATA), and one or more standard POTS telephones, and you're ready to go. Fast, easy, and pretty neat, but there's nothing wireless in that equation.

The simplest way to add a wireless element to this equation is to hook a cordless telephone system like the Siemens Gigaset models (www.siemens-mobile.com/gigaset) into the POTS phone jack on your VoIP ATA. The key here is to look for a cordless phone system that provides for multiple handsets on a single base station — otherwise, you'll have to spend time trying to wire your ATA into your existing home phone wiring.

Cordless phone systems work well, but there are even cooler solutions to going wireless with your VoIP: Wi-Fi VoIP phones. These phones look like cordless or mobile phone handsets, and they have both Wi-Fi chips and the circuitry to support SIP built right in. With a Wi-Fi VoIP phone, you don't even need the ATA; you just need a Wi-Fi connection to the Internet and you're set.

UTStarcom F1000

The phone that Vonage is launching for their VoIP Wi-Fi (sometimes called VoWi-Fi — Voice over Wi-Fi) service is the UTStarcom F1000. This phone, pictured in Figure 15-4, looks and feels like a cellphone and has all the standard cellphone features you might expect — like an address book, call holding, call waiting, call forwarding, and more. The big difference between this phone and a cellphone is that the F1000 works on Wi-Fi, not a cellular network. You can find more data about the F1000 on UTStarcom's site at the following URL: `www.utstar.com/Solutions/Handsets/WiFi/`.

Like most Wi-Fi phones to date, the F1000 is 802.11b-compliant — which means that you can use it on any 802.11b network and any 802.11g network that's been set up to support a mixed mode (the default for all 802.11g APs we know of — see Chapter 7 for more info on this).

The F1000 is also SIP-compliant, which means that it should work on any SIP-enabled VoIP phone network (like Vonage). The phone will initially be available only as part of a package with a VoIP service provider — so it will come preconfigured to connect to their network — but you can use onscreen menus to configure the phone for other networks if you desire.

Figure 15-4:
The UTStarcom F1000 takes your VoIP to a new wireless level.

Like most VoWi-Fi phones, the F1000 supports WEP, but not WPA. As we discuss in Chapter 8, WEP isn't really all that secure (even the 128-bit variants supported by the F1000 can be broken by hackers using tools that anyone can download for free on the Internet) — so we highly recommend that you use WPA in your network whenever possible.

This leaves you with a bit of a dilemma. You can't mix and match WPA and WEP on a network — it's one or the other. Our personal recommendation is to use WPA (WPA Enterprise if you can) on your main data wireless network and run a separate AP on a separate channel with WEP for your VoIP phones. If you have an old 802.11b AP and you've upgraded to a newer WPA-equipped 802.11g AP, you're set — just take the old AP out of retirement! If you don't, consider buying the cheapest 802.11g AP you can find for your VoIP network. You probably won't have to spend more than $30 or $40 if you just shop for what's on sale at your local Fry's or Best Buy.

The F1000 has one security function that we think is pretty awesome, and that's support for 802.1X authentication. The F1000 doesn't support the full WPA Enterprise standard, but it can support a WEP and 802.1X combination — something that many businesses have put together for their corporate Wi-Fi networks. If your network (or a client's or partner's) is architected this way, you could bring the F1000 to the office with you.

The F1000 is new to the market (we've been able to play with a beta unit, but haven't seen the final production units as we go to press in mid-2005), so the final pricing has not been set. Expect it to be priced competitively with a mobile phone or high-end cordless phone.

ZyXEL P-2000W v.2

The folks at ZyXEL make a lot of really cool wireless gear. The company has long been focused on selling equipment to businesses and service providers, so they're not a household name like Linksys, NETGEAR, or D-Link, but they actually sell a broad range of Wi-Fi gear, and lots of it!

One thing that really caught our eye was the P-2000W v.2 (not the slickest name ever) Wi-Fi phone. Like the UTStarcom F1000, this is a cellphone-sized Wi-Fi phone (and like the F1000, it's got the "candy bar" form factor rather than being a flip phone) with all of the standard convenience factors you'd expect from a mobile or cordless phone.

And like the F1000, the P-2000W (we're going to drop the *v.2* because version 1 is no longer on the market) is a SIP-based 802.11b phone with WEP support. The biggest difference is that you can buy a P-2000W today from places like Office Depot (www.officedepot.com) or Newegg (www.newegg.com) for about $250 without going through a service provider.

Figure 15-5 shows the P-2000W in all its Wi-Fi glory!

Figure 15-5:
You can toss
out your
"cordless"
phones and
go Wi-Fi
with the
P-2000W.

Making VoIP Work on Your Network

VoIP on your wireless network — whether it's a Wi-Fi phone or just a softphone client on a wireless laptop, desktop, or handheld computer — should *just work*. The beauty of VoIP is that it's just another type of data moving across the network, like Web pages, file downloads, and e-mail.

But voice data is less tolerant of network problems than are other types of data. For example, if a bit of data from a Web page download comes into your PC out of order, who cares? If your e-mail takes an extra ten seconds to download, no big deal. But voice is a very real time application, dependent on timing and *latency* (or delay).

Dealing with QoS

Unlike "pure" data applications, where you can retransmit bits and bytes that get lost due to network errors, voice has no tolerance for delays and retransmits. If the bits that represent a word don't come through the network in time, you can't get them back, at least not until the other party says, "Could you say that again?"

So Wi-Fi VoIP (and all VoIP, for that matter) is dependent on a network with low latency and a low rate of errors that require retransmission. On that front, we've got some good news and some bad news.

The bad news first: Only a handful of Wi-Fi products support the WMM standard (Wi-Fi MultiMedia), which can provide QoS (Quality of Service) across the Wi-Fi portion of a network. *None* of these products are VoIP phones or related products. At the time of this writing, no products that ensure that the quality of service is maintained on your wireless network are available.

You *can* buy products designed for large businesses from companies like Symbol (www.symbol.com) or SpectraLink (www.spectralink.com) that use their own *pre-standard* or proprietary standard versions of WMM or 802.11e to provide this QoS. Unfortunately, these systems are priced for that market and aren't designed for (or priced for) the home user.

In the near future — very near future as a matter of fact, perhaps even by the time you read this — you'll be able to buy WMM-certified Wi-Fi phones. Keep in mind that you'll also need to have a WMM-certified AP or router on the other end of the connection to gain the advantages of WMM.

To check for products that are WMM-certified, look on the Wi-Fi Alliance Certified Products Web page at www.wi-fi.org/OpenSection/certified_products.asp?TID=2. You can use pulldown menus and check boxes to quickly sort through all of the listed products to find exactly what you're looking for.

WMM is going to be a big help, but it's not a panacea. The underlying protocols beneath 802.11 networks were never designed to provide as robust a QoS environment as is possible in a wired network. You *can* make wireless VoIP sound very good (and work very well), but it will probably never equal a wired connection. We think that the great increase in convenience is worth that small degree of performance loss; we suspect that you'll agree.

The good news is that you *can* deal with the QoS issue at your router, and give your VoIP traffic priority over other data being sent to and from your broadband Internet connection. To do this, you need a SIP *acceleration* or *prioritization* product. These products recognize SIP-based VoIP packets as they pass through the router and automatically assign to them a higher priority. The accelerator delays *other* data packets from entering the Internet connection if they would cause delay in the transmission of voice.

You'll find two forms of SIP acceleration products for your home or small office network:

✔ **Stand-alone devices:** Stand-alone devices like the D-Link DI-102 Broadband Internet/VoIP Accelerator (`www.dlink.com/products/?pid=426`), which retails for about $60, are installed *inline* between your broadband Internet connection and your primary router (wired or wireless). All traffic entering and leaving your home network travels through the accelerator, which then prioritizes the VoIP traffic. The D-Link Net Accelerator is shown in Figure 15-6.

✔ **Built into a router:** Some vendors are beginning to incorporate this VoIP acceleration functionality right into their routers. For example, the ZyXEL P-334WT wireless router includes ZyXEL's Media Session Routing Technologies (MSRT), which prioritize SIP and other protocols. You can even go into the router configuration Web pages for the P-334WT to customize this prioritization (so you can add other applications, like online gaming, to the priority list, as well as set the bandwidth reserved for voice to an appropriate level — like 90 Kbps for Vonage). This router retails for about $60 — roughly the same price as some of the stand-alone SIP acceleration devices.

Figure 15-6: Make your SIP calls zip through your network with an accelerator.

Dealing with XP issues

One issue to keep in mind with wireless VoIP if you're a Windows XP user is a behavior of XP's Wireless Zero Configuration system. Zero Config is a *great* tool for finding wireless networks and getting online — it's so easy and so integrated into the OS that we use it all the time, instead of using the software included with our wireless client adapter hardware.

Feedback on feedback

Some folks we know try to use the microphones and speakers that are built into their laptop or desktop computers for making peer-to-peer or softphone calls when they're on the road. Although this works — just barely — the quality of the call is really subpar. That's because you usually need to end up using a lot of echo cancellation within your softphone program to keep your speaker's output from feeding back into the microphone. The result is laggy and less clearly audible audio output.

You can buy an analog headset to plug into the microphone and headphone minijacks found on many (but not all!) laptop computers. These devices really improve your sound quality and give you privacy for your calls, for just a few bucks (you can buy many headsets for $20 or less).

An even better option is to invest in a USB headset like the Plantronics Audio 45 (www. plantronics.com/north_america/en_ US/products/cat640035/cat1430032/ prod5020014). For less than $60, you get a plug-and-play headset that works with Windows XP or Mac OS X automatically (just plug it in!), and that includes a noise-canceling microphone and a DSP (digital signal processing) system that gives you better audio quality than you could ever have imagined. Combine this with a high bit-rate codec (like a high bandwidth Skype call), and it will sound *better* than any cellphone or landline call you've ever made.

But Zero Config has one issue that can be a pain. If you're in a less-than-great coverage area, and Zero Config has you connected at a less-than-full-speed (Excellent or Very Good coverage) connection, Zero Config "looks around" for a better connection every few minutes.

In this process, you may sometimes actually drop your Wi-Fi connection for just a second. This dropping of the connection is utterly unnoticeable for downloading Web pages or checking e-mail, but for real-time, latency-sensitive applications like VoIP (or for online gaming, for that matter), it can be a real pain.

If your signal is strong, this won't be an issue. If it's not, you have a couple of choices:

✔ You can use different client software (the software included with your PC's Wi-Fi hardware) to control your connections.

✔ You can turn off Zero Config after you are connected to the AP.

To turn off Zero Config after you're connected to the AP, simply follow these steps:

1. **Open the Control Panel window by selecting Start➪Control Panel.**

   If you're in the Category view of the Control Panel window, click the Switch to Classic View link in the left pane of the window.

2. **Double-click the Administrative Tools icon.**

3. **Double-click the Services icon in the window that opens.**

4. **Double-click Wireless Zero Configuration.**

   The Wireless Zero Configuration Properties window opens, as shown in Figure 15-7.

5. **Click the Stop button and then click OK.**

   Zero Config is turned off until you restart your computer or manually restart it using these same steps, substituting the Start button for the Stop button in Step 5.

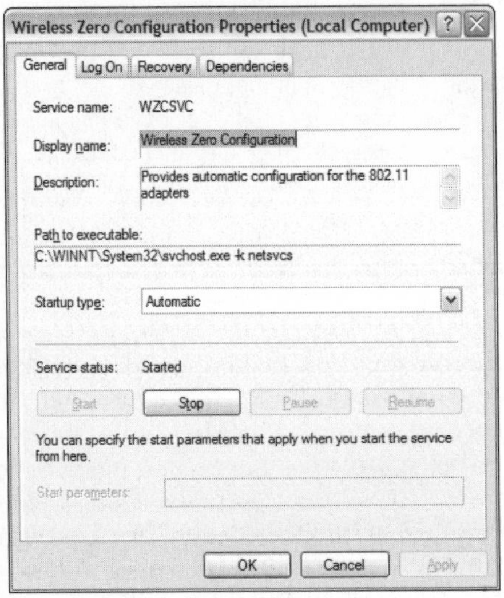

Figure 15-7:
Turning off
Zero Config
when you're
making IP
calls.

VoIPing on the Road

Wi-Fi and VoIP in the home or office is pretty cool and can have a great convenience factor, but we think that the really awesome application for wireless VoIP is on the road. Imagine going into a hot spot and making free phone calls to anyone in the world. Or pulling out your Wi-Fi phone at a convention center and having all of your calls to your home or office number ring you right where you are, with no per-minute charges. Or staying in a hotel overseas and calling folks back in the states (or receiving calls from them) by just dialing U.S. numbers — as part of your U.S. and Canada "unlimited" plan.

All of these things are possible with VoIP and Wi-Fi. Read on!

Using softphones

The easiest way to combine VoIP and Wi-Fi on the road is to simply use your PC, Mac, or handheld computer with a softphone program to place and receive calls.

For example, you can use Skype (or a similar program, as we listed above) to make peer-to-peer calls and to "call out" to regular numbers. There's nothing to this process really. Just log into the hot spot as we discuss in Chapter 9 and start up Skype. Because Skype isn't tied down to any particular geographical location, when you go online, you'll be reachable by your normal Skype username. If you have a SkypeIn account, other people can dial that number with any regular phone and reach you at the hot spot.

You don't have to use Skype to make this work, either — most hardware-based VoIP services include a softphone client as an optional component. For example, Vonage offers a softphone service as an add-on to its basic hardware-based services. For an additional $9.99 a month, you get the softphone client software, an additional number for your laptop, and 500 local and long distance minutes. Vonage has even inked a deal with Boingo (we discuss Boingo in Chapter 9) to integrate the softphone and Boingo's hot spot services.

 If softphones sound like a good deal to you, shop around carefully when you choose your VoIP provider — more and more companies are starting to include the softphone as a freebie service using your main plan's minutes.

 If you travel to a particular location very frequently and make or receive a lot of local calls in that area, you might consider getting a second phone number from your VoIP provider that's in that local area code. Many providers offer a second phone number service for just a few bucks a month (and for the Vonage softphone example we mentioned above, a second phone number is part of the package — in fact, the Vonage phone is a completely separate number from your home Vonage line, so you'll have a custom number to use on the road).

 If you're interested in learning more about softphones, check out Xten Networks (www.xten.com). They make the softphone clients used by many different VoIP providers (including Vonage).

Bringing your VoIP handset on the road

Softphones work well, but you do tend to look a bit dorky talking into your laptop and USB headset while you're in a coffee shop or hotel lobby. And booting up a laptop is just not all that convenient for a quick call. That's where a Wi-Fi VoIP handset can come in handy.

The two handsets we discuss earlier in this chapter (the UTStarcom and ZyXEL models) can both be used in hot spot and public Wi-Fi network environments. Both support up to 128-bit WEP encryption, so even if the hot spot uses that form of encryption, you can still get online.

Both phones offer a simple keypad-based method for inputting ESSID and WEP keys for networks that need them, and both automatically search for open networks that broadcast their SSIDs. We weren't able to play with the beta units of the UTStarcom phone in a hot spot environment, but the ZyXEL phone is particularly easy to use — you can just scroll through a list of available networks and click a button on the phone to connect. The phone even maintains memory of ESSIDs and WEP keys — which can be very handy if you're returning to the same place multiple times, or using a hot spot network that has the same ESSID in every location.

After you connect to the hot spot, the phone automatically connects back to your service provider's SIP proxy server, which brings your phone online. You can make and receive phone calls at that point just as if you were back in your home or office. The only thing cooler than that is the next generation of combined cellular/Wi-Fi phones that we discuss in the sidebar entitled, "Coming soon: Dual-mode cellular/Wi-Fi handsets."

Coming soon: Dual-mode cellular/Wi-Fi handsets

The real future of Wi-Fi and VoIP is not the stand-alone Wi-Fi VoIP phones we discuss in this chapter. Instead, we're beginning to see *dual-mode* phones that incorporate both Wi-Fi and traditional cellular in a single unit. So you could hop onto your VoIP service provider's network when you're at home, in the office, or at a Wi-Fi hot spot, and then flip over to your CDMA or GSM mobile network when you're on the road.

The real trick here is handling the *handoff* between these two networks. Say you're on a Wi-Fi VoIP call within a hot spot and you need to step outside to hail a taxi. What happens as you move out of range of the hot spot is crucial — making a seamless transition from Wi-Fi to cellular without dropping the call is an engineering task that is relatively complex — and is occupying the attention of many cellular and Wi-Fi networking companies as they work on these new dual-mode phones.

One of the first to be announced is Motorola's CN620 (`www.motorola.com/wlan/solution_cn620.html`). This soon-to-be-released phone combines 802.11a Wi-Fi (including industrial strength 802.1X and WPA security) with a GSM mobile phone. Motorola has partnered with a number of companies to provide an entire solution (for the mobile phone and Wi-Fi network operators) that lets the CN620 seamlessly roam among different access points and between the Wi-Fi and GSM mobile networks without dropping calls or even causing an audible break in the conversation.

Every big cellular handset manufacturer we know of has some product on the drawing boards like this. It's the future of mobile telephony!

Chapter 16

That's Not All: Other Cool Wireless Toys

In This Chapter

▶ Sharing your digital camera pictures wirelessly

▶ Making hotel room broadband wirelessly available to the whole room

▶ Finding a Wi-Fi signal when you need it

▶ Getting a start on RFID

▶ Getting a firm handle on your firmware

A gazillion wireless toys and gadgets are on the market. We don't think of these as wireless per se because they are often associated with specific activities or tasks. We don't really think a lot about a wireless remote-controlled toy car from Radio Shack or that oh-so-special remote control fart machine that Danny got from his brother (thanks, David) — because these are not devices that deal with a higher level network at all.

This book is all about building out your home's wireless infrastructure and then taking advantage of that. So put another way, if you've got this great standardized wireless superhighway running through your house, why not see what else you can do with it?

You had to ask, didn't ya? Read on! We tell you about other devices that you can use at home, on the road, in the air, and anywhere else there are wireless networks to hop on and off of!

Digital Cameras with Wi-Fi

The battle for the hearts and minds of the digital consumer is raging when it comes to taking pictures. Many cellphones today are outfitted with pretty decent megapixel cameras that allow you to snap a picture and then instantly send it to someone you want to make insanely jealous.

The camera manufacturers have taken notice of this and of the fact that Wi-Fi is just about everywhere these days. You guessed it — they've merged the two together.

Kodak has its EASYSHARE-ONE Wi-Fi camera (www.kodak.com, $599 retail plus $99 for a Wi-Fi card). The EASYSHARE-ONE, shown in Figure 16-1, is a 4-megapixel CCD camera with a 3-inch LCD screen, 256MB of onboard memory, and optional 802.11b Wi-Fi compatibility made available by an SDIO 802.11b Wi-Fi card.

Figure 16-1:
Kodak's
EASY-
SHARE-ONE
is easy
to share
wirelessly.

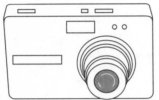

With the wireless capability, you can e-mail photos from any hot spot and order prints from the Kodak EasyShare Gallery (www.kodakgallery.com) with the click of a button. You can also print wirelessly to a Kodak printer dock, or upload the files for later access from your computer — clearing up space on your camera to take more pictures. The EASYSHARE-ONE uses a technology known as Zeroconf (Zero Configuration — also known to Apple users as Rendezvous or, with the advent of OS X 10.4 Tiger, Bonjour) to automatically find devices within a close range of the camera. These devices include printers, camera phones, other cameras, and computers — any device the user would want to transfer images to or from. Think of the freedom that allows!

For the not-so-average photographer, Nikon and Canon both have launched 802.11 cards for their high-end products. Nikon has its WT-2/2A 802.11g (www.nokiausa.com, $650) and its WT-1/1A 802.11b wireless adapters ($450), which tuck underneath its professional digital cameras, such as the D2X or D2-Hs models — cameras that cost around $5,000 each. With Nikon's Capture 4.2 software, you can wirelessly control your camera.

Canon has a similar add-on option, the WFT-E1A (www.canon.com, $850), which can transmit over both the 802.11b and 802.11g protocols. It fits Canon's $8,000 EOS-1Ds cameras.

Expect to see most cameras with wireless connectivity soon, in the same way that most cellphones are moving to have cameras integrated as well. Picture perfect in our book!

Extra Storage Anywhere You Want

Now it's easy to take a ton of pictures and send them back to your home's network — but where are you going to store them? Why, on your home's wireless *network attached storage* (NAS), of course. NAS devices give you all the benefits of a huge hard drive on your network, without the overhead of having to maintain another computer or server in the home. Users can have read/write access at the same time, giving anyone on the network additional storage whenever they need it. You can integrate NAS into your home network as a media storage server backing up music, photos, and videos, for instance. It can also be used as a file server — NAS devices typically include backup software that allows for scheduling unattended backup tasks.

Storage is like money — you want a lot of it and in large denominations so it's easy to handle. You want to buy a NAS with as much memory as you can get, for as reasonable a price as you can get. When buying NAS for your home network, you won't need a lot of fancy features, so look at the cost per GB of storage as a gauge for how cost-effective a unit is. For example, a 120GB wireless NAS device that costs $80 ends up running about $.66 per gigabyte — a pretty good rate. Some NAS devices also ship with an integral print server, so you get some extra great functionality for those small offices like Pat's. (Check out the next section on why you want a print server in your house.)

Tritton Technologies, Inc. (www.trittonsales.com), offers 120GB ($299) and 200GB ($329) NAS with full 802.11g access points onboard, as shown in Figure 16-2. Iomega (www.iomega.com) NAS 100d, likewise, has an integral 802.11g access point — you can get models with 250GB for $400 and 160GB for $330.

D-Link offers several wireless NAS units, such as the 40GB MediaLounge Wireless G Central Home Drive DSM-624H (www.dlink.com, $429), but at almost $10 per gigabyte, it's a pricey option to choose.

We mention the wireless options first because, well, this is a wireless book. With wireless, you have total freedom to decide where you want to put it. But NAS can sit anywhere on your network — the key is being able to hop onto your network to get to it. If you have an access point and wireless connection to your LAN already, you don't need the integral access point that comes in the NAS. And if you have space near a wired connection, you have no special reason to have wireless NAS, as opposed to wired NAS. Wired NAS options cost less, so you get more for your money. So unless you have some specific wireless requirement — like you want to put it in your car — check out your wired options as well.

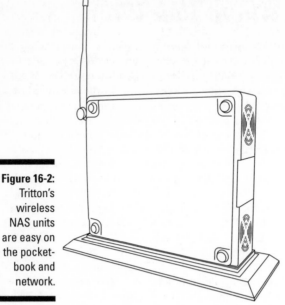

Figure 16-2:
Tritton's
wireless
NAS units
are easy on
the pocket-
book and
network.

A lot of wireless adjunct gear — including NAS but not just limited to those devices — does not support the latest wireless security protocols embodied in WPA. (See Chapter 9 for more info on WPA.) If your access points and other wireless gear are WPA and you buy a wireless NAS that only supports WEP, you either have to step everything down to WEP, or create a separate segment on your wireless LAN for WEP — either is a pain. So make sure you have a handle on your wireless security strategy when buying peripherals to add to your network.

You *really* don't want to use security more minimal than WPA on a NAS device if you don't have to. WEP is not all that secure (see Chapters 8 and 9 for more on this), and a NAS device is something that may have very important and confidential data on it. Best to go "wired" if you can't find a WPA NAS unit.

It's a Print (Server)

Printing anything these days requires processing resources on your PC and network. High-resolution cameras yield high-resolution images that yield large file sizes that have to be moved through your computer's processing resources to the printer. If your target printer is attached to a remote computer, that computer's resources will get tied up printing the picture. Multiply this by several kids, at homework time, all doing graphically intense projects, and your printer-hosting computer can become noticeably affected.

Enter the print server. The print server's role is to offload processing to a specialized device that simply manages all the print jobs bound for a particular printer. You can place a printer anywhere in range of your wireless devices using a wireless print server. You no longer have to be within a cable's distance of a host PC. Just hook up a printer to the wireless print server as you would to a PC, and off you go. Often, you can find a better place to put a printer. Because printers are noisy beasts and can churn for a long time, a lot of us would not mind getting them off our desks.

Print servers aren't all that expensive either. Some access points, switches, and NAS devices come with a print server built into the device. The D-Link DI-824VUP ($130), for instance, is a four-port wireless Ethernet broadband router with a built-in print server. NETGEAR's 54 Mbps Wireless Print Server with 4-Port Switch ($80) houses the server functionality at your main switching location. So you can put your switch, printers, and other gear all in one place and connect it back to your cable modem or DSL connection wirelessly.

You can also get stand-alone wireless print servers focused on that one task — D-Link's DP-G321 Wireless Multi-Port Print Server ($89) features two USB 2.0 ports and one parallel port, which allows everyone on the network to access and share up to three printers off the one device. You could set up a printer farm with that!

The nice thing about going wireless is that any 802.11 wireless device can print directly to the print server, making it easy for visitors to print out their recipes for lobster flambé.

When you choose a print server, look for one that supports 802.11g and USB 2.0. Supporting these standards isn't important if you're printing a single text-only page, but if you're doing something more demanding, such as printing photos across the network, you really want (and need) some speed!

A complementary and related idea is the Bluetooth print server. This allows Bluetooth devices to camp on and print — particularly handy for PDAs and cellphones outfitted with Bluetooth. You can use a Bluetooth print server and Bluetooth USB adapter to accomplish three things:

- ✔ Get rid of the PC-printer cable snaking across the floor.
- ✔ Make your PC Bluetooth-capable.
- ✔ Open up the printer to be shared by any other Bluetooth-capable device in your home.

Iogear (www.iogear.com) makes some nice Bluetooth adapters. Their GBP302 kit ($120) contains the USB 2.0 adapter for your PC and the combo adapter for your printer. Almost any online computer store has Bluetooth print server kits as well.

Bluetooth is a short-range technology. Although some variants of Bluetooth can reach 100 feet or more, most real-world Bluetooth connections go only 25 or 30 feet. So a Bluetooth print server might only be useful if you're accessing it from within the same room.

Travel Routers

In the beginning, when travel routers first came out, they were just cool. Now they are a *necessity* for any laptop warrior. *Travel routers* are small wireless access points with a built-in router that enable you to connect to a hotel or other broadband Ethernet connection and share it with others via Wi-Fi. Before travel routers, you had to connect to the room's broadband connection via a cable, which is a pain: Most room modems are on a desk on one side of the room, whereas you want to work on your laptop watching television on the other side of the room. What's worse, the cables provided by the hotels are usually pretty short.

Travel routers change all of this because they are designed to interwork seamlessly with these forms of broadband connections, and they also allow you to share that wireless connection among all your roomies (especially the grumpy ones like Pat who get mad when you hog the broadband connection).

So if you travel and bring your wireless-enabled gear with you, and you want to access that broadband connection easily, travel routers are for you. They are about as expensive as a normal access point — starting at about $50.

When checking out travel routers, here are some things to look for:

✓ **What it does:** Travel routers can be about a lot more than just connecting to a broadband connection. Some, like Apple's AirPort Express, shown in Figure 16-3, can stream music from iTunes, allow computers to share printers, and bridge AP traffic. (And AirPort Express can be used with Macs and PCs alike! See the sidebar titled, "Apple doesn't mean just Macs anymore.") D-Link's DWL-G730AP (www.dlink.com, $60) is another very compact and powerful device — it's an 802.11g access point, router, and wireless client all in one. You change among the three modes via a switch on the bottom of the device. SMC's SMCWTK-G (www.smc.com, $90) travel router also sports an Ethernet bridge and repeater capability.

✓ **What interfaces it has:** D-Link's DWL-G730AP not only has a USB connection, but it can be powered from it too. The AirPort Express also has audio and USB connections. The more interfaces, the more roles it can play when you use it.

Apple doesn't mean just Macs anymore

When it comes to travel routers, Apple's AirPort Express (www.apple.com/airport express/, $129) defies easy description because it's . . . well . . . sort of a . . . quasi-access point, printer server, music hub, wireless repeater type of device. And it works for Macs *and* PCs alike. Cool!

It's 802.11g, which means it supports your 802.11b as well. It's an access point and a bridge. It supports WPA and 128-bit WEP encryption as well. Want to share a printer? No problem: The AirPort Express has a built-in print server for any USB-connecting printer. Have an iPod and iTunes on your network? Connect your sound system to the audio port on the AirPort Express Base Station using an audio cable. A bundled software program — AirTunes — lets you wirelessly stream your iTunes music through your stereo or powered speakers. iTunes automatically detects the connection of your remote speakers. To play a music file, just select it in the iTunes window and click Play.

To top it all off, you don't have to worry about an AC adapter — it's built into the device.

Some functions are only supported by Macs. For instance, the bridge mode was designed for enhancing the AirPort product alone. But if you are a Mac user and you want to connect to the Internet with your PowerBook in an area that lies beyond the range of your AirPort Express or AirPort Extreme Base Station, you can use AirPort Express as a wireless bridge to extend the range of your primary base station. Simply place AirPort Express within the range of your primary base station and near the area where you'd like to enjoy your wireless connection, and the AirPort Express links to that base station.

Apple's AirPort Express is the first device to pack wireless networking, audio, printing, and bridging capabilities into a single, well-priced, portable unit. Well done.

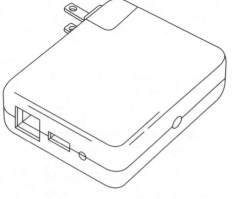

Figure 16-3:
Apple's
AirPort
Express
works with
PCs and
Macs alike.

If you are likely to be in places without a broadband connection but still want to share a dial-up connection because there's only one phone line (beach house, anyone?), the WiFlyer from Always On Wireless is for you (www.alwaysonwireless.com, $150). Although substantially pricier than the other travel routers, it's the only one we know of with dial-up that is designed for travel. It supports 802.11g and 802.11b wireless clients.

We bet that a travel router will become as important to your trip as your passport and your ATM card. Don't leave home without it.

Wi-Fi Finders

Say you're buying into our theme of Wi-Fi all over the place, and you're on the road with Wi-Fi to the hilt . . . so where can you log on? In Chapter 10, we told you about roaming networks and other Wi-Fi tips for the road. But if you had a Wi-Fi finder in your pocket, you wouldn't need to boot up to figure out where your nearest hot spot is.

A *Wi-Fi finder* is a divining rod for wireless access. It looks like that plastic remote control for the car locks that you get with new cars these days. Operating a finder is usually a matter of pressing a button. It sniffs the air for wireless signals that it can log onto, and alerts you via lights and other indicators that you're in range of an AP's signal.

When shopping for a Wi-Fi finder, here are some things to think about:

✓ **Signal indicators:** The whole point of this device is to communicate that you are in range of a Wi-Fi signal, so how it does it is pretty important. Most have a signal strength LED indicator to tell you that a signal is around and how strong it is. Kensington's WiFi Finder Plus (www.kensington.com, $29), Smart ID's WiFi Trekker (www.smartid.com.sg, $29), and Chrysalis California's WiFi Seeker (www.wifiseeker.com/, $29) each have LED signal strength indicators. Smart ID's device lets you put it in auto-scanning mode. In auto-scanning mode, the WiFi Trekker alerts you that it has found a signal with flashing lights and a built-in buzzer. But for those of you who think like we do — that lights are not enough — look for a finder with an LCD screen that can really tell you something. The Digital Hotspotter from Canary Wireless (www.canary wireless.com, $59), shown in Figure 16-4, has an LCD screen; when it finds a network, it horizontally scrolls the SSID name, signal strength, encryption status, and channel number across the one-line LCD display. The signal strength is shown via the same bar motif found on your cell-phone. (The LCD is not backlit, but we hope it will be in the future.)

The encryption status is displayed either as *Open* or *Closed. Closed* means the network is encrypted using WEP or WPA. *Open* doesn't necessarily mean you've just found a free ticket onto the Internet, however. Commercial networks like Boingo, Wayport, and T-Mobile show up as *Open,* but route you to a Web page for payment before you can actually surf via them.

✔ **Multiple network feedback:** A signal indicator is nice, but how do you interpret the signal when multiple networks are present? The Canary Wireless device scrolls the different networks available for your perusal. Pick the one you like best!

✔ **Signals detected:** All of the Wi-Fi finder's we've seen detect 802.11b and g signals; some, like the Kensington and SmartID devices, detect Bluetooth. Some try to filter out non–Wi-Fi signals — the Canary Wireless device blocks out 2.45 GHz signals — such as Bluetooth networks, cordless phones, and microwaves — that may be worthless to you. Be sure to buy a device that detects what you are looking for.

✔ **Batteries:** What batteries does it use? Kensington's WiFi Finder Plus uses two CR2016 coin cell batteries, which can be tough to find on the road. Other detectors use standard AAA batteries, so you won't have a hard time buying replacement batteries pretty much anywhere in the world.

✔ **Extra features:** Kensington's WiFi Finder Plus includes a built-in flashlight for those dark nights roaming the streets for Wi-Fi. Hawking Technologies HWL1 802.11b/g WiFi Locator (www.hawkingtech.com, $30) has a flip-open Hi-Gain Directional Antenna that helps you determine exactly where the signal source is coming from.

We think the Canary Wireless Digital Hotspotter is the "must-have" device for our high-tech tastes. As hot spots proliferate, you simply need to know which network is which, and the Hotspotter is the only device on the market that tells you this.

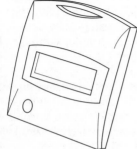

Figure 16-4:
Canary
Wireless's
Digital
Hotspotter
with LCD.

All-in-one finders with *more power*

The folks at Hawking Technologies (www.hawkingtech.com) have launched one of the cooler Wi-Fi finders that we've yet seen, although it's so new that we've not had a chance to test it out ourselves yet. The HWL2/HWL2A models (the "A" model is designed for use with Apple computers) combine Hawking's high-gain antenna Wi-Fi finder technology (from the HWL1 model) with a built-in USB 2.0 802.11g Wi-Fi network adapter. So you can use the directional Wi-Fi finder to locate the hot spot, and then just plug the same device into an available USB 2.0 port on your PC or Mac to get online. Pretty handy, if you ask us.

Technology in this space changes frequently, so check out sites like The Gadgeteer (www.the-gadgeteer.com/) or Engadget (www.engadget.com) for their take on the latest devices.

Jumping into RFID

RFID is going to change your life. It may not be obvious at first, but it will get more and more visible as it takes over the world. Radio Frequency Identification is merely a way to put a radio-frequency-sensitive tag into everything that moves. This tag, when queried by a specific radio frequency, reveals all sorts of information about itself. Cars may speak RFID to their mechanics, the package of Oreos in your pantry will be able to tell your home network that it needs to be reordered because it's stale, and — brace yourself — you'll be able to match clothing with the right kid's pile and combine socks with the right mate — because the IDs within the clothing tell you all about them.

We're not there yet, but it's coming. Wal-Mart is one of the leaders in forcing its suppliers to adopt RFID so it can track when it needs to order more Crest toothpaste or know where that pallet of new PS3 gaming platforms is located because there's a riot in Albuquerque due to shortages. By putting RFID readers throughout its shipping chain, it can scan a shipping container electronically from the outside and know everything that is inside.

As RFID tags get cheaper and built into more things, you'll be able to do more with them to simplify your life, so you'd better get started, now. You need an RFID Starter Kit from iAutomate.com (www.iautomate.com, $480), as shown in Figure 16-5. With this kit, you can start reading RFID tags that you install and ones that are installed in other products as well.

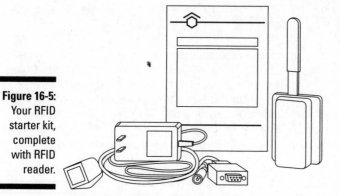

Figure 16-5:
Your RFID
starter kit,
complete
with RFID
reader.

The kit includes a long-range RFID reader — the device that sends out the RFID queries and reads the responses — and the software to help you take advantage of the RFID information after you have it — home automation software from HomeSeer (www.homeseer.com). All you need to do is add any RFID tags to cars, people, backpacks, you name it, and you can start tracking and automating things around your house. Attach an RFID keyfob to your keychain to have the system "see" when you drive up the driveway and automatically open the garage door, turn on the lights, and buzz the spouse to meet you at the door with a kiss. Okay, that last part is a stretch, but once HomeSeer is triggered, any one of many programmable activities can take place because HomeSeer is basically a home automation program for controlling anything in the home.

You can hide range-adjustable antennas in walls, ceilings, and doorways to identify and track tag activity. You can daisy-chain additional readers on one system to give your home more reading area for RFID sensors. The antennas are range-adjustable, meaning that you can control the readable area to limit the application to a specific room, for instance. The readers can simultaneously read multiple RFID tags at ranges of up to 450 feet and can also register and report the disappearance or unauthorized movement of individual RFID tags. It's definitely applicable for anything that has a sign above it reading, "Keep your filthy hands off!"

The readers are compatible with wired or wireless Ethernet systems. You connect to them with standard CAT-5e cabling, and the cable plugs into an RS-232 adapter that plugs into a serial port on your PC.

RFID is something you will hear a lot more about, so now is as good a time as any to get your feet wet with a starter kit. What we've covered in this book is just the tip of the iceberg. For more information, pick up *RFID For Dummies* by Patrick J. Sweeney (Wiley).

Adding New Firmware for Your AP

Sveasoft Inc. (www.sveasoft.com) has an interesting point of view — why slug it out in the consumer access point market where the margins are razor-thin and making money is hard? They instead focus on the software side of the equation, developing state-of-the-art firmware upgrades that *replace* the manufacturer's own firmware loads. In doing so, they create an annual recurring revenue stream for their software (about $20 per year) without having to build a distribution channel for hardware. Pretty ingenious, we think.

So how can a small company build better software than a large company like Linksys or Belkin? They pick and choose what models they want to enhance and focus just on those models. Sveasoft has come out with neat enhancements like mesh networking and VoIP functionality that rides on top of the wireless hardware as if it were there from the start. Sveasoft developed a means to provide the same level of functionality as on the normal system but in two-thirds of the space, giving them room to download more programming to your access point for new functionality.

We especially like the hot spot and mesh networking products. The hot spot build adds an onboard hot spot and billing module, including an onboard RADIUS server and SQL server for user authorization and data storage. You can also link your AP to external RADIUS servers if you want.

The mesh routing build adds the ability to auto-configure based on link strength and distance to Internet feeds. Using WPA, the mesh build enables instant neighborhood networks with little or no configuration. So if you and your neighbors want to create a neighborhood area network, you can do so, and share Internet connections as well.

The firm is initially focusing on two Linksys products, the Linksys WRT54G and WRT54GS wireless routers, but they are quickly adding new vendors' gear to their list. You should check it out to see what they have to offer before you pay a lot of money for a much pricier packaged product that performs the same functions.

Updating your firmware is a tricky process when you are merely installing the next version, much less putting a whole new vendor's firmware onboard. It's not for a beginner — and most of the functionality Sveasoft adds is not for beginners either — so only attempt this if you are truly an advanced wireless user.

More, More, and More Wireless

The integration of wireless into all devices is continuing apace — we can hardly keep up with it. Here's a snapshot of other types of devices on the market:

✔ **Combo Wi-Fi/Flash USB keychain gear:** There are USB keychain storage devices, and USB Wi-Fi clients — as Reese's did with chocolate and peanut butter, it's inevitable that someone would figure out that they're two great tastes that taste great together. We like to keep units separate so you can get the best keychain storage device out there and the best Wi-Fi adapter out there, but some people might be limited by USB space or just have simpler needs. In this case, check out products like KingByte's Wireless PenDrive (www.kingbyte.com), — an 802.11b unit with capacities up to 256MB.

✔ **Cellphone Wi-Fi cards:** If you have a cellphone with an SD slot, you may be able to add a Wi-Fi card or add-on device. There are a lot of "ifs" about adding Wi-Fi to your phone:

- If your phone does not already have Wi-Fi onboard, and

- If your phone has an SD I/O (SDIO) slot for accepting third-party devices, and

- If your phone has available drivers for the SDIO-enabled device, then you may be able to add Wi-Fi to your phone

You may, for example, have heard about the difficulties of adding Bluetooth SD cards to a Treo 600 because there are no drivers for the phone, although the phone has an SD slot and there are SD Bluetooth cards on the market. The same is true for Wi-Fi in this instance.

The best way to find out about adding Wi-Fi to your cellphone is to check out your cellphone manufacturer's site first, and *then* visit your service provider's site to make sure they have not corrupted the capability on your phone. Search for your phone model and the term *Wi-Fi*. If that doesn't give you useful search results, try the FAQ or Support areas of the site.

Have heart. There are specific products to help add Wi-Fi to your phone — you just might have to dig for them. Enfora (www.enfora.com, $150), for instance, has launched a Wi-Fi Sled that attaches to the backside of Treo 600 — and this uses the SD slot as its interface. If you have a phone or PDA based on the Palm or Windows OS, there's a good chance you can get some sort of add-on capability.

Depending on how the SD interface is actually integrated into the cell-phone's circuitry and other processor-related issues, you may find that you won't get anywhere near Wi-Fi speeds with your cellphone. Check out places like *Tom's Networking* (www.tomsnetworking.com) for updates on Wi-Fi performance with cellphones, as they tend to cover that topic a lot.

We talk about the Treo a lot because of its massive penetration and the desire of so many Treo users for add-on wireless connectivity. If you want to get Wi-Fi on your Treo phone no matter what your stinky service provider tells you, check out the Wi-Fi driver hacks created by "Shadowmite" at www.shadowmite.com. Read more about it in this forum at the Treo Central site, discussion.treocentral.com/forumdisplay.php?f=38.

✔ **Decorative Wi-Fi APs:** For some of us, the gray, plastic, antenna-riddled look of an access point is just fine. Others who have a more refined aesthetic sensibility may want something more akin to On-Q's in-ceiling 802.11g Wireless Access Point (www.onqhome.com, $280). (See Figure 16-6.) It looks much like a smoke detector and has a low-impact form factor. It can be line-powered so a single CAT-5e cable hooks it into your home's network.

✔ **Wi-Fi videophones:** You can use Wi-Fi to videoconference as well. With the DVC-1100 Wireless Broadband VideoPhone (www.dlink.com, $220), you can turn your TV into a videoconferencing screen. No computer is needed; you just connect the videophone to your TV using standard composite RCA connectors, configure the device to hop on your wireless network (the DVC-1100 uses 802.11b), and you're ready. You need a DVC-1100 (or compatible D-Link video conferencing device) on each end of the call.

Figure 16-6: OnQ's nicely designed in-ceiling AP.

You can attach a telephone handset to the device for the audio portion of the call, which we recommend. Otherwise, you get a fair amount of feedback from the voices coming from the TV being re-fed back into the microphone as originating audio. Lots of companies are doing some substantial research and development trying to come up with a good way to talk to your TV set for just this application.

🖛 **Power over Ethernet:** You're not always lucky enough to have an electrical outlet near your Ethernet cabling port for your remote access point, so products like D-Link's DWL-P100 and P200 models (www.dlink.com, $30 to $40) really save the day. You can add power at the front end of the connection and split it back off when you get to the access point. (See Figure 16-7.) The DWL-P200 transfers data on CAT-5e cable pairs 1/2 and 3/6; power is transmitted on unused Ethernet pairs 4/5 and 7/8.

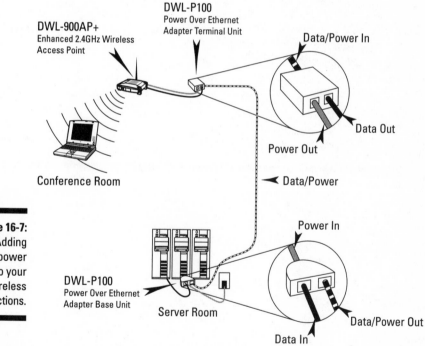

Figure 16-7:
Adding some power to your wireless connections.

Part V
The Part of Tens

The 5th Wave   By Rich Tennant

EXPERIMENTING WITH THE
WIRELESS LASER BEAM NETWORK

@RICHTENNANT

"Okay–did you get that?"

In this part . . .

We always enjoy making lists. Without them, we'd never get anything done. So we think you might enjoy our lists that will help you get more done with your wireless network. In this Part, we give you Top Ten lists designed to tickle your brain and whet your appetite for wireless. First, we list our ten favorite sites for keeping current on wireless trends, and then we answer the most frequently-asked questions of advanced wireless users.

Chapter 17

(Almost) Ten Sites for Advanced Wireless Topics

*W*ireless news and information is everywhere. Pat's mom even calls him to discuss wireless articles she reads in her hometown newspaper. These days, wireless is simply an everyday topic for the everyman (and woman).

Certain sites, however, we track regularly in order to stay up to speed on the latest and greatest tips, tricks, reviews, news, blogs, pictures, and wacky stories that just make our day more fun and informative at the same time.

In this chapter, we tell you about almost ten (we can't count too well, but our editors keep us honest) key sites to visit if you have questions or just want to see what's new. We bet you'll visit them often if you visit them once!

No one site will tell you everything you need to know about advanced wireless topics. At best, you can get great reviews from one site, terrific gadget news coverage from another site, wonderful and responsive forums on another site, and so on. The patchwork of Web site content combines to give you a well-rounded view each day as you seek wireless truth. The wireless gurus are in: Bring on the wireless truthseekers!

Wi-Fi Net News

Wi-Fi Net News (www.wifinetnews.com) is an interesting roundup of the wireless topics that intrigue the editors. Because we're usually intrigued by what they pick to write about, we bet you'll like it too. Wi-Fi Net News covers a variety of advanced wireless topics, including VoIP and WiMax. They also have WNN Europe, which is a Europe-focused news reporting area of their site.

Wi-Fi Net News, like many other sites, now supports *RSS feeds*. If you don't know about RSS, you will soon. Most news and information sources (even E! Online, for all you closet Demi/Ashton fans) offer RSS feeds to tell you about the latest news and features on their Web sites. RSS feeds are electronic feeds that contain basic information about a particular item, like the headline, posting date, and summary paragraph about each news item on the site. You use a program called an RSS reader, such as NewsGator Online (www.newsgator.com) or any of dozens of other free RSS Readers, to reach out and access these feeds on a regular basis. Some RSS readers load into your e-mail program, browsers, instant messaging programs, and so on. These readers allow you to scan the headlines and click on the ones you want to read. You could set up an RSS reader to access the RSS feeds of each of these sites and stay current on everything wireless. We highly recommend RSS.

Tom's Networking

Tom's Networking (www.tomsnetworking.com) is a go-to source for us and many others. It includes practical advice on wireless issues ("How can I get my wireless notebook to automatically connect to the AP with the strongest signal?") and fun-loving stories that push the edge of networking ("Building a BlueSniper Rifle – Part 1"). Tom (and there *is* a Tom) even mimics the *For Dummies* Part of Tens concept with his "Top Tens" area that details things like the top ten most-read articles, the top ten most popular FAQ items, and more.

But what we love about Tom's is the detailed reviews that show detailed product views and take you through all the aspects of setting up and using the products. If you want to know what to expect with a wireless product, Tom's Networking tells you the pros and cons of the product, installation issues, and even looks under the hood to cover chips, boards, and all of that techie stuff that we love.

If you like this site, check out his other site, Tom's Hardware Guide (www.tomshardware.com).

JiWire

JiWire (`www.jiwire.com`) is a terrific online resource for all things hot spot–oriented. We think you'll be traveling with your wireless gear all over the place, and logging into hot spots is going to become a religious experience for you.

What's great about JiWire's Web site is that it's wholly focused on the traveling user. JiWire's goal is to build the world's largest database of Wi-Fi hot spots — you can find reviews of wireless PC cards, for instance, that are optimal for traveling users, not just home offices. There are how-to stories about using VoIP over Wi-Fi on the road. (The news on the site is not homegrown — it comes from Wi-Fi Net News.)

JiWire is also branching out to offer services specifically designed for Wi-Fi users on the go. The company recently launched a service designed to automatically and securely connect to Wi-Fi access hot spots. You can read more about this in Chapter 10.

FreeNetworks.org

FreeNetworks.org (`www.freenetworks.org`) is — you guessed it — devoted to the proliferation of free networks around the world. A *free network* is any computer network that allows free local connectivity to anyone who wants it.

If you have fun with wireless, this organization might be for you. It's all volunteer-run, and the people involved believe in the freedom of the airwaves for anyone who wants to log on. Building a community network, as we discuss in Chapter 12, can be quite an undertaking, and FreeNetworks.org provides you with peering agreements, advice, and community discussion groups to help move your community towards wireless communism. What would Lenin say?

Robert Hoskins' Wireless Super Sites

Robert Hoskins, a broadband wireless enthusiast, has a series of almost 20 sites all based around the wireless industry — 802.11a/b/g/i, Bluetooth, broadband wireless . . . you name it. Most of these sites are designed to be a capsule on what's happening on each topic. For instance, 80211info (`www.80211info.com`) lists the latest news, articles, white papers, research reports, events, books, and other content on, you guessed it, 802.11. Robert also offers some Buyer's Guides and Business Directories, but these do not tend to be as populated as some other sites.

Want to find RSS feeds?

The Google of the RSS kingdom is Syndic8 (www.syndic8.com). This is a listing of user-submitted/Syndicat8-authenticated RSS feeds that you can subscribe to in your RSS reader.

Just enter your keyword in the Search area and Syndicat8 displays all of the listings of available publications and sources with that phrase in their description. Check it out!

We like these sites because you can get a concise listing of all the latest articles and news on one topic — without all the extraneous information you find with a Google or CNET search. So if we want to know all the latest Bluetooth articles that have been published in the tech industry, we just hop over to www.bluetoothdailynews.com, and we're happy. And best of all, his sites support RSS too.

Wi-Fi Planet

Brought to you by the folks at Jupitermedia, the same people who publish Internet.com, Wi-Fi Planet (www.wi-fiplanet.com) is a well-rounded news and features site on Wi-Fi topics. We like this site because they always have interesting and useful stories, whether it's giving advice about hardware ("Used Routers Can Create Whole New Problems") or about brand-new services to check out ("Enterprise Authentication at Home"). In particular, Wi-Fi Planet has two areas focused just on WiMax and VoIP to keep you current on those topics.

The site also sports wireless reviews, tutorials, and an insights section that gives views on different topics. The forums (which don't get a lot of traffic) and product listings (which tend to be more commercials for vendors than really meaty listings) are the site's weak spots. Stick with the news, features, and tutorials for the best use of this destination.

Checking In on CNET

CNET (www.cnet.com) should be a primary news source (next to this book, of course) for tracking the latest in wireless networking happenings. CNET *News* is a source reputable enough for even the *Wall Street Journal* to reference. The Networking sections of the CNET site offer a well-rounded view of news, reviews, software downloads, and buying tips based around the products on the market each day.

URLs change a lot, but as of the time of this writing, CNET offers Networking and Wi-Fi information at `http://reviews.cnet.com/Networking/2001-3243_7-0.html?tag=co`. This part of the site gives you feature specs, reviews, and price comparisons of leading wireless gear. (CNET even certifies vendors listed, so you know they pass at least one test of online legitimacy.)

At `wireless.cnet.com`, the CNET editors summarize their view of what you should be doing wireless-wise in your life, through feature stories focused on wireless use. Overall, CNET is a sound resource for wireless networking news and reviews.

We talked about RSS reader programs earlier in the chapter; you can find CNET's reviews of the popular RSS readers here: `http://reviews.cnet.com/4520-10088_7-5143606.html?tag=nav`.

Practically Speaking

Practically Networked (`www.practicallynetworked.com`) is run by the folks at Jupitermedia Corporation, who you might recognize by all the other sites they run as well, like Internet.com. This site offers reviews, Q&A forums, features, and tips for the novice wireless reader. If you are buying a piece of gear, you might check out the reviews on this site to see what they found in their practical use of the gear, pun intended. The forums are also very helpful — we've seen fairly quick and knowledgeable responses from participants.

We like this site, but we wish they'd put more effort into keeping parts of it more current. The troubleshooting and tutorial sections of the site seem very dated, at least at the time of this writing. We don't recommend those areas.

Read About the Gadgets

If you have not figured this out by now, we love gadgets. So do you, we bet. So if you love gadgets, you will love these gadget-tracking sites:

- Gizmodo (`www.gizmodo.com`): Dubbed the Gadget's Weblog, Gizmodo tracks all sorts of cutting-edge gadgets. We usually see a lot of stuff we want right now, except it's only available in Asia. But the pictures and write-ups are simply wonderful and you never know what you are going to find. Nothing fancy here, just listings of gadget after gadget. (At the time of this writing, the top piece is a "USB Memory with Ghost Detection" device — it displays a particular LED sequence when a real ghost is nearby!

We think it's scarier that someone even created a USB storage unit with a ghost detector in it. (Not that we believe in ghosts, mind you. Boo!) Danny's favorite is the ""iPoo GPS Toilet Locator," available in the U.K. for finding the nearest loo.

✔ Engadget (www.engadget.com): Gizmodo was the first major Web presence we know of that tracked gadgets, but then one of the major editors from Gizmodo left and formed Engadget. The site is similar to Gizmodo, but with longer posts and reader comment streams for each article.

✔ EHomeUpgrade (www.ehomeupgrade.com): EHomeUpgrade has a little broader scope of coverage than Gizmodo or Engadget, talking about software, services, and even industry trends.

Chapter 18

Top Ten Wi-Fi Security Questions

*I*n this book, we've written a fair amount about issues of wireless security. There's a method to our madness here — wireless security is a really big deal, and although today's systems can be made quite secure, a secure network takes effort.

Avoiding steps that don't add much security but only lure users into a false sense of security takes knowledge. That's the worst place to be — feeling safe enough to do things like online banking or shopping without actually having a secure system in place. In this chapter, we answer ten common questions folks have about security, and separate some of the myths from the facts.

If I'm Using WEP, I'm Safe, Right?

For several years, Wi-Fi systems have shipped with Wired Equivalent Privacy (or WEP) as the primary means of securing the network and *encrypting* (or scrambling) data being sent over the airwaves. The reason behind this is very sound — whether you like it or not, your wireless LAN signals can be intercepted by bad guys, and the bad guys can use these intercepted signals to monitor everything you do on your network. Encryption (like WEP) theoretically solves this problem by scrambling your data and making it unreadable without the encryption *key*.

The problem with WEP is that it's not hard for a cracker to figure out what your key is. Due to some design problems with the way the *RC-4* encryption cipher is implemented in WEP, it is almost trivially easy to crack with widely available tools. In fact, we recently read at Tom's Networking Web site (`www.tomsnetworking.com`) — we discuss this site more in Chapter 17 — that an FBI computer forensics team demonstrated an attack that broke a full 128-bit WEP key (generated with a random password) in about three minutes.

This attack used tools that anyone (anyone!) can freely download from the Web and have up and running in a few minutes. The bottom line here is that WEP can't be considered secure — if someone wants to break into your WEP-encrypted wireless LAN and monitor your communications, they can.

The solution is to switch to the newer WPA system. Although some variants of WPA also use the RC-4 cipher, the way WPA manages and uses the encryption keys makes it significantly harder to crack — almost impossible if you use a good password.

Can't I Just Hide My Network?

Some folks recommend that you "secure" your network by turning off the *SSID broadcast* feature found on most access points. SSID broadcast basically advertises the existence of your access point to the world — it's what lets all nearby wireless clients know about the existence of the wireless LAN.

When SSID Broadcast is turned on (this is a setting in your AP or router's configuration page), your AP automatically sends out a short unencrypted signal with the network's name (the SSID), which anyone with a Wi-Fi–equipped device can pick up. You can probably see where this is going: The thought is that if you're not broadcasting the network's existence with SSID, the network is effectively hidden from potential hackers, crackers, identity thieves, and other assorted bad folks.

Actually, that's not really true. Turning off SSID broadcast is sort of like hiding the key to the house under the front door mat. Honest folks who are wandering by and not looking to get in, won't. People who *are* trying to infiltrate your network (or your house) can figure out how to get in with just a moment's work. Network scanning tools let anyone willing to spend 45 seconds of scanning time find your network, regardless of the status of SSID Broadcasts.

When SSID Broadcast is off, someone needs to know the network's SSID ahead of time to connect to the network. They won't be able to select your network from a list of available networks, but they'll be able to easily type in the SSID and find it (and connect to it if they have the right WPA credentials).

Now we're not telling you that you shouldn't turn off SSID Broadcast if you want to. Doing so can help keep basically honest people from trying to break into your network, but anyone with NetStumbler, Kismet, or MacStumbler is going to get around this "security" measure in a few seconds.

Can I Secure My Network by Filtering for Friendly MAC Addresses?

Another "security" measure that many folks recommend for wireless LANs is to turn on MAC address filtering. The *Media Access Control* address is an identifier that's unique to an individual piece of networking hardware (like a wireless LAN network adapter). And if the identifier is really unique, you could "filter" users on your wireless LAN so that only users with pre-identified MAC addresses can get on. Theoretically, this could provide a secure means of controlling access to your LAN: Just put all of your own MAC addresses on the "allowed" list (almost all APs or wireless routers have this feature in their configuration software).

You can find the MAC address of most Wi-Fi adapters by simply looking for a label on the outside of the adapter. For adapters built into a PC, check for a sticker on the bottom (laptop) or back (desktop) of the PC itself.

Unfortunately, the relationship between a MAC address and the hardware it identifies is not so rigid. In fact, MAC addresses can be *spoofed* or impersonated — so a wireless client with MAC address x can be set up to look like the client with MAC address y. This is a pretty easy task to perform, and in fact, the client software that comes with many Wi-Fi network adapters lets you do it.

Finding MAC addresses to spoof isn't hard either — any of the sniffer programs, such as NetStumbler, give you the MAC addresses of computers attached to and actively communicating with a wireless LAN.

Some security systems fight spoofed MAC addresses by noticing any conflicts in the network (like when the spoofer and spoofee try to connect to the AP at the same time). But these systems are pretty rare and usually work only when there's an active conflict (for example, if the same MAC address connects to the network from two different computers). They don't protect your network from someone who captures an "allowed" MAC address and uses it at some time in the future.

The bottom line is that MAC address filtering makes your network a bit harder to use (any guests or new users need to be configured in your "allowed MAC address" list) and doesn't provide a lot of security. MAC filtering doesn't hurt, but, in our opinion, the benefit isn't worth the effort.

What's the Difference between Personal and Enterprise WPA?

If you read the first section of this chapter, we hope that you're convinced that WPA (Wi-Fi Protected Access) and not WEP is the very minimum starting point for wireless network security. The improved encryption key management in WPA (called TKIP, or Temporal Key Integrity Protocol) eliminates the biggest flaws in WPA and provides a strong encryption of all data flowing across the network. As long as you choose a reasonably random and complex passphrase (called the *shared secret*), you can rely upon WPA to keep your data secure.

But there's more to a wireless network's security than just encryption, and that's why there's more than one variant of WPA. A truly secure network goes beyond shared secrets (which often don't remain secret — particularly in a larger network environment where lots of people have access to the secret) and adds in a layer of user authentication. *User authentication* is nothing more than a cryptographic system that verifies that everybody within a wireless network is exactly who they say they are.

This user authentication (using the 802.1X system we describe in Chapter 9) is the big difference between WPA-Personal and WPA-Enterprise Wi-Fi equipment. WPA-Personal equipment is more common (and usually less expensive), but it doesn't support the 802.1X authentication protocol. WPA-Enterprise gear, on the other hand, *does* support connections to a RADIUS server and allows you to use the 802.1X protocol to confirm the identity of all users connected to a wireless network.

Why do you care? Well, for a small home network, nothing's wrong with the *PSK* (pre-shared key) approach taken by WPA-Personal. But the PSK model starts to break down when you want to add guest users to your network — like a relative visiting town or a coworker who's come over to help finish off a project over the weekend. You have to give out that same PSK to *everyone* who is joining your network, and if you decide for security purposes that you want to change the key, you need to change it on *every* PC and device attached to the LAN. It can be a real pain.

A WPA-Enterprise network eliminates this problem by using the 802.1X authentication system to assign each user (or device) connecting to the network its own password, each time it authenticates itself. You can let your Uncle Bill bring his laptop and get on the network without compromising your PSK. There's a downside of course — you need to put a little more effort (or money) into your network by running (or paying for the use of) a RADIUS server.

How Can 1 Use 802.1X When 1 Don't Know Anything About 1t?

Most folks who have wireless networks have never even heard of 802.1X or WPA-Enterprise and don't know much about RADIUS servers and *AAA* (Authentication, Authorization, and Accounting) systems. Why would they? This is really obscure stuff, but if you want to have a truly secure network, particularly in a dynamic environment like a small business, it makes sense to take advantage of these systems.

Luckily, you can do this without having to learn a thing about EAP types and RADIUS server configurations and certificate authorities — just outsource! Heck, everyone outsources these days — why not join the crowd?

In Chapter 9, we discuss some services that let you get all of the advantages of WPA-Enterprise and the strong authentication it offers, without any of the configuration headaches and steep learning curves of doing it yourself. For a relatively low monthly fee, you can have all the security that big corporations have on their wireless LANs (more than many have, as a matter of fact)!

With services like WiTopia (www.witopia.net) and WSC Guard (www.wirelesssecuritycorp.com), you can cheaply buy access to a remote RADIUS server that provides secured and just about fail-safe authentication and authorization of all users of your wireless LAN. To make this work, however, you need a reliable and always-on Internet connection (like cable or DSL) to provide the connectivity between your router and remote RADIUS server.

What's the Difference between WPA and WPA2?

The latest generation of wireless gear is starting to come equipped with WPA2 security systems. Just when we were starting to all understand the difference between WEP and WPA (and the benefits of WPA over WEP), along comes a new development. Keeping up with advances in the wireless world is nothing if not difficult!

So here's the scoop: WPA was always an *interim* step along the path of Wi-Fi security. As soon as Wi-Fi became the mega-hit billion dollar business that it is today, researchers and hackers (the good kind!) discovered that the WEP encryption system was totally inadequate. This led to crackers finding ways to defeat the encryption system in almost no time.

The folks at the Wi-Fi Alliance, who represent just about all manufacturers of Wi-Fi gear, decided to take the bold step of "fixing" WEP by adding (among other things) a system called TKIP that would change the encryption key on a rapidly occurring basis.

This fix was never intended to be permanent, as an entirely new 802.11 standard (802.11i) was on the horizon, with an even stronger and more permanent fix to the encryption problems of WEP. WPA2 is this 802.11i standard come to life. In WPA2, the RC-4 cipher and TKIP protocol are replaced by the AES encryption system — which is, with today's technologies, basically uncrackable for anyone short of a government spy agency.

As a wireless LAN user, what matters to you is that WPA2 is backwards-compatible with WPA. So you can seamlessly slot new WPA2-enabled gear into your existing WPA network. Eventually, when all your gear is WPA2 ready, you can turn your encryption up a notch, from TKIP to AES.

How Can I Stay Safe When I'm Away from My Home Network?

As more and more of us travel with laptops (or handheld computers), we find opportunities to get online at hot spots in airports, hotels, coffee shops, and other locations. We also find that requiring "guest" Wi-Fi access at a client or business partner's office or even a friend's home becomes more common.

All of this access brings with it a security risk. Setting up a secure network within the confines of your home or office is one thing; remaining secure in locations where you have almost no control over the rest of the network is quite another.

In Chapter 10, we discuss some solutions for staying secure in "unknown" wireless environments. The most effective step you can take is to utilize a VPN (virtual private network) connection whenever you're using an unsecured wireless network. A VPN encrypts every bit of data you send across the network so that eavesdroppers are unable to make heads or tails of it. You can set up a VPN through your corporate VPN network (if you've got one), use hot spot client software (like Boingo's), or even buy an inexpensive (less than $10 a month) VPN service that's designed specifically to secure your hot spot connections.

There are a bunch of VPN services available (we discuss several in Chapter 9). Our current favorite of the bunch is WiTopia's personal VPN service (www. witopia.net).

Can I Use My Credit Card Online When I'm Using Wi-Fi?

Many folks worry about using a credit card (for online shopping) or connecting to their online banking and commerce sites when they're wirelessly connected. After all, there's so much discussion about wireless insecurity — it can't be a good idea to send such personal information over a wireless connection!

The short answer is this: You don't have to sweat it, as long as you exercise some caution. You should always start off with the basic assumption that your wireless data can be intercepted by someone somewhere (the antennas we talk about in Chapter 7 make picking up Wi-Fi signals from great distances without being detected possible). As one security expert said, "Always assume that the bad guy has a bigger antenna."

If you think this way (it's not paranoia, really!), make sure that you take the right steps to avoid misuse of your personal data. First off, if you possibly can, use a secure WPA network. The encryption in WPA keeps most folks from ever gleaning important private information from the data that they intercept.

Second, and just as importantly, make sure that you're connecting to secure Web sites (using SSL security — sites whose URL begins with https). Don't just assume when the little yellow padlock shows up in your browser's status bar that everything is okay — double-click that padlock and check out the certificates. Make sure they have been issued to the organization that you are trying to communicate with (like your bank). Double-check that they've been issued by a reliable certificate authority like Verisign, Thwate, or Equifax.

You want to use SSL for these types of transactions and communications because your security threats are *not* just on the wireless LAN — there are plenty of scams and threats that affect the wired part of the Internet too!

Never send your vital information in an e-mail or an IM, unless you're using some sort of encryption (like PGP — www.pgp.com).

How Can I Let My Friends Use My Network without Losing Security?

Guest access is one of the most vexing problems in Wi-Fi security. The whole idea behind setting up a secure Wi-Fi network is to create some secret that is shared amongst a very limited number of people — a secret that unlocks the data flowing across the network. The more widely you share this secret (think: password or passphrase), the more likely it is to fall into the wrong hands.

Guest access causes a disruption here because you have two choices. You can either turn off security (and allow *anyone* to get into your network — not a good idea), or pass on your shared secret to more and more people as they need guest access. If you take the latter approach, pretty soon you realize that your secret isn't so secret any more, and you need to start all over again, and reset your network security.

That's no fun. You can take a couple of approaches to resolve this, however.

If you've got a WPA-Enterprise network, your problem is solved — these types of network are set up to allow an administrator to quickly and easily grant time-limited guest access to users, and to also take away this access at any time. And when a users' access has expired (or been revoked) in this network, they haven't got a key or shared secret that can compromise your network in the future.

Another approach to take is to follow some of the advice we offer in Chapter 12 for setting up a hot spot — using a separate access point or a specialized public/private gateway access point. You can maintain your own internal network using a secured, WPA-enabled AP, and create a segregated "open" AP for guest access.

Having a second AP for public access may seem to be a bit extravagant. But a second AP may only cost you $30 or $40. A great way to have a second AP is to save your old 802.11b AP when you upgrade to 802.11g — and set up this lower-speed AP as your guest network. Be sure to follow the tips in Chapters 5 and 6 for avoiding radio interference and for properly segregating the IP network to avoid performance issues.

How Do I Stay Secure If Not All of My Equipment Is WPA?

One of the dirty little secrets of the Wi-Fi world is that although WPA has been on the market for two years (and counting . . .), a lot of Wi-Fi equipment being sold does not yet support WPA. Although WPA support is becoming common on most access points, wireless routers, and wireless network adapters for PCs, it is still rare on devices like media adapters for audio and video, Ethernet bridges for game consoles, wireless Web cams, and the like. Basically, Wi-Fi peripheral devices (all the stuff we discuss in Part III of the book) are simply a few years behind the curve when it comes to security.

By itself, that's not necessarily a big problem. These devices, for the most part, are not carrying data that is exceptionally personal or private (watch where you aim the Web cams, though!). You're probably not doing your online banking, for example, through any of these devices. But when you try to connect WEP devices to a WPA network, you run into the real issue — you need to turn the encryption of the entire network down to WEP. You can't mix and match — the AP either uses WEP or WPA. Your least common denominator limits your security.

What's the solution? There isn't an easy one. We recommend using a completely separate network — a different AP on a different channel — for these WEP devices. Keep your PCs secure with a WPA Wi-Fi network, and let this less important data ride over the WEP network. With the low prices of APs these days, this won't cost you an arm and a leg. And if you're doing a lot of multimedia stuff (like video) over the network, you may want to do this anyway, for network performance reasons.

Index

• Z •

Notes

Notes

Notes

Notes

Notes

BUSINESS, CAREERS & PERSONAL FINANCE

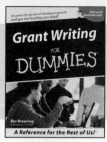

0-7645-5307-0

0-7645-5331-3 *†

Also available:

- Accounting For Dummies †
  0-7645-5314-3
- Business Plans Kit For Dummies †
  0-7645-5365-8
- Cover Letters For Dummies
  0-7645-5224-4
- Frugal Living For Dummies
  0-7645-5403-4
- Leadership For Dummies
  0-7645-5176-0
- Managing For Dummies
  0-7645-1771-6

- Marketing For Dummies
  0-7645-5600-2
- Personal Finance For Dummies *
  0-7645-2590-5
- Project Management For Dummies
  0-7645-5283-X
- Resumes For Dummies †
  0-7645-5471-9
- Selling For Dummies
  0-7645-5363-1
- Small Business Kit For Dummies *†
  0-7645-5093-4

HOME & BUSINESS COMPUTER BASICS

0-7645-4074-2

0-7645-3758-X

Also available:

- ACT! 6 For Dummies
  0-7645-2645-6
- iLife '04 All-in-One Desk Reference
  For Dummies
  0-7645-7347-0
- iPAQ For Dummies
  0-7645-6769-1
- Mac OS X Panther Timesaving
  Techniques For Dummies
  0-7645-5812-9
- Macs For Dummies
  0-7645-5656-8

- Microsoft Money 2004 For Dummies
  0-7645-4195-1
- Office 2003 All-in-One Desk Reference
  For Dummies
  0-7645-3883-7
- Outlook 2003 For Dummies
  0-7645-3759-8
- PCs For Dummies
  0-7645-4074-2
- TiVo For Dummies
  0-7645-6923-6
- Upgrading and Fixing PCs For Dummies
  0-7645-1665-5
- Windows XP Timesaving Techniques
  For Dummies
  0-7645-3748-2

FOOD, HOME, GARDEN, HOBBIES, MUSIC & PETS

0-7645-5295-3

0-7645-5232-5

Also available:

- Bass Guitar For Dummies
  0-7645-2487-9
- Diabetes Cookbook For Dummies
  0-7645-5230-9
- Gardening For Dummies *
  0-7645-5130-2
- Guitar For Dummies
  0-7645-5106-X
- Holiday Decorating For Dummies
  0-7645-2570-0
- Home Improvement All-in-One
  For Dummies
  0-7645-5680-0

- Knitting For Dummies
  0-7645-5395-X
- Piano For Dummies
  0-7645-5105-1
- Puppies For Dummies
  0-7645-5255-4
- Scrapbooking For Dummies
  0-7645-7208-3
- Senior Dogs For Dummies
  0-7645-5818-8
- Singing For Dummies
  0-7645-2475-5
- 30-Minute Meals For Dummies
  0-7645-2589-1

INTERNET & DIGITAL MEDIA

0-7645-1664-7

0-7645-6924-4

Also available:

- 2005 Online Shopping Directory
  For Dummies
  0-7645-7495-7
- CD & DVD Recording For Dummies
  0-7645-5956-7
- eBay For Dummies
  0-7645-5654-1
- Fighting Spam For Dummies
  0-7645-5965-6
- Genealogy Online For Dummies
  0-7645-5964-8
- Google For Dummies
  0-7645-4420-9

- Home Recording For Musicians
  For Dummies
  0-7645-1634-5
- The Internet For Dummies
  0-7645-4173-0
- iPod & iTunes For Dummies
  0-7645-7772-7
- Preventing Identity Theft For Dummies
  0-7645-7336-5
- Pro Tools All-in-One Desk Reference
  For Dummies
  0-7645-5714-9
- Roxio Easy Media Creator For Dummies
  0-7645-7131-1

SPORTS, FITNESS, PARENTING, RELIGION & SPIRITUALITY

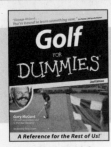

0-7645-5146-9

0-7645-5418-2

Also available:
- Adoption For Dummies
  0-7645-5488-3
- Basketball For Dummies
  0-7645-5248-1
- The Bible For Dummies
  0-7645-5296-1
- Buddhism For Dummies
  0-7645-5359-3
- Catholicism For Dummies
  0-7645-5391-7
- Hockey For Dummies
  0-7645-5228-7
- Judaism For Dummies
  0-7645-5299-6
- Martial Arts For Dummies
  0-7645-5358-5
- Pilates For Dummies
  0-7645-5397-6
- Religion For Dummies
  0-7645-5264-3
- Teaching Kids to Read For Dummies
  0-7645-4043-2
- Weight Training For Dummies
  0-7645-5168-X
- Yoga For Dummies
  0-7645-5117-5

TRAVEL

0-7645-5438-7

0-7645-5453-0

Also available:
- Alaska For Dummies
  0-7645-1761-9
- Arizona For Dummies
  0-7645-6938-4
- Cancún and the Yucatán For Dummies
  0-7645-2437-2
- Cruise Vacations For Dummies
  0-7645-6941-4
- Europe For Dummies
  0-7645-5456-5
- Ireland For Dummies
  0-7645-5455-7
- Las Vegas For Dummies
  0-7645-5448-4
- London For Dummies
  0-7645-4277-X
- New York City For Dummies
  0-7645-6945-7
- Paris For Dummies
  0-7645-5494-8
- RV Vacations For Dummies
  0-7645-5443-3
- Walt Disney World & Orlando For Dummies
  0-7645-6943-0

GRAPHICS, DESIGN & WEB DEVELOPMENT

0-7645-4345-8

0-7645-5589-8

Also available:
- Adobe Acrobat 6 PDF For Dummies
  0-7645-3760-1
- Building a Web Site For Dummies
  0-7645-7144-3
- Dreamweaver MX 2004 For Dummies
  0-7645-4342-3
- FrontPage 2003 For Dummies
  0-7645-3882-9
- HTML 4 For Dummies
  0-7645-1995-6
- Illustrator CS For Dummies
  0-7645-4084-X
- Macromedia Flash MX 2004 For Dummies
  0-7645-4358-X
- Photoshop 7 All-in-One Desk
  Reference For Dummies
  0-7645-1667-1
- Photoshop CS Timesaving Techniques
  For Dummies
  0-7645-6782-9
- PHP 5 For Dummies
  0-7645-4166-8
- PowerPoint 2003 For Dummies
  0-7645-3908-6
- QuarkXPress 6 For Dummies
  0-7645-2593-X

NETWORKING, SECURITY, PROGRAMMING & DATABASES

0-7645-6852-3

0-7645-5784-X

Also available:
- A+ Certification For Dummies
  0-7645-4187-0
- Access 2003 All-in-One Desk
  Reference For Dummies
  0-7645-3988-4
- Beginning Programming For Dummies
  0-7645-4997-9
- C For Dummies
  0-7645-7068-4
- Firewalls For Dummies
  0-7645-4048-3
- Home Networking For Dummies
  0-7645-42796
- Network Security For Dummies
  0-7645-1679-5
- Networking For Dummies
  0-7645-1677-9
- TCP/IP For Dummies
  0-7645-1760-0
- VBA For Dummies
  0-7645-3989-2
- Wireless All In-One Desk Reference
  For Dummies
  0-7645-7496-5
- Wireless Home Networking For Dummies
  0-7645-3910-8

HEALTH & SELF-HELP

Diabetes FOR DUMMIES
0-7645-6820-5 *†

Low-Carb Dieting FOR DUMMIES
0-7645-2566-2

Also available:

- Alzheimer's For Dummies
  0-7645-3899-3
- Asthma For Dummies
  0-7645-4233-8
- Controlling Cholesterol For Dummies
  0-7645-5440-9
- Depression For Dummies
  0-7645-3900-0
- Dieting For Dummies
  0-7645-4149-8
- Fertility For Dummies
  0-7645-2549-2

- Fibromyalgia For Dummies
  0-7645-5441-7
- Improving Your Memory For Dummies
  0-7645-5435-2
- Pregnancy For Dummies †
  0-7645-4483-7
- Quitting Smoking For Dummies
  0-7645-2629-4
- Relationships For Dummies
  0-7645-5384-4
- Thyroid For Dummies
  0-7645-5385-2

EDUCATION, HISTORY, REFERENCE & TEST PREPARATION

Spanish FOR DUMMIES
0-7645-5194-9

The Origins of Tolkien's Middle-earth FOR DUMMIES
0-7645-4186-2

Also available:

- Algebra For Dummies
  0-7645-5325-9
- British History For Dummies
  0-7645-7021-8
- Calculus For Dummies
  0-7645-2498-4
- English Grammar For Dummies
  0-7645-5322-4
- Forensics For Dummies
  0-7645-5580-4
- The GMAT For Dummies
  0-7645-5251-1
- Inglés Para Dummies
  0-7645-5427-1

- Italian For Dummies
  0-7645-5196-5
- Latin For Dummies
  0-7645-5431-X
- Lewis & Clark For Dummies
  0-7645-2545-X
- Research Papers For Dummies
  0-7645-5426-3
- The SAT I For Dummies
  0-7645-7193-1
- Science Fair Projects For Dummies
  0-7645-5460-3
- U.S. History For Dummies
  0-7645-5249-X

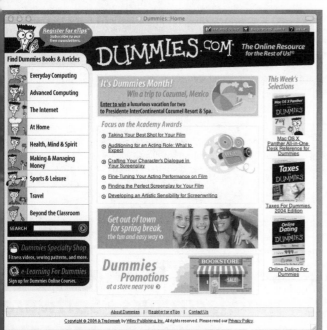

Get smart @ dummies.com®

- **Find a full list of Dummies titles**
- **Look into loads of FREE on-site articles**
- **Sign up for FREE eTips e-mailed to you weekly**
- **See what other products carry the Dummies name**
- **Shop directly from the Dummies bookstore**
- **Enter to win new prizes every month!**

Separate Canadian edition also available
Separate U.K. edition also available

Available wherever books are sold. For more information or to order direct: U.S. customers visit www.dummies.com or call 1-877-762-2974. U.K. customers visit www.wileyeurope.com or call 0800 243407. Canadian customers visit www.wiley.ca or call 1-800-567-4797.